Visit us at

www.syngress.com

Syngress is committed to publishing high-quality books for IT Professionals and delivering those books in media and formats that fit the demands of our customers. We are also committed to extending the utility of the book you purchase via additional materials available from our Web site.

SOLUTIONS WEB SITE

To register your book, visit www.syngress.com/solutions. Once registered, you can access our solutions@syngress.com Web pages. There you may find an assortment of valueadded features such as free e-books related to the topic of this book, URLs of related Web sites, FAQs from the book, corrections, and any updates from the author(s).

ULTIMATE CDs

Our Ultimate CD product line offers our readers budget-conscious compilations of some of our best-selling backlist titles in Adobe PDF form. These CDs are the perfect way to extend your reference library on key topics pertaining to your area of expertise, including Cisco Engineering, Microsoft Windows System Administration, CyberCrime Investigation, Open Source Security, and Firewall Configuration, to name a few.

DOWNLOADABLE E-BOOKS

For readers who can't wait for hard copy, we offer most of our titles in downloadable Adobe PDF form. These e-books are often available weeks before hard copies, and are priced affordably.

SYNGRESS OUTLET

Our outlet store at syngress.com features overstocked, out-of-print, or slightly hurt books at significant savings.

SITE LICENSING

Syngress has a well-established program for site licensing our e-books onto servers in corporations, educational institutions, and large organizations. Contact us at sales@syngress.com for more information.

CUSTOM PUBLISHING

Many organizations welcome the ability to combine parts of multiple Syngress books, as well as their own content, into a single volume for their own internal use. Contact us at sales@syngress.com for more information.

SYNGRESS®

The Real MCTS/MCITP Exam 642 Network Infrastructure Configuration Prep Kit

Brien Posey Technical Editor

Susan Snedaker
Jeffery Martin
John Karnay

Ira Herman
Dustin Hannifin
Shawn Tooley

KEY	SERIAL NUMBER
001	HJIRTCV764
002	PO9873D5FG
003	829KM8NJH2
004	BPOQ48722D
005	CVPLQ6WQ23
006	VBP965T5T5
007	HJJJ863WD3E
008	2987GVTWMK
009	629MP5SDJT
010	IMWQ295T6T

PUBLISHED BY
Syngress Publishing, Inc.
Elsevier, Inc.
30 Corporate Drive
Burlington, MA 01803

The Real MCTS/MCITP Exam 70-642 Prep Kit

Printed in the United States of America
1 2 3 4 5 6 7 8 9 0

ISBN 13: 978-1-59749-246-1

Publisher: Andrew Williams
Acquisitions Editor: David George
Technical Editor: Brien Posey
Project Manager: Gary Byrne

Page Layout and Art: SPI
Copy Editors: Audrey Doyle, Judy Eby, Adrienne Rebello
Indexer: Nara Wood
Cover Designer: Michael Kavish

For information on rights, translations, and bulk sales, contact Matt Pedersen, Commercial Sales Director and Rights, at Syngress Publishing; email m.pedersen@elsevier.com.

Technical Editor

Brien Posey is a freelance technical writer who has received Microsoft's MVP award four times. Over the last 12 years, Brien has published more than 4,000 articles and whitepapers, and has written or contributed to more than 30 books. In addition to his technical writing, Brien is the cofounder of Relevant Technologies (www.relevanttechnologies.com) and also serves the IT community through his own Web site at www.brienposey.com.

Prior to becoming a freelance author, Brien served as CIO for a nationwide chain of hospitals and healthcare facilities and as a network administrator for the Department of Defense at Fort Knox. He has also worked as a network administrator for some of the nation's largest insurance companies.

Brien wishes to thank his wife, Taz, for her love and support throughout his writing career.

Contributing Authors

Susan Snedaker, (MCSE, MCT) principal consultant for VirtualTeam Consulting, LLC (www.virtualteam.com), is an accomplished business and technology consultant, speaker, and author. During her career, she has held executive and technical positions with companies such as Microsoft, Honeywell, Keane, and Apta Software. As a consultant, she has worked with small, medium-sized, and large companies, including Canyon Ranch, University of Arizona, National University, Sabino Investment Management, Pyron Solar, University of Phoenix, DDB Ventures, ShopOrganic.com, and the Southern Arizona AIDS Foundation.

Susan's latest book, *Business Continuity and Disaster Recovery for IT Professionals*, Syngress (978-1-59749-172-3) was released in the spring of 2007. Additionally, Susan has written four other books and contributed chapters to 11 books. She has also written numerous technical articles on a variety of technology, information security, and wireless technologies. Susan is an experienced trainer, facilitator, and speaker.

Susan holds a Master of Business Administration (MBA) and a Bachelor of Arts in Management (BAM) from the University of Phoenix. In 2006, she received an Executive Certificate in International Management from Thunderbird University's Garvin School of International Management. Susan also holds a certificate in Advanced Project Management from Stanford University and attained Microsoft Certified Systems Engineer (MCSE) and Microsoft Certified Trainer (MCT) certifications. Susan is a member of the Project Management Institute (PMI) and the Information Technology Association of Southern Arizona (ITASA).

Jeffery A. Martin MS/IT, MS/M (MCSE, MCSE:Security, MCSE: Messaging, MCDBA, MCT, MCSA, MCSA:Security, MCSE:Messaging, MCP+I, MCNE, CNE, CNA, CCA, CTT, A+, Network+, I-Net+,

Project+, Linux+, CIW, ADPM) has been working with computer networks for more than 20 years. He is an editor, coeditor, author, or coauthor of more than 15 books and enjoys training others in the use of technology.

John Karnay is a freelance writer, editor, and book author living in Queens, NY. John specializes in Windows server and desktop deployments utilizing Microsoft and Apple products and technology. John has been working with Microsoft products since Windows 95 and NT 4.0 and consults for many clients in New York City and Long Island, helping them plan migrations to XP/Vista and Windows Server 2003/2008. When not working and writing, John enjoys recording and writing music as well as spending quality time with his wife, Gloria, and daughter, Aurora.

Ira Herman (MCSE, CCAI, CCNA, CNA, A+, Network+, i- Net+, CIW Associate) is co-chief executive officer and cofounder of Logic IT Consulting (www.logicitc.com), a consulting firm specializing in business information technology solutions with an emphasis on work-life balance, stress-free productivity, and efficiency training and coaching. Prior to founding Logic IT Consulting, Ira held various technical and executive positions with companies such as Microsoft, Keane, The University of Arizona, Xynetik, and Brand X LLC. Ira has written and delivered technical training for Logic IT Consulting and its clients as well as various organizations, including Pima Community College, JobPath, and SeniorNet. Ira holds Microsoft Certified Systems Engineer (MCSE and MCSE+I), Cisco Certified Academy Instructor (CCAI), Cisco Certified Network Associate (CCNA), Certified Novell Administrator (CNA), CompTIA A+ Certified Computer Service Technician (A+), CompTIA Network+, CompTIA Internetworking (i-Net+), and ProsoftTraining Certified Internet Webmaster Associate (CIW Associate) certifications as well as Microsoft internal endorsements in Windows NT 4 Fundamentals (Workstation), Windows NT 4 Advanced (Server), Microsoft TCP/IP on Windows NT 4, Windows 2000 Foundational Topics, and Windows 2000 Setup Specialty.

Dustin Hannifin (Microsoft MVP—Office SharePoint Server) is a systems administrator with Crowe Chizek and Company LLC. Crowe (www.crowechizek.com) is one of the nation's leading public accounting and consulting firms. Under its core purpose of "Building Value with Values®," Crowe assists both public and private companies in reaching their goals through services ranging from assurance and financial advisory to performance, risk, and tax consulting. Dustin currently works in Crowe's Information Services delivery unit, where he plays a key role in maintaining and supporting Crowe's internal information technology (IT) infrastructure. His expertise resides in various Microsoft products, including Office SharePoint Server, System Center Operations Manager, Active Directory, IIS, and Office Communications Server. Dustin holds a bachelor's degree from Tennessee Technological University and is a founding member of the Michiana IT Professionals Users Group. He regularly contributes to technology communities, including his blog (www.technotesblog.com) and Microsoft newsgroups. Dustin, a Tennessee native, currently resides in South Bend, IN.

Shawn Tooley owns a consulting firm, Tooley Consulting Group, LLC, that specializes in Microsoft and Citrix technologies, for which he is the principal consultant and trainer. Shawn also works as network administrator for a hospital in North Eastern Ohio. Shawn's certifications include Microsoft Certified Trainer (MCT), Microsoft Certified System Engineer (MCSE), Citrix Certified Enterprise Administrator, Citrix Certified Sales Professional, HP Accredited System Engineer, IBM XSeries Server Specialist, Comptia A+, and Comptia Certified Trainer. In his free time he enjoys playing golf.

Contents

Foreword

This book's primary goal is to help you prepare to take and pass Microsoft's Exam 70-642, *Windows Server 2008 Network Infrastructure, Configuring*. Our secondary purpose in writing this book is to provide exam candidates with knowledge and skills that go beyond the minimum requirements for passing the exam and help to prepare them to work in the real world of Microsoft computer networking.

What Is MCTS Exam 70-642?

Microsoft Certified Technology Specialist (MCTS) Exam 70-642 is both a stand-alone test for those wishing to master Active Directory technology and a requirement for those pursuing certification as a Microsoft Certified Information Technology Professional (MCITP) for Windows Server 2008. Microsoft's stated target audience consists of IT professionals with at least one year of work experience on a medium-sized or large company network. This means a multisite network with at least three domain controllers running typical network services such as file and print services, messaging, database, firewall services, proxy services, remote access services, an intranet, and Internet connectivity.

However, not everyone who takes Exam 70-642 will have this ideal background. Many people will take this exam after classroom instruction or self-study as an entry into the networking field. Many of those who do have job experience in IT will not have had the opportunity to work with all of the technologies covered by the exam. In this book, our goal is to provide background information that will help you to understand the concepts and procedures described even if you don't have the requisite experience, while keeping our focus on the exam objectives.

Exam 70-642 covers the basics of managing and maintaining a network environment that is built around Microsoft's Windows Server 2008. The following task-oriented objectives are included:

- **Configuring IP Addressing and Services** This objective includes configuring IPv4 and IPv6 addressing, configuring Dynamic Host Configuration Protocol (DHCP), configuring routing, and configuring IPsec.

- **Configuring Name Resolution** This objective includes configuring a Domain Name System (DNS) server, configuring DNS zones, configuring DNS records, configuring DNS replication, and configuring name resolution for client computers.

- **Configuring Network Access** This objective includes configuring remote access, configuring Network Access Protection (NAP), configuring network authentication, configuring wireless access, and configuring firewall settings.

- **Configuring File and Print Services** This objective includes configuring a file server, configuring Distributed File System (DFS), configuring shadow copy services, configuring backup and restore, managing disk quotas, and configuring and monitoring print services.

- **Monitoring and Managing a Network Infrastructure** This objective includes configuring Windows Server Update Services (WSUS), capturing performance data, monitoring event logs, and gathering network data.

Path to MCTS/MCITP/MS Certified Architect

Microsoft certification is recognized throughout the IT industry as a way to demonstrate mastery of basic concepts and skills required to perform the tasks involved in implementing and maintaining Windows-based networks. The certification program is constantly evaluated and improved, while the nature of information technology is changing rapidly; consequently, requirements and specifications for certification can also change rapidly. This book is based on the exam objectives as stated by Microsoft at the time of writing; however, Microsoft reserves the right to make changes to the objectives and to the exam itself at any time. Exam candidates should regularly visit the Certification and Training Web site at www.microsoft.com/learning/mcp/default.mspx for the most updated information on each Microsoft exam.

Microsoft currently offers three basic levels of certification on the technology level, professional level, and architect level:

- **Technology Series** This level of certification is the most basic, and it includes the **Microsoft Certified Technology Specialist (MCTS)** certification. The MCTS certification is focused on one particular Microsoft technology. There are 19 MCTS exams at the time of this writing. Each MCTS certification consists of one to three exams, does not include job-role skills, and will be retired when the technology is retired. Microsoft Certified Technology Specialists will be proficient in implementing, building, troubleshooting, and debugging a specific Microsoft technology.

- **Professional Series** This is the second level of Microsoft certification, and it includes the **Microsoft Certified Information Technology Professional (MCITP)** and **Microsoft Certified Professional Developer (MCPD)** certifications. These certifications consist of one to three exams, have prerequisites from the Technology Series, focus on a specific job role, and require an exam refresh to remain current. The MCITP certification offers nine separate tracks as of the time of this writing. There are two Windows Server 2008 tracks, Server Administrator and Enterprise Administrator. To achieve the Server Administrator MCITP for Windows Server 2008, you must successfully complete one Technology Series exam and one Professional Series exam. To achieve the Enterprise Administrator MCITP for Windows Server 2008, you must successfully complete four Technology Series exams and one Professional Series exam.

- **Architect Series** This is the highest level of Microsoft certification, and it requires the candidate to have at least 10 years' industry experience. Candidates must pass a rigorous review by a review board of existing architects, and they must work with an architect mentor for a period of time before taking the exam.

> **NOTE**
>
> Those who already hold the MCSA or MCSE in Windows 2003 can upgrade their certifications to MCITP Server Administrator by passing one upgrade exam and one Professional Series exam. Those who already hold the MCSA or MCSE in Windows 2003 can upgrade their certifications to MCITP Enterprise Administrator by passing one upgrade exam, two Technology Series exams, and one Professional Series exam.

Prerequisites and Preparation

There are no mandatory prerequisites for taking Exam 70-642, although Microsoft recommends that you meet the target audience profile described earlier.

Preparation for this exam should include the following:

- Visit the Web site at www.microsoft.com/learning/exams/70-642.mspx to review the updated exam objectives.

- Work your way through this book, studying the material thoroughly and marking any items you don't understand.

- Answer all practice exam questions at the end of each chapter.

- Complete all hands-on exercises in each chapter.

- Review any topics that you don't thoroughly understand.

- Consult Microsoft online resources such as TechNet (www.microsoft.com/technet/), whitepapers on the Microsoft Web site, and so forth, for better understanding of difficult topics.

- Participate in Microsoft's product-specific and training and certification newsgroups if you have specific questions that you still need answered.

- Take one or more practice exams, such as the one included on the Syngress/Elsevier certification Web site at www.syngress.com/certification.

Exam Day Experience

Taking the exam is a relatively straightforward process. Prometric testing centers administer the Microsoft 70-642 exam. You can register for, reschedule, or cancel an exam through the Prometric Web site at www.register.prometric.com. You'll find listings of testing center locations on these sites. Accommodations are made for those with disabilities; contact the individual testing center for more information.

Exam price varies depending on the country in which you take the exam.

Exam Format

Exams are timed. At the end of the exam, you will find out your score and whether you passed or failed. You will not be allowed to take any notes or other written materials with you into the exam room. You will be provided with a pencil and paper, however, for making notes during the exam or doing calculations.

In addition to the traditional multiple-choice questions and the select and drag, simulation and case study questions, you might see some or all of the following types of questions:

- *Hot area* questions, in which you are asked to select an element or elements in a graphic to indicate the correct answer. You click an element to select or deselect it.

- *Active screen* questions, in which you change elements in a dialog box (for example, by dragging the appropriate text element into a text box or selecting an option button or checkbox in a dialog box).

- *Drag and drop* questions, in which you arrange various elements in a target area.

Test-Taking Tips

Different people work best using different methods. However, there are some common methods of preparation and approach to the exam that are helpful to many test-takers. In this section, we provide some tips that other exam candidates have found useful in preparing for and actually taking the exam.

- Exam preparation begins before exam day. Ensure that you know the concepts and terms well and feel confident about each of the exam objectives. Many test-takers find it helpful to make flash cards or review notes to study on the way to the testing center. A sheet listing acronyms and abbreviations can be helpful, as the number of acronyms (and the similarity of different acronyms) when studying IT topics can be overwhelming. The process of writing the material down, rather than just reading it, will help to reinforce your knowledge.

■ Many test-takers find it especially helpful to take practice exams that are available on the Internet and with books such as this one. Taking the practice exams can help you become used to the computerized exam-taking experience, and the practice exams can also be used as a learning tool. The best practice tests include detailed explanations of why the correct answer is correct and why the incorrect answers are wrong.

■ When preparing and studying, you should try to identify the main points of each objective section. Set aside enough time to focus on the material and lodge it into your memory. On the day of the exam, you be at the point where you don't have to learn any new facts or concepts; instead, you'll need simply to review the information already learned.

■ The value of hands-on experience cannot be stressed enough. Exam questions are based on test writers' experiences in the field. Working with the products on a regular basis—whether in your job environment or in a test network that you've set up at home—will make you much more comfortable with these questions.

■ Know your own learning style and use study methods that take advantage of it. If you're primarily a visual learner, reading, making diagrams, watching video files on CD, etc., may be your best study methods. If you're primarily auditory, classroom lectures, audiotapes you can play in the car as you drive, and repeating key concepts to yourself aloud may be more effective. If you're a kinesthetic learner, you'll need to actually *do* the exercises, implement the security measures on your own systems, and otherwise perform hands-on tasks to best absorb the information. Most of us can learn from all of these methods, but have a primary style that works best for us.

■ Although it may seem obvious, many exam-takers ignore the physical aspects of exam preparation. You are likely to score better if you've had sufficient sleep the night before the exam, and if you are not hungry, thirsty, hot/cold or otherwise distracted by physical discomfort. Eat prior to going to the testing center (but don't indulge in a huge meal that will leave you uncomfortable), stay away from alcohol for 24 hours prior to the test, and dress appropriately for the temperature in the testing center (if you don't know how hot/cold the testing environment tends to be, you may want to wear light clothes with a sweater or jacket that can be taken off).

■ Before you go to the testing center to take the exam, be sure to allow time to arrive on time, take care of any physical needs, and step back to take a deep breath and relax. Try to arrive slightly early, but not so far in advance that you spend a lot of time worrying and getting nervous about the testing process. You may want to do a quick last-minute review of notes, but don't try to "cram" everything the morning of the exam. Many test-takers find it helpful to take a short walk or do a few calisthenics shortly before the exam to get oxygen flowing to the brain.

- Before you begin to answer questions, use the pencil and paper provided to you to write down terms, concepts, and other items that you think you may have difficulty remembering as the exam goes on. Then you can refer back to these notes as you progress through the test. You won't have to worry about forgetting the concepts and terms you have trouble with later in the exam.

- Sometimes the information in a question will remind you of another concept or term that you might need in a later question. Use your pen and paper to make note of this in case it comes up later on the exam.

- It is often easier to discern the answer to scenario questions if you can visualize the situation. Use your pen and paper to draw a diagram of the network that is described to help you see the relationships between devices, IP addressing schemes, and so forth.

- When appropriate, review the answers you weren't sure of. However, you should change your answer only if you're sure that your original answer was incorrect. Experience has shown that more often than not, when test-takers start second-guessing their answers, they end up changing correct answers to the incorrect. Don't "read into" the question (that is, don't fill in or assume information that isn't there); this is a frequent cause of incorrect responses.

- As you go through this book, pay special attention to the Exam Warnings, as these highlight concepts that are likely to be tested. You may find it useful to go through and copy these into a notebook (remembering that writing something down reinforces your ability to remember it) and/or go through and review the Exam Warnings in each chapter just prior to taking the exam.

- Use as many little mnemonic tricks as possible to help you remember facts and concepts. For example, to remember which of the two IPsec protocols (AH and ESP) encrypts data for confidentiality, you can associate the "E" in encryption with the "E" in ESP.

Pedagogical Elements

In this book, you'll find a number of different types of sidebars and other elements designed to supplement the main text. These include the following:

- **Exam Warning** These sidebars focus on specific elements on which the reader needs to focus in order to pass the exam (for example, "Be sure you know the difference between symmetric and asymmetric encryption").

- **Test Day Tip** These sidebars are short tips that will help you in organizing and remembering information for the exam (for example, "When preparing for the exam on test day, it may be helpful to have a sheet with definitions of these abbreviations and acronyms handy for a quick last-minute review").

- **Configuring & Implementing** These sidebars contain background information that goes beyond what you need to know from the exam, but provide a "deep" foundation for understanding the concepts discussed in the text.

- **New & Noteworthy** These sidebars point out changes in Windows Server 2008 from Windows Server 2003 as they will apply to readers taking the exam. These may be elements that users of Windows Server 2003 would be very familiar with that have changed significantly in Windows Server 2008 or totally new features that they would not be familiar with at all.

- **Head of the Class** These sidebars are discussions of concepts and facts as they might be presented in the classroom, regarding issues and questions that most commonly are raised by students during study of a particular topic.

Each chapter of the book also includes hands-on exercises in planning and configuring the features discussed. It is essential that you read through and, if possible, perform the steps of these exercises to familiarize yourself with the processes they cover.

You will find a number of helpful elements at the end of each chapter. For example, each chapter contains a *Summary of Exam Objectives* that ties the topics discussed in that chapter to the published objectives. Each chapter also contains an *Exam Objectives Fast Track,* which boils all exam objectives down to manageable summaries that are perfect for last-minute review. *The Exam Objectives Frequently Asked Questions* section answers those questions that most often arise from readers and students regarding the topics covered in the chapter. Finally, in the *Self Test* section, you will find a set of practice questions written in a multiple-choice format that will assist you in your exam preparation These questions are designed to assess your mastery of the exam objectives and provide thorough remediation, as opposed to simulating the variety of question formats you may encounter in the actual exam. You can use the *Self Test Quick Answer Key* that follows the *Self Test* questions to quickly determine what information you need to review again. The *Self Test Appendix* at the end of the book provides detailed explanations of both the correct and incorrect answers.

Additional Resources

There are two other important exam preparation tools included with this study guide. One is the DVD included in the back of this book. The other is the concept review test available from our Web site.

- **A DVD that provides book content in multiple electronic formats for exam-day review** Review major concepts, test day tips, and exam warnings in PDF, PPT, MP3, and HTML formats. Here, you'll cut through all of the noise to prepare you for exactly what to expect when you take the exam for the first time. You will want to watch this DVD just before you head out to the testing center!

- **Web-based practice exams** Just visit us at **www.syngress.com/certification** to access a complete Windows Server 2008 concept multiple-choice review. These remediation tools are written to test you on all of the published certification objectives. The exam runs in both "live" and "practice" mode. Use "live" mode first to get an accurate gauge of your knowledge and skills, and then use practice mode to launch an extensive review of the questions that gave you trouble.

## Chapter 1

MCTS/MCITP
Exam 642

IP Addressing and Services

Exam objectives in this chapter:

- Configuring IPv4 and IPv6 Addressing
- Configuring Dynamic Host Configuration Protocol (DHCP)
- Configuring Network Authentication
- Configuring IP Security (IPsec)
- Windows Firewall with Advanced Security in Windows Server 2008

Exam objectives review:

- ☑ Summary of Exam Objectives
- ☑ Exam Objectives Fast Track
- ☑ Exam Objectives Frequently Asked Questions
- ☑ Self Test
- ☑ Self Test Quick Answer Key

Introduction

The Transmission Control Protocol/Internet Protocol (TCP/IP) is a suite of protocols used for communicating across a variety of networks. TCP/IP works well in part because it can send data across dissimilar network types. In this chapter, we'll look at how IP addressing is configured in the Windows Server 2008 environment and we'll also explore the related IP services. Much of the information in this chapter should be familiar to those of you who are already network administrators or who have experience with other Windows Server technologies.

We'll begin by reviewing IPv4 and IPv6 addressing fundamentals as they relate to setting up the network interface on a Windows Server 2008 computer. We'll walk through setting up DHCP as well as configuring network authentication, configuring IPsec, and configuring firewall settings. In each section, we'll cover the basics as well as highlight new features and new areas to focus on for the exam.

This chapter does assume you have a basic familiarity with IP addressing such as how to configure an IPv4 address using the dotted decimal notation and how to create a subnet using the subnet mask. If you're not familiar with these basics or if you're a bit rusty, we'll point you to some resources you can use to brush up on those much-needed networking skills.

Configuring IPv4 and IPv6 Addressing

Windows Server 2008 should install IPv4 and IPv6 by default so that you can configure them on the network interface card (NIC). If they're not already installed, you can install them from the Local Area Connection Properties dialog box. We'll briefly look at configuring IPv4 and IPv6 on the Windows Server 2008 NIC before heading into the DHCP configuration settings, where network IP settings are managed. Although we're assuming you're familiar with IPv4 and IPv6 to some extent, we've included Table 1.1 to give you a quick review of the differences between IPv4 and IPv6. If anything in this table is unfamiliar to you, please take some time out to revisit your IPv4 and IPv6 fundamentals.

TEST DAY TIP

The information in Table 1.1 is a great test day refresher. Even though the exam is not likely to quiz you on these specific details, expect to see a question or two on the exam that uses this information. Often you'll see several answers that are possibly correct and you'll need to have a solid understanding of the differences between IPv4 and IPv6 in order to determine the correct response.

Table 1.1 IPv4 and IPv6 Comparison

Category	IPv4	IPv6
Address length	32 bits	128 bits
Notation style	Four sets of three digits separated by a dot	Eight sets of four digits separated by a colon
Compression	If all three digits are zero, single zero is used	If all four digits are zero, a double colon is used
Types of addresses	Public, private, multicast	Global, local-use unicast, anycast
IPsec support	Optional	Required
Fragmentation	Done by hosts and routers	Done by hosts only
Error reporting and diagnostic	ICMP (for IPv4)	ICMPv6
Router discovery support	Optional	Required
Host configuration	DHCP or manual	Automatic, DHCP or manual
DNS record type for name resolution	A record	AAAA record
DNS record type and location for reverse name resolution	PTR records in IN-ADDR.ARPA domain	PTR records in IP6.ARPA domain

IPv4 Quick Review

You can skip this section if you're familiar with addressing in the IPv4 format. If not, this section will provide a very brief review. If it's not enough information for you, please refer to additional resources (some of which are mentioned throughout this chapter) to make sure you're comfortable with addressing in both schemas.

IPv4 typically uses three classes of network addresses—A, B, and C. A is for large networks (like the Internet), B is for medium networks, and C is for small networks. Each has a maximum number of network IDs and host IDs. In recent years as IP addresses became scarce, network address translation became popular. This method enables companies to use private IP addressing internally and then connect through an Internet Service Provider with a public IP address. This translation allows multiple companies to use the same internal IP addressing and it's only when traffic needs to cross the public network (the Internet) that addressing becomes important—so it gets translated to a unique public IP address for its trip to and from the Internet. Many smaller companies use the Class C 192.168.0.x range of private network addresses, though there are Class A and Class B private network addresses as well. Table 1.2 delineates the Class A, B, and C network ID boundaries along with network and host bits.

Table 1.2 IP Address Classes for IPv4 Networks

Class	Network Bits	Number of Networks	Host Bits	Maximum Number of Hosts
A	8	126	24	16,777,214
B	16	16,384	16	65,534
C	24	2,097,152	8	254

The subnet mask is used to indicate the network portion of an IP address. A subnet mask of 255.255.255.0 indicates that only the right-most eight bits (represented by the 0) are the host ID portion of the IP address, and the other 24 bits (represented by 255.255.255) are the network portion of the IP address. In this case, you have 1 through 254 as potential host IP addresses (i.e., 192.168.0.1 through 192.168.0.254). In many small companies, having 254 IP addresses for computers is more than enough. Many companies use the private network address space for addressing internal to their organization. This provides flexibility in addressing but requires the use of *network address translation*, so that the private IP addresses are translated into public IP addresses only when they cross your router to the Internet service provider's (ISP's) connection to the Internet. This network could be notated as 192.168.0.1/24, indicating the subnet mask or number of bits masked is 24. This style of notation, referred to as network/bits-masked notation is used in the Classless Inter-Domain Routing or CIDR. This same style of notation is used in IPv6 as well.

Configuring & Implementing…

Internet Protocol Basics

If you're not already familiar with IP addressing, you would do well to study this topic before taking the exam. IPv4 is the familiar IP addressing format with four octets. You've probably all seen 192.168.0.1, for example. IPv4 addresses require the use of a subnet mask and use four bytes (32 bits). IPv6 was developed because the world was running out of valid IP addresses under the IPv4 schema. IPv6 uses a different format than IPv4, but the underlying basics are similar, though there are significant differences between the two. IPv6 uses 16 bytes or 128 bits. There are a lot of great resources on IP addressing, but two of my favorites are www.learntosubnet.com and www.tcpipguide.com/free/t_toc.htm (this one unfortunately has a lot of pop up ads, but the information is solid). You can also get a quick refresher on the Microsoft Web site at http://support.microsoft.com/kb/164015. Of course, there are a lot of great books that discuss IP addressing if you really want to get in-depth knowledge in this area.

If you want to brush up on IPv6, you can read an overview article from Microsoft at http://technet2.microsoft.com/windowsserver/en/library/892c53fa-cf13-43d7-8086-11ab9ac1f0e81033.mspx or at http://download.microsoft.com/download/e/9/b/e9bd20d3-cc8d-4162-aa60-3aa3abc2b2e9/IPv6.doc. If you're brand new to IPv6, you might find this basic primer helpful, located on the Microsoft Web site at http://technet.microsoft.com/en-us/library/bb726944.aspx. There are a couple of others you might find helpful at www.windowsnetworking.com/articles tutorials/Crash-Course-IPv6-Part1.html and www.windowsnetworking.com/aritcles tutorials/Get-Ready-Run-IPv6.html to help you get up to speed on IPv6.

Keep in mind that because IPv6 is supported in Windows Server 2008, you can expect to see a lot of IPv6 types of questions. Even if your organization is not planning on going to IPv6 any time soon, you'll need to be familiar with the in's and out's of this protocol in order to successfully navigate the Windows Server 2008 exams.

Configuring Local IPv4 Settings

The Windows Server 2008 computer's network interface card can be configured with IPv4 and IPv6 addressing (see Exercise 1.1). As you know, you can access the computer's network settings in any one of several ways. Figure 1.1 shows the **Local Area Connection Properties** dialog box. IPv4 and IPv6 are both installed and enabled by default in Windows Server 2008 due to the implementation of **Next Generation TCP/IP stack**, which supports a dual IP stack sharing common transport and framing layers. If for some reason IPv6 is not installed and enabled on your Windows Server 2008 computer, you can install it by clicking the **Install** button and following the prompts.

Figure 1.1 Windows Server 2008 Local Area Connection Properties

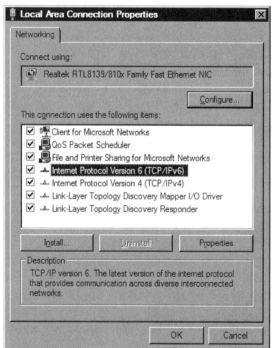

EXERCISE 1.1

CONFIGURING LOCAL IPv4 SETTINGS

To configure IPv4 settings, click to select **Internet Protocol Version 4 (TCP/IPv4)**, then click **Properties**. The **IPv4 Properties** dialog will open, as shown in Figure 1.2. For client computers, you'll typically select "Obtain an IP address automatically" so the client can utilize the DHCP server for dynamic addressing. In the case of a server, however, you typically choose a static IP address. We'll discuss creating a reservation within the DHCP server scope later in this chapter. You create a reservation on the DCHP server to ensure that the static IP address assigned to this server is not used by any other computer on the network. As you can see in this example, the server is manually configured to use 192.168.0.91 with a default gateway located at 192.168.0.2. The subnet mask for this network is 255.255.255.0, the standard subnet mask for a Class C private network address. You can also see that the primary and alternate DNS servers are located at 192.168.0.90 and 192.168.0.91, respectively. **Advanced** options allow you to configure additional DNS options as well as WINS servers, if needed. Click **OK** once you've configured your IPv4 settings.

Figure 1.2 IPv4 Configuration Settings

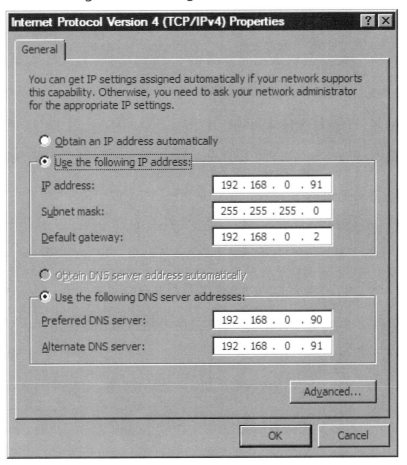

New & Noteworthy...

The Next Generation TCP/IP Stack

A full discussion of the changes to the TCP/IP implementation in Windows Server 2008 is outside the scope of this book but you might be interested in reading about this topic, especially if you plan on implementing IPv6 in your organization anytime soon. Microsoft's TechNet has an article located at www.microsoft.com/technet/community/columns/cableguy/cg0905.mspx that discusses the Next Generation TCP/IP Stack in Windows Vista and Windows Server 2008. There's also an article at www.microsoft.com/technet/community/columns/cableguy/cg1005.mspx that discusses the changes in TCP/IP in Windows Vista and Windows Server 2008. There are, of course, many other references on IPv6 but these are good to start with prior to the Windows Server 2008 exam.

Configuring IPv4 Options

In Windows Server 2008, you can use IPv4, IPv6, or a combination of the two. This is similar to Windows Server 2003, though in Windows Server 2008, IPv6 is enabled by default whereas in Windows Server 2003, you can add IPv6 if needed. Briefly, you should understand your network's physical and logical configuration if you're modifying IP address configurations, such as creating a new subnet. In addition, if you are implementing a new network altogether, you should take time to map out the physical and logical structure as well as create your IP addressing scheme. Planning in advance of implementation is crucial to avoid time-consuming errors. Each IPv4 host computer needs, at minimum, a host ID, a subnet mask, and a default gateway. You can also designate the preferred and alternate DNS server along with the WINS server, if used. Let's start with subnetting for IPv4 networks, since this is the most common IP option used.

Subnetting

IPv4 networks are divided into five types: A, B, C, D, and E though the commonly used are A, B, and C. This system is now referred to as *classful* networking because each range of IP addresses falls into one of these classes. Later implementations of

IPv4 and all implementations of IPv6 are considered *classless*, to distinguish them from this system. We'll discuss the classless system, known as *CIDR*, later in this chapter. Class A networks originally were intended for large organizations that had few networks but millions of hosts. Class C networks, on the other end of the spectrum, were designed for small companies that have perhaps a few hundred hosts. Class D networks are for IP multicast addresses and Class E addresses were not supported by Microsoft as late as Windows Server 2003. In Windows Server 2008, IPv4 and IPv6 are both supported; we'll discuss IPv6 later in this chapter.

Back to our discussion of classes. Class A addresses used 8 bits to define the network address and 24 bits to define host addresses. The left-most bit must be set to zero, so in practice, you can use only the right-most 7 bits of the left-most octet. If you're really good with binary and octal math, you know that there can be only 126 networks in the Class A category—total worldwide. A Class A network, however, can have 16,777,214 hosts in each network. Table 1.2, earlier in the chapter, shows the number of networks and hosts in each class of network.

As you can see, when you use 7 bits for the network ID in Class A, it yields only 126 possible network addresses, but millions of host IDs. When you use 8 bits for the *host* ID, it yields only 254 host IDs. If you recall, there are rules about the use of all ones or all zeros; it explains the discrepancy between the number of IDs and the number of bits used in the right-most and left-most segments of the IPv4 address. There are five rules you have to follow when enumerating IPv4 addresses:

- All bits in the host ID cannot be set to 1. That's reserved for broadcast addresses.

- All bits in the host ID cannot be set to 0. That's reserved for IP network IDs.

- Class A network IDs must have 0 as the left-most bit.

- Class B network IDs must have 10 as the two left-most bits.

- Class C network IDs must have 110 as the three left-most bits.

The host ID must be unique to the network. It makes sense that you can have two IP addresses that are the same only if they are on different networks that never talk to one another. Otherwise, there'd be no way to differentiate between two hosts.

With the increasing popularity of computer networking, at some point it became clear that the world would run out of valid IP addresses. As you can see from Table 1.2, there are only 16,384 possible Class B networks worldwide and there are only 2,097,152 Class C network IDs available. So, there are just over 2.1 million network IDs available and it's not hard to estimate there are far more networks than that in the world. As the number of available IP addresses decreased, private network addressing and network address translation grew in popularity and use.

Today many companies are using private IP addresses internally, then using Network Address Translation (NAT) when communicating across a public network (the Internet). The benefit of NAT is that you can use an internal addressing scheme that suits your company and network traffic cannot be routed outside the network unless it's translated into a public address. Internet service provider's routers will simply discard packets with private IP addresses. In our examples, we'll use the private IP range of 192.168.0.1 through 192.168.0.254 for illustration, but you can utilize any of the private address ranges, which are:

- 10.0.0.0 to 10.255.255.255

- 172.16.0.1 to 172.31.255.255

- 192.168.0.1 to 192.168.255.255

Private network addresses still come in Class A, B, and C flavors, but Company 1 can use a Class B private network address and so can Company 2, 3, 4....*n*. These addresses are not passed through routers heading out to the Internet; instead, they are translated into a public IP address, typically provided by the ISP. This provides a lot of flexibility in terms of addressing for companies and ISPs. In addition, CIDR was introduced, which was a step toward the classless system used in IPv6. More on CIDR later in this chapter.

If you choose to use private network addressing for your network, you will also need to have an ISP provide you with a public IP address and you'll need to utilize either a Proxy Server or NAT Router so that your private addressing can be routed out of the network to the Internet.

Head of the Class...

Subnetting and Active Directory

This chapter doesn't cover Active Directory (AD), but it's important to understand that subnets are assigned to sites through the AD interface. A subnet can belong to only one site; a site can contain more than one subnet. Here's the quick way to create a subnet in Active Directory. Remember, though, that this is different than setting up DHCP options, which we'll discuss later in this chapter.

In Active Directory Sites and Services, shown in Figure 1.3, right-click the **Subnets** icon in the console tree and select **New Subnet** from the menu. The New Object Subnet dialog box is displayed. Enter the address prefix using network prefix notation (address/prefix length). You can enter either IPv4 or IPv6 subnet notation. The dialog box gives two examples—one of IPv4 and one of IPv6—along with a text box into which you can enter the prefix. For example, you might enter 192.168.7.0/24. Select the site with which the subnet should be associated, then click **OK** to apply the change and create a new subnet. When reading an exam question related to subnets, be sure to understand the context so you can decide whether you need to look at AD or DHCP for the answer.

Figure 1.3 Active Directory Sites and Services Console

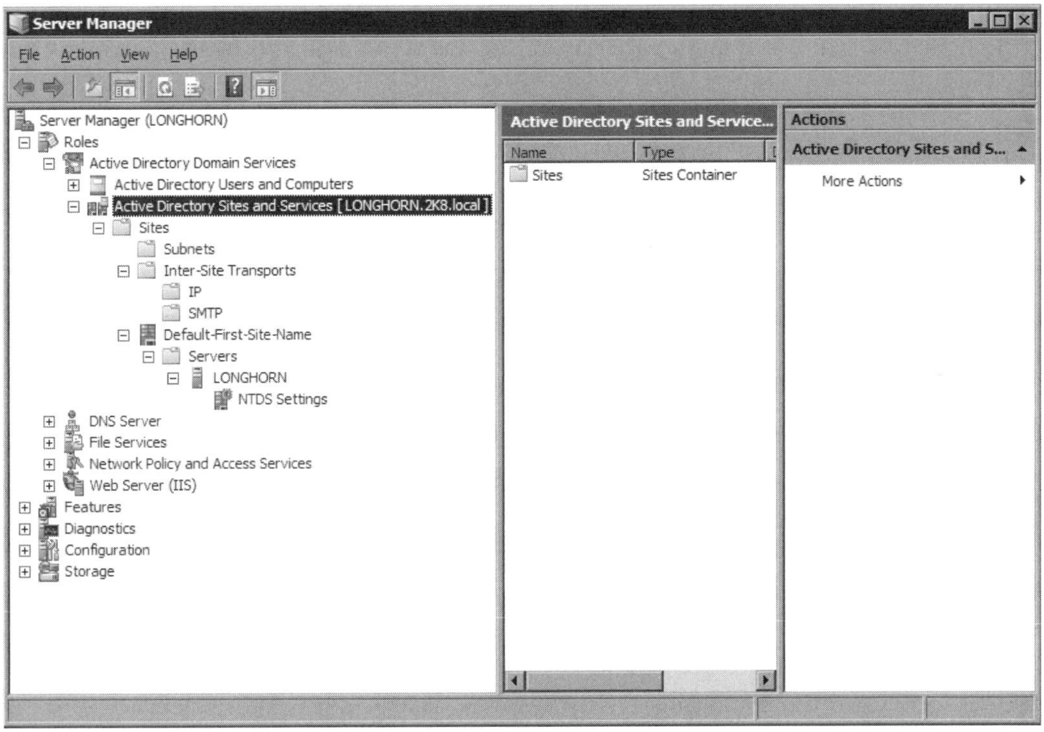

TEST DAY TIP

Remember that subnets are assigned to sites via Active Directory Sites and Services console whereas subnetting options are set up in the DHCP Server role. Also remember that subnets can easily be moved to different sites within the AD Sites and Services console simply by double-clicking the subnet in the Subnets folder and changing the site association in the Site selection list on the General tab. Changing the Site may impact other settings, so clearly you should have a plan in place before modifying these kinds of settings.

Supernetting

Another IP innovation that was developed prior to the implementation of IPv6 is supernetting. Supernetting is the combining of several smaller Class C networks into one larger network in order to accommodate the need for a network larger than Class C but not as large as a Class B. It is, in essence, the opposite of subnetting. This is also called *Classless Inter-Domain Routing* (CIDR) and is used to express a range of Class C networks at a single route. A super-netted subnet mask contains fewer network ID bits than a standard IPv4 subnet mask. CIDR sometimes is thought of as a group or range of Class C networks, but with the introduction of IPv6, CIDR is perhaps more fittingly viewed as an address space in which multiple classful networks are combined into a single, classless network.

If you consider a supernet as a range of Class C network IDs, you can easily understand supernetting. In order to create a supernet, you must have contiguous Class C network IDs (i.e., they must be sequential) and the number of Class C network IDs must be expressed as a power of 2 (due to the use of weighted binary in IPv4 addressing). Typically, a subnet mask for a Class C network would be 255.255.255.0 or it could be notated as the network ID with /24 indicating that 24 bits were used for the network ID.

Again, we're assuming you have a basic understanding of IP addressing including subnetting and supernetting—we're providing this information as a basic review for you. The Windows Server 2008 exam is likely to focus less on IPv4 than on the coexistence of IPv4 and IPv6 in the enterprise, so that's where your focus should be. Understanding the evolution of IPv4 helps you understand the new features of IPv6.

Alternative Configuration

Automatic alternate configuration is an enhancement to TCP/IP that allows for a valid static IP address configuration on DHCP configured machines. Without an alternate configuration defined, a computer that is unable to obtain an IP address lease from a DHCP server would automatically receive an Automatic Private IP Address (APIPA) from the 169.254.0.0/16 pool. If you're troubleshooting network connectivity (or answering a question about network connectivity on the exam) and you see that an address in this range has been assigned, it indicates the host was unable to obtain a valid IP lease. When answering questions about IP addressing on the exam, always think through the address provided and what the implications of that address might be.

Internet Protocol Version 6 (IPv6)

A discussion of IPv6 could take up an entire chapter and the focus of this chapter is configuring IPv6, so we're working on the assumption you have some familiarity with IPv6. That said, we'll spend just a bit of time here reviewing some of the basics to give you a quick refresher. If you're fully up to speed on IPv6, feel free to skip this section. If there are any concepts you're not familiar with, you should do additional research to fill in any gaps. Earlier in the chapter, we provided several links to resources you might want to look at it improve your IPv6 skills if you're not already conversant with the IPv6 addressing requirements.

IPv6 Address Format

As you know, IPv6 provides an alternative to the shortage of IPv4 addresses. As such, it uses 128 bits instead of the 32 bits used in IPv4. This enables 75 trillion trillion (yes, two *trillions* follow the number 75) potential unique IP addresses (or 2^{96}). Much of the newer hardware and software now supports IPv6 addressing (IPv6 has been around a while) but you can't simply plug in IPv6 equipment and expect everything to work. There are numerous transition technologies available, a full discussion of which is outside the scope of this chapter.

Typically, the IPv6 address is divided in half—64 bits for the network component and 64 bits for the host component. However, the IPv6 addressing format also used the CIDR notation, so that an address might look like this: 2424:DC8:4138::/48 indicating that the network is identified using 48 bits.

Each section of an IPv6 address is four digits, which are in hexadecimal format. That means that numbers can range from zero to F (0–F) in each place. F in hexadecimal is 15 and numbers 0 through F produces 16 numbers (hence the term hexadecimal).

There are eight groups of numbers and hypothetically, each can range from 0000 to FFFF (as with IPv4 addressing, there are rules about zeros and ones that we won't go into at the moment). Thus, an example of an IPv6 address is 4F5C:0000:0000:0000: BA59:093C:D102:4612. You can omit leading zeros and consecutive groups of zeros. When you omit groups of zeros, you use a double colon (::) notation. To determine how many groups of zeroes were omitted, you simply count the number of groups and subtract from eight. Thus, the address 4F5C:0000:0000:0000:BA59:093C:D102:4612 can be represented as 4F5C::BA59:93C:D102:4612.

IPv6 Address Types

Briefly, there are several types of IPv6 addresses. If you're not familiar with these, you'll need to do a bit of independent reading to fill in the gaps.

- **Local-link addresses**. Addresses that are accessible only on the local network segment.

- **Unique local IPv6 unicast addresses**. Routable on your network but not accessible from the Internet.

- **Global unicast addresses**. Addresses that can be routed on the IPv6 Internet (a portion of the Internet that uses IPv6).

- **Multicast addresses**. Single host can communicate with multiple recipients.

- **Anycast addresses**. Addresses that can be assigned to multiple interfaces, such as assigning a single IPv6 address to a multihomed computer.

- **Special addresses**. Includes special purpose addresses like loopback and others.

A **local link address** is used like a private address in IPv4. As such, it is not routable because the network prefix is always the same. In IPv6, the first left-most 10 digits are always 1111 1110 10. The next 54 bits are always 0. This comprises the 64-bit unroutable network ID. The right-most 64 bits are the host portion of the address. Thus, the local-link address is written as FE80::/64. If you run the **ipconfig /all** command from the command line on a Windows Server 2008 computer, you'll see the local link address listed.

Global addresses are like IPv4 public addresses and are routable across the Internet. The first three bits of a global address are 001, the next 45 bits are used for the global routing prefix, followed by 16 bits for the subnet ID. The remaining 64 bits identify the host segment of the address. This creates an address prefix notated in this way: 2000::/3.

A few of the **special addresses** include the following:

- **::1/128** (or just ::1). Local loopback address, refers to the local computer.

- **::FFFF:0:0/96**. Prefix used for IPv4 mapped addresses.

- **2002::/16**. Used for 6to4 addressing (discussed later in this section).

- **FE80::/64**. A local-link address. Seeing this address assigned to an interface indicates there was no DHCPv6 server available.

Note that almost all hosts can self-configure IPv6 local-link addresses themselves without contacting a DHCP server (or other infrastructure component), but additional configuration information is required for unique local addresses, global addresses, and other address types and that information typically does come from the DHCP server or other infrastructure component. IPv4 clients will look for a local DHCP server when they start up. By contrast, IPv6 clients will try to get address information from a router and perform a DHCP query only if instructed by the router to perform a stateful configuration.

IPv6 Autoconfiguration Options

Depending on how your IPv6 routers are set up, autoconfiguration of an IPv6 client can happen in three ways: stateless, stateful, and both. In *stateless* mode, an IPv6 client configures its own IPv6 address by using IPv6 Router Advertisements. In *stateful* mode, an IPv6 client will get its addressing information from a DHCPv6 server when it receives Router Advertisement messages with no prefix options (and when certain other conditions are met). This also occurs if no IPv6 routers are available. The *both* option uses stateful and stateless together. The most common example of this is an IPv6 client using stateless autoconfiguration to obtain an IPv6 address and using stateful autoconfiguration to get DNS and other IP configuration information from a DHCPv6 server.

In addition, addresses can be nontemporary (the equivalent of static IP addresses in IPv4) or temporary. Routers, gateways, and other devices may need these types of addresses and, just as with IPv4, you can allow a host to autoconfigure or you can manually set up the IPv6 addressing.

IPv6 Transition Technologies

Since the transition to IPv6 won't happen overnight (or even anytime soon), there are numerous ways companies can transition to IPv6. For more information, you can visit the Microsoft Web site and query the title "IPv6 Transition Technologies" for more information.

- **Dual IP Layer architecture**. Allows computers to communicate using both IPv6 and IPv4. This is required for ISATAP and Teredo hosts and for 6to4 routers.

- **IPv6 over IPv4 tunneling**. Places IPv6 packet data inside of an IPv4 header with an IP Protocol value of 41. This tunneling technique is used with ISATAP or 6to4.

- **Intra–Site Automatic Tunnel Addressing Protocol (ISATAP)**. Allows IPv6 hosts to use IPv6 over IPv4 tunneling to communicate on intranets.

- **6to4**. Allows IPv6 hosts to communicate with the IPv6 Internet. A 6to4 router with a public IPv4 address is required.

- **Teredo**. Allows IPv4/IPv6 hosts to communicate with the IPv6 Internet even if they are behind a network address translator (NAT).

Head of the Class…

Rolling Out IPv6

As you can imagine, it's a major job to roll out IPv6 in an organization. Windows Server 2008 and Windows Vista natively understand IPv6, but older operating systems, software programs, and hardware devices may not. Before you decide to run with IPv6, set up a test lab, configure it to use IPv6 and test your hardware, software, routers, and other network infrastructure in a closed environment. If you roll it out into a live environment, you are all but guaranteed that something will not work as expected. There are numerous tools available via the Microsoft Web site (and others) that will help you plan, assess, and manage your transition.

Configuring IPv6 Settings

When you access the local area connection properties of the Windows Server 2008 computer, you also have the option of configuring IPv6 settings if IPv6 is installed (it is installed by default in Windows Server 2008, so it should be there). You should be able to access IPv6 settings from the **Local Area Connection Properties** dialog box. If IPv6 is not shown, the protocol is not installed. Click the **Install** button and follow the on-screen prompts to install IPv6. Then, access the Local Area Connection Properties to configure the settings.

In the **Local Area Connection Properties** dialog box, shown in Figure 1.1 you can configure IPv6 addressing options by selecting Internet Protocol Version 6 (IPv6) and clicking **Properties**. The IPv6 Properties dialog box will open, as shown in Figure 1.4.

Figure 1.4 IPv6 Properties and Address Configuration

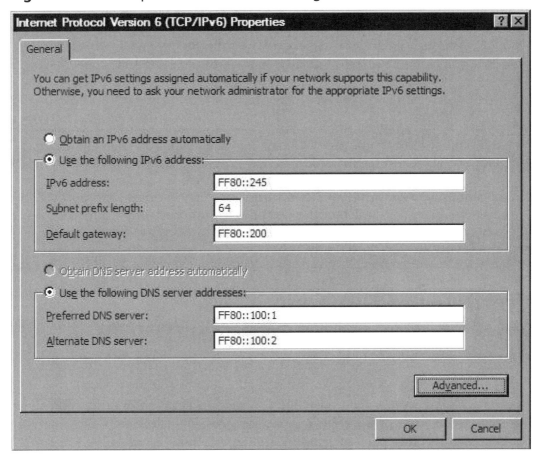

As with IPv4, you would typically allow host computers to obtain an IPv6 address automatically from the DHCP server. However, since this computer is a server, you may want to assign a *nontemporary* IP address to it (recall that nontemporary is the IPv6 equivalent of a static IP address in IPv4). If you choose to use a nontemporary address, you could click the radio button next to "Use the following IPv6 address:"

and enter the specifics. Also remember that if you set a nontemporary IP address here, you should create a reservation for this address in the DHCP server so that this address does not get assigned to another computer on the network. Best practices typically include creating your DHCP server scope and reservations before activating the DHCP server, then activating the DHCP server and assigning nontemporary (and static) IP addresses. This helps avoid potential problems with IP address assignments.

Let's look at how to configure IPv4 and IPv6 options in DHCP in Windows Server 2008. We're assuming you've enabled the DHCP Server role from within the Windows Server 2008 management console. If not, do so now but keep in mind that you want to do this on a test network or in a lab setting. As you know, activating more than one DHCP server on a network can cause the whole thing to crash, so be sure you're not connected in a way that will cause real-world problems.

EXAM WARNING

Be familiar with IP notation in both IPv4 and IPv6. You're likely to see more on IPv6 and transitioning to IPv6 than on standard IPv4 notation. If you're not up to speed on IPv6, you might want to take some time to thoroughly understand IPv6 and transition technologies before heading into the exam. The Microsoft exams pull questions from a pool of possible questions, so you might not see any questions in this topic area, but if you do, you'll be ready.

Configuring Dynamic Host Configuration Protocol (DHCP)

Dynamic Host Configuration Protocol (DHCP) allows DHCP servers to assign (lease) IP addresses to computers (hosts) and other devices on the network that are enabled as DHCP clients. We're assuming you have a solid foundation in DHCP, but we'll discuss some of the basics in this section as a quick review.

DHCP servers have pools of addresses defined, called scopes, which are handed out to (leased) DHCP clients on the network. The configuration information provided by the DHCP server to the DHCP client includes the IP address, subnet mask, default gateway, DNS server(s), WINS server(s) if any, and other options. The DHCP client will attempt to renew its IP address about halfway through the lease duration. If the DHCP server is online when that occurs, the renewal typically goes through and the lease period restarts. If the DHCP server is not online at the time of the lease renewal request, the client will continue to try to renew its lease periodically. If the lease is not renewed when 87.5% of the lease period has elapsed, the client will start looking for another DHCP server to provide the IP address. This may mean the client receives a new IP address or new configuration information based on the configuration of the new DHCP server it uses.

EXAM WARNING

Questions about DHCP on the exam will likely fall into one of three types—DHCP server questions, DHCP relay agent questions, and DHCP lease questions. DHCP servers should be highly available so you should have more than one on a network and you should try to avoid having clients get IP addresses from a DHCP server across a WAN link. Keep in mind that if you have more than one DHCP server per subnet, you must ensure the scopes are configured properly to avoid overlap and IP addressing issues. Look for questions with that type of scenario. DHCP relay agents should be configured on each network segment that does not have a DHCP server. This enables DHCP clients to contact DHCP servers on other network segments to obtain IP configuration data. Remember, the DHCP relay agent doesn't provide the lease, it simply forwards DHCP traffic to facilitate in the lease process. DHCP relay agents are typically routers on the network. Finally, lease duration questions might pop up and here's why. The longer the DHCP lease duration, the less DHCP traffic on the network. That's good. However, the longer the DHCP lease duration, the more likely it is that unused or inactive computers will hold onto IP addresses. That's bad. So, if your network is comprised largely of desktop computers, go for a longer lease period. If it's mostly mobile users with laptops coming on- and offline, set the duration lower to make better use of your IP addresses.

The short version of deploying DHCP is this: add the role, configure the scopes, options, and exclusions, then authorize the DHCP server. Configure routers as DHCP relay agents as needed. OK, now that we've got that all laid out, let's step through it in a bit more detail.

Adding the DHCP Server Role

DHCP is managed by the DHCP Server role in Windows Server 2008, as it was in Windows Server 2003. Once you've installed Windows Server 2008, you can select various roles to install on that computer, and DHCP is one. Install the role from the Server Manager interface (**Start | Server Manager**) or from the command line. We'll go over command line options later in this section. You can add the DHCP role to the server, but keep in mind that you should have a well thought out DHCP deployment plan before installing the DHCP server role on any computer. Scopes, reservations, and exclusions also should be planned out and set up on all DHCP servers before activating them so they don't overlap and accidentally assign identical IP addresses to different hosts on the network. You can see that the DHCP role in the Server Manager console, shown in Figure 1.5, includes both IPv4 and IPv6 configuration and options. Note that there are server options that can be configured at the DHCP Server level (click DHCP Server in the left pane and choose **Action** from the menu or **More Actions** from the right pane) or at the scope or reservation level. In Figure 1.5, we're looking at server-level options. We'll look at scope options in a moment.

Figure 1.5 DHCP Server Role with IPv4 and IPv6 Options

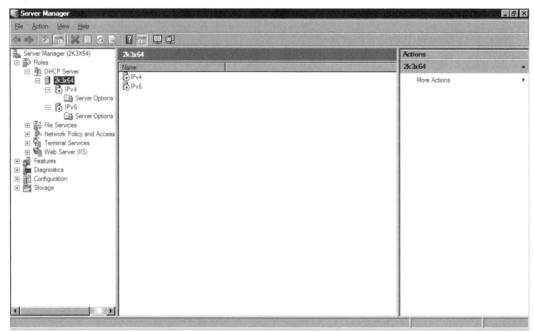

After you install the DHCP server role, you need to configure the DHCP settings. In the sections that follow, we'll look at:

- Scopes
- Scope options
- Creating new options
- Reservations

- Exclusions
- Authorizing the DHCP server

Notice that the server isn't authorized on the AD domain until it's been properly configured. Adding a DHCP server to the AD domain with improper configuration will likely cause massive problems on the network, so *configure*, *activate*, and *authorize*, in that order. We'll step through IPv4 first, then go back and step through IPv6 settings afterward. The reason for this is that when you're walking through the set up screens on the DHCP server, you set up all the IPv4 options at once. Of course, you can always go back in and modify settings but it will make more sense to walk through IPv4 completely and then step through IPv6.

Configuring DHCP Scopes

Scopes are groups of IPv4 or IPv6 addresses that can be dynamically assigned to hosts on the network. You can also assign *static* IPv4 addresses for servers, routers, and other network devices that require a permanent IP address, *nontemporary* addresses in IPv6 addressing space. Every subnet for which a DHCP server provides IP address configuration information, including remote subnets using a DHCP relay agent, must have a DHCP scope configured.

Scopes are created to specify IP address ranges available for lease by DHCP clients. For example, you could create a scope called Main Office and assign a range of addresses from 192.168.15.2 to 192.168.15.200. Any device on the Main Office network will contact the DHCP server and be assigned an IP address within that range. Note that scopes can use public or private IPv4 addresses.

A DHCP server can manage multiple scopes, which can be used for various purposes. In addition, there are three types of scopes with IPv4 addresses you can use:

- **Normal**. Normal scopes are ranges of IPv4 address pools from Class A, B or C networks.
- **Multicast**. Multicast IPv4 addresses are defined as Class D networks and are reserved for multicast traffic.
- **Superscopes**. Superscopes are essentially buckets into which you can put scopes to better manage groups of scopes.

Configuring IPv4 Scopes and Options

You're probably familiar with the basic configuration of IPv4 addressing in a DHCP server, so configuring DHCP IPv4 in Windows Server 2008 will be easy for you. Let's take a quick look at how to configure the scope and options in the IPv4 section of DHCP.

To configure IPv4 within DHCP, open the Server Manager console and click **DHCP Server**. Click **IPv4** in the left pane, then click **Action** from the menu and select **New Scope**. This initiates the New Scope Wizard. The first screen is the Welcome screen; click **Next**. The second step is to define the IP address range for the scope, as shown in Figure 1.6, where the private address range of 192.168.10.1 through 192.168.10.254 is shown. The subnet mask was calculated automatically for the range by the operating system and the suggested length of 24 bits with a subnet mask of 255.255.255.0 is the default and can be used. You can change this here or click **Next** to continue.

Figure 1.6 Creating a New DHCP IPv4 Scope

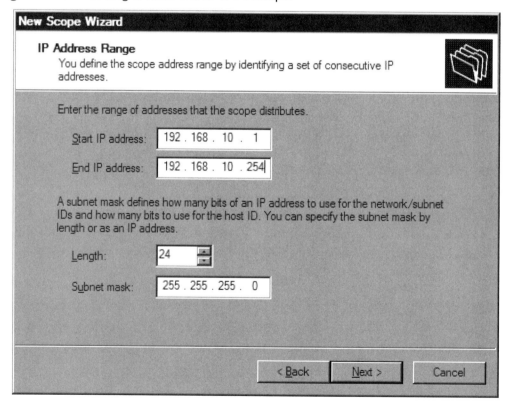

In the third screen, you can add exclusions. Ranges of IP addresses typically are excluded so that static IP addresses can be assigned to devices such as servers, routers, or printers that may require a static IP address. In Figure 1.7, you can see that two ranges have been excluded: 192.168.10.10 to 192.168.10.20 and 192.168.10.100 to

192.168.10.120. Addresses within these ranges will not be assigned automatically to dynamic DHCP clients. When you've completed entering any exclusions, click **Next**.

Figure 1.7 Excluded DHCP IPv4 Ranges

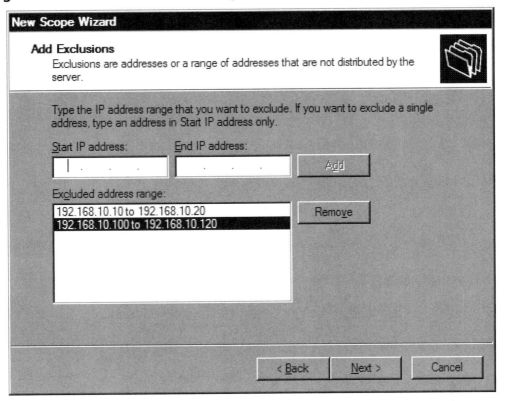

The next screen is the lease duration. This should be relatively short for networks that have a lot of mobile clients and relatively long for networks with mostly stable clients (desktops, etc.). If you have a mixture, a lease duration of two to four days might make the most sense. The default value is eight days and we'll leave it at the default for this example. The lease duration screen is self-explanatory and is not shown here.

After you've selected the lease duration, click **Next** to continue to the following screen where you can configure DHCP options. You can choose to set these now or later; we'll go through them later in the DHCP section. Click the radio button next to "No, I will configure these options later" then click **Next** and then **Finish**. Remember that before any clients can receive addresses from this DHCP server, you need to add any scope-specific options (which includes default gateway, among other things) and you need to activate the scope.

DHCP IPv4 Reservations

To reserve an address, you create a reservation and specify the Media Access Control (MAC) address of the host. This permanently reserves the designated IPv4 address for that MAC address. As you can see from Figure 1.8, this is a very straightforward process. Remember to set the IP address on the device to match this reservation. If the device is set to obtain an IP address automatically, it will be dynamically assigned an IP address that will not match the reservation. As you can imagine, this can cause problems on the network if static routes have been defined or if computers on the network are looking for a server at a specific IP address.

Figure 1.8 DHCP IPv4 Reservation

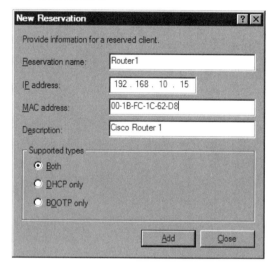

Configuring DHCP Scope Options

Before you can activate the scope, you need to set the scope options. Though we chose not to do this during the previous scope configuration, in the real world, you would most likely choose to set up the options at the same time you create the scope. We elected not to so that you can see how the scope options look in Server Manager. Keep in mind that there are three types of DHCP options—server, scope, and reservation, as shown in Figure 1.9.

Server Options

Server options are those set for the DHCP server. These options apply to all clients that use this DHCP server. Values set here apply to all scopes managed by this server.

These values can be overridden if those values are set at either a scope, options class, or reserved client level.

Scope Options

As the name implies, scope options are those set just for a particular defined scope on the DHCP server. Values set here can be overridden by values set at either an options class or reserved client level. We'll discuss scope options in more detail in a moment.

Reservation Options

Options set here are specific to a client reservation (reserved client level). Though it seems obvious, you must first add a reservation before you can configure options. Only properties manually configured at the client computer can override options assigned at this level.

When using any of the option configuration dialog boxes (Server Options, Scope Options, or Reservation Options), you can click the **Advanced** tab to set options for assignment to identifying member clients of a specified user class or vendor class. The available options are dependent upon whether you're configuring server, scope, or reservation options.

Figure 1.9 DHCP Server IPv4 Options

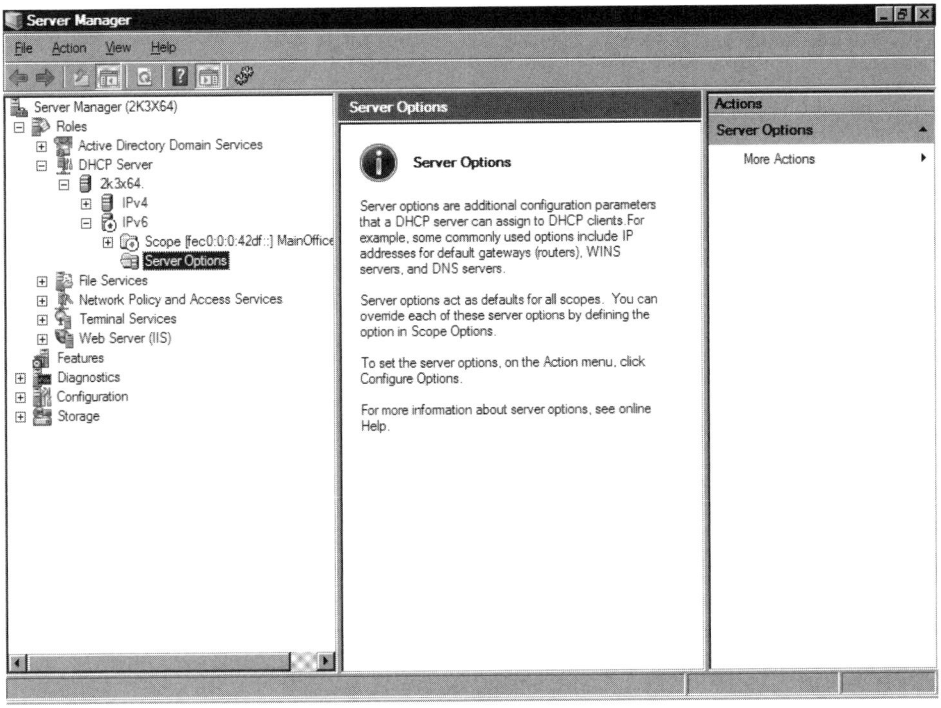

Setting Scope Options

To set up scope options, select the scope you want to configure, click **Scope Options** in the left pane, then click **Action | Scope Options** from the Server Manager menu.

To set an option, select it from the Available Options by clicking the checkbox to the left of the option. A brief description is shown to the right of each option. When you click an option, the data entry elements below are enabled and you can enter the server name and IP address. There is a long list of scope options that can be set here. A list and brief description of these is included in Table 1.3. You can also click the **Advanced** tab to select more advanced DHCP scope options. The Vendor class options include DHCP Standard Options, Microsoft Options, Microsoft Windows 2000 Options, and Microsoft Windows 98 Options. In addition to Vendor class options, you can select from among various user class options. These are Default BOOTP Class, Default Network Access Protection Class, Default Routing and Remote Access Class, and Default User Class. The data options beneath the Available Options section change depending on the option selected. These options should be modified only if you have a specific need to do so. In most cases, the default scope options are adequate.

Table 1.3 Scope Options List

Option Name	Settings	Notes
Router/Default Gateway	IP address	Identifies the default gateway for clients within this DHCP scope.
Domain Name and DNS Server	Parent domain, server name, IP address	Identifies the parent domain, the DNS server name, and IP address for clients within this DHCP scope.
WINS Node Type	Node type	The preferred NetBIOS name resolution method for the DHCP client to use such as b-mode for broadcast only or h-node for hybrid.
WINS Server(s)	Server name, IP address	If you have clients within the network that require the use of WINS name resolution, you should define your WINS server(s) here. This will be added to the DHCP option information provided to DHCP clients within this scope. A primary and secondary WINS server can be specified.

Most of the scope options available in Windows Server 2008 are the same as they were in Windows Server 2003. However, there are a lot of options available and if you're not familiar with these options, you can visit the Microsoft Web site to review details of each option to determine whether any of these more advanced options are appropriate for your network. Head up to http://technet2.microsoft. com/windowsserver/en/library/7f9261b1-92ef-40aa-a3b6-1dd9ab97c46e1033. mspx for more details.

Configuring IPv6 Scopes

As you know, IPv6 provides far more addresses than IPv4. Many firms use Network Address Translation so they can utilize private IP addressing on their local networks and then use public IP addresses to connect to the Internet. IPv6 can be used in a similar manner—it has both global and local IP addresses that correspond to public and private IP addresses. Site local addresses begin with FFE0, local link addresses begin with FE80. These can be used internally and are not routed by ISPs to the public domain.

Just as with IPv4 scopes in DHCP, the scope options for IPv6 are accessed through the Server Manager. Click **Server Manager | Roles | DHCP Server | IPv6** to configure IPv6 options. Click **IPv6** and then click **Action | New Scope** from the Server Manager menu. Like the IPv4 scope configuration process, this launches the New Scope Wizard. Click **Next** to continue from the Welcome screen. The next screen prompts you to type a name and description of the scope. Using a descriptive name and short description will help you keep your scopes organized. Click **Next** after entering the name and description. The following screen, shown in Figure 1.10, prompts you to enter the **Scope Prefix** as well as a **Preference** value for the scope. The CIDR notation is, by default, /64 and is provided by Windows automatically. In IPv6, note that /64 is a subnet identifier, /48 is a route identifier, and /8 is an address range.

Figure 1.10 DHCP IPv6 Scope Prefix Dialog Box

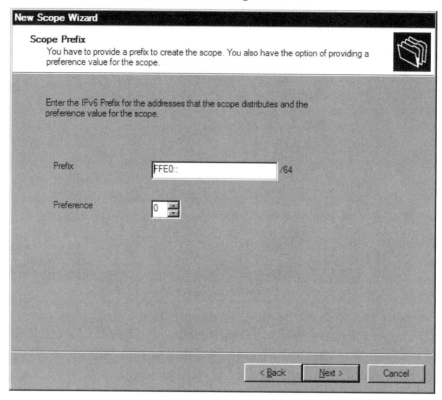

The preference value is optional and it sets the preference for a particular scope, meaning addresses will be assigned from the scope with the lowest preference first. This is an optional setting. Unless you're sure how to use this feature, leave the default value at 0.

When you've completed entering your scope data, click **Next** to access the **Add Exclusions** screen. As with the IPv4 wizard, you are prompted to enter the start and end IPv6 address for exclusions. When you've entered the range to exclude, click **Add** to add that range of addresses to the exclusions. If you want to remove an excluded range, select it and click **Remove**. When you're finished configuring exclusions, click **Next**. In the following screen, the **Scope Lease** screen, you're prompted to configure both temporary and nontemporary scope leases, as shown in Figure 1.11. As with IPv4 address leases, best practices include setting the lease duration equal to the average time a computer is connected to the same physical network. If you have a large number of mobile users, set the lease time to a shorter duration.

Figure 1.11 DHCP IPv6 Scope Lease Settings

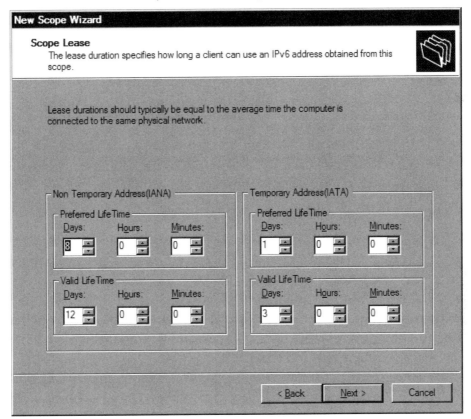

When you've completed setting the temporary and nontemporary lease duration settings, click **Next** to complete the scope configuration. The settings you've selected are recapped for you and if you've made a mistake, you can click **Back** to change them now. You can also choose to activate the scope at this point by selecting **Yes**. The scope is not available for leasing until the scope is activated, but if you want to configure all your scopes before activating, you can click **No** and come back and activate this scope later. We'll select **No** so you can see what it looks like when a scope is not yet activated. To activate the scope, click on the scope and choose **Action | Activate** from the Server Manager menu. The scope is activated and its status changes from inactive to active. You can deactivate the scope by clicking the scope and selecting **Action | Deactivate** from the menu. If you try to deactivate an active scope, you'll get a warning message reminding you that if you deactivate an active scope, clients will be unable to obtain a lease from that range of IP addresses.

Configuring IPv6 Scope Options

The options available in the IPv6 scope settings are different than those available in the IPv4 options section. When you select an IPv6 scope and click **Scope Options**, you can select from among numerous options listed here:

1. SIP Server Domain Name List
2. SIP Servers IPV6 Address List
3. DNS Recursive Name Server IPV6 Address List
4. Domain Search List
5. NIS IPV6 Address List
6. NIS+ IPV6 Address List
7. NIS Domain List
8. NIS+ Domain Name List
9. SNTP Servers IPv6 Address List

SIP stands for Session Initiation Protocol and a SIP server is an outbound proxy server. See the IEFT draft on SIP and DHCPv6 for more information (www3. tools.ietf.org/html/draft-ietf-sip-dhcpv6-01).

NIS stands for Network Information Service (and Network Information Service Plus, NIS+). You can read more about the NIS RFC specification at www. faqs.org/rfcs/rfc3898.html, where they discuss DHCP configuration options NIS, NIS+, NIS Domain List, and NIS+ Domain List.

As with the IPv4 options, you can configure individual options by clicking the checkbox to the left of the option in the Available Options section, then entering the specific data in the data entry section. The Advanced tab contains the same Vendor class and User class options as the IPv4 scope options dialog box and those options were previously described. Refer back to the section on Advanced IPv4 scope options for details on these options. When you're finished configuring scope options, click **OK**.

DHCP IPv6 Client Reservation Configuration

The client reservation configuration for IPv6 is very similar to the IPv4 configuration, though you have a few different options, as shown in Figure 1.12. The DUID is the device unique identifier, which in more common language is the device's MAC address. You can find the MAC address by opening a command prompt (**Start | Run | cmd**) on the client computer and typing in **ipconfig /all**.

The IAID is the *identity association identifier* that sets a unique identifier prefix for the client computer. This is typically a 9-digit value. The description is just a short description to help you identify the device. When you've configured the reservation, click **Add**.

Figure 1.12 DHCP IPv6 Client Reservation Configuration Options

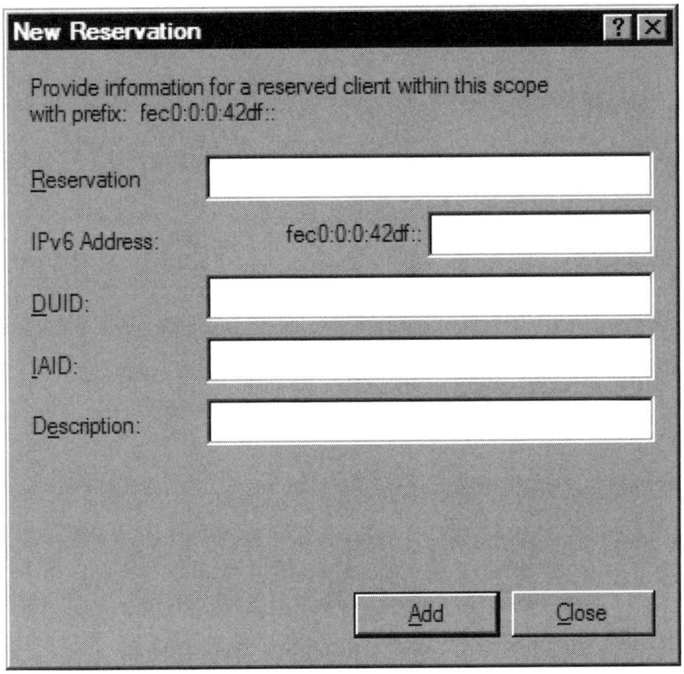

Creating New Options

You can create new options in DHCP through the interface or through the command line. Add or define new custom option types only if you have new software or applications that require a nonstandard DHCP option. There are vendor-defined classes, which are used to manage DHCP options assigned to clients by vendor type, and there are user-defined classes, which are used to manage DHCP options assigned to clients by a common need for similar DHCP configuration information. Note that after defining a new option class, you must configure your individual scopes with any class-related options that need to be provided to DHCP clients.

New Options Using the Windows Interface

Right-click the DHCP server in the left pane of Server Manager and select New User Class or New Vendor Class from the shortcut menu. Once you configure the new class, you can open the selected scope; right-click and choose **Scope Options** then **Configure Scope Options**. Click **Advanced** then click the check boxes next to the items you want to use with the new classes and click **OK** to accept changes, or **Cancel** to exit without accepting changes.

New Options Using the Command Line

You can add a new DHCP option type through the command line. This can be helpful if you want to use a batch file to add this option to multiple servers across the enterprise. Clearly, adding DHCP options is not for the faint of heart (or for the novice net admin), but the syntax is included here. You can query the Microsoft Web site for more information on adding DHCP options via the command line. This is accomplished through the command mode interface by typing **netsh dchp**. From the dhcp> prompt, you can enter this command to add a new option type:

```
add option defOptCode OptName{BYTE | WORD | DWORD | STRING | IPADDRESS}
[[IsArray=]{0 | 1}] [vendor=VendorClass] [comment=OptComment] [DefValue]
```

Exclusions

Exclusions are used to prevent a range of addresses from being handed out from within the scope. There are numerous reasons you might do this, but clearly you want to ensure your reservations are part of the excluded range of IP addresses. This helps manage static IP addresses for devices that should remain stable such as servers, routers, and other hardware devices that always need to be found. If an IP address is reserved but not excluded, the device using the static IP address will get the reserved IP address, but the DHCP server may also hand that same IP address out through normal DHCP activities. This would cause connectivity issues for one or both devices.

Exclusions are fairly straightforward and again, a bit of advanced planning goes a long way in making sure you set up your DHCP server right the first time. Typically, you'll set exclusions when you're setting up a new scope. From within the New Scope Wizard, you'll be prompted to set exclusions. If you have no ranges to exclude, you can skip this step by leaving the Start IP address and End IP address boxes blank and clicking **Next**. The New Scope Wizard in IPv4, shown in Figure 1.13, is similar in IPv6.

Figure 1.13 Setting DHCP Exclusions

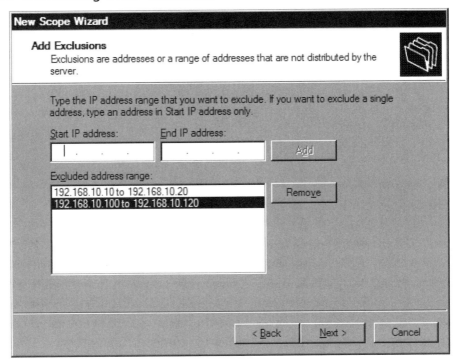

In this example, you can see that two ranges have been excluded. In this case, 192.168.10.10 through 192.168.10.20 is the first range excluded. The second range excluded is 192.168.10.100 through 192.168.10.120. The first range specifically excludes addresses (last octet) 10 through 20, providing 11 excluded addresses. The second range specifically excludes 100 through 120, providing 21 excluded addresses. These excluded addresses can be assigned as static IP addresses to servers, routers, printers and other devices requiring set IP addresses through setting reservations.

EXAM WARNING

All DHCP traffic uses the User Datagram Protocol (UDP). Messages from the client to the server use UDP port 68 as the source port and port 67 as the destination port. Messages from the server to the client use just the reverse—UDP port 67 as the source and UDP port 68 as the destination. If you see questions using UDP ports 67 or 68, think *DHCP*. Authorizing DHCP Server in Active Directory.

In order to help prevent the placement of rogue DHCP servers on the network, an Active Directory network requires that a DHCP server be specifically authorized to fill that role (see Exercise 1.2). Stated differently, in the AD environment, a Windows-based DHCP server will not start unless authorized. In older operating systems, it was possible to place a rogue DHCP server on the network and cause it to come to a crashing halt. This often was done erroneously but certainly there were intentional instances as well. Even in Windows Server 2008, it is possible to activate a non–Windows-based DHCP server (such as a Linux-based DHCP Server) on the network and introduce a rogue DHCP server. So, even though any Windows-based DHCP servers will not work without authorization, it is still possible to introduce a DHCP server on the network. Although it may be fairly unlikely to occur in your network environment, it's important to know it can happen and it's even more important to be aware of this for the exam. In order to prevent that, AD requires that the DHCP server be authorized. The steps for authorizing the DHCP server in AD are the same as in Windows Server 2003 and are provided in the *Configuring & Implementing* section that follows. DHCP servers should be authorized only after you've designed your DHCP configuration for the network and set up your scopes, exclusions, and reservations. Remember, too, that scopes can be configured but not activated, so you have three basic steps: *configure*, *activate*, and *authorize*.

EXERCISE 1.2

AUTHORIZE A DHCP SERVER

The following exercise will walk you through authorizing a new DHCP server on the domain. **CAUTION:** This should be done in a test environment or with a DHCP server that is properly configured to join the domain.

1. Log on as a member of the Domain Admins group.
2. Click **Start | Administrative Tools | DHCP**.
3. Under DHCP, right-click the server name and click **Authorize**.
4. Right-click the server name again and click **Refresh**.

A DHCP Server that is not yet authorized will have red arrows next to the IPv4 and IPv6 icons in the DHCP console. Figure 1.14 shows the red icon to the left of the specific IPv4 scope (the scope is in reversed type) and green icons to the left of the IPv4 and IPv6 DHCP server icons (although the color won't show up in this book, you can see where the icons are located). After you **Authorize** the DHCP server and click

Refresh, the red arrows should be gone, indicating the server has been authorized. The server will now begin handing out IP addresses for the scopes it manages. If you want to deauthorize a DHCP server, use the same steps, except in step three, the option will be **Unauthorize** instead.

Figure 1.14 DHCP Scopes—Activated and Not Activated

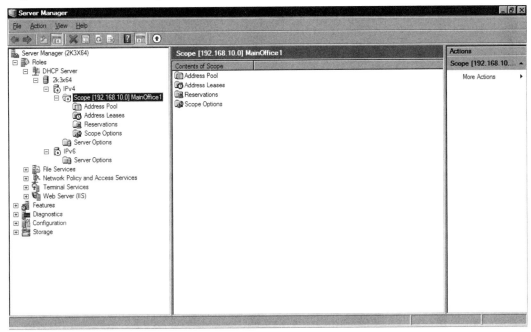

You can also authorize a DHCP server using a script. Run the following command with Domain Admin privileges: **netsh dhcp add server** *ServerName* *[ServerIPv4Address]*.

TEST DAY TIP

Only Windows-based DHCP servers must be authorized in an Active Directory domain. If someone wanted to install a non-Windows-based DHCP server (such as a Linux-based DHCP server) on the network, they could start it up and start handing out IP configuration data to unsuspecting DHCP clients. Check your answers on DHCP to ensure the server specified is (or is not) Windows-based.

DHCP Relay Agents

A DHCP relay agent is a network device configured specifically to relay DCHP traffic to a nearby DHCP server. Essentially, you must have a DHCP relay agent or a DHCP server on every network segment where DHCP client computers reside. In Windows Server 2008, the DHCP relay agent is enabled in the Routing and Remote Access Server role. Note that a computer cannot be configured as both a DHCP server and a DHCP relay agent. The DHCP relay agent is, essentially, a routing protocol that is installed on an appropriate device. Typically, a router is set up as a DHCP relay agent so that DHCP discovery traffic will be routed to the appropriate DHCP server.

PXE Boot

Let's begin by discussing the basics of the PXE Boot. The Pre-Boot Execution Environment, or PXE Boot, is a standard created by Intel to provide a consistent set of functionality prior to booting the operating system. These capabilities are stored in the boot firmware on the computer. The primary objective of the PXE Boot is to enable a client computer to boot up and receive a network boot program (NBP) from a server. PXE is used as part of the Windows Deployment Services feature because it enables remote computers without an operating system (new install or repair) to connect to the network and install the OS from a network share. If the OS is damaged, a computer can still be connected to the network to download repair tools. You can also use computers on the network that have no hard drive storage by booting to the network and downloading the software image needed to run a particular program.

Here's how PXE works. The computer's firmware contains the PXE Boot instructions, which allow the computer to boot and contact a DHCP server for an IP address using the normal DHCP discovery process. As part of the DHCP discovery process, the computer identifies itself as PXE Boot enabled so the PXE Server, which is a protocol extension of DHCP, knows it needs to service a PXE client. Any PXE server on the network can service the PXE client by providing the IP address of the PXE server to the PXE client. The initial communication also provides the name of a boot file the client should request if it wants service from that server.

After the PXE client has a valid IP address, it will attempt to connect to the PXE server and download the network boot program (NBP). The NBP is transmitted to the PXE client using the Trivial File Transfer Protocol (TFTP) from the PXE server and the client computer then executes the NBP file.

The PXE boot is able to obtain an IP address through the use of specific data fields (called options) in the DHCP packet. If you implement the Windows Deployment Services PXE Server (WDSPXE), you can place it on the same physical server as the DHCP Server though the default (and preferred) configuration is to place the PXE Server and the DHCP Server on different physical servers. If you're going to configure them to run on the same physical server, you need to make two changes:

1. You must configure WDSPXE not to listen to UDP Port 67, which is used by the DHCP Server.

2. You must add the DHCP option tag 60, set to the PXEclient string, and it has to be added to all active DHCP scopes. By doing so, you enable PXE booting clients to be notified of WDSPXE from the DHCP Server. However, setting DHCP option tag 60 has another effect you should know about—clients booting from the network will always be notified that WDSPXE is available, even if the server is out of service.

Head of the Class…

Network Boot Program Quick Facts

Windows Deployment Services uses the NBP feature extensively. Here are a few quick facts you should know. NBPs are both architecture- and firmware-specific. According to the PXE specification, on BIOS computers the NBP is a 16-bit real-mode application and can therefore be used both on the x86-based and x64-based operation system platforms. Windows Deployment Services provides a number of different NBP programs. For example, PXEboot.com, which is the default, requires users to press the F12 key to perform the PXE boot. PXEboot.n12 does not require the F12 key and will boot automatically. Windows Deployment Services is discussed later in this book, but since we were on the topic of DHCP, it was appropriate to introduce PXE Boot here. For very detailed information on PXE specification, see www.pix.net/software/pxeboot/archive/pxespec.pdf.

DHCP and Network Access Protection (NAP)

Network Access Protection (NAP) is a platform supported by over 100 independent software vendors (ISVs) and independent hardware vendors (IHVs). It is managed by Windows Server 2008 and works with Windows Vista clients natively. Support for NAP in Windows XP clients is part of Service Pack 3 (SP3). Network access protection is designed to prevent computers that are lacking appropriate security measures including service updates and service packs as well as up-to-date antivirus definition files. NAP is discussed in detail in Chapter 6, but since we're looking at DHCP, we'll take a quick detour to understand how DHCP and NAP interact (see Exercise 1.3). Keep in mind that NAP can be enforced in different ways but that using DHCP is one of the weaker forms since users with administrator-level access can override certain settings with respect to DHCP and NAP enforcement.

EXERCISE 1.3

CREATING A NAP AND DHCP INTEGRATION POLICY

If you haven't already, install the Network Policy Server (NPS) role on your DHCP server via the **Server Manager | Add Roles** function. In the left pane, select **NPS** (Local) then click **Configure NAP** in the main pane. This launches the **Configure NAP Wizard.**

1. In the **Network Connection Method** list, select Dynamic Host Configuration Protocol (DHCP) as the connection method you want to deploy for DHCP clients. The default policy name provided is NAP DHCP. You can accept this name or create another name. Click **Next** to continue.

2. The next screen is **Specify NAP Enforcement Servers Running DHCP**. Identify all the remote DHCP servers on your network by clicking **Add** and in the **Add New RADIUS client** box, type a friendly name of the remote server in the **Friendly Name** box. Enter the DNS name or IP address of the remote DHCP server in the **Address** box. Click **Verify** to validate the entered information before proceeding.

3. In the **Shared Secret** panel (of the **Specify NAP Enforcement Servers Running DHCP** dialog), select **Generate** then click **Generate** to create a long, shared secrete keyphrase. You'll use this same keyphrase in the NAP DHCP Policy on all remote DHCP

servers so be sure to make a note of it so you can locate it when needed. Click **OK**, then **Next** to continue.

4. In the **Specify DHCP Scope** page of the setup wizard, identify the scope(s) to which you want this policy to apply. If you do not specify any scopes, the policy is applied to all NAP-enabled scopes on the selected DHCP server(s). Click **Next**. On the next screen, you can **Configure Groups**. We'll skip this and click **Next** to continue.

5. The next screen is the **Specify NAP Remediation Server Group and URL** page, which allows you to specify where a client should go if it has problems with NAP. You can select a Remediation Server or click **New Group** to define a remediation group and select servers to handle the remediation. Note: Remediation Servers store software updates for NAP clients that need them. In the text box, provide a URL NAP clients can access with information on bringing their computers up to NAP health policy requirements. Click **Next** to continue.

6. The final screen of the wizard is the **Define NAP Health Policy** page. The default settings on this page are fine for most applications, but you can modify the defaults if you have reason to do so. Otherwise, accept the defaults and click **Next**, then **Finish**. These default settings essentially have the NAP-ineligible clients are denied network access, checked for compliance then automatically remediated by downloading and installing software updates from the remediation location you specified in Step 5.

In addition to enabling NAP, you can set NAP settings globally or on a per scope basis. To modify or view settings in Server Manager on the server you want to work with, right-click **IPv4** and select **Properties**. Click the **Network Access Protection** tab and either **Enable on all scopes** or **Disable on all scopes**. You can also specify how DHCP server should behave when if the NPS server is unavailable. You can choose from three options:

- **Full Access**. Allows DHCP clients full, unrestricted access to the network.

- **Restricted Access**. Allows DHCP clients restricted access to the network. Clients can work only with the server to which they are connected.

- **Drop Client Packet**. This is another way of saying No Access. When the server is instructed to drop client packets, all packets from the client will be dropped and the client will not be able to connect to a server or to the network.

When you've finished configuring these settings, click **OK** to accept changes or **Cancel** to exit without accepting changes.

Although integrating DHCP and NAP is the easiest method of enforcing NAP, it's also the weakest. To harden the implantation, you should combine DHCP enforcement with another form of enforcement such as 802.1x or IPsec.

EXAM WARNING

Microsoft exams are notorious for extensive testing on new features. In Windows Server 2008, there are two notable new features related to DHCP. The first is support for **Dynamic Host Configuration Protocol for IPv6 (DHCPv6),** which is defined by the IETF's RFC 3315 specification. It provides stateful address configuration for IPv6 hosts on a native IPv6 network. In Windows Server 2008 and Windows Vista, the DHCP client service supports DHCPv6. A computer running either of these operating systems can perform *stateful* and *stateless* configuration of DHCPv6. *Stateful configuration* includes both addresses and configuration settings whereas *stateless configuration* is configuration settings only.

The second important change related to DHCP is the addition of Network Access Protection (NAP) enforcement support. DHCP enforcement in the NAP platform requires that the DHCP client prove it's healthy before it can receive an address configuration for unlimited access.

Network Access Protection in Windows Server 2008, Windows Vista, and Windows XP SP3 (with NAP Client for Windows XP) provides policy enforcement elements to ensure computers connecting to or communicating across a network are "healthy," meaning they comply with administrator-defined requirements for system health. One common example is that a computer must have the latest operating system updates and antivirus signature files installed before connecting to the network. This helps reduce the probability of a systemwide virus, for example, and helps isolate potential problems by preventing unhealthy computers from connecting.

DHCP Configuration via Server Core

You can enable and manage DHCP through the Server Core command-line interface. This can be helpful when remotely managing a DHCP server across a slower WAN link or when creating batch files to perform repetitive DHCP tasks. We'll include some of the commands you can use in Windows Server 2008 Core, but a more extensive listing of command line commands can be found in the Windows Server 2008 Help file or online at the Microsoft Windows Server 2008 Web site.

The **netsh** command can be implemented via the command line. Open a command window and type:

`netsh dhcp` (then press **Enter**)

to begin command line management of DHCP. Once you've done this, the command prompt line will show **dhcp>**. Commands include:

> Add Server (Adds a DHCP server to the domain)
>
> Syntax = **add server** DNSname IPaddress
>
> Example = **add server dhcpsrv1.example.microsoft.com 10.2.2.2**

Change Command Line focus to different DHCP Server

> Syntax = **server** IPaddress (or **server** \\path)
>
> Example = **server 10.0.0.1**

Add Scope

> Syntax = **add scope** ScopeAddress SubnetMask ScopeName [ScopeComment]
>
> Example = **add scope** 10.2.2.0 255.255.255.0 MainOfficeScope

You can manage the server scope from the netsh command as well. In the command line window, type:

`netsh dhcp server scope` (then press **Enter**)

This will result in a **dhcp server scope>** prompt. From there, you can utilize the following commands. You can get syntax assistance by using the ? variable.

- add excluderange
- add iprange
- add reservedip
- delete excluderange
- delete iprange
- delete lease

- delete optionvalue
- delete reservedip
- delete reservedoptionvalue
- dump
- initiate reconcile
- set comment
- set name
- set optionvalue
- set reservedoptionvalue
- set scope
- set state
- set superscope
- show clients
- show clientsv5
- show excluderange
- show iprange
- show optionvalue
- show reservedip
- show reservedoptionvalue
- show scope
- show state

TEST DAY TIP

Be sure to familiarize yourself with the command line options. Even though you won't have to memorize every command and all its syntax to pass the exam, you should expect to see a fair amount of emphasis on command line usage. Understanding the basics of how to use the command line window, which is the user interface for the Windows Server 2008 Core installation, will help you answer these types of questions, and they might be the difference between passing and just squeaking by (or not).

Configuring Network Authentication

Let's start with a quick review of the basics to set the foundation for this discussion of network access and authentication. Windows Server 2008 authentication is a two-part process involving authentication of the user (interactive login) and access control to network resources. When a user logs in, their identity is verified through Active Directory (AD) Domain Services and this provides controlled access to Active Directory objects. As the user attempts to access various network resources, their network authentication credentials are used to determine whether or not the user has permission to access those resources. Also part of AD are user accounts and groups that impact network access. Authentication can also occur through a public key infrastructure (PKI), which uses digital certificates and certification authorities to verify and authenticate entities including users, computers, and services. Group Policy is used to manage configuration settings for servers, clients, and users. Remote Authentication Dial-In User Service (RADIUS) is a protocol that originally was created for dial-in authentication and authorization service. Now, its role has expanded to include wireless access point access, authenticating Ethernet switches, virtual private network servers, and more. In Windows Server 2008, the RADIUS function is now handled by the Network Policy and Access Services role.

As you can see from Figure 1.15, the Network Policy and Access Services role installs Network Policy Server (NPS) and Routing and Remote Access (RRAS). Under the NPS node, you'll find RADIUS Clients and Servers, Policies, Network Access Protection (NAP) and Accounting. Under the Routing and Remote Access node, you'll find Network Interfaces, Remote Access Logging & Policies, IPv4 and IPv6.

Back to NPS: NPS allows you to configure and manage network policies from a centralized location. You can configure and manage RADIUS server, RADIUS proxy, and Network Access Protection (NAP) policy server from within this role. With NPS, you can authorize and authenticate network connections through different access servers such as 802.1x, wireless access points (WAP), virtual private network server (VPN), dial-up servers, and computers running Windows Server 2008 with Terminal Services Gateway (TS Gateway).

Network Policy Server creates and enforces organizationwide access policies for clients. These services include client health, connection request authentication, and connection request authorization. You can also use NPS as a RADIUS proxy to forward connection requests for authentication and authorization to NPS or other RADIUS servers. As part of NPS, routing and remote access services can also be installed. This provides users access to resources connecting remotely through VPN or dial–up connections. RRAS can also be used to provide routing services on small networks or to connect two private networks across the Internet.

To summarize, authentication in Windows Server 2008 is provided by numerous infrastructure components including Active Directory Domain Services, Group Policy, Public Key Infrastructure, and RADIUS. These interact with Network Policy Server (NPS). For example, in Active Directory, you can configure user or computer accounts to either *Allow Access* or *Control Access Through NPS Network Policy (recommended)*. In Windows Server 2008, the *Control Access Through NPS Network Policy (recommended)* is selected by default. When using groups to manage access, you can then use your existing groups and create network policies in NPS that either allow access (with or without restrictions) or deny access based on existing groups. For example, you can configure a policy in NPS that specifies the Marketing group have unrestricted VPN access. You might also configure another NPS policy that specifies that Vendors can never have VPN access.

TEST DAY TIP

Numerous authentication and communication-based protocols are no longer supported in Windows Server 2008 (and Windows Vista). We've listed a few here, but for the full list (and subject to change until the final version of Windows Server 2008 is released), refer to the Microsoft Web site. Support has been removed for:

- X.25
- SLIP-based connections (automatically updated to PPP-based connections)
- ATM
- NWLinkIPX/SPX/NetBIOS Compatible Transport Protocol
- Service for Macintosh
- OSPF
- SPAP, EAP-MD5-CHAP and MS-CHAPv1 authentication protocols

NTLMv2 and Kerberos Authentication

Starting with Windows 2000, Kerberos Version 5 (Kerberos) was supported as the default authentication protocol in Active Directory. The NT LAN Manager (NTLM) protocol is still supported for authentication with clients that required NTLM (i.e., for backward compatibility only). You can control how NTLM is used through

Group Policy. The default authentication level in most cases is "Send NTLMv2 Response Only." With this level of authentication, NTLMv2 is used with clients that use this authentication protocol and session security only if the server supports it.

You can configure Kerberos to utilize different methods of authentication, and these can be set via NPS for the network as well as in the IPsec Settings tab of the Windows Firewall with Advanced Security Properties, which we'll discuss a bit later in this chapter.

To begin, install this role on your Windows Server 2008 computer, if it's not already installed. To do so, open Server Manager, choose **Add Roles** from the interface option, then select **Network Policy and Access Services**. Follow the on-screen prompts to complete configuration, which are self-explanatory. In order to install *Health Registration Authority* (HRA) and *Host Credential Authorization Protocol* (HCAP), you also need to have web services (IIS) installed. For our purposes, we will disregard these two options and focus just on network access. Once Network Policy and Access Services are installed, you can access the services through the Server Manager interface. As shown in Figure 1.15, you can start, stop, or check the status of a service as well as set Preferences. Note that you can deploy NPS in a number of ways at various points in your forest or domain. It is beyond the scope of this chapter to discuss these options in detail.

Figure 1.15 Network Policy and Access Services Server Manager Interface

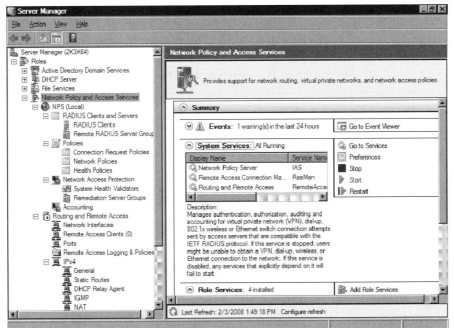

WLAN Authentication Using 802.1x and 802.3

NPS is responsible for network security and is used to provide secure wireless access through NPS. Windows Server 2008 also provides features that enable you to deploy 802.1x authenticated wired service for IEEE 802.3 Ethernet network clients. In conjunction with 802.1x capable switches and other Windows Server 2008 features, you can control network access through Wired Network Policies in Windows Server 2008 Group Policies. Recall that NPS is used to configure remote connections. The 802.3 wired network specification allows you to use the 802.1x specification to provide wired networking access. This is configured via NPS and uses Protected Extensible Authentication Protocol (PEAP) authentication. It is outside the scope of this book to discuss how to plan, configure, and deploy a WLAN authentication method, but we will discuss these concepts to the extent you need to understand the changes in the Windows Server 2008 environment.

TEST DAY TIP

Group Policy and Network Policy Server are two Windows Server 2008 areas with which you should be familiar. Understand the role of Group Policy versus the role of Network Policy Server in securing the network. Be able to explain in your own words what these two features do in Windows Server 2008. If you can describe them in your own words, there's a good chance you understand their functionality and will be able to distinguish right and wrong answers on the exam.

Let's start with some definitions as a review. The 802.11 standard defined the shared key authentication method for authentication and Wired Equivalent Privacy (WEP) for encryption for wireless communications. 802.11 ultimately ended up being a relatively weak standard and newer security standards are available and recommended for use. The 802.1x standard that existed for Ethernet switches was adapted to the 802.11 wireless LANs to provide stronger authentication than the original standard. 802.1x is designed for medium to large wireless LANs that have an authentication infrastructure, such as AD and RADIUS in the Windows environment. With such an infrastructure in place, the 802.1x standard supports dynamic WEP, which are mutually determined keys negotiated by the wireless client and the RADIUS server. However, the 802.1x standard also supports the stronger Wi-Fi

Protected Access (WPA) encryption method. The 802.11i standard formally replaces WEP with WPA2, an enhancement to the original WPA method.

Wireless and Wired Authentication Technologies

Windows Server 2008 supports several authentication methods for authenticating that a computer or user is attempting to connect via a protected wireless connection. These same technologies support 802.1x authenticated wired networks as well. These Extended Authentication Protocols (EAP) methods are:

- EAP–TLS
- PEAP–TLS
- PEAP–MS–CHAPv2

Extended Authentication Protocol–Transport Layer Security (EAP–TLS) and Protected Extended Authentication Protocol–Transport Layer Security (PEAP–TLS) are used in conjunction with Public Key Infrastructure (PKI) and computer certificates, user certificates, or smart cards. Using EAP–TLS, a wireless client sends its certificate (computer, user, or smart card) for authentication and the RADIUS server sends its computer certificate for authentication. By default, the wireless client authenticates the server's certificate. With PEAP–TLS, the server and client create an encrypted session before certificates are exchanged. Clearly, PEAP–TLS is a stronger authentication method because the authentication session data is encrypted.

If there are no computer, user, or smart card certificates available, you can use PEAP-Microsoft Challenge Handshake Authentication Protocol version 2 (PEAP-MS-CHAPv2). This is a password-based authentication method in which the exchange of the authentication traffic is encrypted (using TLS), making it difficult for hackers to intercept and use an offline dictionary attack to access authentication exchange data. That said, it's the weakest of these three options for authentication because it relies on the use of a password.

A Windows-based client running Windows Vista or Windows Server 2008 can be configured in the following ways:

- Group Policy
- Command line
- Wired XML profiles

Using Group Policy, you can configure the Wired Network (IEEE 802.3) Policies Group Policy extension, which is part of Computer configuration Group

Policy that can specify wired network settings in the AD environment. The Group Policy extension applies only to Windows Server 2008 and Windows Vista computers. The command line can be used within the **netsh** context using the **lan** command (**netsh lan**). You can explore the available comments by typing **netsh lan /?** at the command line prompt. Wired XML profiles are XML files that contain wired network settings. These can be imported and exported to Windows Server 2008 and Windows Vista clients using the **netsh** context as well. You can use **netsh lan export profile** or **netsh lan add profile** to export or import a wired profile using the command line.

For Windows XP SP2 or Windows Server 2003-basec computers, you can manually configure wired clients by configuring 802.1x authentication settings from the Authentication tab of the properties dialog box of a LAN connection in the Network Connections folder, as shown in Figure 1.16, which shows the Network Connections Properties dialog box from a Windows XP Pro SP2 computer.

Figure 1.16 802.1x Settings on Wired Windows XP SP2 Client

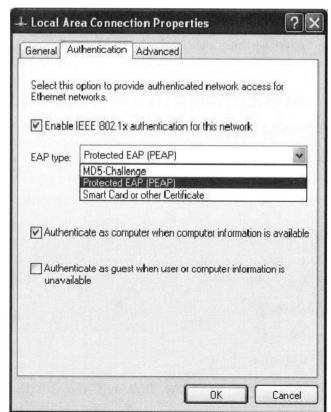

Implementing Secure Network Access Authentication

Although it's outside the scope of this chapter to go into the details of PKI, it is useful to look at some of the ways PKI can be used as part of a Windows-based authentication infrastructure for secure network access using the protocols discussed in this section.

- When using PEAP–MS-CHAPv2 for network access authentication, configure Group Policy for autoenrollment of computer certificates to install computer certificates on the NPS servers.

- When using certificates for computer-level network access authentication, you should configure Group Policy for autoenrollment of computer certificates. This applies if you're using EAP–TLS or PEAP–TLS for computer-level wireless authentication.

- When using certificates for user-level network access authentication, configure a certificate template for user certificates and also configure Group Policy for autoenrollment of user certificates. As with computer-level certificates, this is needed when using EAP–TLS and PEAP–TLS.

Group Policy is also an important part of securing network access and authenticating computers and users. You can use Group Policy to deploy settings to install a root certificate on a domain member computer to validate computer certificates of the NPS servers. It can also be used to autoenroll user and computer certificates on domain member computers for user- and computer-level certificate-based authentication.

In addition to being useful in the deployment of certificate-based authentication, Group Policy is also useful in deploying configuration settings for:

- 802.11 wireless network profiles

- 802.1x wired network profiles

- Windows Firewall with Advanced Security connection security rules to protect traffic

- NAP client configuration

New & Noteworthy...

Changes to Authentication Protocols

PPP-based connections no longer support the SPAP, EAP-MD5-CHAP and MS-CHAPv1 authentication protocols. Remote access PPP-based connections now support the use of Protected EAP (PEAP) with PEAP-MS-CHAP v2 and PEAP-TLS. Keep this in mind as you plan out your new Windows Server 2008 remote access options.

EAPHost architecture in Windows Server 2008 and Windows Vista includes new features not supported in Windows Server 2003 and Windows XP including:

- Support for additional EAP methods
- Network discovery (as defined in RFC 4284)
- RFC 3748 compliance and support for expanded EAP types including vendor-specific EAP types
- Coexistence of multiple EAP types (Microsoft and Cisco, for example)

EXERCISE 1.4

CONFIGURING 802.1X SETTINGS IN WINDOWS SERVER 2008

You can configure wired policies form the **Computer Configuration | Policies | Windows Settings | Security Settings | Wired Network (IEEE 802.3) Policies** node in the **Group Policy Management Editor snap-in** via the MMC. By default, there are no wired policies in place. To create a new policy, use the following steps:

1. Right-click the **Wired Network (IEEE 802.3) Policies** in the console tree of the GP Editor snap-in.

2. Click **Create A New Windows Vista Wired Policy**.

3. The **New Windows Vista Wired Policy Properties** dialog is displayed, shown in Figure 1.17. It has two tabs: General and

Security. The **General** tab is selected by default. Enter the policy name and description and ensure the checkbox for "Use Windows Wired Auto Config service for clients" is checked.

Figure 1.17 New Vista Wired Network Policy Properties Security Tab

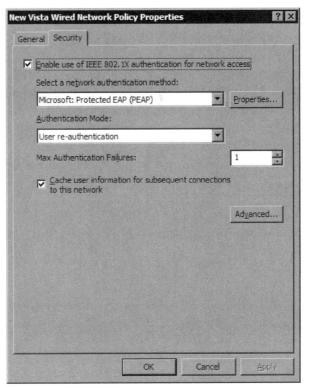

4. Click the **Security** tab to set security options. On this tab, click the checkbox next to "Enable use for IEEE 802.1X authentication for network access" then click the dropdown box to select a network authentication method (EAP, PEAP, MS-CHAPv2). Also select the "Authentication Mode" from the second dropdown box. The options are User re-authentication, computer only, user authentication, or guest authentication. Also select the number of times the authentication can fail before it is abandoned (1 is the default). The last setting in the Security tab is a checkbox whether to "Cache user information for subsequent connections to this network." If this checkbox is cleared, the credential data is removed when the user logs off. If the checkbox is checked, the credential data will be cached after user log off.

5. To access advanced settings, click the **Advanced** button on the Security tab. There are two Advanced segments: **IEEE 802.1X** and **Single Sign On**, shown in Figure 1.18.

Figure 1.18 Advanced Settings for new Vista Wired Network Policy Properties

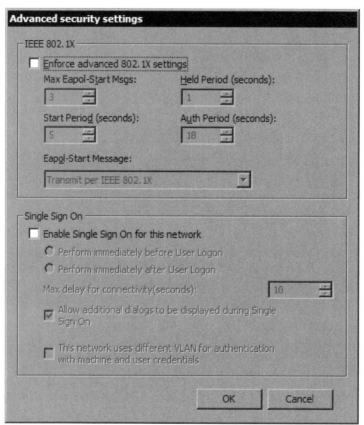

6. In the **IEEE 802.1X** section, click the checkbox to the left of "Enforce advanced 802.1X settings" to enable these options: Max Eapol-Start Msgs:, Held Period (seconds), Start Period (seconds), Auth Period (seconds), Eapol-Start Message. In most cases, the default settings are fine; it you believe you need these advanced settings, check the Microsoft documentation for details on how to set these.

7. In the **Single Sign On** section, click the checkbox next to "Enable Single Sign On for this network" to enable the following options: Perform immediately before User Logon, Perform immediately

after User Logon, Set Max. delay for connectivity (seconds), Allow additional dialogs to be displayed during Single Sign On, and This network uses different VLAN for authentication with machine and user credentials. Again, as with the IEEE 802.1X Advanced settings, these can be modified if you have a specific need to do so. Check Microsoft documentation for details on using these options within your network environment. A good starting place is www.microsoft.com/technet/technetmag/issues/2008/02/CableGuy/default.aspx.

8. Click **OK** to accept configuration; click **Cancel** to exit without saving changes.

Routing and Remote Access Services (RRAS) Authentication

Routing and Remote Access Services (RRAS), installed via the NPS, enables users to be authenticated and to connect to the network remotely. RRAS services are similar to those in Windows Server 2003, though there are a few updates to be aware of. For details of the Windows Server 2008 changes, read the New & Noteworthy section that precedes this section.

As we've mentioned, EAP-TLS and PEAP-TLS are supported in Windows Server 2008 and the less secure PEAP-MS-CHAPv2 is supported when certificates are not available. RRAS policies are configured here as well as via Group Policy in AD.

We're assuming you already have an understanding of a security infrastructure (AD, PKI, etc.), so we'll build on that knowledge. As you know, RRAS can be configured via Group Policy so you can control access based on group membership—whether that's a computer or user group. The most popular method of remote connection these days is through a Virtual Private Network (VPN) connection. You can secure that connection of a remote computer and the local network in different ways. The three methods in Windows Server 2008 are:

- Point-to-Point Tunneling Protocol (PPTP)

- Layer Two Tunneling Protocol with Internet Protocol security (L2TP/IPsec)

- Secure Socket Tunneling Protocol (SSTP)

Point-to-Point Tunneling Protocol (PPTP) uses PPP authentication methods for user-level authentication and it uses Microsoft Point-to-Point Encryption (MPPE) for data encryption. Layer Two Tunneling Protocol with Internet Protocol security (L2TP/IPsec), like PPTP, uses PPP for user-level authentication but it uses IPsec for computer-level security that includes peer authentication, data authentication, data integrity, and data encryption. Secure Socket Tunneling Protocol (SSTP) also uses PPP for user-level authentication and it uses Hypertext Transfer Protocol (HTTP) encapsulation over a Secure Sockets Layer (SSL) channel (Transport Layer Security) for data authentication, data integrity, and data encryption.

A remote client makes a remote connection via VPN to a private network through a VPN server, which provides access to the network to which that VPN server is connected. During the connection process, the VPN client authenticates itself to the VPN server. Depending on how VPN connections are configured, the VPN server may also authenticate itself to the client.

New & Noteworthy...

Changes to PPTP and L2TP/IPsec Protocols

Warning: This section refers to modifying the Windows registry file. Using Registry Editor incorrectly can cause serious problems that may make the system unstable or unusable and that may require you to reinstall the Windows operating system. There is no guarantee that problems resulting from the incorrect modification of the Registry file can be solved. Edit or modify the Registry at your own risk and do not do this on a live server unless you know exactly what you're doing and have a backup of the Registry. Always make a backup of the Windows Registry file before you modify any settings. You can back up the entire Registry or a single portion of the Registry using REGEDIT. For more information on backing up and restoring the Registry file, visit http://support.microsoft.com/kb/136393.

By default, Windows Server 2008 and Windows Vista have MPPE encryption with 40-bit and 56-bit keys disabled. Instead, the stronger 128-bit encryption is enabled. You can configure Windows Server 2008 to use 40-bit and 56-bit keys if you have a need to connect with Windows Server 2003 or Windows XP SP2-based computers. This can be enabled by setting the *HKEY_LOCAL_MACHINE\system\CurrentControlSet\Services\Rasman*

parameters\AllowPPTPWeakCrypto registry value to 1 and restarting the computer. Keep in mind, however, that this is a weaker encryption system and generally is not recommended.

As mentioned previously, support for the Message Digest (MD5) hash has been discontinued in L2TP/IPsec. Now, Windows Server 2008 supports only 3DES encryption and the Secure Hash Algorithm-1 (SHA1) hashed method authentication code (HMAC) by default. Support for the Advanced Encryption Standard (AES) using 128-bit or 256-bit keys has been added. As with MPPE encryption, you can enable MD5 support for interoperability, but this also is not recommended. If you have reason to enable this, you can access it via the following registry key and setting the value to 1: *HKEY_LOCAL_MACHINE\system\CurrentControlSet\Services\Rasman\ parameters\AllowL2TPWeakCrypto*.

Any time you modify a registry key, you need to restart the computer before the setting takes place. Again, these changes are not recommended as they weaken security, but they can be modified if needed.

Configuring IP Security (IPsec)

The IP Security (IPsec) protocol is a standard that provides cryptographic security services for IP traffic. IPsec is an end-to-end security solution. The only two nodes aware of IPsec traffic on the network are the two peers communicating with each other. IPsec packets are forwarded by routers like any other packet on the network. As you probably recall, IPsec provides the following properties:

- **Peer authentication**. IPsec verifies the identity of a peer computer before data is sent.

- **Data origin authentication**. Each IPsec packet has an encrypted checksum in the form of a keyed hash. It ensures that only one computer could have sent the packet, preventing a malicious user from masquerading as the sender.

- **Data integrity**. The IPsec protocol protects the contents of the packet through the encrypted checksum. The receiver of the data can verify the data is unmodified by checking the checksum value. A malicious intruder would be unable to properly modify both the packet's data and it's cryptographic checksum.

- **Data confidentiality**. IPsec uses secret key encryption techniques that protect the data being sent in the packet. If the packet is intercepted, only the packet's encrypted contents can be viewed.

- **Anitreplay**. Each protected packet has a sequence number that prevents an intruder from getting in the middle of the communications and modifying packet data.

- **Key management**. IPsec provides a secure way of deriving initial keying data and to periodically change the keys used for secure communications to prevent the key from being discovered through any other method than brute force.

IPsec does not provide nonrepudiation security service for data, meaning that the sender can later deny having sent the packet. IPsec uses a shared secret key, called a symmetric key, and since two peers share a key, nonrepudiation is not provided by IPsec.

IPsec can operate in either transport mode or tunnel mode. The transport mode protects communications between hosts and it encrypts the User Datagram Protocol/Transmission Control Protocol (UDP/TCP) protocol header and original data but not the IP header itself. In tunnel mode, IPsec protects host-to-network communications like that in virtual private networks (VPN). Since IPsec changes the IP packet, the original version of Network Address Translation did not support IPsec. However, the newer version, Network Address Translation–Traversal (NAT–T) is used. It allows IPsec traffic to pass through NAT–T compatible servers that are configured to allow traffic on UDP port 4500. All versions of Windows that support IPsec also support NAT–T.

IPsec supports numerous authentication and encryption standards, so two IPsec-capable computers might not support the same sets of standards. And, not all computers can support IPsec. So, before an IPsec connection can be made, whether in transport or tunnel mode, an IPsec negotiation is established to determine if the IPsec supported by the two end points (host-to-host or host-to-server) are supporting the same standards.

IPsec provides security by enveloping the data (the *IP payload*) in an additional header or trailer that provides data origin authentication, data integrity, data confidentiality, and antireplay protection. The IPsec protocol uses two elements, the authentication header (AH) and the encapsulating security payload (ESP) header and trailer. Applying the AH or ESP to an IP datagram transforms the packet into a secure datagram. As a result, AH and ESP sometimes are referred to as *transforms*.

ESP is widely supported and is therefore the preferred IPsec protocol, but AH is the fallback protocol if both hosts cannot support ESP. Let's look briefly at the AH and ESP protocols.

IPsec Authentication Header (AH)

The Authentication Header protocol provides data origin authentication, data integrity, and antireplay protection for the entire IP datagram. It does *not* provide data confidentiality (for that, use ESP, discussed in the next section). AH can be used in transport or tunnel mode. The packet format for both is shown in Figure 1.19. Notice that when AH is used in transport mode (Figure 1.19A), the AH header is added just after the IP header. The IP header is modified to indicate the presence of AH (the Protocol field is set to 51). This packet type is forwarded by routers just as any other standard IP packet would be. However, firewalls look for the modification of the IP header and might not allow this traffic through due to the modification of the Protocol field in the IP header. For that reason, some firewalls might need to be configured to forward data in which the IP header Protocol field is set to 51.

In Figure 1.19B, the tunnel mode for AH is shown. In this case, the IP packet is included without modification and the entire packet is authenticated, including the new IP header, the AH header, and the original IP header and payload. This added header allows the packet to pass through firewalls more easily but it does generate more network traffic by adding to the packet size.

Figure 1.19 AH in Transport and Tunnel Mode

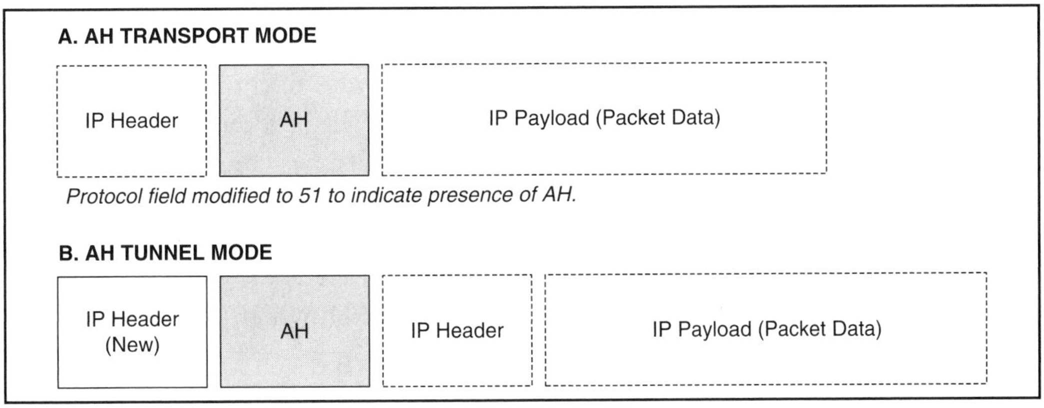

A. AH TRANSPORT MODE

| IP Header | AH | IP Payload (Packet Data) |

Protocol field modified to 51 to indicate presence of AH.

B. AH TUNNEL MODE

| IP Header (New) | AH | IP Header | IP Payload (Packet Data) |

Head of the Class…

IPsec Headers and Footers

A security association (SA) is the combination of security services used by communicating peers. This typically includes security services, protection methods, and cryptographic keys. The SA contains the information needed to negotiate a secure communications between peers. Two types of SAs are created when IPsec peers communicate in a secure mode: ISAKMP SA and IPsec SA.

The Internet Security Association and Key Management Protocol (ISAKMP) SA also is known as the *main mode* SA and is used to protect IPsec security negotiations themselves. The IPsec SA also is known as the *quick mode* security association (SA). The IPsec SA cipher information is protected by the ISAKMP SA. In IPsec packets, no information about the type of traffic or the protection mechanisms is sent as plaintext. Recall that for a pair of IPsec peers, there are always two IPsec SAs—one for inbound and one for outbound traffic. The inbound SA for one IPsec peer is the outbound SA for the other IPsec peer.

IPsec Encapsulating Security Payload (ESP)

Encapsulating Security Payload (ESP) provides both a header and a trailer for an IP datagram that secures the packet. ESP provides data origin authentication, data integrity, antireplay, and data confidentiality protection for the ESP-encapsulated portion of the packet. Figure 1.20 shows the format of the ESP header in transport mode and Figure 1.21 shows the ESP header in tunnel mode. We've also included what the packet looks like if you use both AH and ESP, shown in Figure 1.22, though typically ESP is used as the default method of security the packet unless you have reason to use AH, which does not provide data confidentiality.

Figure 1.20 ESP in Transport Mode

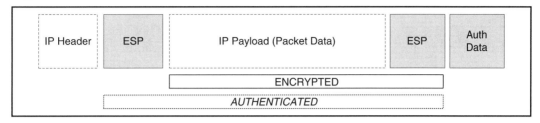

Figure 1.21 ESP in Tunnel Mode

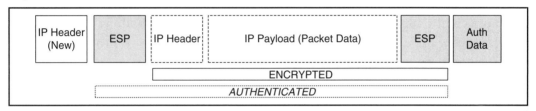

Figure 1.22 AH and ESP Packet Format

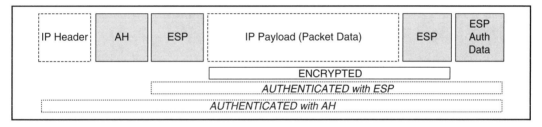

Now that we've refreshed your skills on the format of the IPsec AH and ESP data, let's get back to the practical IPsec skills needed to configure a Windows Server 2008 computer network.

Configuring IPsec in Windows Server 2008

IPsec is configured via Group Policy in Active Directory as well as through Windows Firewall with Advanced Security. In Windows Firewall with Advanced Security, IPsec inbound and outbound traffic rules can be configured along with connection security rules. In this section, we'll look briefly at IPsec in Group Policy and then we'll take a more detailed look at the integration of IPsec in Windows Firewall with Advanced Security since this is a new feature in Windows Server 2008.

In Windows Server 2003, configuring IPsec and configuring the Windows Firewall were configured separately and in two different places. This led to the possibility of conflicting settings. In Windows Server 2008, IPsec and the Windows Firewall functionality have been combined, removing the possibility of conflicting settings. IPsec and Windows Firewall are now configured via the Windows Firewall with Advanced Security snap-in. Note that the command line options, within the **netsh advfirewall** context, can be used for command line configuration of both firewall and IPsec behavior. Again, the command line options are helpful when setting up scripting, batch files, or when administering a remote server—so it's useful to make note of the commands you're most likely to need. You'll also see some of the more commonly used command line commands on the Windows Server 2008 exam, so we're including them when it seems likely you'll see it on the exam.

New & Noteworthy...

IPsec in Windows Server 2008

There are many new improvements to the IPsec implementation in Windows Server 2008. According to the Microsoft Web site, these are:

- Integrated firewall and IPsec configuration
- Simplified IPsec policy configuration
- Client-to-DC IPsec protection
- Improved load balancing and clustering server support
- Improved IPsec authentication
- New cryptographic support
- Integration with Network Access Protection
- Additional configuration options for protected communication
- Integrated IPv4 and IPv6 support
- Extended events and performance monitor counters
- Network Diagnostics Framework support

[Source: http://technet.microsoft.com/en-us/library/bb726965.aspx]

In the Window Server 2008 exam, expect to see questions that test your knowledge and understanding of the latest implementation of IPsec. Most notably, be familiar with how IPsec is integrated into and configured in the firewall. Also be aware of the Simplified IPsec policy configuration, which will likely show up on your exam in one form or another. Finally, be familiar with the integrated IPsec support with IPv4 and IPv6. Refer to the Microsoft Web site if you need to dig into the vast detail of IPsec in Windows Server 2008.

Creating IPsec Policy

IPsec policy is created either in Active Directory as a Group Policy or via the Windows Server 2008's Windows Firewall with Advanced Security. Clearly, IPsec settings in these two areas are related but are not interchangeable. Policy set in Active Directory is applied according to policies set at the domain level and will take precedence over local IPsec policy located on a member computer. IPsec policy will be applied according to AD and Windows Firewall with Advanced Security settings on a Windows Server 2008 computer.

We won't go into too much detail about AD IPsec policy here but we will discuss IPsec in Windows Firewall with Advanced Security in more detail later in this chapter. You can open the IP Security Policy Management console through the MMC snap-in. To open the MMC Console, click **Start | Run** and type **mmc**, then click **OK**. This opens the MMC console from which you can select the IPSecurity Management Snap-in. Right-click **IP Security Policies** in the left pane then choose **Create IP Security Policy** from the menu to launch the IPsec Security Policy Wizard.

IPsec Using the Command Line

As with many other functions in Windows Server 2008 management, you can configure IPsec policy via the command line. This section briefly outlines some of the more commonly used IPsec commands. However, you may want to explore the command line options for IPsec on your own so you're familiar with these options. You can configure static mode and dynamic mode options, as shown in Table 1.4. You can type **netsh ipsec /?** to get a full list of command line options related to IPsec.

Table 1.4 IPsec Command Line Options

IPsec Command	Details
netsh ipsec static add policy *name*	Creates an IPsec policy with the specified name.
netsh ipsec static delete *[option]*	Deletes the specific IPsec policy. Can be used with the switch *all* to remove all IPsec policies, filter lists, and filter actions.
netsh ipsec dynamic set policy *name*	Sets a policy name immediately.
netsh ipsec dynamic delete *name*	Removes a specific policy immediately.
netsh ipsec dynamic export policy *name*	Exports all IPsec policies to a specified file.
netsh ipsec dynamic show *all*	Used to view IPsec policy and statistics.
netsh ipsec dynamic set config ipsecdiagnostics 7	Enables IPsec driver logging of dropped inbound and outbound packets.
netsh ipsec dynamic set config ipsecloginterval 60	Used to change the default interval the IPsec log file writes entries to the log file. This example sets the interval to 60 seconds. This can be helpful in troubleshooting IPsec issues/.

Head of the Class…

Saving Command Line Output to a File

Sometimes the output of a command line command, such as a "show all" command, can be quite lengthy and can scroll off the screen making it hard to locate needed information. You can save the output to a file by using this sequence of commands. Although the example is used for the **netsh ipsec** context, this works anywhere in the command line context.

At the netsh command line context, type **set filename** *filename.txt* (where filename.txt is the file you want to create). Then, type **ipsec static**

show all. Finally, type **set file close**. The contents of the ipsec static show all command have been saved to the filename you specified.

Even faster is the command from the standard command line context (not within netsh): **netsh ipsec static show all >*filename.txt*.** Saves time, saves your data.

If you want to see the entire output without dumping it to a file, you can use the |more switch so the command would be **netsh ipsec static show all |more**.

IPsec Isolation Policy

Server and domain isolation is accomplished through configuring IPsec computers to require protection for inbound traffic (or attempts at inbound traffic) and to request but not require protection for outbound traffic. Trusted computers in an isolation scenario use fallback to clear to initiate communication with hosts on their intranets that are not IPsec-enabled. However, beginning in Windows Server 2003 (and continued in Windows Server 2008), the Simple Policy Update changes the IPsec negotiation process. IPsec negotiation failures will still fallback to clear but because negotiation falls back to clear, it's possible for two peers using IPsec who cannot validate each others' credentials to allow unsecured communication with non-IPsec aware computers (if this setting is enabled) or to accept unsecured communication but always respond using IPsec (if the setting is enabled).

Exam Warning

A concept you should be familiar with is *defense-in-depth*. This refers to a network security strategy that uses layers of security methods to provide security at several different layers of the network. For example, on a server, you have various applications and services that are running and can be configured to require authentication for access or use. You also have a firewall application that filters traffic to and from the server based on configured settings. You can also use IPsec to protect traffic to and from that server (though there are some important considerations to review before implementing that) and you can use network access protection (NAP) at the network layer to protect the network (and servers) from computers that do not meet health requirements. On the client side, you use login credentials for access to the client, you may use a local firewall for filtering, and you also can use IPsec for IP security and tunneling or VPN for secure point-to-point communications. All these combined create a deep security framework that helps protect network resources. Though it's outside the scope of this chapter to discuss this in-depth, all the elements discussed in this chapter come into play with a defense-in-depth strategy and you are very likely to see these kinds of questions on the exam.

Windows Firewall with Advanced Security in Windows Server 2008

Firewalls can run on a network's perimeter to protect computers on the network via filtering both inbound and outbound traffic. Firewalls can also run on a host computer to protect that host. Let's look briefly at these two types of configurations.

Network Perimeter Firewalls

Network perimeter firewalls provide a variety of services to protect network traffic. They're typically either hardware- or software-based, some are both. Some perimeter firewalls also provide application proxy services as well. These perimeter firewalls typically provide the following services:

- Management and control of network traffic through stateful packet inspection, connection monitoring, and application-level filtering.

- Stateful connection analysis by inspecting the state of communications by computers on the network.

- Virtual private network (VPN) gateway functionality providing IPsec authentication and encryption services along with Network Address Translation-Transversal (NAT-T) to allow IPsec traffic to pass through the firewall between public and private IP addresses.

Host–based Firewalls

Although perimeter firewalls protect the network from traffic flowing into and out of the network itself, they cannot protect internal network traffic. Host-based firewalls are used to protect host computers from threats internal to the network itself. You can configure a firewall to block specific types of incoming and outgoing traffic to provide an extra layer of security for the host computer.

New Features in Windows Firewall with Advanced Security

Before we look at the specifics of Windows Firewall with Advanced Security, let's take a look at the new features. Be sure to explore these features fully on your

Windows Server 2008 computer since, as we've stated several times, the new features are the most likely to be tested on an exam.

1. IPsec Integration
2. Support for IPv6
3. Support for Active Directory user, computer, and groups
4. Location-aware profiles
5. Detailed rules
6. Expanded authenticated bypass

IPsec Integration

This is a pretty significant change from previous versions of Windows. In Windows Server 2008, IPsec is integrated into firewall functionality, as shown in Figure 1.23. In the Windows Firewall with Advanced Security snap-in, firewall filtering and IPsec rule configuration are integrated. Note, however, that if you want to configure IPsec for computers running an operating system prior to Windows Server 2008 or Windows Vista, you'll need to use the IPsec Policy Management snap-in instead.

Figure 1.23 Windows Firewall with Advanced Security Properties with IPsec Integration

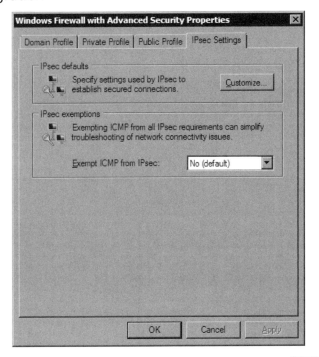

Support for IPv6

The firewall function in Windows Server 2008 provides native support for IPv6. Of course, it also still fully supports IPv4 as well as IPv6 to IPv4 (6 to 4) and the new NAT traversal for IPv6 called Teredo (discussed briefly in this chapter).

Support for Active Directory User, Computer, and Groups

You can create various firewall rules and these rules can filter connections by user, computer, or groups in Active Directory. These connections must be secured with IPsec using a credential that carries the AD account information. Kerberos V5 is the default for Windows Server 2008 and is an example of a credential that carries the AD account information.

Location-Aware Profiles

There are three built-in profiles in the firewall software that allow you to create location-aware profiles. The three profiles are domain, private, and public. If you enable all three of these profiles, the software will determine which profile to utilize based on your location (and connection). The domain profile is used when the computer is authenticated via AD and is active when all interfaces can authenticate to a domain controller. The private profile is used when the computer is connected to a private network behind a private gateway or router. The public profile is used when the computer is connected to a public network or unidentified connection, such as those found at airports and coffee shops. Clearly, you would likely never use the public profile on a server unless it happens to be in a DMZ on the network. Windows Vista and Windows Server 2008 are based on the same code, so the public profile is geared primarily toward Windows Vista-based computers rather than Windows Server 2008-based computers. You might choose to disable the public profile on your Windows Server 2008-based computers.

Detailed Rules

By default, Windows Firewall with Advanced Security is enabled for both inbound and outbound traffic. The default settings block most incoming traffic and allow outgoing traffic. This version of the firewall software enables you to configure detailed rules for filtering any Internet Assigned Numbers Authority

(IANA) protocol numbers. Previous versions supported only filtering UDP, TCP, and ICMP protocols. In addition, the firewall software in Windows Server 2008 supports configuration of AD domain service accounts and groups, application names, TCP, UDP, ICMPv4, ICMPv6, local and remote IP addresses, interface types and protocols, and ICMP type and code filtering. The good news, though, is that the default settings are a very good starting point and you now have the capability to be very detailed in configuring traffic rules if you have a need to do so.

Expanded Authenticated Bypass

Previous versions of the firewall software provided an "all or nothing" style of configuration. Either you could allow a computer full access to another computer if it was configured to use IPsec, but you couldn't specify ports or protocols, for example. In Windows Server 2008 (and Windows Vista), you can provide much more detailed authenticated bypass rules that will allow you to specify which ports or programs can have access and which computers or groups of computers can have access. This keeps computers protected while providing rule-based exceptions as needed.

Network Location–Aware Host Firewall

In Windows Server 2008, the Windows Firewall with Advanced Security can act both as a network location-aware host firewall and as part of a server and domain isolation strategy. Let's look at these two scenarios in detail to understand the considerations for these deployment options.

Windows Server 2008 (as well as Windows Vista) includes network awareness APIs that enable applications to sense changes to network configurations. What that means is that a corporate laptop that is placed into standby or hibernate and later fires up connected to a home network or a public hotspot will sense that it's on a new network and the firewall settings will be modified accordingly. The network awareness APIs handle that function. This function is clearly less useful on a Windows Server 2008 computer permanently connected to a corporate network. It's really intended for use on mobile computers (which could run Windows Server 2008, of course) that might be running Windows Vista as the client operating system. Although this functionality is included in Windows Vista, we'll refer to it within the Windows Server 2008 context. Windows Server 2008 identifies and remembers network connections and can apply settings according to these configurations. Applications can query for characteristics of networks including:

- **Connectivity**. Is the computer connected to a network, is it connected locally or to the Internet?

- **Connections**. Is the computer connected to the network by one or more connections?

- **Category**. What type of network is the computer connected to? Each network is assigned a category in Windows Server 2008 that helps identify the network type. Firewall settings can be applied based on the category assigned.

There are three network location types used in Windows Firewall with Advanced Security:

- **Domain**. A network on which the Windows Server 2008 (and Windows Vista) computer can authenticate via Active Directory.

- **Private**. A network is categorized as private if a user or application identifies it as such. Only networks behind a NAT device should be identified as private networks.

- **Public**. All other domain networks to which a computer connects. This includes public connections such as those found at airports, hotel lobbies and coffee shops (typically used for Windows Vista, not Windows Server 2008, though available in both operating systems).

Although all three profiles can be enabled simultaneously, only one profile is applied at a time and in this order:

1. If all connections (interfaces) are authenticated to the domain controller for the domain of which the computer is a member, then the **domain** profile is applied.

2. If all connections (interfaces) are authenticated to the domain controller or connected to networks identified as private, then the **private** profile is applied.

3. If either of the two previous scenarios does not apply, the **public** profile is applied.

Clearly, the public profile is the most restrictive and is applied in cases where the computer is not authenticated on its native domain or not connected to a private (and therefore somewhat protected) network. In all profiles, most incoming traffic is blocked by default with the exception of core networking traffic. With the private network profile applied, core networking traffic along with network discovery and remote assistance traffic is allowed. Default settings on all profiles also allow almost all out bound traffic; you must create specific rules to block outgoing traffic to suit your needs.

You might choose to configure specific rules for outbound traffic on your network. Although it's fairly clear why you'd block unsolicited incoming traffic, blocking outbound traffic can be extremely useful in preventing malware from "phoning home" and transmitting data back to a malicious source.

Server and Domain Isolation

As an experienced network administrator, you're probably familiar with the concept and practice of isolation. You know that you can physically and/or logically isolate network segments for a variety of reasons. You can use these segments to speed up the network by keeping local traffic local or you can use these segments as a way to increase network security. In a Windows Server-based network, you can isolate server and domain resources to limit access to authenticated and authorized computers to prevent unauthorized computers (and programs) from gaining access to resources. There are two primary types of isolation available in this regard: server and domain.

Server Isolation

A server can be configured to require secure authenticated communications only (IPsec). This means that the server will respond only to certain types of requests such as a database server that will respond only to a web application server. In this way, the only traffic allowed to the server is traffic coming from a specific computer or computers.

Domain Isolation

Domain isolation uses IPsec policy to provide protection for traffic sent between computers on a domain, including client (host) and server computers. Active Directory domain membership is used to ensure that computers that are members of the domain accept only secure, authenticated traffic (IPsec) from other members of the domain.

Configuring Windows Firewall with Advanced Security

Windows Firewall with Advanced Security is a *stateful* firewall and as such, it inspects all packets for all IP traffic (IPv4 and IPv6). The default setting is that all incoming traffic is blocked automatically unless it is a response to a host request (called *solicited traffic*) or unless it specifically has been allowed. Specific traffic can be allowed by configuring firewall rules to allow specific traffic by configuring the port number, application name, service name, and other settings.

Figure 1.24 shows the Windows Firewall with Advanced Security as viewed from within Server Manager. You can see the three profiles (Domain, Private, and Public) are all "on," but keep in mind that only one profile at a time is applied based on the connection type. The default settings for each profile are often adequate to start with. Notice in the right pane under Actions, you can import and export policies as well as restore defaults, a handy feature in the event you tweak your settings and create a problem that you can't pinpoint.

Notice also that you can access Inbound Rules, Outbound Rules, Connection Security Rules, as well as Monitoring (with additional options beneath Monitoring) from this screen. Keep in mind that the Windows Firewall with Advanced Security settings here are server-specific, meaning, these settings are applied to this server's connections. You can configure additional options by accessing the Windows Firewall with Advanced Security snap-in via the MMC console. We'll discuss that later in this chapter.

Figure 1.24 Windows Firewall with Advanced Security—
Server Manager View

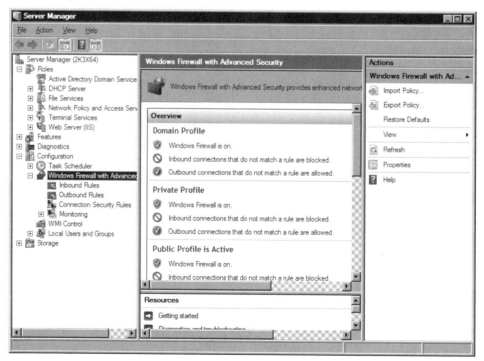

EXAM WARNING

Microsoft recommends enabling Windows Firewall with Advanced Security for all three profiles. You may see an exam question on this topic implying that you can enable only one profile at a time. You can configure these profiles by right-clicking **Windows Firewall with Advanced Security** in the left pane of Server Manager, then clicking **Properties**. You can also access the properties from the **Action** menu item, the Action pane on the right, or the center pane, when the folder is selected. All three profiles should be *enabled*, but only one will be *applied* based on the Network Awareness API functionality.

Incoming and Outgoing Traffic Filtering

Firewall rules are configured for incoming and outgoing traffic to determine which packets will be allowed and which will be blocked. When incoming traffic is blocked, an entry is made into the firewall log and the packet is discarded. The firewall options are numerous and we'll look briefly at these options.

In each profile (domain, private, and public), you can set rules regarding action taken for inbound and outbound connections. However, this is not the same thing as inbound and outbound rules for the firewall, though they certainly work together to provide security.

Firewall Rules

Rules can be configured for **inbound** or **outbound** traffic, for computers, users, programs, services, ports, and protocols. You can also specify which types of network adapters rules will apply to—local area connections, wireless, remote (VPN), and so on. You can also create a rule that is applied when a specific profile is used.

Inbound and outbound rules explicitly allow or block traffic that matches the criteria of the rule. For inbound traffic, you can configure rules that allow inbound traffic secured by IPsec, for example, but block traffic that is not secured by IPsec. You can also configure Windows Firewall with Advanced Security to take a specific action (to block or allow connections) when no inbound rules apply. Inbound traffic is blocked by default and must explicitly be allowed after installing Windows Firewall with Advanced Security.

Outbound rules can be used to block outbound traffic from a particular computer or group of computers, for example, or to block particular traffic types or through specific ports. Outbound traffic is allowed by default, so you must create an outbound rule to block any outgoing traffic.

By default, Windows Firewall with Advanced Security blocks all incoming unsolicited TCP/IP traffic. That's a good thing for security but usually creates connectivity problems of some sort in many networks. You may need to create rules for programs and services that act as servers, listeners, or peers. Program, port, and service rules have to be actively managed as server roles and configurations change. Therefore, less is more when creating rules. Create only the rules you need to get the job done and note which are likely to require on-going monitoring and maintenance versus those that you can set and forget.

The default behavior of Windows Firewall with Advanced Security is to dynamically open and close ports required by various programs. The recommended method, then, for allowing unsolicited incoming TCP/IP traffic through the firewall is to add programs to the rules list. That way, when a program is running, the needed traffic is allowed in. When the program is not running, traffic for that program is blocked. In Exercise 1.5, you can step through creating new inbound and outbound rules. Be sure to become familiar with setting up Windows Firewall with Advanced Security. Some of the new features are highly likely to end up as exam questions.

EXERCISE 1.5

CREATE NEW INBOUND AND OUTBOUND RULES

In this exercise, we'll walk through creating a new inbound and outbound rule. Begin by accessing the Windows Firewall with Advanced Security folder in the left pane of Server Manager (located under Configuration if the tree is collapsed). Expand the Windows Firewall node and right-click on Inbound Rules (or click New Rules in the Actions pane to the right) and select **New Rule**. The New Inbound Rule Wizard will launch.

1. The first screen gives you four options for a new rule: *Program, Port, Predefined*, and *Custom*. Select **Program** and click **Next**.

2. The Program screen prompts you to create a rule for all programs or for a particular program. If you want to set a rule for a particular program, click **This program path:** and the click **Browse** to locate the program file. We'll select **All programs** and click **Next**.

3. The next screen defines the Action to be taken. The choices are: Allow the connection; Allow the connection if it is secure (require the connection to be encrypted, override block rules), and Block the Connection. If you Allow the connection, all connections for

all programs will be allowed. If you Allow the connection if it is secure, you can require IPsec be used but you'll have to separately enable IPsec I the Connection Security rule node (more on that in a moment). You can require the connection be encrypted—this provides privacy along with data integrity and authentication. You can also specify that the rule override block rules. This can be helpful in using remote administration tools that might otherwise be blocked. However, to use this option, you must also specify an authorized computer or computer group. Select **Block the connection** (we're assuming your Windows Server 2008 is on a test network and not a live network for all exercises), then click **Next**.

4. In the Profile screen, you can apply this rule to any of the three profiles (domain, public, and private). The default setting selects all three profiles. Accept this setting by clicking **Next**.

5. The final screen of the New Inbound Rule Wizard is to create a name for the rule. Tip: Using a short descriptive name will help immensely if you want to manage the firewall rules via the command line netsh commands. For this rule, type **All Programs Blocked** in the Name: text box and leave the description blank. Click **Finish** to create this rule. Figure 1.25 shows the resulting new rule added to the Inbound Rules section. Notice that you can Disable Rule, Delete, check Properties, and get Help for the inbound rule you just created.

Figure 1.25 New Inbound Rule

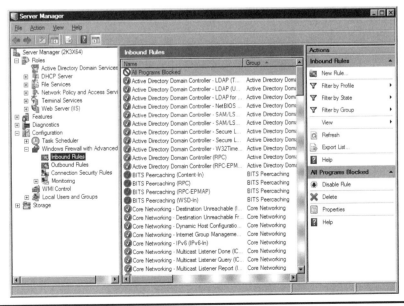

When you configure a new rule and select Port (instead of Program), you'll be prompted to create a rule for a specific TCP or UDP port. Once you select TCP or UDP, you can apply the rule to all local ports or just specific ports by entering port number(s). The Wizards for creating inbound and outbound rules have the same options and they're pretty straightforward. Keep in mind that you should start out with the default rules and add rules as you need them.

Connection Security Rules

Connection security rules are different than inbound and outbound traffic rules. Firewall rules allow traffic through the firewall based on rules you've configured, but they do not enforce connection security. To secure traffic with IPsec, you must create connection security rules. Note that the creation of connection security rules does not allow the traffic to pass through the firewall. These are two separate but interrelated concepts. Connection security rules are not applied to programs or services, they are applied only between the two computers trying to communicate.

Connection security rules work in conjunction with inbound and outbound rules. To create a new rule, click the **Connection security rules** node in the left pane and choose **New Rule** from the right pane (or click **Action** on the menu and select **New Rule** or right-click **Connection security rules** and select **New Rule** from the shortcut menu). When the New Connection Security Rule Wizard starts, you'll have several options. Figure 1.26 shows the Rule Type screen.

Figure 1.26 New Connection Security Rule Wizard

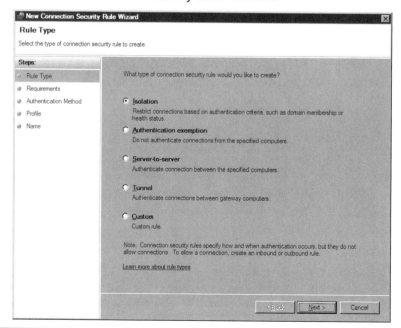

Your options on this screen are:

- **Isolation**. Restrict connections based on authentication criteria, such as domain membership or health status.

- **Authentication exemption**. Do not authenticate connections from specific computers.

- **Server-to-server**. Authenticate connections between the specified computers.

- **Tunnel**. Authenticate connections between gateway computers.

- **Custom**. Create a custom rule.

Remember, connection security rules specify how and when authentication and security occurs, but they do not allow or block connections; this is managed through inbound and outbound rules.

The options for the remaining screens of the wizard change depending on the option selected on the Rule Type screen. However, once you've made the Rule Type selection, the remaining configuration options are fairly straightforward (and vary depending on your Rule Type selection). If you choose to create a custom rule, you'll be prompted to provide Endpoint information for the computers creating the connection.

Firewall Profiles

You can configure different settings for different profiles. As mentioned earlier, there are three profiles: domain, private, and public. Figure 1.27 shows the Windows Firewall with Advanced Security Properties accessed by right-clicking Windows Firewall with Advanced Security and selecting **Properties** from the menu. You can see the three profiles in this dialog box: domain, private, and public. This is also where you can set IPsec Settings (not to be confused with AD IPsec policy).

Figure 1.27 Windows Firewall with Advanced Security Properties

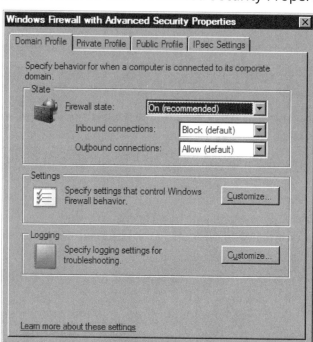

IPsec Settings

If you click the IPsec Settings tab in the Windows Firewall with Advanced Security Properties dialog box, you'll be able to access the IPsec settings, as shown in Figure 1.28. The key exchange (using ISAKMP if you recall the earlier discussion of IPsec basics) is the main mode. You can use the default settings or customize these settings by clicking the radio button to the left of **Advanced**, then clicking the **Customize** button, which will be enabled if you select Advanced. The quick mode (for data protection) also has Default and Advanced settings and advanced settings can be customized here. The Authentication Method can be configured to authenticate the computer, user, computer and user, computer certificate, or advanced. You can click the link at the bottom of the dialog box to learn more about your options or to understand what, exactly, the default settings are. In most cases, the default values are fine and you should start with these first. As you probably know, setting incorrect IPsec settings can interrupt communications. Also keep in mind that IPsec policy from Active Directory will also interact with these settings, so default settings is the best place to start unless you have a specific need to modify these settings.

Figure 1.28 IPsec Settings in Windows Firewall with Advanced Security

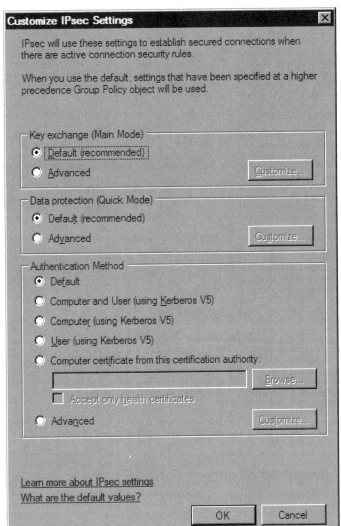

Though the default settings are fine in most cases, we've included a few screenshots of the advanced settings to give you an idea of just how much you can customize these settings. Be sure to scan these just so you're familiar with them. Although you probably won't see any questions on the exam testing your specific knowledge of the **Advanced** settings, it's good background knowledge to have in answering questions related to IPsec and firewall settings. Figure 1.29 shows the Advanced settings under the Main Mode (key exchange) section.

Figure 1.29 Main Mode Advanced Settings

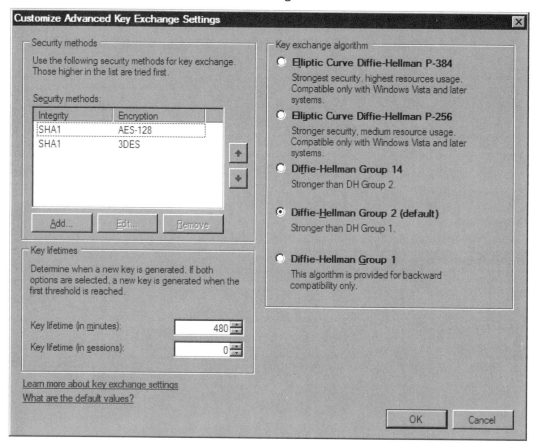

Figure 1.30 shows the Advanced settings for Quick Mode (data protection). As you can see, you can configure data integrity algorithms as well as data integrity and encryption algorithms in this area. You can add, remove, and edit these settings as well as move the algorithms up (or down) in the list. As stated in the dialog box, those algorithms higher in the list are tried first.

Figure 1.30 Quick Mode Advanced Settings

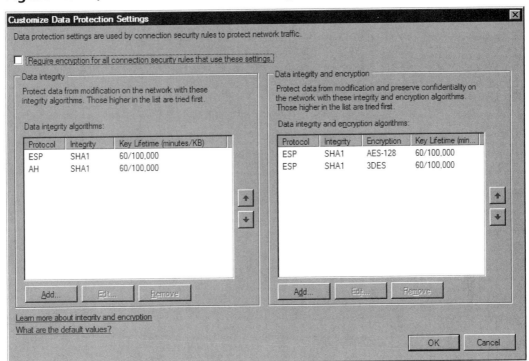

The third area of Advanced settings you can configure are the Authentication Method settings. If you click the **Advanced** radio button then click **Customize**, you'll see the settings shown in Figure 1.31. Notice that you can set a first and second authentication method but you cannot set a second authentication method if you specify a preshared key as the first authentication method. It doesn't matter where in the list the preshared key method is in the first authentication method list. If it's in the first authentication method list, you cannot specify a second authentication method.

Figure 1.31 Advanced Authentication Method Settings

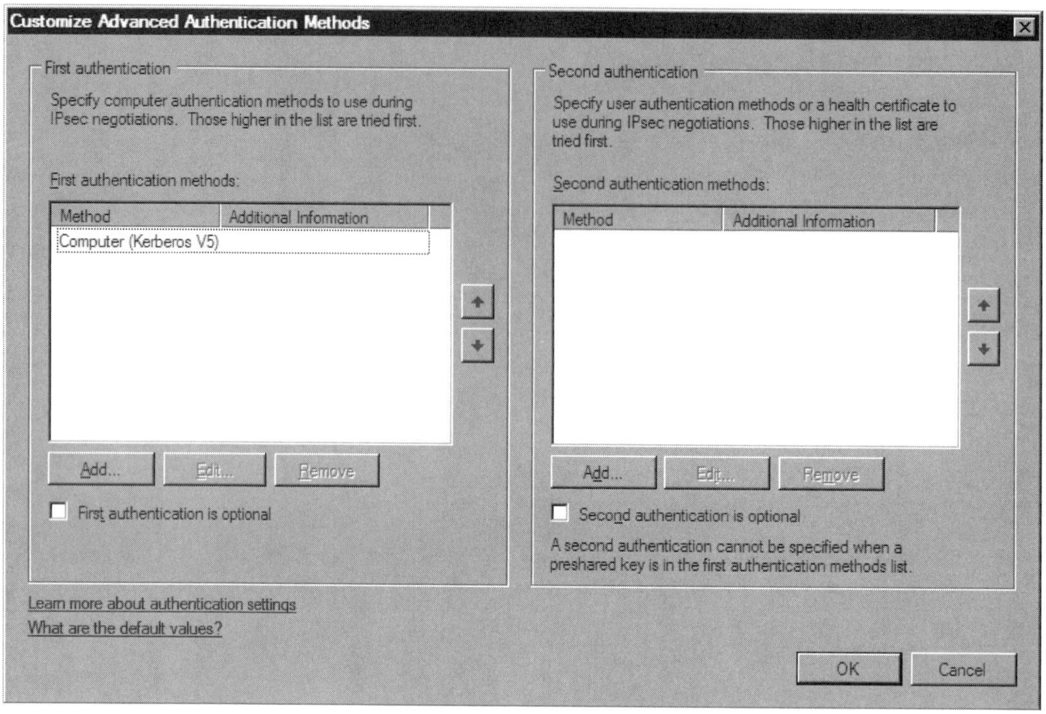

Monitoring

The monitoring folder under Windows Firewall with Advanced Security provides access to firewall, connection security rules and security associations monitoring features, shown in Figure 1.32. By default, when you select this folder in the left pane of Server Manager, you will see the three profiles in the center pane (domain, private, public). Each section can be collapsed and expanded as needed and the profile that is active will be shown as Active.

You can click **Firewall** in the left pane and see all the rules and traffic filtering in place. If you kept the All Programs Blocked rule we created earlier, you should see this rule in the list with a red circle with a line through it. Blocking rules show up with this red circle icon. Allow rules are displayed with a green circle and white checkmark so you can quickly locate Allow and Block rules.

Figure 1.32 Windows Firewall with Advanced Security Monitoring

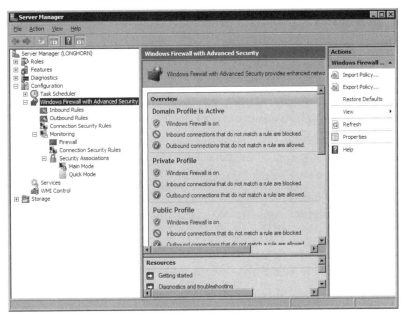

If you click **Connection Security Rules**, you can see all rules you created for connection security. If none are present, you are not requiring secure connections even if you allow or block secured traffic.

The last folder in the Monitoring tree is the Security Associations folder. It shows two modes: Main mode and Quick mode. Main mode lists all the Main mode security associations (SA) with detailed information about their settings and endpoints. You can view IP address of endpoints here. Quick mode lists all the Quick mode SAs with detailed information about them including IP addresses of endpoints. If you recall from our earlier discussion of IPsec, you have two SAs—Main mode (key exchange) and Quick mode (data protection).

Managing Windows Firewall with Advanced Security via Group Policy

In Microsoft operating systems prior to Windows Server 2008, local Group Policy was processed in the following order:

- Computer policies processed when the computer boots up.

- User policies processed when the user logs in.

- Computer and user policies refreshed at intervals.

Windows Server 2008 also provides the following:

- Computer and user policies processed when a computer establishes a VPN connection with a remote site.

- Computer and user policies processed when a computer comes out of hibernation or standby.

As you can see, these two additional processes are extremely helpful in maintaining a secure host through ensuring the computer has the most recent Group Policy settings related to the specific configuration of its connections.

To configure Windows Firewall with Advanced Security using Group Policy, access the Windows Firewall with Advanced Security snap-in from within the Group Policy Management Console. Note that if you deploy Windows Firewall with Advanced Security via Group Policy and block outbound connections, you'll have a problem unless you enable the Group Policy outbound rules. Otherwise, you might prevent all computers that receive the policy from updating the policy in the future, unless you manually update them, which defeats the purpose of using Group Policy to distribute settings.

Identifying Ports and Protocols

In some cases, you can't add the program or the service to the rules list. In these cases, you'll have to figure out which ports the program or service uses and add the port(s) to the rules list. When you add a port to the rules list, you have to specify the port number and protocol. You can specify ports only using TCP and UDP protocols.

EXAM WARNING

Here's a key take away for working with Windows Firewall with Advanced Security (and don't be surprised to see a question related to this on the exam). When you allow or block unsolicited traffic by creating a TCP or UDP port rule, that action will be taken any time Windows Firewall is running. This differs from creating a rule for a program in which the action is taken only when the program is running. So, if you create a rule to allow UDP 1443 traffic, that rule will be enabled when the firewall is enabled (which should be all the time). Contrast that to a program rule that specifies that it needs UDP 1443 traffic. In that case, the firewall will allow only UDP 1443 traffic when the program is running—a much more secure setting and the recommended method, whenever possible.

Command Line Tools for Windows Firewall with Advanced Security

As with just about any other server feature in Windows Server 2008, you can use the command line to adjust firewall settings. Once you've opened the command window (**Start | Run | cmd**), you use the **netsh** context with the **advfirewall** command. As with other commands, you can use the **netsh advfirewall /?** command to get a list of available options and switches. We've listed a few here for your convenience; all commands here begin with **netsh advfirewall** followed by the option shown.

- **Export**. Exports the current firewall policy to a file.

- **Import**. Imports a policy from a specified file.

- **Reset**. Restores Windows Firewall with Advanced Security to default settings.

- **Show**. Shows properties of a particular file including:

    - Show allprofiles

    - Show domainprofile

    - Show privateprofile

    - Show publicprofile

- **Help**. Displays a list of available commands.

In addition, you can use the subcontext commands as well. These are shown with their full syntax as an example of how they can be used:

- **netsh advfirewall consec /?** Shows the options available for the connection security settings within Windows Firewall with Advanced Security.

- **netsh advfirewall firewall /?** Shows the options available for configuring firewall rules.

- **netsh advfirewall monitor /?** Shows options available for configuring monitoring settings.

Exam Warning

Whenever you run server-type commands from the command line, you have must have Administrator-equivalent rights. Depending on the server and its roles, you may need Domain Administrator rights rather than local Administrator rights. That said, keep in mind that best practices suggest you log onto a server using a standard user account and log in using the Administrator account only by using the **Run As Administrator** option. This helps maintain tight security on your network. If you see questions on the exam that use the **Run As** option, chances are good it's a correct answer (or among possible correct answer candidates).

Windows Firewall with Advanced Security is a stateful host-based firewall that blocks incoming and outgoing traffic based on default profiles (domain, private, public) and based on connections using the Network Awareness API, which in Windows is called Network Location Awareness (NLA). You can configure the firewall on the local server via the Server Manger interface; advanced configuration must be done via the Microsoft Management Console (MMC) Windows Firewall with Advanced Security snap-in. IPsec is now integrated with firewall functions to help avoid conflicting settings between these two protective features.

Summary of Exam Objectives

Windows Server 2008 includes many of the IP features you're familiar with from Windows Server 2003, but there are important changes and additions as well. In order to score well on the exam, you'll need to have a solid foundation of IPv4 addressing and at least a basic understanding of IPv6. As with other Microsoft exams, the skills tested are not memorization of facts but the application of those facts in real world scenarios. In configuring IPv4 and IPv6, you're likely to see questions that test your knowledge and understanding of how you might transition to IPv6 or how you might incorporate IPv6 in an IPv4-based network. Knowing the length of IPv4 and IPv6 addresses along with how they are configured into network and host segments as well as how different network infrastructure components handle IP packets is important and will be tested. Concepts in IPv6 such as local-link addressing, global unicast, multicast, and anycast addressing and special addressing will likely show up in exam questions.

The role of DHCP server should be one that is familiar to you and as with IP in Windows Server 2008, many of the features and options are similar to Windows Server 2003. New features will be highlighted and you're likely to see questions regarding the implementation of DHCP in a mixed (IPv4 and IPv6) environment. Look for questions on configuring the DHCP server, especially in an IPv6 setting (scope, reservations, exclusions) and in a mixed environment. DHCP server, relay agent, and lease settings will be the most likely areas to be tested.

DHCP integrates with Network Access Protection (NAP), a new feature that enforces computer health through a variety of mechanisms. DHCP and NAP can be used to enforce client health through granting full access, restricted access, or no access (drop client packet) based on your network's unique needs.

With the release of the Windows Server 2008 Core, you're likely to see questions related to using the command line. Though you won't be expected to memorize every single command line command and all the options, you should be conversant with using the command line and with the general syntax of those commands. Also be prepared to answer questions that test your understanding of how command line commands can be utilized for security and efficiency such as using batch files that run various commands to configure and control remote devices.

Network authentication in Windows Server 2008 is managed through the familiar tools including Active Directory and Group Policy as well as through the latest addition, Network Policy and Access Services. Network Policy and Access services includes Network Policy Server (NPS), Routing and Remote Access (RRAS), Remote Authentication Dial In User Service (RADIUS) server,

RADIUS proxy, and Network Access Protection. This consolidation of network access services helps in managing network access and authentication. Just as with Windows Server 2003, Kerberos is the default authentication method through Active Directory. However, there are numerous settings for local, remote, wired, and wireless access to the network. Most of the changes involved upgrading authentication protocols and removing support for older, less secure protocols. In order to do well in the exam, you should be familiar with the basic mechanics of user and computer authentication as well as protocols used in various scenarios. The 802.11 and 802.1X standards are likely to be well-represented on the exam as will the 802.3 Wired Network Policies options. Familiarity with EAP, PEAP, MS-CHAPv2, PPTP, L2TP/IPsec, and SSTP will be needed in order to successfully navigate through network authentication questions.

Internet Protocol Security (IPsec) is being used by more and more organizations due to the ability to protect and encrypt network traffic through transport and tunnel modes. Your understanding of how to implement IPsec, especially through Active Directory Group Policy (as in Windows Server 2003 and prior) as well as through the Windows Firewall with Advanced Security, is likely to be highlighted. IPsec configuration for inbound and outbound traffic is now integrated in the firewall capabilities, and settings for domain, public, private, and IPsec can be configured through the firewall properties. A key takeaway is the understanding how IPsec Group Policy and IPsec settings in firewall interact to provide a secure framework for IP traffic. As with other technologies in Windows Server 2008, you can configure and check IPsec settings via the command line and you should have a solid understanding of the more commonly used IPsec command line options.

Another area highlighted in the exam is the Windows Firewall with Advanced Security. The addition of advanced security options provides new security methods that were not previously integrated into the firewall functionality. Understanding the new features, including how network perimeter firewall settings versus host-based firewall settings may differ; how to configure the firewall settings to enable IPsec, IPv6 and support for AD user, computer, and groups will be key to successfully navigating exam questions and answers. Again, the integration with IPsec settings will likely show up on your exam as well. Expect to see questions related to how you could configure the firewall to support various security scenarios such as preventing external users from pinging an internal server or how to limit DNS name resolution to internal computers only. This also includes the ability to configure inbound and outbound rules, set IP filtering, create connection security rules, and monitor results. Rule types are likely to be prominent in this section of your exam, so pay special attention to isolation, authentication exemption, server-to-server and tunnel rule types along with the associated authentication methods. Give some thought to various scenarios (especially based on your prior experience with the Microsoft exam style) to be sure you're comfortable with configuring firewall settings in Windows Firewall with Advanced Security.

If you're familiar with the Microsoft exam style, you know that questions are pulled from a pool of available questions, so no two exams are completely alike. However, Microsoft does have several reliable patterns and one is that questions typically focus more on new features, and questions test you on how you would use these in real-world scenarios. As you review material prior to the exam, keep that in mind and you should find yourself focusing on the highest priority topics.

Exam Objectives Fast Track

Configuring IPv4 and IPv6 Addressing

- ☑ IPv4 addressing uses 32-bits and a subnet mask to identify the network and host portions of the address.

- ☑ IPv6 addressing uses 128 bits and the network information is contained in the left-most 64 bits, host information in the right-most 64 bits. IPv6 uses hexadecimal notation.

- ☑ Supernetting uses the Classless Inter-Domain Routing (CIDR) notation, and this notation is also used in IPv6.

- ☑ IPv6 address types include local-link, unique local IPv6 unicast, global unicast, multicast, anycast, and special addressing. Local-link maps to IPv4 private addressing, global unicast maps to IPv4 public addressing.

- ☑ The local loopback address in IPv6 is ::1/128; FF80::/64 is used for local-link addressing.

- ☑ IP4 to IP6 transition technologies include dual IP layer architecture, IPv6 over IP4 tunneling, Intra-Site Automatic Tunneling Addressing Protocol (ISATAP), 6to4, and Teredo.

Configuring Dynamic Host Configuration Protocol (DHCP)

- ☑ The DHCP server role in Windows Server 2008 includes native support for IPv6 as DHCPv6.

☑ Scope, reservations, exceptions, and scope options are configured in IPv6 much the same as they are in IPv4.

☑ A DHCP server should have its scope and configuration data set, the scope should be activated, and the server should be authorized in the Active Directory domain in order to bring a new DHCP server online.

☑ DHCP and Network Access Protection (NAP) are integrated in Windows Server 2008, providing the ability to deny or limit access to network resources based on the client computer's health status. Health status includes having the latest operating system updates and antivirus signatures installed.

☑ DHCP can be configured using command line commands. This is helpful for managing DHCP servers remotely across the network.

Configuring Network Authentication

☑ Network authentication is managed through Active Directory and uses Kerberos as the default authentication protocol. NTLMv2 is supported for backward compatibility and should be used only if needed.

☑ Network Policy and Access Services is a role that can be installed on the Windows Server 2008 computer. It includes Network Policy Server (NPS), Routing and Remote Access Server (RRAS), Remote Authentication Dial In User Service (RADIUS), RADIUS proxy, and Network Access Protection (NAP).

☑ WLAN access and authentication follows 802.11, 802.1X, and 802.3 standards. Associated protocols include EAP-TLS, PEAP-TLS, PEAP-MS-CHAPv2, PPTP, and SSTP.

☑ Support for SPAP, EAP-MD5-CHAP, and MS-CHAPv1 has been removed in Windows Server 2008. EAPHost architecture includes new features not supported in earlier operating systems including support for additional EAP methods, network discovery, vendor-specific EAP types, and coexistence of multiple EAP types across vendors.

☑ Routing and remote access supports the use of IPsec through transport and tunnel modes. Point-to-point tunneling protocol (PPTP), Microsoft Point-to-Point Encryption (MPPE), Layer 2 Tunneling Protocol with IPsec (L2TP/IPsec), and Secure Socket Tunneling Protocol (SSTP) are supported for data authentication, integrity, encryption, and confidentiality.

Configuring IP Security (IPsec)

☑ Internet Protocol Security (IPsec) provides peer authentication, data origin authentication, data integrity, data confidentiality, antireplay, and key management. Due to increasing needs for network security, IPsec is being implemented with greater frequency.

☑ The AH and ESP protocols within IPsec provide different types of security. Data encryption is provided by ESP, not by AH, making it the preferred protocol.

☑ IPsec is integrated with Windows Firewall with Advanced Security and is also managed through Group Policy in the Active Directory context.

☑ IPsec can be configured via command line commands within the **netsh ipsec** context.

☑ IPsec can be used to provide server and domain isolation to ensure secure IP traffic remains secure.

Windows Firewall with Advanced Security in Windows Server 2008

☑ Windows Firewall with Advanced Security in Windows Server 2008 includes numerous new features to simplify and enhance both network perimeter and host security.

☑ New features include IPsec integration, support for IPv6, integration with Active Directory user, computer, and group settings, location aware profiles (for mobile computers), detailed rules, and expanded authenticated bypass capabilities.

☑ Inbound and outbound rules along with connection security rules provide the network administrator with the ability to create finely tuned rules to protect the network and the host.

☑ Connection security rules including isolation, authentication exemption, server-to-server, and tunnel rules can be configured with requirements, authentication methods, and profiles to manage and restrict connections on the network.

☑ IPsec settings, including Main Mode and Quick Mode (computer and user authentication, respectively), can be configured to use a variety of authentication methods.

☑ Customized IPsec data protection settings allow you to configure data protection to use the ESP and AH IPsec protocols. Advanced authentication methods, including the ability to provide primary and secondary authentication methods (Kerberos, certificates, NTLMv2, etc.), can also be configured within the IPsec settings of Windows Firewall with Advanced Security.

☑ Windows Firewall with Advanced Security can be configured using the snap-in from the Group Policy Management console.

☑ You can use command line options for configuring, managing, and monitoring Windows Firewall with Advanced Security.

Exam Objectives
Frequently Asked Questions

Q: I'm pretty solid with IP addressing in IPv4 but I'm not really well-versed in IPv6. How much do I need to know for the exam?

A: If you're familiar with Microsoft exams, you'll know that the questions are pulled from a pool of questions and that they'll progressively test you on various elements. So, the short answer is that there's no guarantee you'll see any questions about IPv6 on the exam, whether directly or indirectly, but there's a high likelihood you will need to be comfortable with IPv6 in order to navigate one or more questions on the exam. You should understand the basics such as the address format; how networks, hosts, and ranges are specified; as well as where you configure IPv6 settings. Also be clear about the terminology, such as temporary and nontemporary, specific to IPv6 and be sure to be familiar with site local, link local, and other IPv6 formats and naming conventions.

Q: I've been reading a bit about Windows Server 2008 online and there's a lot of discussion about the Core version. What do I need to know about this?

A: Throughout this chapter, we've included brief references to the Core installation and specifically to the command line commands available to you. Expect to see questions about using the command line on the exam. Command line options have always been available, but the release of the Core version of Window Server 2008 will certainly bring this to the forefront. Where applicable, we've included command line commands to demonstrate how these commands can be used. Don't expect the exam to test you on syntax necessarily, but do expect to see questions related to using the command line options for frequently used features.

Q: DHCP is pretty basic stuff, though the addition of IPv6 makes it a bit different. What should I expect in the way of DHCP questions on the exam?

A: Expect to see questions that test your understanding of DHCP configuration and settings as well as questions that test your understanding and knowledge of new DHCP features. Since IPv6 is just being rolled into organizations, you can expect to see some IPv6-based questions related to DHCP.

Q: There are tons of protocols—sometimes it's like alphabet soup—MS-CHAP, MS-CHAP v2, EAP, PEAP, PPP, Kerberos V5, and the list goes on. I'm having a hard time keep all these straight and remembering how they're used (or not) in Windows Server 2008. Any tips you can share?

A: It does seem like every new release from Microsoft comes with a lot of new acronyms to learn, so the ALC (acronym learning curve) can be a bit daunting. You're probably familiar with some of these protocols from previous versions of Windows. If not, you might want to brush up on those before heading in to Windows Server 2008. However, there are some basics that might help. First, divide protocols into those used to authentication users locally (Kerberos, etc.) and those used to authentication users remotely (PPP, EAP, PEAP). It can be helpful to divide the protocols according to these areas so you can better keep track of what they do and when they're used. Also, spend time in the Routing and Remote Access Server segment of Windows Server 2008 as well as in the Windows Firewall with Advanced Security section. The more you see the various protocols being used in the default screens, the more they should sink in. That said, there are a lot of acronyms and thankfully, Microsoft exams don't test you on acronyms. Most of the time, the item will be spelled out the first time you see it (as we do in this book). If it's not, then it's a pretty common acronym such as AD for Active Directory or IP, IPsec, or DHCP.

Q: I'm not sure I'm clear on the difference between IPsec settings in the Windows Firewall with Advanced Security and the IPsec settings in Active Directory Group Policy. I've reread the material in this chapter, but I am still a bit confused. Can you provide any additional information that might help?

A: Yes. Group Policy in AD is going to specify how computers, users, and groups much be configured or must interact with the network. If you specify IPsec within Group Policy for a set of computers, you are requiring that all computers to which that policy is applied must use IPsec to communicate with other computers (for example). Windows Firewall with Advanced Security, on the other hand, can be configured to require IPsec for inbound and/or outbound connections. So, the computers to which the IPsec Group Policy has been applied (we'll call them the GP computers for short here) can communicate with other GP computer or other computer using IPsec all day long and have no interaction with the IPsec rules in the Windows Firewall on the Windows Server 2008. Suppose, however, that one of those computers needs to access an application or service running on that Windows Server 2008 computer or access something on the other side of that server. Now the firewall rules come into play. Since the GP computer is already using IPsec, it's likely it will conform to the firewall rules and its communications will be conducted security. On the other hand, if the GP computer tried to communicate via the server to a computer elsewhere that was not IPsec compliant, either the GP policy or the firewall rules would prevent that (depending on configuration). GP will apply IPsec rules to computers and groups on your network. IPsec rules in Windows Firewall with Advance Security applies to inbound and outbound traffic on the server itself. Together, these can create a secure solution and unlike previous versions of Windows Firewall, the IPsec configuration is integrated to prevent unintentional gaps in IPsec settings.

Self Test

1. You need to set up a network in the lab for a training class. You want to isolate the lab network from the rest of the corporate network so students don't inadvertently do something that takes the entire network down. What IP addressing method would you use?

    A. Private network addressing

    B. Public network addressing

    C. Network Address Translation

    D. Subnet isolation through subnet mask

2. Your boss asked you to subnet a network in the lab for an upcoming class. He hands you a piece of paper while he's on the phone and it simply says "192.168.10.x/25. 4 subnets." What is the subnet mask and the first address in each subnet?

    A. 255.255.255.0/ 192.168.10.1, 192.168.10.32, 192.168.10.64, 192.168.10.128

    B. 255.255.255.252/ 192.168.10.0, 192.168.10.32, 192.168.10.64, 192.168.10.128

    C. 255.255.255.240/ 192.168.10.0, 192.168.16.0, 192.168.24.0, 192.168.32.0

    D. 255.255.255.128/ 192.168.10.1, 192.168.10.33, 192.168.10.65, 192.168.10.97

3. You have a growing network that originally was configured using the private Class C address space. However, you're now about to grow beyond the maximum number of devices and need to expand but you don't anticipate needing more than a total of 290 addresses. What action would you take to solve this problem that would create the least disruption to your network?

    A. Install a router. Create two new scopes on your DHCP Server and reassign IP addresses.

    B. Change the default subnet mask to 255.255.252.0.

    C. Change the IP addressing scheme from Class C to Class B.

    D. Assign new computers on the network IP addresses from the existing address pool.

4. Your company's president comes to you and says that he understands IPv6 is fully supported in Windows Server 2008. He will approve your IT budget if it includes plans to transition to Windows Server 2008 and IPv6. However, he wants to know how quickly you can transition to IPv6. What should you tell him?

   A. There is no fast and easy way to transition to IPv6. Much of the Internet's backbone is running on IPv4, so transitional technologies will be required. You'd recommend setting up IPv6 segments and using a tunneling protocol for the transition to begin.

   B. The transition to IPv6 on the Internet backbone has been completed and as soon as the company upgrades to Windows Server 2008 and replaces its routers, you're good to go.

   C. There is no reasonable way to transition to IPv6 for this organization since all hardware and software would have to be replaced to run Windows Server 2008 or Windows Vista. The cost would be prohibitive and is therefore not recommended.

   D. The transition to IPv6 requires the installation of new hardware and software on all subnets using IPv6 exclusively. In the meantime, IPv4 can be used on older subnets and IPv6 can be used on newer subnets and a specific IPv4 to IPv6 router can be installed to bridge the two.

5. You open Windows Server 2008 DHCP Server role and examine the scope settings one of your staff members created, shown in Figure 1.33. Based on this information, which statement is true?

Figure 1.33 Windows Server 2008 DHCP Configuration

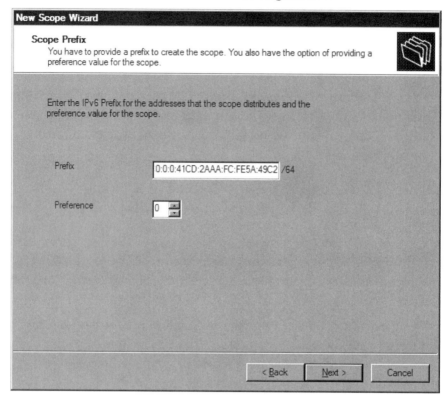

A. The Preference Value is incorrect. It must be set to 1 for all addresses that use the /64 option.

B. The Prefix Value is incorrect. It cannot begin with 0:0:0:.

C. The Prefix Value is too long. It should contain fewer digits.

D. Both B and C are correct.

E. The Prefix value and Preference values are correct.

6. You've asked Justin, a junior member of your IT staff, to install Windows Server 2008 on a spare computer in the lab and set up the DHCP role so you can teach a class on what's new in DHCP. Justin hesitates and asks how he should set the scope settings so it doesn't take the network down. What should you tell Justin?

A. DHCP in Windows Server 2008 cannot be installed on a computer attached to a network with a live DHCP server. Remove the server's network connection before installing DHCP.

B. Only one DHCP can exist on a network. He should configure the server as a DHCP relay agent instead.

C. A new DHCP server must be authorized in AD before it can perform the DHCP role.

D. Adding a new DHCP server could not take the network down.

7. You need to expand your network and create a new subnet for a new research project. You want the traffic for the research group to remain local to the subnet. None of the computers for the research project are installed yet. What's the fastest and easiest way to go about creating this subnet and keeping local traffic local?

A. Add the computers to the network, assign them a different subnet mask, enable IPsec through Group Policy, and assign it to the research project subnet.

B. Create a scope on the DHCP server that will provide addresses to just those computers, install a router, assign it a static IP address, and use that router as the default gateway for the computers on that subnet.

C. Install a new router and configure it as the DHCP Relay Agent for the existing scope using a static IP address. Then, connect the new computers to the network through the new router.

D. Modify the existing scope options on the DHCP server so that the subnet addresses for the new research subnet are excluded from the scope. Install a new router and configure it with a static IP address from the same range as the excluded IP addresses. Last, connect the new computers to the subnet and check that they are configured to automatically get IP configuration data.

8. The company has just leased a nearby building so it can expand operations. You've been asked to configure the network infrastructure in the new building. You configure the DHCP server that will go on this new network segment with the following options:

- Scope: 192.168.10.0 to 192.168.15.0

- Subnet mask: 255.255.252.0

- Default gateway: 192.168.10.1

- Exclusions: 192.168.12.0 to 192.168.12.20

- Reservations: 192.168.10.1 DNS server, 192.168.12.2 DNS server, 192.168.12.5 WINS server, 192.168.12.6 Router8

You set Router 8 to have a static IP address of 192.168.12.6 and configure it to be a DHCP relay agent. What's wrong with your set up?

A. You can't have two DNS servers on one subnet, the scope and the subnet mask do not match, you can't set up a router as DHCP relay agent.

B. Your scope cannot have a zero in the last place, your subnet mask is wrong, your default gateway and your DNS server share the same IP address and may slow down the subnet, you don't need a WINS server.

C. Your default gateway and your DNS server use the same IP address. You cannot have a DHCP relay agent (your router) and a DHCP server on the same subnet. Your excluded range and your reservations settings are mutually exclusive.

D. The default gateway has the wrong IP address and all network traffic will be sent to the Router, causing all local traffic to be routed to the main network and back again, causing too much unneeded network traffic. You don't need a DHCP server on this subnet and should simply enable the server as a RRAS server to handle remote traffic to the main corporate site.

9. You've set up a new subnet with a DHCP server. After a few days, mobile users begin complaining they can't log onto the network when they're locally connected (at their desks, for example). What would you check in your DHCP settings?

A. Scope settings

B. Exclusions

C. Subnet mask or default gateway

D. Lease duration

10. A recent change to the network infrastructure configuration was completed over the weekend. Monday morning, users begin complaining that the network is terribly slow. The Help Desk phones are lit up and there's a rumble in the building as users start going to others' desks asking if they're having any luck using network resources and getting out to the Internet. The new configuration is shown in Figure 1.34. What would you change in order to best resolve this problem?

Figure 1.34 New Network Configuration

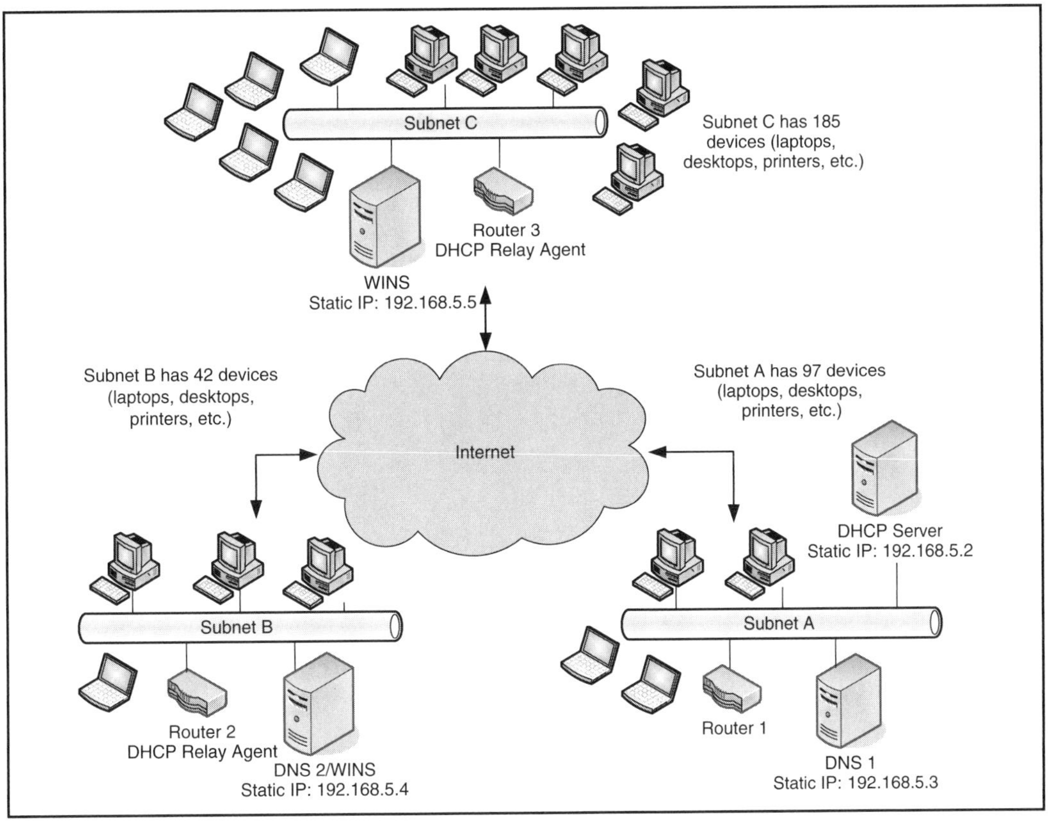

A. Add a DNS Server to Subnet C.

B. Remove the DHCP Relay Agent role from either Router 2 or Router 3.

C. Add a DHCP Server to Subnet C and remove Router 3.

D. Both A and C.

E. Add a DHCP Server to Subnet C.

Self Test Quick Answer Key

1.	**D**	6.	**C**
2.	**D**	7.	**B**
3.	**B**	8.	**C**
4.	**A**	9.	**D**
5.	**D**	10.	**E**

## Chapter 2

MCTS/MCITP
Exam 642

Configuring DNS

Exam objectives in this chapter:

- An Introduction to Domain Name System (DNS)
- Configuring a DNS Server
- Creating DNS Zones
- Configuring and Managing DNS Replication
- Creating and Managing DNS Records
- Configuring Name Resolution for Client Computers

Exam objectives review:

- ☑ Summary of Exam Objectives
- ☑ Exam Objectives Fast Track
- ☑ Exam Objectives Frequently Asked Questions
- ☑ Self Test
- ☑ Self Test Quick Answer Key

Introduction

Today, most of the computers in the world are identified by IP address. Although computers are great at working with numbers, humans generally have an easier time remembering names than long strings of numbers. This is where Domain Name Servers (DNS) comes into play. DNS is responsible for resolving host names to IP addresses, so that we do not have to remember each individual host's IP address.

DNS is by far one of the most important parts of most networks, and the exam covers DNS heavily. There are several reasons why DNS is so important. For starters, there are countless computers on the Internet, and new ones are being added all the time. There is no way that a single database could possibly maintain a list of all these machines, and keep the list up to date. DNS takes a hierarchical approach to name resolution, making it ideal for keeping up with vast numbers of hosts. When you enter an Internet domain into your Web browser, it is the DNS server that figures out the IP address that's associated with Web site you have requested.

DNS is also important on Windows networks, because the Active Directory is completely dependent on DNS. You cannot even create an Active Directory forest without having a DNS server on your network.

In this chapter, we will start with the basics, by talking more in depth about what DNS is and what it does. As the chapter progresses, we will cover fundamental concepts such as forward and reverse lookup zones, forwarders, root hints, and dynamic DNS updates. The chapter will also discuss some of the more common types of DNS records, and explain how DNS fits in with legacy host name resolution mechanisms.

An Introduction to Domain Name System (DNS)

The domain name system allows the use of user-friendly names to locate hosts on IP networks. Since Windows Server 2003 and Windows XP DNS has been the primary method used to resolve names into IP addresses on Windows networks. In addition to hostname resolution, DNS also facilitates reverse lookup of IP addresses into hostnames, as well as the location of network services such as domain controllers. Windows Server 2008 includes major updates to DNS that allow it to fully support IPv6 addresses.

Name resolution on IP networks originally took place using *hosts* files that were originally stored centrally and later locally on every host. Most hosts, including all Windows computers, still contain these files and can use them for name resolution. The files were nothing more than long lists consisting of every hostname on the network and its corresponding IP address. Over time the ability of these single, flat files began to hinder performance and became far too difficult to manage.

The domain name system solved these problems by allowing for a partitioning of the global hostname space. This partitioning occurs on two levels, the logical and the physical. The logical portion is covered in this section. The physical portion is covered in the section entitled *Creating DNS Zones*. Logically, DNS is divided into tiers of domains and subdomains. Technically, there is no name for the domain at the very top, but often it is represented as the "." domain. Every fully qualified domain name (FQDN) has a period (.) at the end of it, though most users never see it because it is entered for them automatically in the background. When a user types *www.syngress.com* into a web browser, the actual name resolution request that goes out onto the network is *www.syngress.com.*, with the period being added by either the browser or name resolution (DNS) client software.

A FQDN tells you everything you need to know about what a host is called and where it is located within DNS. The previous example, *www.syngress.com*, means that the user is looking for the *www* host in the *syngress.com* domain. Typically the left-most portion of a FQDN is a hostname. Sometimes, however, you will see a domain name without the host and it will look just like a FQDN. For example, a FQDN might be *host1.authors.syngress.com*, but you might see only *authors.syngress.com* referred to. It's easy to think that *authors* is a hostname in circumstances like this, and really there is no way to differentiate it. You just have to be on your guard as to whether a domain name is being referred to or a FQDN (which includes the hostname).

The domain portion of the FQDN lets you know the location of the host on the network. *Host1.authors.syngress.com* tells you that the host is located in the *authors* subdomain, of the *syngress* subdomain, of the *com* domain. Often you will see portions of the name space being referred to differently. For example, you might see the *com*, *net*, *org*, and other upper level namespace domains being referred to as top-level domains (TLDs). The major TLDs are listed in Table 2.1. Countries also typically have their own TLDs; a sample of these can be found in Table 2.2. It is appropriate to refer to them as TLDs or domains; we will use domain in this book because Microsoft's software uses only the terms domain and subdomain.

Table 2.1 Internet Top-Level Domain Names

TLD	Designated Use
.aero	Air-transport industry related
.asia	Asia-Pacific region
.biz	Business related
.cat	Catalan language or culture related
.com	Originally designated for commercial purposes, but now in wide use for any purpose; this is the most commonly used TLD
.coop	Cooperatives as defined by the Rochdale Principles
.edu	Educational, generally limited to institutions of learning, such as 2- and 4-year colleges and universities
.gov	U.S. government entities and agencies
.info	Information
.int	International organizations, offices, and programs that are endorsed by a treaty between two or more nations
.jobs	Used by companies with jobs to advertise
.mil	United States Military
.mobi	Mobile-compatible sites
.museum	Museums
.name	Individuals, by name; registrations may be challenged if they are not by individuals, or the owners of fictional characters, in accordance with the domain's charter
.net	Originally designated for use by a network, but now in wide use for any purpose
.org	Originally designated for use by nonprofit organizations, but now in wide use for any purpose
.pro	Professions, currently reserved for licensed doctors, attorneys, and certified public accountants
.tel	Internet communication services
.travel	Travel and tourism industry related sites

Table 2.2 Country Top-Level Domain Names

TLD	Country
.au	Australia
.cn	Mainland China
.ca	Canada
.de	Germany
.es	Spain
.eu	European Union
.uk	United Kingdom
.us	United States

Understanding Public Name Resolution

Different servers are often responsible for the various logical domain partitions seen in a FQDN. When a user takes an action that requires name resolution, such as typing a FQDN into a web browser, a flurry of activity is set in motion on the network. Each host is configured to communicate with one or more DNS server(s). If the first DNS server is contacted successfully, any additional DNS servers are not used. This is true even if the first DNS server contacted isn't able to successfully resolve the FQDN to an IP address.

The first server contacted may physically contain the record being requested. For example, your host (host1.syngress.com) may be attempting to locate a second host (host2.syngress.com) that is part of the same logical portion of the domain namespace. It's likely that the DNS server your host is configured to use is *authoritative* for the domain your computer belongs to (syngress.com). This means that it physically contains the information that maps host, service, and other names to IP addresses within the domain. If this is the case, your DNS server will return the requested information and the name resolution process ends.

If, however, your server doesn't contain the needed information, a longer process is initiated. Let's say that your host (host1.syngress.com) is attempting to contact *www.elsevier.com*. Because the *elsevier* domain is different than your *syngress* domain, it is unlikely that your DNS server contains the needed information for it.

Remember that all FQDNs have a period (.) appended to them. When a DNS server cannot directly answer a request, it next contacts a name server for this "." domain. By default, DNS servers contain *root hints* that tell the server who these "." name servers are, and where they can be found. The "." domain name server examines the request and attempts to determine if there is any part of it that it can answer. In this case, it is likely to be configured for high-level domain name servers such as *com*, *net*, *org*, *edu*, and so forth; and will return a list of the name servers for the *com* domain to your DNS server.

Your DNS server will next send a request to one or more of the name servers for the *com* domain. These name servers will examine the request and attempt to determine if they have information relating to any portion of the requested FQDN. Assuming the *elsevier* domain is registered properly through an Internet name registrar, and not simply made up by someone, the *com* DNS servers will know where to find the *elsevier* domain name servers. The addresses for these DNS servers will be returned to your DNS server.

Finally, your DNS server will contact one or more *elsevier* DNS server(s). Because these name servers should contain the information for the *www* host, your DNS server finally receives the IP address that your computer needs to contact. It caches the information locally for a period of time so it can answer other potential requests for the same resource more rapidly, and returns the requested information to your computer. Your computer also caches it for a period of time so that it doesn't have to continue to ask the DNS server for the information each time you type the FQDN into your web browser. With the IP address now in hand, your computer can contact the host.

Understanding Private Name Resolution

The previous example used a host with Internet access attempting to resolve the name of a publicly accessible web server with a publicly registered domain name. Not all name resolution involves publicly resolvable names, however. It is also possible for a DNS namespace to be private, and not connected to the Internet. For example, a highly sensitive network may not allow external connections for security reasons. These may include governmental, research and development, and similar types of networks. When this is the case, it is not necessary to use publicly registered names.

Private DNS networks are configured with the equivalent of their own "." name servers. These are private DNS servers that sit at the top of the organization's network. DNS servers in the organization typically are configured to query them when they don't have the information a client is requesting. Accordingly, the DNS administrators for the organization configure these servers to know where at least one other level of the logical domain name space resides. Although more flexibility can be accommodated, essentially, these administrators build a structure of DNS servers that mirrors the publicly resolvable namespace. Very small organizations might have everything required on just one or two DNS servers. Large multinational organizations may have layers of DNS servers that rival the complexity of the public name servers. Regardless of which is the case, clients and DNS servers follow the same resolution process as the one covered in the previous section.

Understanding Microsoft's DNS Terminology

Much of the terminology Microsoft uses for DNS is standard across the industry, but some of it isn't. Now that you have a good idea of how DNS works, in this section you'll get an overview of the official terminology that accompanies the preceding process as well as a bit more detail for some of them. The local DNS software on a Windows host is referred to as the *resolver*. When a user makes a request, such as for a Web page, the resolver first checks the local cache to see if it contains the needed information. Next, the local hosts file is checked. Finally, a query is sent to the first DNS server that the resolver is configured to use.

Microsoft calls this step a *client-to-server query*. This query involves the client asking for very specific information. In the case of a Web site, it would be the IP address that matches a FQDN. If the DNS server queried does not have the information needed, it contacts other DNS servers attempting to locate it.

Server-to-server queries are also called *recursive queries*. These differ from client-to-server queries in that they ask two questions to the receiving DNS server. The first is for the specific information needed, such as the IP address to match a FQDN. The second is for any information that may get the requesting DNS server closer to obtaining the specific information that is being requested by the client. This later aspect of recursive queries is what results in a DNS server for a domain (such as *com*) sending the name servers for the next domain in the FQDN if it knows it (such as elsevier).

TEST DAY TIP

In addition to caching responses from DNS servers containing the requested resources (called positive caching), the local resolver also caches negative responses. These result from a failure to locate DNS resources. When a server returns a request to a client's query that contains a negative response, the local resolver caches it and will not request it again for a period of time. Temporary DNS problems can thus become longer term issues until this cached record expires. You can manually purge the client's resolver cache using the following command: **ipconfig /flushdns**.

Configuring a DNS Server

DNS servers can be complex to configure. Midsize to large organizations often have dedicated DNS administrators because of the specialized knowledge required. In this section, we'll examine the core configuration steps at the server-level of the DNS role in Windows Server 2008. We'll begin by installing the role itself, and then look at the components it offers to direct queries without using locally stored records. This will include where to configure the "." name servers (called root hints), as well as how to bypass them and direct server-to-server queries to other DNS servers instead.

Installing the DNS Server Role

To install the DNS Server role, follow these steps:

1. Open Server Manager by clicking **Start | Server Manager**.

2. In the right pane, scroll down to **Roles Summary** and click **Add Roles**.

3. In the **Add Roles Wizard** dialog, read the **Before You Begin** page and click **Next**.

4. On the **Select Server Roles** wizard page, select **DNS Server** and click **Next**. See Figure 2.1.

Figure 2.1 Selecting the DNS Server Role

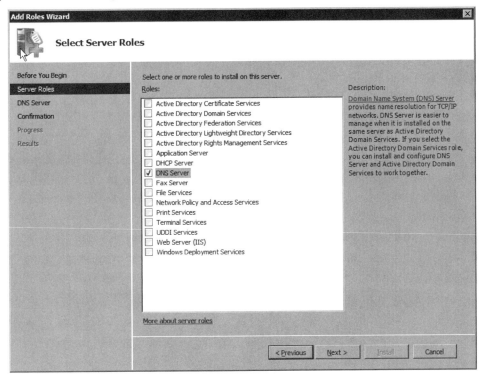

5. Review the information provided on the **DNS Server** wizard page and click **Next**.

6. Review the information provided on the **Confirm Installation Selections** wizard page and click **Install**.

7. Review the information provided on the **Installation Results** wizard page and click **Close**.

Understanding Cache-Only DNS Servers

The DNS Server role installs without any zones or forwarding configured, as a caching-only DNS server. This means that it can resolve client requests only by locating and querying other DNS servers using root hints. Root hints are discussed in the next section. Once a client request has been resolved, the server caches information for the DNS record received. Administrators can clear this cache manually using the following steps:

1. Open DNS Manager by clicking **Start | Administrative Tools | DNS**.

2. In the left pane, right-click the server's node and select **Clear Cache**.

Configuring Root Hints

There are two primary ways to use root hints. By default, root hints comes configured with the Internet root servers specified. This allows the DNS server to locate DNS records for publicly resolvable domain names. Larger organizations often have complex hierarchies of DNS servers, only some of which are configured to resolve public domain names. Many of the DNS servers will be configured to locate domains and subdomains that belong to the organization. Those servers will often have their root hints configured so that they point to higher level DNS servers within the organization, rather than Internet root servers. There are several graphical configuration options available in DNS Manager for root hints: adding and removing records, editing existing records, and copying a list of root hints addresses from another server. The root hints records are stored in an editable text file: %systemroot%\System32\Dns\ Cache.dns. Figure 2.2 displays the servers Properties dialog and the Root Hints tab.

Figure 2.2 The Root Hints Tab

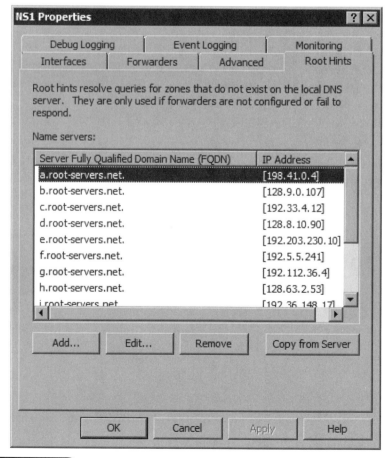

Adding Root Hint Records

Follow this procedure to add a new Root Hint:

1. Open DNS Manager by clicking **Start | Administrative Tools | DNS**.
2. In the left pane, right-click the server you want to configure and select **Properties**.
3. Click the **Root Hints** tab to bring it forward. See Figure 2.2.
4. Click the **Add...** button.
5. In the New Name Server Record dialog box, type the fully qualified domain name (FQDN) in the Server fully qualified domain name (FQDN): text box, and click **Resolve**. See Figure 2.3.

Figure 2.3 The New Name Server Record Dialog

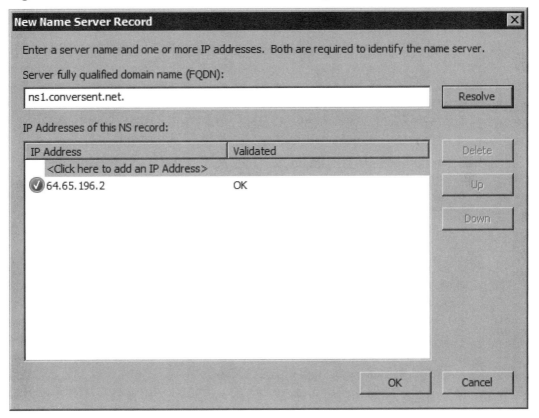

6. If you wish to manually add an IP address, you can click **<Click here to add an IP Address>** and enter it in the text field that appears. Resolved IP addresses can also be modified by clicking them. If multiple IP addresses are configured for the record, you can determine the priority they will be used in by ordering them with the **Up** and **Down** buttons. IP addresses can also be removed using the **Delete** button.

7. Click **OK** to finish adding the record.

Editing Root Hints Records

Follow this procedure to edit an existing root hints record:

1. Open DNS Manager by clicking **Start | Administrative Tools | DNS**.

2. In the left pane, right-click the server you want to configure and select **Properties**.

3. Click the **Root Hints** tab to bring it forward. See Figure 2.2.

4. Select the record you want to edit and click the **Edit...** button.

5. In the **Edit Name Server Record** dialog box (see Figure 2.4), you can:

   - Change the FQDN for the record by typing it in the **Server fully qualified domain name (FQDN):** text box, and clicking **Resolve**.

   - Manually add an IP address, by clicking **<Click here to add an IP Address>** and entering it in the text field that appears.

   - Modify an existing IP address by clicking it and modifying it in the text field that appears.

   - Specify the order that the IP addresses will be used in by ordering them with the **Up** and **Down** buttons.

   - Remove one or more IP addresses by using the **Delete** button.

Figure 2.4 The Edit Name Server Record Dialog

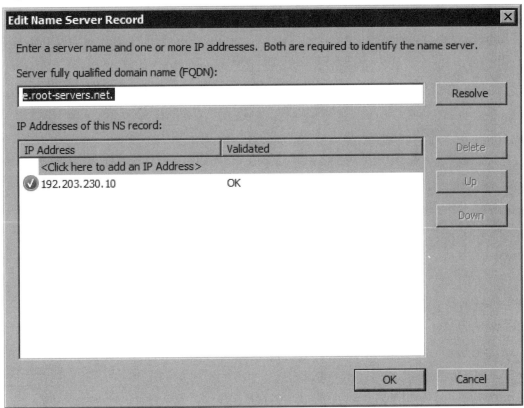

6. Click **OK** when you are finished making changes.

Removing Root Hints Records

Follow this procedure to remove an existing root hints record:

1. Open DNS Manager by clicking **Start | Administrative Tools | DNS**.

2. In the left pane, right-click the server you want to configure and select **Properties**.

3. Click the **Root Hints** tab to bring it forward. See Figure 2.2.

4. Select the record you want to delete and click the **Remove** button.

5. Click **OK**.

Copying Root Hints from Another Server

You can add a list of root hints records from another server. The imported records will be added to your existing list, if any, and will not overwrite existing records. Follow this procedure to copy a list of root hints records from another server:

1. Open DNS Manager by clicking **Start | Administrative Tools | DNS**.

2. In the left pane, right-click the server you want to configure and select **Properties**.

3. Click the **Root Hints** tab to bring it forward. See Figure 2.2.

4. Click the **Copy from Server** button.

5. In the Server to Copy From dialog box enter the FQDN or IP address of the server that you want to copy the root hints records from, then click **OK**.

6. If requested, provide the appropriate logon credentials.

7. Click **OK**.

Configuring Server-Level Forwarders

For security reasons, organizations often do not want to enable their internal DNS servers to directly resolve queries for pubic domain names. One strategy employed when this is the case is to configure all internal DNS servers to point to a DNS server that has been designated as a forwarder. This server typically resides outside the organization's firewall. Restricted communication is allowed between it and the organization's internal DNS servers. If the external forwarder becomes compromised, the internal servers remain safe and function normally. By default, DNS servers are already configured as forwarders. They install without zones, and with the correct root hints. The configuration to use forwarders is done on the DNS servers that will send queries to the forwarders. To manually configure a Windows Server 2008 DNS Server role holder to use forwarding, follow these steps:

1. Open DNS Manager by clicking **Start | Administrative Tools | DNS**.

2. In the left pane, right-click the DNS server you want to configure and select **Properties**.

3. Click the **Forwarders** tab to bring it forward. See Figure 2.5.

Figure 2.5 The Forwarders Tab

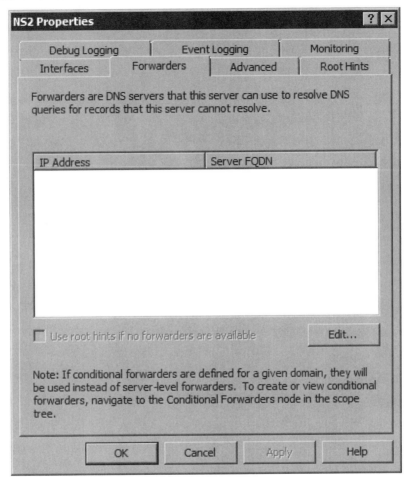

4. In the **Properties** dialog box, click **Edit....**

5. In the **Edit Forwarders** dialog box, click **<Click here to add an IP Address or DNS Name>** and enter a FQDN or IP address for the server queries will be forwarded to. Although multiple addresses can be specified, this is only for failover. The server will try to find a responding DNS forwarder by working its way down the list. If the first forwarder

does not respond to the query, the DNS server will try the next one. If the first forward does respond, but is not able to resolve the query, the DNS server does not try other servers in the list. They are used only in the event of server failure. The amount of time a DNS server waits to hear back from each forwarder is specified by the value in the Number of seconds before forward queries time out: text box. See Figure 2.6.

Figure 2.6 The Edit Forwarders Dialog

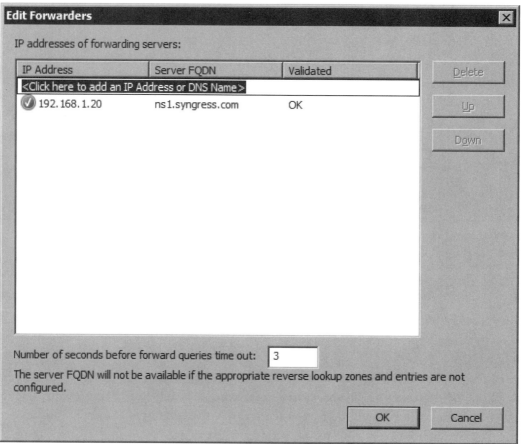

6. Click **OK**.

7. In the **Properties** dialog box, the Use root hints if no forwarders are available box is now available and selected. If you do not want root hints to be used by this server, deselect it.

8. Click **OK** in the Properties dialog box to finish.

EXERCISE 2.1

INSTALLING THE DNS SERVER ROLE AND CREATING A SERVER FORWARDER

In this exercise, you will install the DNS Server role and create a server forwarder. You'll need a server running Windows Server 2008 and an administrative logon. Internet access and a static IP address are also desirable. The static IP address can be private and behind a firewall, as long as the server can access the Internet.

1. Open Server Manager by clicking **Start | Server Manager**.

2. In the right pane, scroll down to **Roles Summary** and click **Add Roles**.

3. In the **Add Roles Wizard** dialog box, read the **Before You Begin** page and click **Next**.

4. On the **Select Server Roles** wizard page, select **DNS Server**, and click **Next**.

5. Review the information provided on the **DNS Server** wizard page and click **Next**.

6. Review the information provided on the **Confirm Installation Selections** wizard page and click **Install**.

7. Review the information provided on the **Installation Results** wizard page and click **Close**.

8. Open **DNS Manager** by clicking **Start | Administrative Tools | DNS**.

9. In the left pane, right-click the DNS server you want to configure and select **Properties**.

10. Click the **Forwarders** tab to bring it forward.

11. In the **Properties** dialog box, click **Edit….**

12. In the **Edit Forwarders** dialog box, click **<Click here to add an IP Address or DNS Name>** and enter the IP address of your ISP's DNS server.

13. Click **OK**.

14. In the **Properties** dialog box, deselect the **Use root hints if no forwarders are available** box.

15. Click **OK** in the **Properties** dialog box to finish.

Configuring Conditional Forwarding

In Windows Server 2003, Microsoft added another level of forwarding that provides much greater flexibility for forwarding queries. When configured for server level forwarding, all queries are sent from a configured DNS server to the forwarder. Conditional forwarding allows an administrator to send requests that deal with different domains to different forwarders. So, for example, a request for host1. authors.syngress.com could be sent to a different forwarder than a request for server1.billing.syngress.com. The system will take its best guess if the exact domain name is not listed. If you have configured a forwarder for the authors.syngress.com domain and client requests resolution for computer1.mcse.authors.syngess.com the request will be forwarded to the closest match, in this case the forwarder configured for the authors.syngress.com domain. If both conditional and server-level forwarding are configured on a server, conditional forwarding is used. To configure conditional forwarding, see the following steps.

Creating Conditional Forwarders

To specify one or more domains for conditional forwarding, follow these steps:

1. Open DNS Manager by clicking **Start | Administrative Tools | DNS**.

2. In the left pane, expand the node representing the server you want to configure, right-click **Conditional Forwarders**, and select **New Conditioner Forwarder….** See Figure 2.7.

Figure 2.7 Creating a New Conditional Forwarder

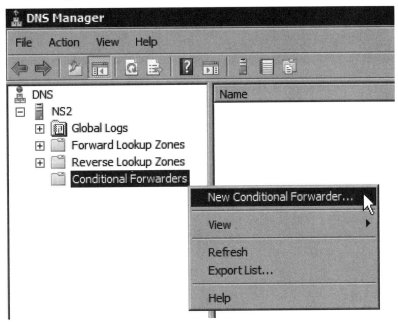

3. In the **New Conditional Forward** dialog box, in the **DNS Domain:** text box, type the name of the domain you want queries forwarded to. For example, if you want to configure a forwarder to resolve queries for authors.syngress.com enter it in this box. See Figure 2.8.

4. In the IP addresses of the master servers: entry area specify the FQDN or IP addresses for the DNS server(s) that will serve as forwarders for the specified domain by clicking **<Click here to add an IP Address or DNS Name>** and entering it in the text field that appears. Although forwarders can be specified, this is only for failover. The server will try to find a responding conditional forwarder by working its way down the list. If the first forwarder does not respond to the query, the DNS server will try the next one. If the first forwarder does respond, but is not able to resolve the query, the DNS server does not try other servers in the list. They are used only for failovers in the event of a forwarding server's failure. The amount of time a DNS server waits to hear back from each forwarder is specified by the value in the Number of seconds before forward queries time out: text box. Entries can be modified by clicking on them. If multiple forwarders are configured, you can determine the priority they will be used by ordering them with the **Up** and **Down** buttons. Entries can also be removed using the **Delete** button. See Figure 2.8.

Figure 2.8 The New Conditional Forwarder Dialog

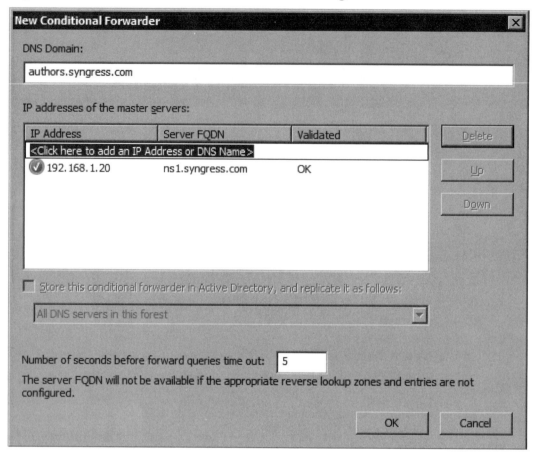

5. Click **OK**.

EXAM WARNING

A server cannot be configured to conditionally forward for a domain if it has a zone configured on it that includes the same portion of the domain name space. For example, if a DNS server hosts the authors.syngress.com zone, it cannot also have conditional forwarding setup for the authors. syngress.com domain.

Managing Conditional Forwarders

To modify the existing configuration for conditional forwarding, follow these steps:

1. Open DNS Manager by clicking **Start | Administrative Tools | DNS**.

2. In the left pane, expand the node representing the server you want to configure, expand the **Conditional Forwarders** node, and right-click the domain name representing the conditional forwarder you want to modify. See Figure 2.9.

Figure 2.9 A Conditional Forwarder's Right-Click Menu

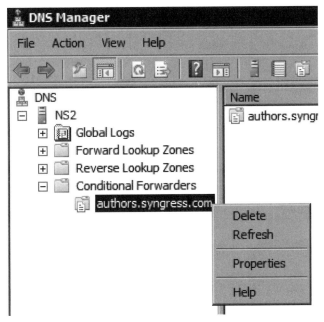

3. To delete the forwarder, click **Delete**. To modify the forwarder, click **Properties**.

4. In the **Properties** dialog box, click **Edit**.

5. In the **Edit Conditional Forwarder** dialog box, make the necessary changes. In the IP addresses of the master servers: entry area specify the FQDN or IP addresses for the DNS server(s) that will serve as forwarders for the specified domain by clicking **<Click here to add an IP Address**

or DNS Name> and entering it in the text field that appears. Although forwarders can be specified, this is only for failover. The server will try to find a responding conditional forwarder by working its way down the list. If the first forwarder does not respond to the query, the DNS server will try the next one. If the first forwarder does respond, but is not able to resolve the query, the DNS server does not try other servers in the list. They are used only as failovers in the event of a forwarding server's failure. The amount of time a DNS server waits to hear back from each forwarder is specified by the value in the Number of seconds before forward queries time out: text box. Entries can be modified by clicking on them. If multiple forwarders are configured, you can determine the priority they will be used by ordering them with the **Up** and **Down** buttons. Entries can also be removed using the **Delete** button. See Figure 2.10.

Figure 2.10 The Edit Conditional Forwarder Dialog

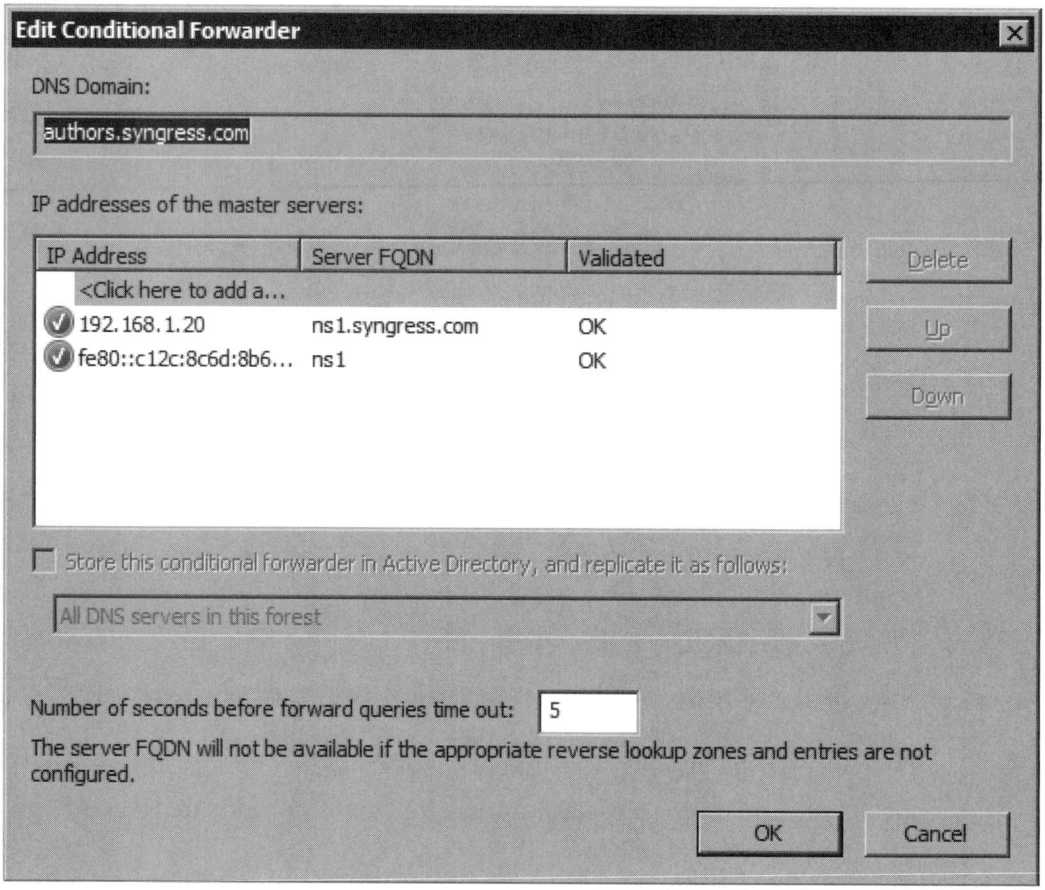

6. Click **OK** to close the **Edit Conditional Forwarder** dialog and **OK** again to close the **Properties** dialog.

Server Core

A Windows Server 2008 Core Server Installation can be used for multiple purposes. One of the ways that Server Core can be used is to provide a minimal installation for DNS. You can manipulate, manage, and configure DNS servers through the various Windows Server 2008 DNS Graphical User Interfaces (GUIs)–DNS Manager and the Server Manager tool.

However, there are no GUIs provided with Windows Server 2008 Core Server. There are a number of advantages to running DNS within Server Core, including:

- **Smaller Footprint.** Reduces the amount of CPU, memory, and hard disk needed.

- **More Secure.** Fewer components and services running unnecessarily.

- **No GUI.** No GUI means that users cannot make modifications to the DNS databases (or any other system functions) using common/user-friendly tools.

If you are planning to run DNS within a Server Core install, there a number of steps you must perform prior to installation. The first step we must take is to set the IP information of the server. To configure the IP addressing information of the server:

1. First we need to identify the network adapter. In the console window, type **netsh interface ipv4 show interfaces** and record the number shown under **Idx** column.

2. Next, we will set the IP address, Subnet Mask, and Default Gateway for the server. To do this, type **netsh interface ipv4 set address name="<ID>" source=static address=<StaticIP> mask=<SubnetMask> gateway= <DefaultGateway>**. **ID** represents the interface number from step 1, **<StaticIP>** represents the IP address we will assign, **<SubnetMask>** represents the subnet mask, and **<Default Gateway>** represents the IP address of the server's default gateway.

3. Lastly, we need to assign the IP address of the DNS server. If this server were part of an Active Directory domain and replicating Active-Directory integrated zones (we will discuss those next), we would likely point this server to another AD-integrated DNS server. If it is not, we would point it

to another external DNS server—commonly the Internet provider of your company. From the console, type **netsh interface ipv4 add dnsserver name="<ID>" address=<DNSIP> index=1. >. ID** represents the number from step 1, **<StaticIP>** represents the IP address of the DNS server.

Once the IP address settings are completed—you can verify this by typing **ipconfig /all**—we can install the DNS role onto the Core Server installation.

4. To do this, from the command line type **start /w ocsetup DNS-Server-Core-Role**.

5. To verify that the DNS Server service is installed and started, type **NET START**. This will return a list of running services.

6. Next, we can use the **dnscmd** command line utility to manipulate the DNS settings. For example, you can type **dnscmd /enumzones** to list the zones hosted on this DNS server.

7. We can also change all the configuration options that we modified in the GUI section earlier by using the **dnscmd /config** option. For example, we can enable BIND secondaries by typing **dnscmd <servername> /config /bindsecondaries 1**. You can see the results in Figure 2.8.

There are many, many more things you can do with the dnscmd utility. For more information on the dnscmd syntax, visit http://technet2.microsoft.com/WindowsServer/en/library/d652a163-279f-4047-b3e0-0c468a4d69f31033.mspx.

Creating DNS Zones

DNS zones are the actual boundaries of the records that are stored in DNS. They may or may not map to domain names. For example, records for syngress.com and authors.syngress.com could be housed in a single zone (syngress.com) or divided into separate zones that are configured to know about each other (syngress.com and authors.syngress.com). Traditionally zones have been divided to ease the amount of network traffic required to replicate the records between DNS servers, and also to move a relevant portion of the records closer to the users who most often use them. These reasons are less relevant today, because Microsoft recommends the use of Active Directory integrated zones. AD integrated zones provide much more efficient replication than previous zone types because they use the AD directory services database and replication architecture. When a portion of a domain, such as the authors subdomain, is hosted in a separate zone file, it is referred to as being delegated. A Windows Server 2008 DNS server can host a single zone or a large number of them, and the parent and delegated zones can be stored in the same server.

There are several types of zones that can be configured using the DNS Server role in Windows Server 2008, including standard primary, standard secondary, forward lookup, reverse lookup, Active Directory integrated, stub, and GlobalNames. You don't need to understand these at a deep level for a configuration test such as this one, but you should possess some basic knowledge about each. Generally, zones are either forward or reverse lookup zones. Forward lookup zones host records that allow for resolution from a FQDN or NetBIOS name to an IP address. Reverse lookup zones host records that allow for resolution from an IP address to a FQDN or NetBIOS name. Standard primary and secondary zones store records in actual text files, while AD integrated zones store them in the AD database. Standard primary and AD integrated zones can be modified; standard secondary zones are read-only copies of either a standard primary or AD integrated zone. Microsoft recommends primarily using AD integrated zones because of their enhanced efficiency and security.

You will also see the term *master* associated with DNS servers. A master server is any server with a primary, secondary, or AD integrated zone on it that transfers its zone information to another DNS server. If the organization has only one DNS server with a standard primary zone for the organization's domain, this server is a standard primary zone holder, but it is not a master. If the company installs a second DNS server and configures it with a standard secondary zone for their domain, the original DNS server can now be referred to as a master. Secondary zones can initiate zone transfers from standard primary, other secondary, or AD integrated zones.

Stub zones contain records only for name servers. These zones are used most often in conjunction with delegation. If DNS server A hosts the syngress.com zone, and DNS server B hosts the authors.syngress.com zone, these two servers need to know where to find the records for each other's domain. Placing a stub zone for syngress.com, for example, on DNS server B will keep an up-to-date list of DNS servers available to tell server B where it can find the records for the parent (syngress.com) domain.

Finally, GlobalNames is a new type of zone in Windows Server 2008. Microsoft has been trying to get its customers to migrate away from WINS name resolution for several years, and this is a new tool they are providing toward this end. It actually isn't a separate zone type. Rather you let Windows know you want to use the GlobalNames feature at the command line, name a zone *GlobalNames* while creating it, and the Windows Server 2008 DNS Server role takes it from there. Let's see how to configure each of these options.

Head of the Class...

Standard vs. Active Directory Integrated Zones

Microsoft encourages you to use AD integrated zones whenever possible. Standard zones are stored in text files on the DNS server. The only security possible with these types of records is standard NTFS permissions on the zone files themselves. Windows 2000 and later DNS servers support incremental zone transfers for standard secondary zones. When a zone transfer between occurs, all records that have been added or changed will transfer across the network. Previous version transferred the entire zone file for each update. Even though this incremental type of transfer cuts down on network traffic, it is still significantly less efficient than replication using an AD integrated zone.

AD integrated zones store their records within Active Directory. Individual records as well as zones themselves are objects within directory services. This allows for much greater security because Windows Server 2008 and administrators can use object level permissions. In addition, replication of zone records occurs using standard AD replication. Rather than transferring an entire record, as incremental transfers involving standard zones do, only the property within the record that changed is transferred across the network. So, if the IP address in a record changes, with AD integrated zones only the IP address is replicated, not the entire record. An additional benefit of DNS using the AD replication process is that AD replication traffic is encrypted and highly compressed, which adds an additional level of security and efficiency.

Both types of zones are capable of using dynamic updates, however only AD integrated zones have the object-level permissions required to make them secure. When updates are not secure they open the door to attacks that corrupt the DNS database. Although Microsoft includes an option for nonsecure updates, they do not recommend using it. Microsoft always recommends the use of AD integrated zones with secure dynamic updates, when DDNS is desired.

Continued

One final important difference between standard and AD integrated zones involves where changes to records can be made, and fault tolerance. In a standard primary/secondary DNS configuration, the primary zone exists only on one DNS server. If something happens to that server, either the database will not be updated until it is available again, or one of the secondary servers must be converted into the primary zone holder. This single point of failure for updating records is eliminated with AD integrated zones. All AD integrated zones are primary zones, and can accept updates dynamically from clients (if configured) as well as administrators. This *multimaster* model significantly increases fault tolerance. If one of the AD integrated zone DNS servers goes offline, updates to the database are still possible through any other AD integrated zone holder.

Standard secondary zones can be used with AD integrated zones. Standard primary zones cannot. AD integrated zones serve as primary zone holders and do not integrate with standard primary zones. When a secondary zone transfers information from an AD integrated zone, none of the features available with AD replication apply.

Creating a Standard
Primary Forward Lookup Zone

Follow these steps to create a primary, forward lookup zone:

1. Open DNS Manager by clicking **Start | Administrative Tools | DNS**.

2. In the left pane, expand the node representing the server you want to configure, right-click **Forward Lookup Zones**, and click **New Zone....**

3. Read the welcome page of the **New Zone Wizard** dialog box and click **Next**.

4. On the **Zone Type** wizard page, leave the default selection of **Primary zone** and click **Next**. See Figure 2.11.

Figure 2.11 The Zone Type Wizard Page

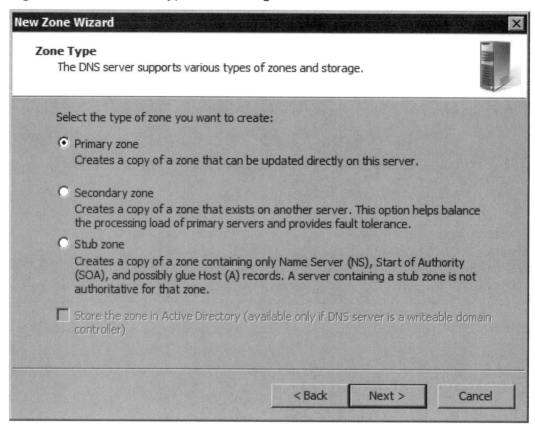

5. On the **Zone Name** wizard page, enter the name of your domain in the **Zone name:** text box and click **Next**. See Figure 2.12.

Figure 2.12 The Zone Name Wizard Page

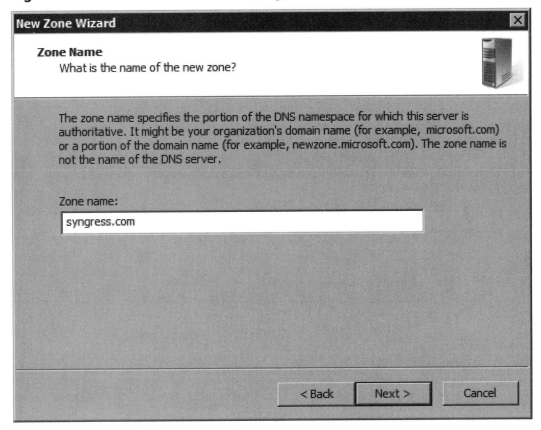

6. On the **Zone File** wizard page, you can select one of the following options (see Figure 2.13):

   ■ **Create a new file with this file name.** This option, which is filled in with a recommended setting by default, is used when you need to create a zone file.

   ■ **Use this existing file.** If you have a preexisting zone file that is configured and ready to use, select this option. The file must be located in the %systemroot%\System32\dns directory.

Figure 2.13 The Zone File Wizard Page

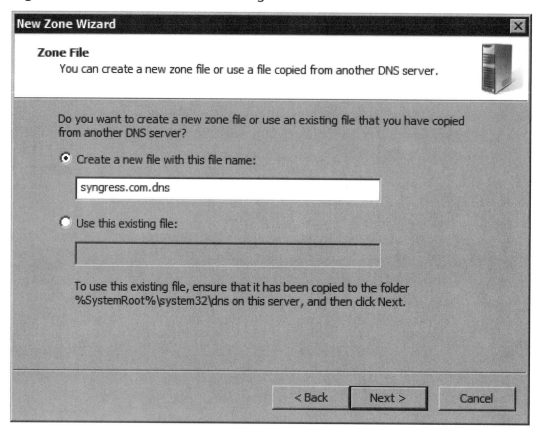

7. Click **Next**.

8. On the **Dynamic Update** wizard page, you can select from the following
    options (see Figure 2.14):

    ■ **Allow both secure and non–secure dynamic updates.** The DNS
    Server role in Windows Server 2008 supports dynamic DNS (DDNS).
    If this option is selected, computers can communicate with the DNS
    server to create and manage their own records. If the zone is AD inte-
    grated, a third option with enhanced security is available. A standard
    primary zone has reduced security when using DDNS that make it
    easy for attackers to specify faulty DNS record information when this
    option is enabled. Microsoft does not recommend enabling this option.

- **Do not allow dynamic updates.** This option prevents the use of dynamic DDNS. Records for this primary zone will need to be managed manually if it is selected. This is the default option.

Figure 2.14 The Dynamic Update Wizard Page

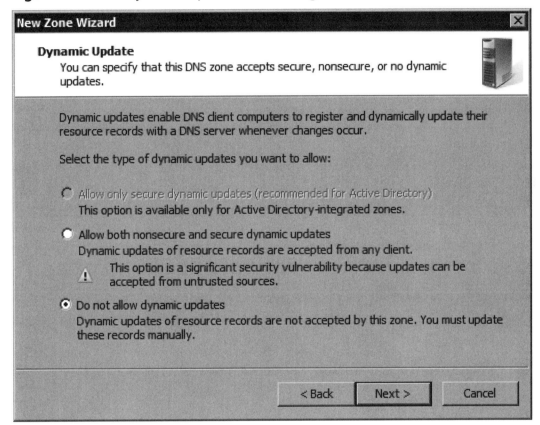

9. Click **Next**.

10. On the **Completing the New Zone Wizard** page, review the information provided and click **Finish**.

11. In the left pane under **Forward Lookup Zones** a new node representing the zone you created should appear. Click that zone.

12. In the right pane, you should see that at least two records have been created automatically (SOA and NS). See Figure 2.15.

Figure 2.15 DNS Manager Utility with the Created Forward Primary Zone

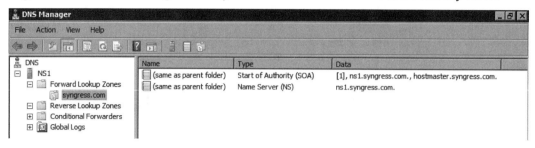

Beware of Microsoft's default options. Sometimes they represent Microsoft's recommended settings, such as with dynamic updates in step 8. Other times a nonrecommended setting is selected by default. On the test, never assume that a default option or setting is a recommended one.

Creating a Secondary Forward Lookup Zone

Follow these steps to create a secondary, forward lookup zone:

1. Open DNS Manager by clicking **Start | Administrative Tools | DNS**.

2. In the left pane, expand the node representing the server you want to configure, right-click **Forward Lookup Zones**, and click **New Zone....**

3. Read the welcome page of the **New Zone Wizard** dialog box and click **Next**.

4. On the **Zone Type** wizard page, select **Secondary zone** and click **Next**. See Figure 2.11.

5. On the **Zone Name** wizard page, enter the name of the domain in the Zone name: text box. This must match the primary zone's name. See Figure 2.12.

6. Click **Next**.

7. In the **Master DNS Servers** wizard page, enter the name of one or more DNS servers from where this secondary zone will take transfers. Enter the master server's IP address or FQDN by clicking on **<Click here to add**

an IP Address or DNS Name>. Secondary zones can be transferred from standard primary, AD Integrated, and other secondary zones. For fault tolerance, more than one master server can be specified. All servers are not used by default. If the first server on the list is successfully contacted, for example, the rest of the list will be ignored. Servers can be ordered using the **Up** and **Down** buttons, and removed from the list using the **Delete** button. See Figure 2.16.

Figure 2.16 The Configured Master DNS Servers Wizard Page

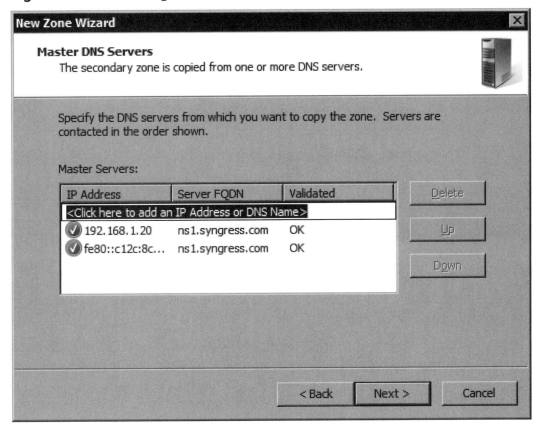

8. Click **Next**.

9. On the **Completing the New Zone Wizard** page, review the information provided and click **Finish**.

Creating an Active Directory Integrated Forward Lookup Zone

Follow these steps to create an AD integrated forward lookup zone:

1. Open DNS Manager by clicking **Start | Administrative Tools | DNS**.

2. In the left pane, expand the node representing the server you want to configure, right-click **Forward Lookup Zones**, and click **New Zone....**

3. Read the welcome page of the **New Zone Wizard** dialog box and click **Next**.

4. On the **Zone Type** wizard page, leave the default selection of **Primary zone** and leave **Store the zone in Active Directory** (available only if DNS server is a writable domain controller) selected.

5. Click **Next**. See Figure 2.11.

6. On the **Active Directory Zone Replication Scope** wizard page, select one of the following options (Figure 2.17.):

   - **To all DNS servers in this forest.** This option replicates the zone information to the AD database on all Windows Server 2003 and later domain controllers in the forest. Domain controllers receive, store, and replicate the zone information even if they are not DNS servers.

   - **To all DNS servers in this domain.** This option replicates the zone information to the AD database on all Windows Server 2003 and later domain controllers in domain controller's AD domain. Domain controllers receive, store, and replicate the zone information even if they are not DNS servers.

   - **To all domain controllers in this domain (for Windows 2000 compatibility).** This option replicates the zone information to the AD database on all Windows Server 2000 and later domain controllers in domain controller's AD domain. Domain controllers receive, store, and replicate the zone information even if they are not DNS servers. This option reduces functionality available to Windows Server 2003 and later domain controllers, and should be used only if your network contains Windows 2000 Server domain controllers that must act as DNS servers.

- **To all domain controllers specified in the scope of this directory partition.** This option replicates the zone information based on the settings for a specific application directory partition. See the *Creating an Application Directory Partition* section for more information.

Figure 2.17 The Active Directory Zone Replication Scope Wizard Page

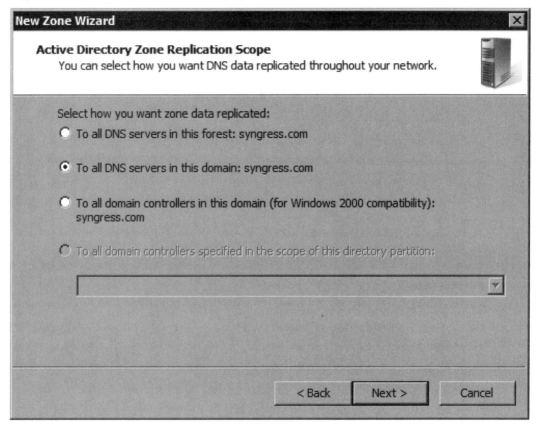

7. Click **Next**.

8. On the Zone Name wizard page, enter the name of your domain in the **Zone name:** text box and click **Next**. See Figure 2.12.

9. Click **Next**.

10. On the **Dynamic Update** wizard page, you can select from the following options (see Figure 2.18):

- **Allow only secure, dynamic updates.** The DNS Server role in Windows Server 2008 supports dynamic DNS (DDNS). This default option, which is recommended by Microsoft, enables a host to add and manage its own forward and reverse lookup records in DNS. It also enables DHCP to be configured to manage host records. During creation, this option sets additional security on records to prevent them being modified by unauthorized hosts.

- **Allow both secure and non-secure dynamic updates.** If this option is selected, computers can communicate with the DNS server to create and manage their own records. It also enables DHCP to be configured to manage host records. A standard primary zone has reduced security options that make it easy for attackers to specify faulty DNS record information when this option is enabled. When used in conjunction with an AD integrated zone, this option will use additional security when clients are capable of it. Because it also allows unsecure DDNS modification, Microsoft does not recommend enabling this option.

- **Do not allow dynamic updates.** This option prevents the use of dynamic DDNS. Records for this primary zone will need to be managed manually if it is selected. This is the default option.

Figure 2.18 The Dynamic Update Wizard Page

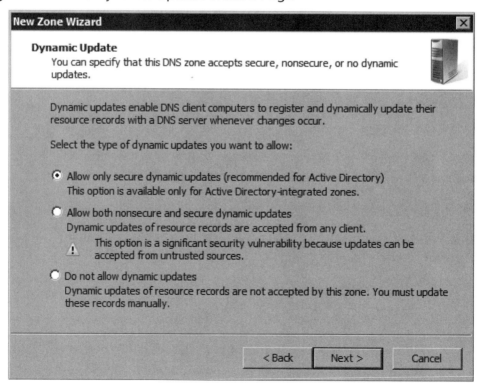

11. Click **Next**.

12. On the **Completing the New Zone Wizard** page, review the information provided and click **Finish**.

Test Day Tip

Be sure to remember that Microsoft recommends and really expects you to use AD integrated zones with secure dynamic updates whenever possible.

Creating a Standard Primary Reverse Lookup Zone

Follow these steps to create a reverse lookup zone:

1. Open DNS Manager by clicking **Start | Administrative Tools | DNS**.

2. In the left pane, expand the node representing the server you want to configure, right-click **Reverse Lookup Zones**, and click **New Zone....**

3. Read the welcome page of the **New Zone Wizard** dialog box and click **Next**.

4. On the **Zone Type** wizard page, leave the default selection of **Primary zone** and click **Next**. See Figure 2.11.

5. On the **Reverse Lookup Zone Name** wizard page, select the appropriate zone type (see Figure 2.19):

   ■ **IPv4 Reverse Lookup Zone.** Select this option if you want the zone to track IPv4 address information. This option is the default.

   ■ **IPv6 Reverse Lookup Zone.** Select this option if you want the zone to track IPv6 address information. This is a new option in Windows Server 2008.

Figure 2.19 The Reverse Lookup Zone Name Wizard Page

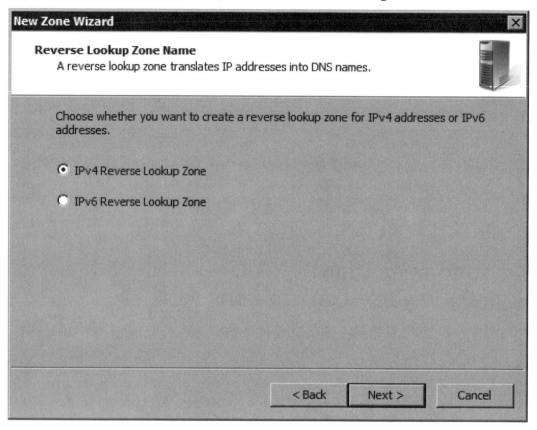

6. Click **Next**.

7. On the second **Reverse Lookup Zone Name** wizard page, select and configure the appropriate option (see Figure 2.20):

   - **Network ID.** This option helps you to properly name the zone. Enter the network portion of the IP address range you want the zone to service. A proper zone name will automatically be filled in under **Reverse lookup zone name:** for you.

   - **Reverse lookup zone name.** If you would prefer to manually enter the zone name, you can do so using this option. You should follow the recommended DNS naming standards for reverse lookup zone names.

Figure 2.20 The Second Reverse Lookup Zone Name Wizard Page

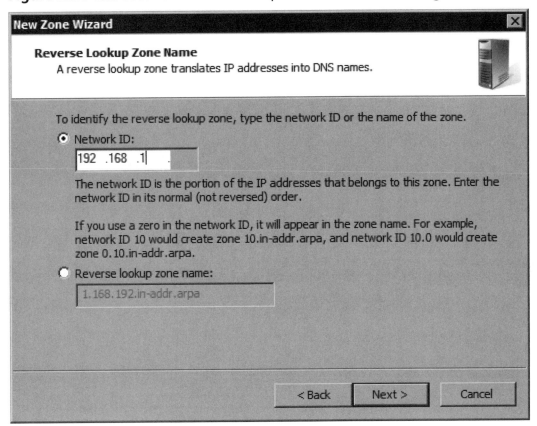

8. On the **Zone File** wizard page, you can select one of the following options (see Figure 2.21):

   ■ **Create a new file with this file name.** This option, which is filled in with a recommended setting by default, is used when you need to create a zone file.

   ■ **Use this existing file.** If you have a preexisting zone file that is configured and ready to use, select this option. The file must be located in the %systemroot%\System32\dns directory.

9. Click **Next**.

Figure 2.21 The Zone File Wizard Page

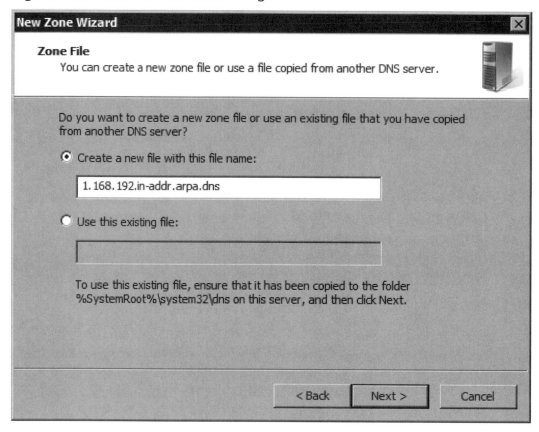

10. Click **Next**.

11. On the **Dynamic Update** wizard page, you can select from the following options (see Figure 2.18):

   - **Allow both secure and nonsecure dynamic updates.** The DNS Server role in Windows Server 2008 supports dynamic DNS (DDNS). If this option is selected, computers can communicate with the DNS server to create and manage their own records. If the zone is AD integrated, a third option with enhanced security is available. A standard primary zone has reduced security options that make it easy for attackers to specify faulty DNS record information when this option is enabled. Microsoft does not recommend enabling this option.

   - **Do not allow dynamic updates.** This option prevents the use of dynamic DDNS. Records for this primary zone will need to be managed manually if it is selected. This is the default option.

12. Click **Next**.

13. On the **Completing the New Zone Wizard** page, review the information provided and click **Finish**.

EXERCISE 2.2

CREATING STANDARD PRIMARY FORWARD AND REVERSE LOOKUP ZONES

In this exercise, you will be creating a standard primary forward and a standard primary reverse lookup zone. You will need a Windows Server 2008 server with the DNS Server role installed, and administrative rights.

1. Open DNS Manager by clicking **Start | Administrative Tools | DNS**.

2. In the left pane, expand the node representing your server, right-click **Forward Lookup Zones**, and click **New Zone.…**

3. Read the welcome page of the **New Zone Wizard** dialog box and click **Next**.

4. On the **Zone Type** wizard page, leave the default selection of **Primary zone** and click **Next**.

5. On the **Zone Name** wizard page, enter the name of your domain in the **Zone name:** text box. If you do not have a domain available, consider searching for an unused one at a domain registrar to use temporarily.

6. Click **Next**.

7. On the **Zone File** wizard page, accept the default options and click **Next**.

8. On the **Dynamic Update** wizard page, select **Do not allow dynamic updates**.

9. Click **Next**.

10. On the **Completing the New Zone Wizard** page, review the information provided and click **Finish**.

11. In the left pane, right-click **Reverse Lookup Zones**, and click **New Zone.…**

12. Read the welcome page of the **New Zone Wizard** dialog box and click **Next**.

13. On the **Zone Type** wizard page, leave the default selection of **Primary zone** and click **Next**.

14. On the **Reverse Lookup Zone Name** wizard page, select **IPv4 Reverse Lookup Zone**.

15. Click **Next**.

16. On the second **Reverse Lookup Zone Name** wizard page, enter the network portion of your IP address in the **Network ID:** box and click **Next**.

17. On the **Zone File** wizard page, leave the defaults and click **Next**.

18. On the **Dynamic Update** wizard page, select **Do not allow dynamic updates**.

19. Click **Next**.

20. On the **Completing the New Zone Wizard** page, review the information provided and click **Finish**.

Creating a Standard Secondary Reverse Lookup Zone

Follow these steps to create a reverse lookup zone:

1. Open DNS Manager by clicking **Start | Administrative Tools | DNS**.

2. In the left pane, expand the node representing the server you want to configure, right-click **Reverse Lookup Zones**, and click **New Zone....**

3. Read the welcome page of the **New Zone Wizard** dialog box and click **Next**.

4. On the **Zone Type** wizard page, select **Secondary zone** and click **Next**. See Figure 2.11.

5. On the **Reverse Lookup Zone Name** wizard page, select the appropriate zone type:

   ■ **IPv4 Reverse Lookup Zone.** Select this option if you want the zone to track IPv4 address information. This option is the default.

   ■ **IPv6 Reverse Lookup Zone.** Select this option if you want the zone to track IPv6 address information. This is a new option in Windows Server 2008.

6. Click **Next**.

7. On the second Reverse Lookup Zone Name wizard page, select and configure the appropriate option (See Figure 2.20):   .

■ **Network ID.** This option helps you to properly name the zone. Enter the network portion of the IP address range you want the zone to service. A proper zone name will automatically be filled in under **Reverse lookup zone name:** for you. This must match the configuration information used when creating the primary reverse lookup zone.

■ **Reverse lookup zone name.** If you would prefer to enter the zone name manually, you can do so using this option. You should follow the recommended DNS naming standards for reverse lookup file names.

8. Click **Next**.

9. On the **Master DNS Servers** wizard page, enter the name of one or more DNS servers that this secondary zone will take transfers from. Enter the master server's IP address or FQDN by clicking **<Click here to add an IP Address or DNS Name>**. Secondary zones can be transferred from standard primary, AD Integrated, and other secondary zones. For fault tolerance, more than one master server can be specified. All servers are not used by default. If the first server on the list is successfully contacted, for example, the rest of the list will be ignored. Servers can be ordered using the **Up** and **Down** buttons, and removed from the list using the **Delete** button. See Figure 2.16.

10. Click **Next**.

11. On the **Completing the New Zone Wizard** page, review the information provided and click **Finish**.

Creating a Zone Delegation

Delegation allows you to transfer authority for a domain to a different zone. For example, an organization with multiple subdomains such as authors.syngress. com, publishers.syngress.com, editors.syngress.com, executives.syngress.com, and so forth may not want to keep all these subdomains in a single syngress.com zone file. Authors and editors might work a different office that has its own DNS server, so moving these parts of the namespace to separate zone files on that server might increase query efficiency, cut down on DNS WAN traffic, and so forth.

When we move subdomains out of their parent domain's zone file, it is called delegating the domains. Follow these steps to create a zone delegation:

1. Open DNS Manager by clicking **Start | Administrative Tools | DNS**.

2. Expand the appropriate server node, expand **Forward Lookup Zones** or **Reverse Lookup Zones**, right-click the zone you want to create a delegation for, and click **New Delegation....** In the example here, we will be using the forward lookup zone *syngress.com*.

3. In the **New Delegation Wizard**, read the welcome page and click **Next**.

4. On the **Delegated Domain Name** wizard page, type the name of the domain in the **Delegated Domain:** text box, and click Next. See Figure 2.22.

Figure 2.22 The Completed Delegated Domain Name Wizard Page

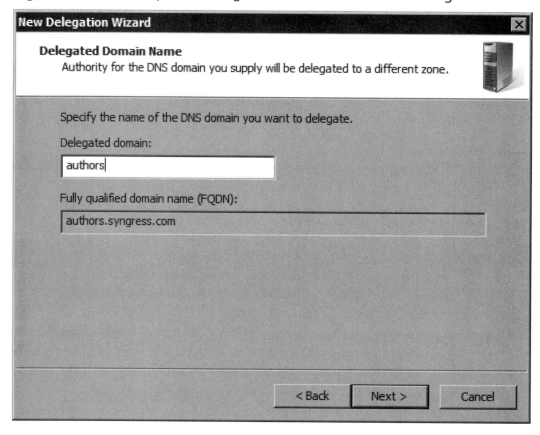

5. On the **Name Servers** wizard page, click the **Add…** button.

6. In the **New Name Server Record** dialog box, type the name of a DNS server that will hold the delegated domain in the **Server fully qualified domain name (FQDN):** text box, and click **Resolve**.

7. In the **IP Addresses of this NS record:** area make any necessary adjustments. If clicking the **Resolve** button didn't locate the IP address of the server you can enter it by clicking **<Click here to add an IP Address>**. You can also click that option to add one or more additional IP addresses that relate to the server but were unresolved. If the DNS server has multiple addresses, you can use the **Up** and **Down** buttons to provide the order that the IP addresses should be contacted. Finally, you can click and remove configured IP addresses using the **Delete** button. The delegated zone must also be configured on the DNS server. This can be done before or after the delegation. If done after it, you'll see the warning message displayed in Figure 2.23.

Figure 2.23 The Completed New Name Server Record Dialog

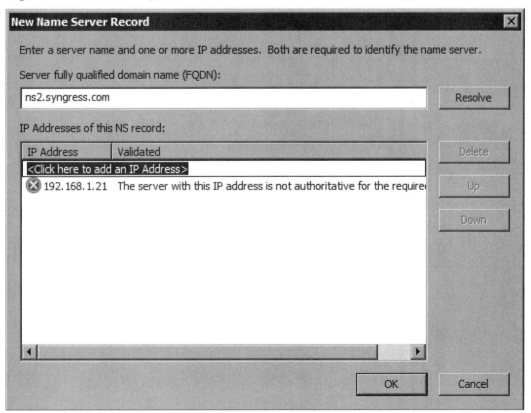

8. Click **OK**.

9. In the **New Name Server Record** dialog box, click **Next**.

10. On the **Completing the New Delegation Wizard** page, click **Finish**.

11. Follow the steps for creating a new forward lookup zone that matches the delegated domain on the DNS server you specified in step 7.

12. Follow the steps to create a stub zone for the parent domain on the DNS server you specified in step 7. This enables the delegated domain to more easily locate its parent domain.

Creating a Stub Zone

Follow these steps to create a stub zone:

1. Open DNS Manager by clicking **Start | Administrative Tools | DNS**.

2. In the left pane, expand the node representing the server you want to configure, right-click **Forward Lookup Zones**, and click **New Zone....**

3. Read the welcome page of the **New Zone Wizard** dialog box and click **Next**.

4. On the **Zone Type** wizard page, leave the default selection of **Stub zone** and click **Next**. See Figure 2.11.

5. On the **Zone Name** wizard page, enter the name of your domain in the **Zone name:** text box and click **Next**. See Figure 2.12.

6. On the **Zone File** wizard page, in the **Create a new file with this file name:** text box, leave the default option or enter a file name for the zone file, then click **Next**.

7. In the **Master DNS Servers** wizard page, enter the name of one or more DNS servers from which this stub zone will take transfers. Enter the master server's IP address or FQDN by clicking **<Click here to add an IP Address or DNS Name>**. Stub zones can be transferred from standard primary, AD Integrated, and secondary zones. For fault tolerance, more than one master server can be specified. All servers are not used by default. If the first server on the list is successfully contacted, for example, the rest of the list will be ignored. Servers can be ordered using the **Up** and **Down** buttons, and removed from the list using the **Delete** button. See Figure 2.16.

8. Click **Next**.

9. On the **Completing the New Zone Wizard** page, review the information provided and click **Finish**.

Using the New GlobalNames Zone Feature

There are two primary forms of name resolution on Windows networks: NetBIOS and DNS. NetBIOS name resolution goes back to the early days of Windows. Recent operating system releases from Microsoft increasingly have moved away from it toward DNS. Although still in wide deployment, Microsoft's NetBIOS name resolution services do not support IPv6. Windows Server 2008 is the first server release from Microsoft that deeply integrates IPv6 technology into all aspects of the operating system and its networking services. In order to allow customers to continue the process of migrating away from NetBIOS name resolution methods, one of the new features Microsoft provides in Windows Server 2008 is the GlobalNames Zone (GNZ) feature.

GNZs are designed to allow administrators to migrate away from WINS servers and move to using DNS for all name resolution. These zones are designed to support single name records that match the NetBIOS computer names on Windows networks. GNZ records are statically configured by administrators, so typically you will use them only for servers that are configured with static IP addresses and are currently located by WINS or LMHOSTS files. See the *Configuring Name Resolution for Client Computers* section of this chapter for more information about LMHOST files and other client name resolution strategies. There are two steps for configuring GNZs:

1. Enable all domain controllers to support GNZs.

2. Create the appropriate name resolution records for the zone. GNZs use CNAME records. Enter the NetBIOS computer name in the **Alias name (uses parent domain if left blank):** field in the CNAME record, and the appropriate FQDN in the Fully qualified domain name (FQDN) for target host field. See the Creating CNAME Records section for more information on this DNS record type.

EXAM WARNING

Only Windows Server 2008 servers support GlobalNames zones.

Enabling a Domain Controller to Support GlobalNames Zones

To enable a domain controller to support GlobalNames Zones, perform the following steps:

1. Open a command prompt by clicking **Start | Command Prompt**.

2. At the command prompt, type **dnscmd <ServerName> /config /Enableglobalnamessupport 1**. For example: dnscmd ad2.syngress.com /config /Enableglobalnamessupport 1 (see Figure 2.24)

Figure 2.24 Enabling GlobalNames Zone Support Using the Command Prompt

Configuring & Implementing...

Configuring Resolution Using GlobalNames Zones

You might be wondering where a GNZ fits with the other name resolution methods available to a DNS server. When a Windows Server 2008 DNS server responds to a query, it first checks its local cache and zone data. If the answer is not found, and a GNZ is configured on the server, it next checks the GlobalNames zone. If the GNZ does not contain the needed information and WINS integration is configured, the server next queries

WINS for the information. The GNZ can be configured as the initial source of information to use when attempting to resolve a query, by using the following steps:

1. Open a command prompt by clicking **Start | Command Prompt**.

2. At the command prompt, type **dnscmd <ServerName> /config /Enableglobalnamessupport 0**. For example: dnscmd ad2. syngress.com /config /Enableglobalnamessupport <order>

   Replacing <order> with a 0 at the end of the command queries the GNZ first.

   Replacing <order> with a 1 will query the local cache and zone records first.

Creating the GlobalNames Zone

To create a GlobalNames Zone, follow these steps:

1. Open DNS Manager by clicking **Start | Administrative Tools | DNS**.

2. In the left pane, expand the node representing the server you want to configure, right-click **Forward Lookup Zones**, and click **New Zone....**

3. Read the welcome page of the **New Zone Wizard** dialog box and click **Next**.

4. On the **Zone Type** wizard page, leave the default selection of **Primary zone** and leave **Store the zone in Active Directory** (available only if DNS server is a writable domain controller) selected.

5. Click **Next**. See Figure 2.11.

6. On the **Active Directory Zone Replication Scope** wizard page, select one of the following options (see Figure 2.17.):

   ■ **To all DNS servers in this forest.** This option replicates the zone information to the AD database on all Windows Server 2003 and later domain controllers in the forest. Domain controllers receive, store, and replicate the zone information even if they are not DNS servers. Microsoft recommends using this option for GlobalNames Zones, but it is not required.

- **To all DNS servers in this domain.** This option replicates the zone information to the AD database on all Windows Server 2003 and later domain controllers in domain controller's AD domain. Domain controllers receive, store, and replicate the zone information even if they are not DNS servers.

- **To all domain controllers in this domain (for Windows 2000 compatibility).** This option replicates the zone information to the AD database on all Windows Server 2000 and later domain controllers in domain controller's AD domain. Domain controllers receive, store, and replicate the zone information even if they are not DNS servers.

- **To all domain controllers specified in the scope of this directory partition.** This option replicates the zone information based on the settings for a specific application directory partition. See the Replication Scope section for more information.

7. Click **Next**.

8. On the **Zone Name** wizard page, in the **Zone name:** text box enter **GlobalNames** (this is not case sensitive) and click **Next**. See Figure 2.12.

9. On the **Dynamic Update** wizard page, select **Do not allow dynamic updates**. This option prevents the use of dynamic DDNS. Although not strictly required, Microsoft recommends this configuration option to ensure that only the proper record types are stored in the zone (see Figure 2.18).

10. Click **Next**.

11. On the **Completing the New Zone Wizard** page, review the information provided and click **Finish**.

EXAM WARNING

Pay careful attention to Microsoft's recommendations regarding GlobalNames zones. Although these zones do not have to be AD integrated, or replicated to all domain controllers in the forest, or configured not to allow dynamic updates—this is how Microsoft expects them to be configured. Often their documentation does not even acknowledge that other configuration options can be used. Play it safe on the exam and give them the answers they want.

Configuring and Managing DNS Replication

Replication for AD integrated zones is managed automatically via AD DS. Once you have specified the replication scope, you don't need to do anything additional to manage zone replication. Standard zones and stub zones, however, have a variety of options that can be configured to control zone transfers. You can manually initiate zone transfers, determine which DNS servers may and may not serve as masters, configure the intervals for replication using a zone's SOA records, and create custom application directory partitions for managing AD integrated zone replication.

Manually Initiating Replication Using DNS Manager

To manually initiate a zone transfer using DNS Manager follow these steps:

1. Open DNS Manager by clicking **Start | Administrative Tools | DNS**.

2. Expand the appropriate server node, expand **Forward Lookup Zones** or **Reverse Lookup Zones**, right-click the desired zone, and click one of the following options:

   - **Transfer from Master.** This option asks the secondary or stub zone to check its master and determine if it is up to date. If it isn't, a zone transfer to obtain any updates will be initiated.

   - **Reload from Master.** This option requests a transfer of the entire zone from the master. It is most often used when some form of corruption has occurred in the secondary or stub zone. Because it transfers all records, it uses more bandwidth and is not recommended except when absolutely necessary.

EXAM WARNING

The server's right-click menu contains a **Reload** option in addition to **Reload from Master**. It's important not to confuse these on the exam. On a secondary zone, the **Reload** option reloads the information in the local zone file. The **Reload from Master** initiates a full zone transfer from a master DNS server and overwrites the records in the zone file.

Configuring DNS Servers to Allow Zone Transfers

For security reasons, by default primary and secondary zones restrict zone transfers. In order to transfer zone information successfully to a standard secondary server, some additional configuration must be done in the properties of a standard primary, AD integrated, or secondary zone on the DNS server that will be the master server. In this section we'll examine how to configure these options, and look at some of the security recommendations Microsoft makes that might turn up on your exam.

Configuring a Standard Primary Zone for Transfers

To configure a primary zone to allow transfers, follow these steps:

1. Open DNS Manager by clicking **Start | Administrative Tools | DNS**.

2. In the left pane, expand the node representing the server you want to configure, expand **Forward Lookup Zones**, right-click the primary zone, and click **Properties**.

3. On the **Properties** dialog, click the **Zone Transfers** tab and select one of the following options (see Figure 2.25):

   - **To any server.** This option is the least secure. It potentially allows anyone to request a zone transfer, which exposes all your DNS records. Potential attackers obtaining this information can receive an enormous amount of information about the network.

   - **Only to servers listed on the Name Servers tab.** The **Properties** dialog has another tab labeled **Name Servers**. This option, the default, uses the list of DNS servers that you have configured on that tab. This is the tab that is used to create NS records for the zone, so by default any server you specify as a name server for the zone is configured automatically for replication. See the *Creating NS Records* section for more information.

   - **Only to the following Servers.** If desired, a separate list can be maintained on the **Zone Transfers** tab. Selecting this option enables the **Edit** button that can be used to add and remove DNS servers.

Larger organizations may require more complexity in how zone transfers are configured. Allowing transfers to any name server for the zone in a global organization might be problematic. Using this option allows for more granular control over which servers can receive zone transfers from the master.

Figure 2.25 The Zone Transfers Tab

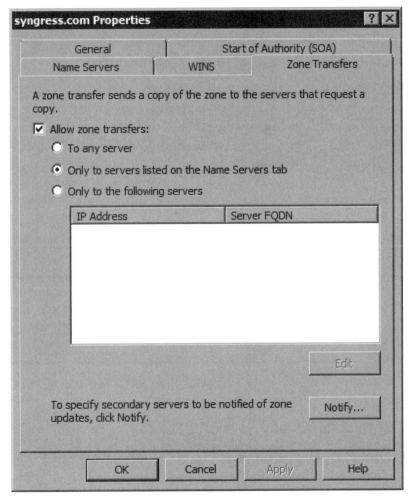

4. Click **OK**.

Configuring an AD Integrated or Secondary Zone for Transfers

By default, AD integrated and secondary zones are configured to prevent zone transfers. To configure these types of zones to allow transfers, follow these steps:

1. Open **DNS Manager** by clicking **Start | Administrative Tools | DNS**.

2. In the left pane, expand the node representing the server you want to configure, expand **Forward Lookup Zones**, right-click the AD integrated or secondary zone, and click **Properties**.

3. On the **Properties** dialog, click the **Zone Transfers** tab.

4. Select **Allow zone transfers:** and configure one of the following options: **To any server**, **Only to servers listed on the Name Servers tab**, **Only to the following Servers**. For more information concerning these options see step 3 in the previous section, *Configuring a Standard Primary Zone for Transfers*. See Figure 2.25.

5. Click **OK**.

EXAM WARNING

Unlike standard primary zones, by default AD integrated and secondary zones are not configured to allow zone transfers. You must check the **Allow zone transfers:** box in the **Zone Transfers** tab in the server's **Properties**.

Configuring the SOA Record

For standard zones, DNS replication relies on the values configured in the Start of Authority (SOA) record. Although it appears as a record when viewing zone information in DNS Manager, the values it contains are actually configured within the zone's properties. To access them, in DNS Manager right-click a zone, select **Properties**, and click the **Start of Authority (SOA)** tab to bring it to the foreground (see Figure 2.26). The following settings can be configured.

- **Serial number.** This text box contains the current version of the zone database. Secondary zones compare their serial number to the one on their master to determine if a zone transfer is needed. You can manually force a zone transfer to all secondary zones by clicking the **Increment** button to manually change this value.

- **Primary Server.** This value specifies the server holding the primary forward lookup zone. When using standard DNS zones, there can only be a DNS server that holds the writable, primary zone.

- **Responsible Person.** This value holds defines Responsible Person (RP) DNS record for the individual who manages the zone.

- **Refresh interval.** This value defines how frequently a DNS server that holds a secondary zone should check for a new version of the zone database. The default value is every 15 minutes.

- **Retry interval.** This value defines how often a DNS server that holds a secondary zone should attempt to check for a new version of the zone database if its initial attempt failed during the standard refresh interval. The default value is every 10 minutes.

- **Expires after.** This value defines how long a secondary zone should retain the zone's records if it cannot contact a master server. Because it is unable to get updates, after a period of time its records may become inaccurate, making it important to ensure they are not being distributed to clients. The default value is one day.

- **Minimum (default) TTL.** This value defines how long a record will be cached by DNS servers and clients that request it. The default value is one hour, which means that any DNS server that obtains this record will return the same information to clients for one hour, and request the record again when that hour is up. Many clients will also cache the record for an hour before asking for an update. As an administrator, you can adjust this value to fit your environment. If IP addresses for requested resources change often, you should keep it low. However, if your resources are fairly static you can increase this value to reduce the load on your DNS servers.

- **TTL for this record.** This option allows the SOA record to have a separate TTL value than the **Minimum (default) TTL** that is applied to all other records in the zone.

Figure 2.26 The Start of Authority (SOA) Tab

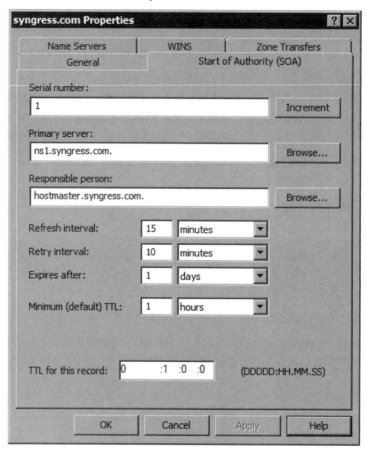

The refresh, retry, and expiration settings on the SOA record apply only to standard secondary zones. AD integrated zones use Active Directory replication and ignore these settings.

EXERCISE 2.3

MODIFYING SOA RECORD PROPERTIES

In this exercise, you will adjust the zone replication intervals in the SOA record for a zone. You'll need to have completed the Exercise 2.2 or have a Windows Server 2008 server with the DNS Server role installed and at least one standard primary forward lookup zone configured on it.

1. Open DNS Manager by clicking on **Start | Administrative Tools | DNS**.
2. In **DNS Manager**, expand your server, expand **Forward Lookup Zones**, right-click a zone, and select **Properties**.
3. In the **Properties** dialog box, click the **Start of Authority (SOA)** tab to bring it to the foreground.
4. Change the **Refresh interval:** to 45 minutes and click **Apply**.
5. Change the **Retry interval:** to 5 minutes and click **OK**.
6. Close DNS Manager.

Creating an Application Directory Partition

In an Active Directory environment, the scope of DNS replication can be narrowly defined while still taking advantage of the benefits of AD replication. You can create an application directory partition, and specify it as where the zone records will be stored during zone creation (see Figure 2.27).

Figure 2.27 The New Zone Wizard with the AD Application Directory Partition Option Enabled

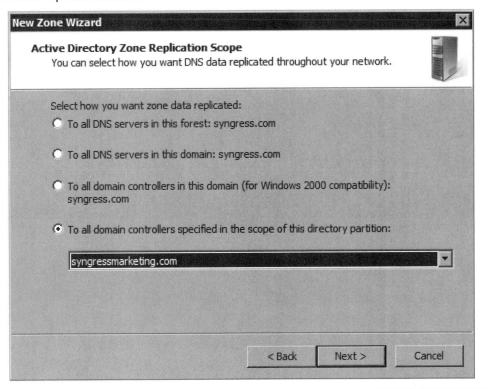

An application directory partition is simply a portion of the Active Directory database that is segregated for replication purposes. When used for DNS, it allows a subset of domain controllers to receive the zone records, rather than the more expansive options of all domain controllers in either the forest or AD domain. You must be a member of the Enterprise Admins group to create partitions. Application directory partitions have uses in AD that extend beyond DNS. They can be created with low level AD management tools such as NTDSUTIL and ADSI Edit. Microsoft makes it easy to create these types of partitions for DNS use by providing an option in their command line DNS management utility, DNSCMD. Follow these steps to create a DNS AD directory partition:

1. Open a command prompt.

2. Type **dnscmd <server name or IP address> /CreateDirectoryPartition <FQDN of the new partition>**. For example: **dnscmd ad2.syngress.com /CreateDirectoryPartition syngressmarketing.com** (see Figure 2.28).

Figure 2.28 Creating an DNS Application Directory Partition Using DNSCMD

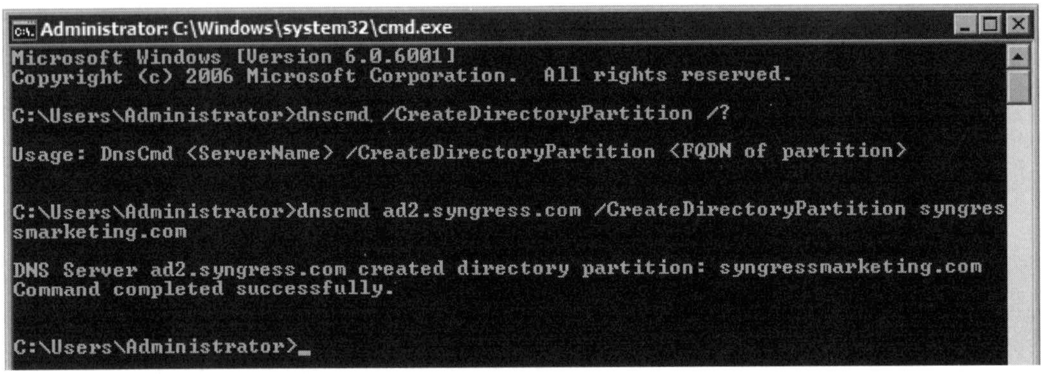

```
Administrator: C:\Windows\system32\cmd.exe

Microsoft Windows [Version 6.0.6001]
Copyright (c) 2006 Microsoft Corporation.  All rights reserved.

C:\Users\Administrator>dnscmd. /CreateDirectoryPartition /?

Usage: DnsCmd <ServerName> /CreateDirectoryPartition <FQDN of partition>

C:\Users\Administrator>dnscmd ad2.syngress.com /CreateDirectoryPartition syngres
smarketing.com

DNS Server ad2.syngress.com created directory partition: syngressmarketing.com
Command completed successfully.

C:\Users\Administrator>_
```

3. Close the command prompt.

Creating and Managing DNS Records

DNS records represent another key DNS management task. In this section we'll see how to manage the major types of DNS records. We'll also take a close look at DNS and WINS integration. On the surface this may not appear to be related to record management, but this integration occurs through the use of WINS and WINS-R records. Finally, we'll take a deeper look at how to manage dynamic DNS.

Managing Record Types

Administrators can manually create a wide range of DNS records. The more commonly used record types are available directly from a zone's right-click menu. All standard RFC record types, plus some used only in Microsoft environments (such as WINS records), can be created with DNS Manager. In this section we examine the major record types and see how to create them.

Creating Host Records

A type host records are used for IPv4 hosts and *AAAA* type host records are used for IPv6 hosts. A computer can have both IPv4 and IPv6 addresses configured on it. Because of this, Windows allows a host to have both A and AAAA host records created for it. Let's examine how to create each type of record.

Creating A Records

To create a new A type host record, follow these steps:

1. Open DNS Manager by clicking **Start | Administrative Tools | DNS**.

2. Expand the node for the server you want to configure, expand the **Forward Lookup Zones** node, right-click the node for the zone to which you want to add the record, and click **New Host (A or AAAA)....** See Figure 2.29.

Figure 2.29 Opening the New Host Dialog

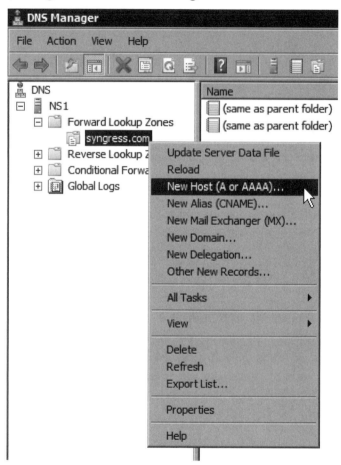

3. In the **New Host** dialog box, type the host's name in the **Name (uses parent domain name if blank):** text area, and the host's IP address in the **IP address:** text area. If you would also like to have a reverse lookup record created, leave the **Create associated pointer (PTR) record** selected. The appropriate reverse lookup zone must be configured for this option to be successful. See Figure 2.30.

Figure 2.30 Configuring the New Host Dialog for an IPv4 Host

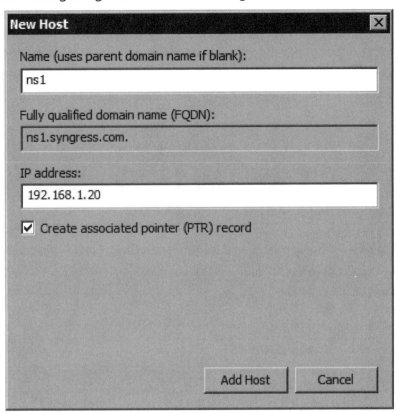

4. Click **Add Host**.

5. In the **DNS** pop-up box that appears to notify you of successful record creation, click **OK**.

6. The **New Host** dialog box stays open with its values cleared so that you can enter another record. Click **Done** to close this dialog.

Creating AAAA Records

To create a new AAAA type host record, follow these steps:

1. Open DNS Manager by clicking **Start | Administrative Tools | DNS**.

2. Expand the node for the server you want to configure, expand the **Forward Lookup Zones** node, right-click the node for the zone to which you want to add the record, and click **New Host (A or AAAA)....** See Figure 2.29.

3. In the **New Host** dialog box, type the host's name in the **Name (uses parent domain name if blank):** text area, and the host's IP address in the **IP address:** text area. If you also would like to have a reverse lookup record created, leave the **Create associated pointer (PTR) record** selected. The appropriate reverse lookup zone must be configured for this option to be successful. See Figure 2.31.

Figure 2.31 Configuring the New Host Dialog for an IPv6 Host

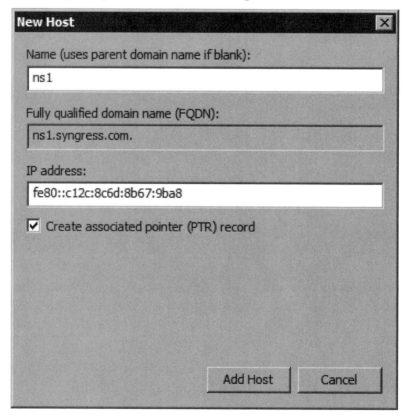

4. Click **Add Host**.

5. In the **DNS** pop-up box that appears to notify you of successful record creation, click **OK**.

6. The **New Host** dialog box stays open with its values cleared so that you can enter another record. Click **Done** to close this dialog.

New & Noteworthy...

Full IPv6 Support

The AAAA record is an excellent example of changes made to Windows Server 2008 to accommodate IPv6. Microsoft has completely reworked Windows networking to ensure that IPv6 is fully incorporated. As a result, both IPv4 and IPv6 are used throughout Windows Server 2008's DNS functionality. Many DNS configuration screens now attempt to automatically resolve both IPv4 and IPv6 addresses for host records, even when IPv6 is not configured and present on the network. Occasionally this can lead to warning messages that aren't relevant for your IPv4 environment.

IPv6 is a new generation of the Internet Protocol. Although it's been available for years, software companies like Microsoft have been slow to support it. It originally was conceived primarily to provide more IP addresses at a time when it looked like the industry was running out of them. However, new technologies such as network address translation solved many of the shortage issues and this greatly slowed the adoption of IPv6. Today, IPv6 runs on some of the largest private networks; however most organizations continue to use IPv4.

Creating Pointer Records

Pointer records are used in reverse lookup zones to resolve IP addresses to host names. As seen in the previous section, they can be added automatically when you create a host record. They can also be created manually using the following procedure:

1. Open DNS Manager by clicking **Start | Administrative Tools | DNS**.

2. Expand the node for the server you want to configure, expand the **Reverse Lookup Zones** node, right-click the node for the zone to which you want to add the record to, and click **New Pointer (PTR)....** See Figure 2.32.

Figure 2.32 Opening the New Pointer Dialog

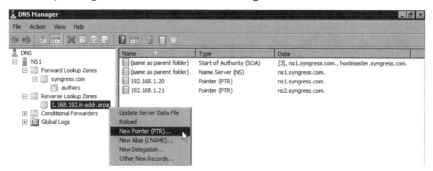

3. In the **New Resource Record** dialog box, type the host's IP address in the **Host IP Address:** text box, and the host's name in the **Host name:** text box. You can also click **Browse...** and select the computer from an existing DNS record, such as an A or AAAA record, if one exists for the host. See Figure 2.33.

Figure 2.33 The Completed New Resource Record Dialog for a PTR Record

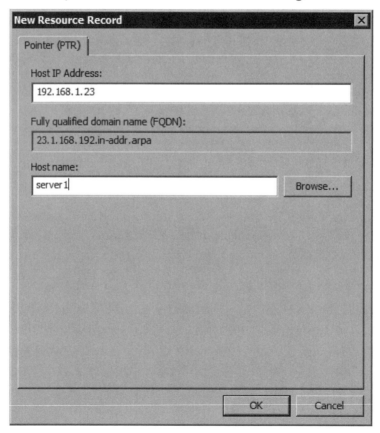

4. Click **OK** to finish adding the record.

EXERCISE 2.4

CREATING A AND PTR RECORDS

In this exercise you will create an A record and a PTR record. You need to have completed Exercise 2.2 or have a Windows Server 2008 server with the DNS Server role installed and standard primary or AD Integrated forward and reverse lookup zones configured on it.

1. Open DNS Manager by clicking **Start | Administrative Tools | DNS**.

2. Expand the node for the server you want to configure, expand the **Forward Lookup Zones** node, right-click the node for the zone to which you want to add the record, and click **New Host (A or AAAA)....**

3. In the **New Host** dialog box, type the host's name in the **Name (uses parent domain name if blank):** text box, and the host's IP address in the **IP address:** text box. If you do not have an additional computer, make up a host name and appropriate IP address for the exercise.

4. Deselect **Create associated pointer (PTR) record**.

5. Click **Add Host**.

6. In the **DNS** pop-up box that appears to notify you of successful record creation, click **OK**.

7. In the **New Host** dialog box, click **Done**.

8. In the **Reverse Lookup Zones** node, right-click the node for the zone to which you want to add the record, and click **New Pointer (PTR)....**

9. In the **New Resource Record** dialog box, type the host's IP address in the **Host IP Address:** text box, and the host's name in the **Host name:** text box. Use the same values you chose for step 3.

10. Click **OK** to finish adding the record.

11. Close DNS Manager.

Creating MX Records

Mail exchanger (MX) records are used to locate email servers. For an email server to be located on the network, an MX record is not enough. An MX record contains only the FQDN of the email server; it does not say where to find it. At a minimum the server must also have an A and/or AAAA record for the email server. It is also recommended that the server have a PTR record. Many spam applications use reverse lookup to verify email servers. To create a new MX record, follow these steps:

1. Open DNS Manager by clicking **Start | Administrative Tools | DNS**.

2. Expand the node for the server you want to configure, expand the **Forward Lookup Zones** node, right-click the node for the zone to which you want to add the record, and click **New Mail Exchanger (MX)....** See Figure 2.29.

3. In the **New Resource Record** dialog box, type the email server's FQDN in the **Fully qualified domain name (FQDN) of mail server:** text box, click **Browse...** and select the server from an existing A or AAAA. See Figure 2.34. If your domain has more than one email server, you can use the **Mail server priority:** value to specify which has priority. The accepted range is 0 to 65535, with priority being given to the lowest number. If that server does not respond, the email server specified in the MX record containing the next highest value is used. If multiple mail servers are configured with the same value, and it is the lowest number, the servers will be used in a random fashion.

Figure 2.34 The Completed New Resource Record Dialog for a MX Record

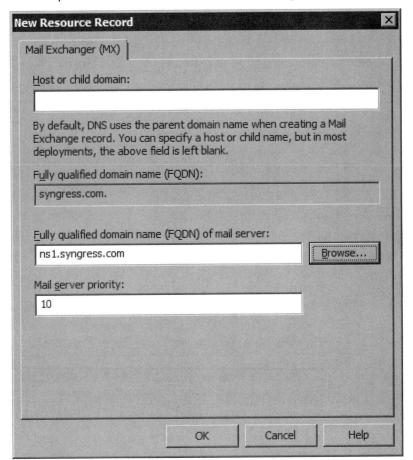

4. Click **OK** to finish adding the record.

Creating SRV Records

Service records are used to specify which server or servers hold certain TCP/IP services in the domain, including finger, ftp, http, Kerberos, ldap, msdcs, nntp, telnet, and whois. Clients that query the domain for the appropriate server to contact for one these services will be responded to based on one or more service record configuration(s). This allows administrators to move the role holders of these services easily if necessary. It also allows for the use of multiple servers with priority and load balancing for any of the services listed. To create an SRV record, follow these steps:

1. Open DNS Manager by clicking **Start | Administrative Tools | DNS**.

2. Expand the node for the server you want to configure, expand the **Forward Lookup Zones** node, right-click the node for the zone to which you want to add the record, and click **Other New Records....** See Figure 2.29.

3. In the **Resource Record Type** dialog box that appears, select **Service Location (SRV)** in the **Select a resource record type:** box, and click **Create Record....** See Figure 2.35.

Figure 2.35 The Resource Record Type Dialog

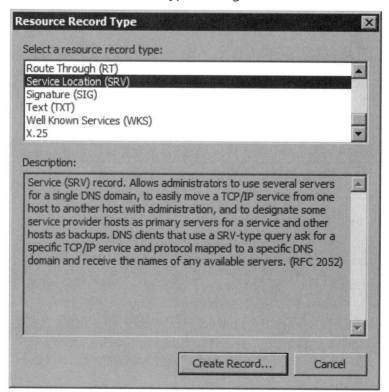

4. In the **New Resource Record** dialog box, configure the following (see Figure 2.36):

   - Drop down the **Service:** box and select the desired service. We'll select _http.

   - Drop down the **Protocol:** box and select the desired protocol, or accept the default for the service you chose.

   - In the **Priority:** text box, leave the default if there will only be one server for this service. If more than one will be used, this box can be used to assign an initial level of priority to the servers. The accepted range is 0 to 65535, with priority being given to the lowest number. If that server does not respond, the server specified in the SRV record containing the next highest value is used. If multiple servers are configured with the same value, and it is the lowest number, the servers will be used in a random fashion unless **Weight:** is configured.

   - In the **Weight:** text box, leave the default value if there will be only one server for this service, if there are multiple servers but only one with this server's assigned **Priority:**, or to specify that it should be used randomly with one or more other servers that are assigned the same **Priority:** and **Weight:** settings. Unlike the **Priority:** setting, the **Weight:** setting uses the record or records configured with higher value first.

   - In the **Port number:** text box, enter the port on which the specified server is configured to respond to the service, or accept the default for the service you selected.

   - In the **Host offering this service:** text box, enter the FQDN of the server. An A or AAAA record must exist for FQDN specified in this box.

   - When dynamic updates are enabled, an additional option may appear on this dialog: **Allow any authenticated user to update all DNS records with the same name.** This option allows an administrator to preconfigure a record for a service host that is not yet online in such a way that the record is allowed to be overwritten dynamically later.

Figure 2.36 The Completed New Resource Record Dialog for a SRV Record

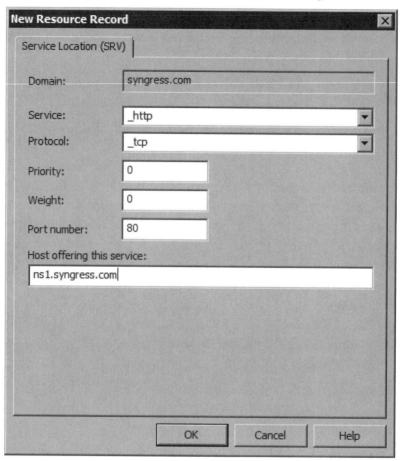

5. Click **OK** to add the record.
6. Click **Done** in the **Resource Record Type** dialog box. A new node that contains the record will appear in the zone. See Figure 2.37.

Figure 2.37 DNS Manager Displaying the New Node and SRV Record

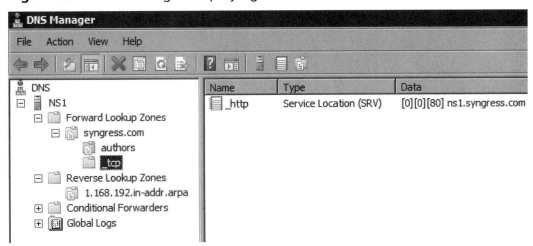

Creating CNAME Records

An Alias (CNAME) record is used when a host needs to be referred to by more than one name. You might have your email and web services running on the same server, for example. It's common for the web server to be resolvable as *www* and for mail servers to be resolvable as *mail*. If the actual configured server name for the Windows Server 2008 server hosting these services is syngress-server, the default host record in DNS may be something like syngress-server.syngress.com. CNAME records can be added so that this server can also be found as www.syngress.com and mail.syngress.com. To configure a CNAME record, follow these steps:

1. Open DNS Manager by clicking **Start | Administrative Tools | DNS**.

2. Expand the node for the server you want to configure, expand the **Forward Lookup Zones** or **Reverse Lookup Zones** node, right-click the node for the zone to which you want to add the record, and click **New Alias (CNAME)…. See Figure 2.29.**

3. In the **New Resource Record** dialog box, type the alias you want to configure into the **Alias name (uses parent domain if left blank):** text box. Type the host's FQDN in the **Fully qualified domain name (FQDN) for target host:** text box, or click **Browse…** and select the server from an existing A or AAAA. See Figure 2.38.

Figure 2.38 A Completed New Resource Record Dialog for a CNAME Record

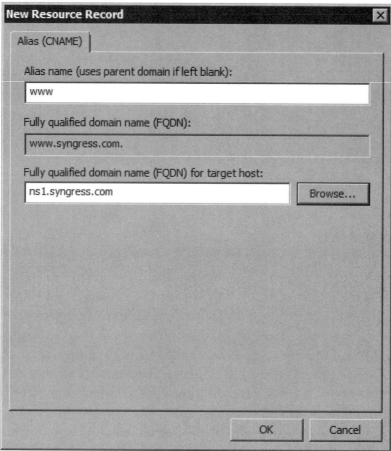

4. Click **OK** to finish adding the record.

Creating NS Records

Name server (NS) records identify DNS name servers for a zone. These records are managed differently than most others. When you specify a name server in the properties of the zone, an NS record is added for the server. To create an NS record, follow these steps:

1. Open DNS Manager by clicking **Start | Administrative Tools | DNS**.

2. Expand the node for the server you want to configure, expand the **Forward Lookup Zones** or **Reverse Lookup Zones** node, right-click the node for the zone to which you want to add the record, and click **Properties**.

3. In the **Properties** dialog box, click the **Name Servers** tab to bring it forward. See Figure 2.39.

Figure 2.39 The Name Servers Tab

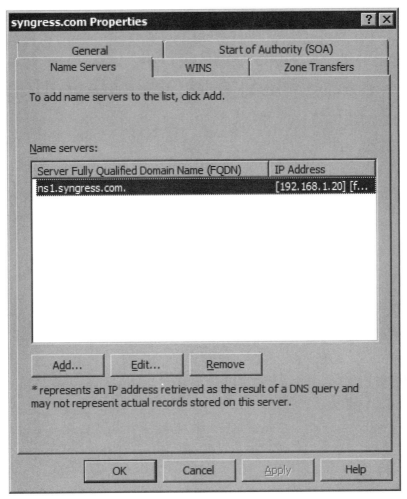

4. Click the **Add...** button.

5. In the **New Name Server Record** dialog box, type the fully qualified domain name (FQDN) in the **Server fully qualified domain name (FQDN):** text box, and click **Resolve**. If you wish to add an IP address manually, you can click **<Click here to add an IP Address>** and enter it in the text field that appears. Resolved IP addresses can also be modified

by clicking them. If multiple IP addresses are configured for the record, you can determine the priority they will be used in with the **Up** and **Down** buttons. IP addresses can also be removed using the **Delete** button. See Figure 2.3.

6. Click **OK**.

7. In the Properties dialog box, click **OK**.

Configuring Windows Internet Name Service (WINS) and DNS Integration

If a DNS client queries a zone that does not have the requested record, you can configure the zone to attempt to resolve the name using WINS. WINS typically is used to resolve NetBIOS names to IPv4 addresses on Windows networks; however it is gradually being phased out. For more information on WINS, see the sections of this chapter titled "Using the New GlobalNames Zone Feature" and "Configuring Name Resolution for Client Computers". Both forward and reverse lookups can be extended to use WINS servers by modifying the zone's properties to create the appropriate DNS record. Let's examine how to create WINS Lookup and WINS Reverse Lookup records.

Creating a WINS Lookup Record

To create a WINS Lookup (WINS) record for a forward lookup zone, follow these steps:

1. Open DNS Manager by clicking **Start | Administrative Tools | DNS**.

2. Expand the node for the server you want to configure, expand the **Forward Lookup Zones** node, right-click the node for the zone to which you want to add the record, and click **Properties**.

3. In the **Properties** dialog box, click the **WINS** tab to bring it forward. See Figure 2.40.

Figure 2.40 A Configured WINS Tab

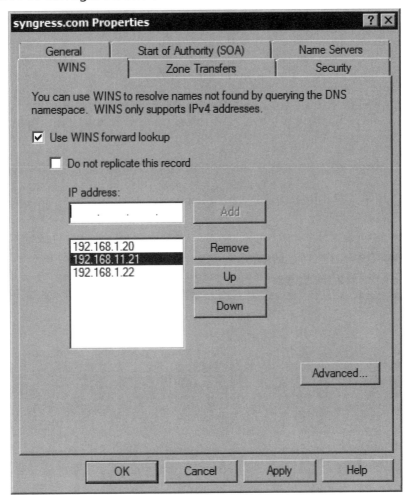

4. By default, the **Use WINS forward lookup** checkbox is not selected on the **Properties** dialog box. To enable WINS lookup and create the needed DNS record, select this option.

5. In the **IP address** area, enter the IPv4 address for a WINS server and click **Add**. If necessary, repeat this step to enter the IP address of more than one WINS server. If multiple IP addresses are configured for the record, you can determine the priority they will be used in with the **Up** and **Down** buttons. IP addresses can also be removed using the **Remove** button.

6. If you use a mix of Windows and non-Windows DNS servers, consider selecting the **Do not replicate this record** option. WINS records are

not standard DNS record types and are not supported by all DNS servers. Attempting to replicate them to DNS servers that do not support them may cause errors.

7. If desired, click the **Advanced...** option to open the **Advanced** dialog box and configure the following additional options (see Figure 2.41):

- **Cache time-out.** This option defines the how long the DNS server remembers any resolved names and returns them from Cache, rather than querying a WINS server again for them.

- **Lookup time-out.** This option defines how long the DNS server will wait to hear from a WINS server before it tries the next one in the list on the WINS tab, or gives up if no more servers are in the list to try.

Figure 2.41 The Advanced Dialog

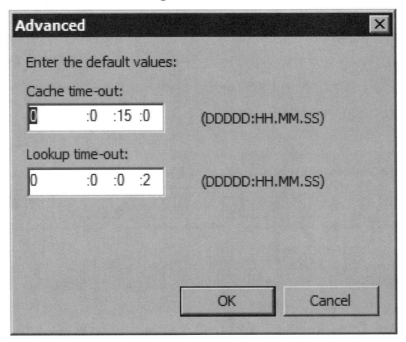

8. Click **OK**.

9. In the **Properties** dialog box, click **OK**.

10. Double-check that the appropriate WINS Lookup record has been created in DNS Manager. See Figure 2.42.

Figure 2.42 Verifying the WINS Record in DNS Manager

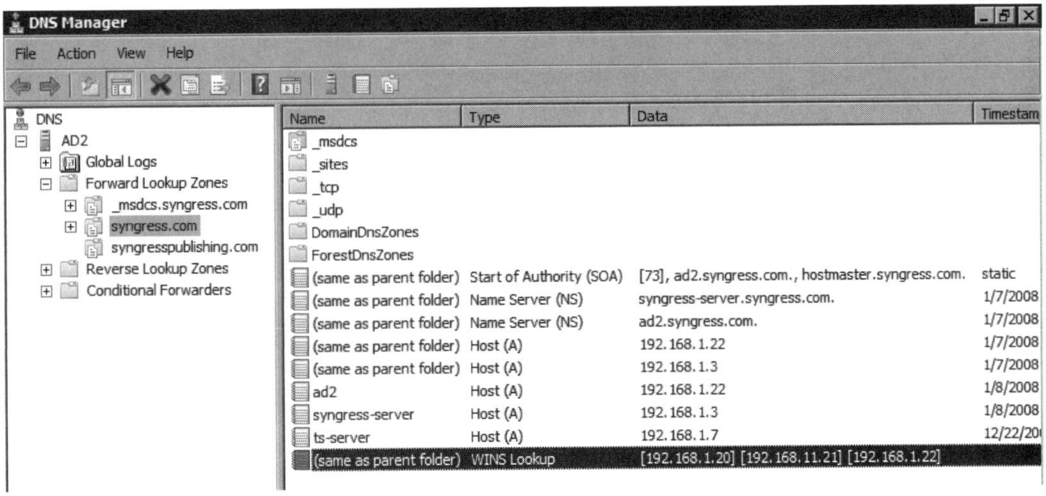

TEST DAY TIP

If you use a mix of Windows and non-Windows DNS servers, consider selecting the **Do not replicate this record** option. WINS records are not standard DNS record types and are not supported by all DNS servers. Attempting to replicate them to DNS servers that do not support them may cause errors.

Creating a WINS Reverse Lookup Record

To create a WINS Reverse Lookup (WINS-R) record for a reverse lookup zone, follow these steps:

1. Open DNS Manager by clicking **Start | Administrative Tools | DNS**.

2. Expand the node for the server you want to configure, the **Reverse Lookup Zones** node, right-click the node for the zone to which you want to add the record, and click **Properties**.

3. In the **Properties** dialog box, click the **WINS-R** tab to bring it forward. See Figure 2.43.

Figure 2.43 The WINS-R Tab

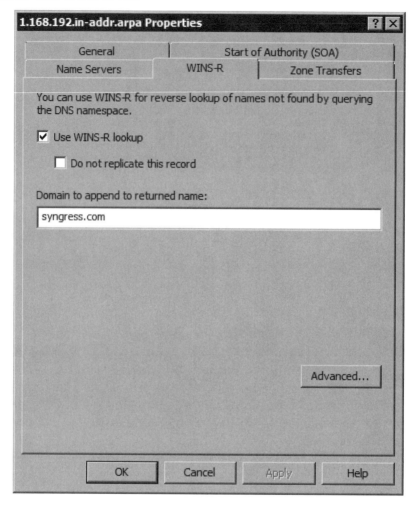

4. By default, the **Use WINS-R lookup** checkbox is not selected on the **Properties** dialog box. To enable WINS reverse lookup and create the needed DNS record, select this option.

5. In the **Domain to append to the returned name:** text box, enter the domain name that you want to have appended to the NetBIOS names returned from WINS. When responding to queries from the DNS server, WINS servers will return NetBIOS computer names. These names will not have DNS suffixes. The suffix that you want appended is entered here.

6. If you use a mix of Windows and non-Windows DNS servers, consider selecting the **Do not replicate this record** option. WINS-R records are

not standard DNS record types and are not supported by all DNS servers. Attempting to replicate them to DNS servers that do not support them may cause errors.

7. If desired, click the **Advanced...** button to open the **Advanced** dialog box and configure the following additional options (see Figure 2.44):

- **Cache time-out.** This option defines the how long the DNS server remembers any resolved names and returns them from Cache, rather than querying a WINS server again for them.

- **Lookup time-out.** This option defines how long the DNS server will wait to hear from a WINS server before it tries the next one in its list.

- **Submit DNS domain as NetBIOS scope.** The NetBIOS namespace had limited partitioning capability, loosely similar to the ability to define top-level domains in DNS. If your network uses these, and they match your DNS domains, select this option. When a lookup request is sent by a client to a DNS server, and the server cannot resolve the query using DNS, the leftmost portion of the FQDN is used as the NetBIOS computer name and the remainder is used as the NetBIOS scope.

Figure 2.44 The Advanced Dialog

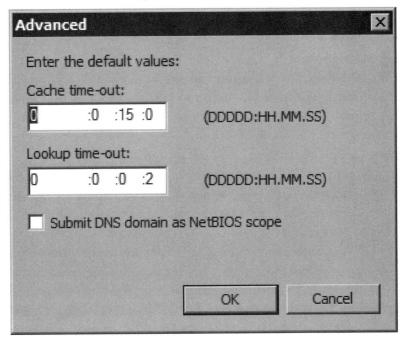

8. Click **OK**.

9. In the **Properties** dialog box, click **OK**.

10. Double-check that the appropriate WINS-R record has been created in DNS Manager. See Figure 2.45.

Figure 2.45 Verifying the WINS-R Record in DNS Manager

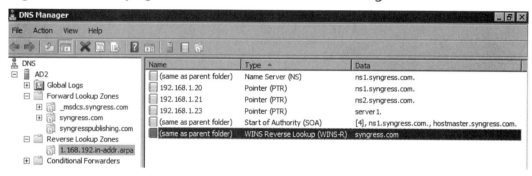

Understanding the Dynamic Domain Name System (DDNS)

Traditionally, DNS record administration had to be performed manually. In some networks with high security requirements this is still the case. Beginning with Windows 2000 Server, Microsoft implemented the ability for hosts and the DHCP network service to dynamically update and manage DNS records. The DDNS feature has remained largely unchanged since its initial release in Windows 2000 Server. In the *Creating DNS Zones* section, we examined the three options that can be specified during the creation of a new forward or reverse lookup zone. These can also be modified after the zone has been created by changing the **Dynamic updates:** option on the **General** tab of the zone's **Properties**.

The use of dynamic records creates potential problems, because hosts do not always remove their records from DNS. If a laptop is not shut down properly, for example, and is restarted on a different network it will leave an invalid DNS record behind on the DNS server for the previous network. Microsoft provides a mechanism known as aging and scavenging to deal with this issue. In this section we'll examine how to configure and use aging and scavenging.

DDNS can conflict with data in the GlobalNames zone. If a GNZ is configured on the DNS server, it is checked first when DDNS requests are received. If a client attempts to register or update a DDNS record using a name that is already specified in the GNZ, the request will fail.

Configuring DDNS Aging and Scavenging

Administrators are responsible for defining when a record should be considered invalid and ready for deletion. Aging settings are used to determine when a record should be removed, and the scavenging process actually deletes it. There are two levels at which aging can be set, the server and the zone. Settings applied at the server level will apply to all AD integrated zones on the DNS server. Settings applied at the zone level override server level settings for AD integrated zones. You do not have to configure zone level settings for AD integrated zones. If you are using standard primary zones, however, you do have to configure aging at the zone level.

When a host or DHCP service registers a record dynamically with DNS, the record receives a timestamp. This timestamp is the foundation for the aging and scavenging process. Once established, records are updated using one of two methods. The first, a record refresh, is performed when a host checks in and lets the DNS server know that nothing has changed and the record is still valid. Most Windows 2000 and later hosts send a refresh every 24 hours. Because the time stamp is updated when a refresh occurs, AD replication (for AD integrated zones) or zone transfers (for standard zones) are triggered. To limit the amount of traffic consumed by DDNS, Microsoft allows administrators to configure a **no-refresh** interval (7 days by default). During this time the DNS server will reject refresh requests for the record.

The second type of communication that hosts and DHCP servers use to dynamically modify DNS records is the record update method. This method is used when a new host joins the network and A (or AAAA) and PTR records are created for it, when a server is promoted to become a domain controller, or when an existing record requires an IP address update. DNS record changes involving the record update method can occur at any time and are not subject to the limits imposed by the **no-refresh** interval. To configure the refresh intervals at either the server or zone level, follow these steps:

1. Open DNS Manager by clicking **Start | Administrative Tools | DNS**.

2. Select one of the following:

    ■   To manage server level aging and scavenging, in the left pane right-click the server node and select **Set Aging/Scavenging for All Zones....**

    ■   To manage zone level aging and scavenging, in the left pane expand the server, expand either the **Forward Lookup Zones** or **Reverse Lookup Zones** node, right-click the zone you want to configure, and click **Properties**. On the **General** tab, click the **Aging** button.

3. In the **Aging/Scavenging Properties** dialog that appears, select the **Scavenge stale resource records** box. See Figure 2.46.

Figure 2.46 The Server Aging/Scavenging Properties Dialog

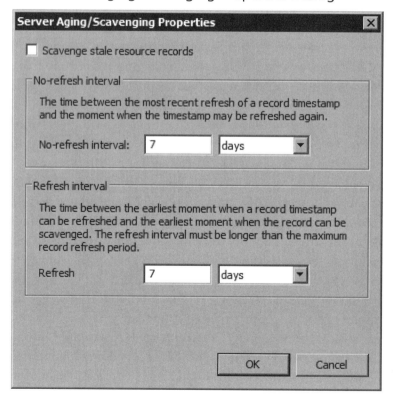

4. Configure the following options:

- **No-refresh interval.** This setting controls when the DNS server rejects refresh requests from hosts and the DHCP service. Most Windows hosts attempt to refresh their records every 24 hours. The DHCP service attempts updates at 50% of the IP address lease time. This option is used to limit the amount of replication traffic required for records that do not change. The default of seven days is acceptable for most networks.

- **Refresh.** This option determines when a DDNS record can be flagged for scavenging (deletion). The default value is seven days. By default, records that are older than the sum of the **no-refresh** and **refresh** intervals will be available for scavenging. This value must be set to a value that is less than the maximum setting for clients to refresh their records. The default is acceptable for most networks; however if you modify your DHCP addresses leases to longer than 14 days, you may want to consider updating this setting to 50% of the configured lease time.

5. Click **OK**.

Enabling Automatic Scavenging

Scavenging is not automatic by default. If you have configured the previous settings, records that exceed the **refresh** interval will be marked only as available for scavenging. To enable automatic scavenging, follow these steps:

1. Open DNS Manager by clicking **Start | Administrative Tools | DNS**.

2. In the left pane right-click the server node, select **Properties**, and click the **Advanced** tab.

3. Select the **Enable automatic scavenging of stale records** box and configure the desired interval, as shown in Figure 2.47.

Figure 2.47 Enabling Automatic Scavenging

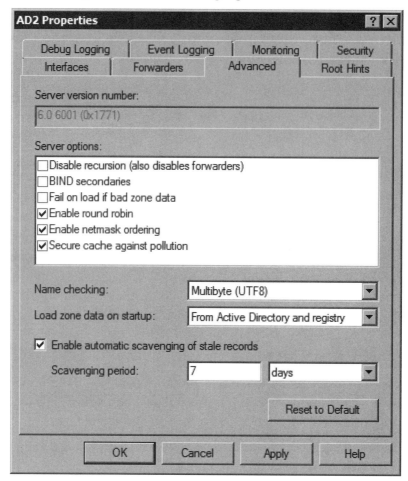

Initiating Manual Scavenging

You can manually initiate the scavenging procedure at any time by following these steps:

1. Open DNS Manager by clicking **Start | Administrative Tools | DNS**.

2. In the left pane right-click the server node and select **Scavenge Stale Resource Records**. See Figure 2.48.

Figure 2.48 Manually Initiating Scavenging

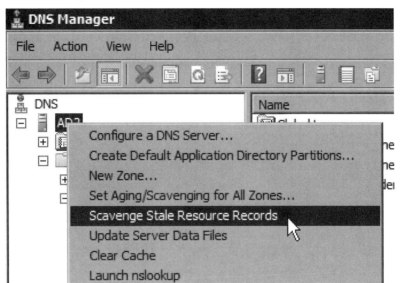

Configuring Name Resolution for Client Computers

There are two primary forms of naming on Windows networks, NetBIOS and host names. NetBIOS name resolution goes back to the early days of Windows. Recent server releases from Microsoft have increasingly moved away from it toward DNS. If a network runs a variety of Windows client and server versions, it's important that both forms of name resolution are configured properly. If the network is comprised primarily of Windows XP and later clients, and Windows Server 2003 and later servers, DNS is most likely supporting many of the network's name resolution needs. In this section, we'll examine how to configure client settings for the maximum name resolution flexibility by examining the options contained in the advanced properties of a Window's Vista client's TCP/IP settings. To access these settings follow this procedure:

1. Click **Start** | **Control Panel** | **Network and Sharing Center** | **Manage network connections**.

2. In the **Network Connections** window's **General** tab, right-click the network connection you want to configure and select **Properties**.

3. In the **Local Area Connection Properties** dialog, select **Internet Protocol Version 4 (TCP/IPv4)** and click **Properties**. See Figure 2.49.

Figure 2.49 The Local Area Connection Properties Dialog

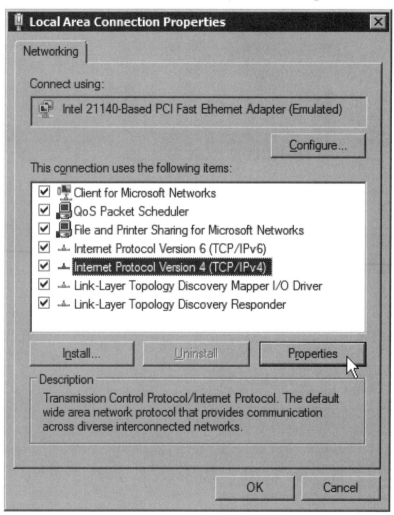

4. In the **Internet Protocol Version 4 (TCP/IPv4) Properties** dialog box, click the **Advanced...** button. See Figure 2.50.

Figure 2.50 The Internet Protocol Version 4 (TCP/IPv4) Properties Dialog

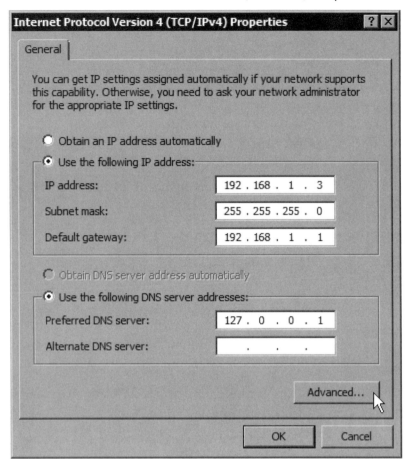

How Name Resolution Works in Windows XP and Later

Although some integration is possible, the NetBIOS and host name resolution methods are very different. Host names are used when a client attempts to use user friendly names (instead of IP addresses) with a TCP/IP utility such as ping, an FTP client, or a web browser. By default, the following name resolution steps are taken when resolving host names: the local host name => the local DNS resolver cache => the local HOSTS file => DNS => the local NetBIOS name cache => WINS => a local network broadcast => the local LMHOSTS file. Additional configuration is needed for all steps to be applied. You must have the address of at least one WINS server configured in the network client properties, for example.

In addition, some steps can be reordered such as checking the LMHOSTS file before sending a network broadcast.

Not all utilities and programs within Windows use host names. For example, if you open the **Start | Run** dialog and attempt to remotely connect to a Windows computer using a command such as **\\servername\sharename**, NetBIOS name resolution will be used. By default, the following name resolution steps are taken when resolving NetBIOS names: the local NetBIOS name cache => WINS => a local network broadcast => the LMHOSTS file => the local host name => the local DNS resolver cache => DNS. Just as with host name resolution, additional configuration is needed for all steps to be used and some can be reordered. Let's examine how to configure the various components of name resolution on a Windows Vista computer.

Configuring the DNS Server List

You can specify one or more DNS servers for a Windows Vista computer to use. When attempting to resolve a DNS query, the servers will be contacted in the order they appear in the list. If a DNS server is contacted successfully, no other DNS servers in the list are queried even if the initial DNS server was unable to resolve the query successfully. The following procedure can be used to configure or manage a list of one or more DNS server:

1. Click **Start | Control Panel | Network and Sharing Center | Manage network connections**.

2. In the **Network Connections** window's **General** tab, right-click the network connection you want to configure and select **Properties**.

3. In the **Local Area Connection Properties** dialog, select **Internet Protocol Version 4 (TCP/IPv4)** and click **Properties**.

4. In the **Internet Protocol Version 4 (TCP/IPv4) Properties** dialog box, click the **Advanced…** button.

5. In the **Advanced TCP/IP Settings** dialog box, click the **DNS** tab to bring it to the foreground.

6. In the **DNS server addresses, in order of use:** section of the page, do one or more of the following (see Figure 2.51):

   ■ Reorder the existing name servers by placing the first one you want used at the top of the list, the second one in the second position on the list, and so forth. To accomplish this, select the name server you wish to reorder and use the up or down arrows to place it in the desired position.

- Add new name servers to the list. To accomplish this, click the **Add...** button and enter the IP address of the new DNS server in the **TCP/IP DNS Server** dialog box, then click **Add**.

- Edit the IP address of an existing server in the list. To accomplish this, click the **Edit...** button, make the desired change in the **TCP/IP DNS Server** dialog box, then click **OK**.

- Remove a DNS server from the list. To accomplish this, select the server you want to remove from the list and click the **Remove** button.

Figure 2.51 The DNS Tab

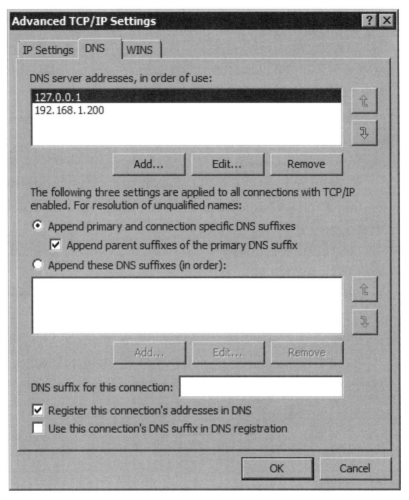

EXAM WARNING

Client DNS server settings can be assigned by group policy. When a client has locally configured DNS servers, and a group policy setting that specifies them, the local server list is ignored.

Configuring the Suffix Search Order

Users don't always type in a fully qualified domain name when attempting to access DNS based resources. For example, your company may have an intranet site that users access by typing **http://companyweb**. Because this is not a FQDN, a name like this is not resolvable. You can configure the DNS suffix search order in Windows Vista to convert a typed name like the earlier example into a FQDN, so that users do not have to type a fully qualified domain name. This can make resources, such as the intranet site name in our example, much easier for users to remember and access. The following procedure can be used to configure or manage the suffix search order:

1. Click **Start | Control Panel | Network and Sharing Center | Manage network connections**.

2. In the **Network Connections** window's **General** tab, right-click the network connection you want to configure and select **Properties**.

3. In the **Local Area Connection Properties** dialog, select **Internet Protocol Version 4 (TCP/IPv4)** and click **Properties**.

4. In the **Internet Protocol Version 4 (TCP/IPv4) Properties** dialog box, click the **Advanced...** button.

5. In the **Advanced TCP/IP Settings** dialog box, click the **DNS** tab to bring it to the foreground and select one of the following options (see Figure 2.51):

   ■ **Append primary and connection specific DNS suffixes.** When this option is selected, the primary DNS suffix is appended to the name the user types, such as our **companyweb** example. The primary DNS suffix for a Windows Vista computer is configured as part of its computer name. If the workstation is configured with a network identity of *workstation1.authors.syngress.com*, its primary domain is *authors.syngress.com*. The computer will attempt to resolve the name **compnayweb.authors.syngress.com**. If a host with this name cannot be located, and the **Append parent suffixes of the primary DNS suffix** option is selected, the parent of the **author** domain, **syngress.com**, will be appended and tried next (**companyweb.syngress.com**). Finally, if a connection-specific DNS suffix is configured, it will be tried. This suffix is configured on this DNS tab in the **DNS suffix for this connection:** text box.

- **Append these DNS suffixes (in order).** This option allows you to specify a list of specific DNS suffixes to append, and does not try to append the primary or connection specific suffixes. You create a list by adding new entries using the **Add...** button, and can edit existing entries using the **Edit...** button. Entries can be removed using the **Remove** button. If you have specified more than one suffix, they will be tried in order. The order the list is in can be modified by selecting an individual suffix and using the up or down arrow buttons to place it in the desired list position. When used for resolution, the first suffix is used. If a host cannot be found that matches the host name plus the name of the first suffix, a second resolution request occurs involving the second suffix, and so forth.

Configuring the HOSTS File

The HOSTS file resides on all Windows computers and can be manually modified by administrators. In Windows Vista and Server 2008, the HOSTS file supports both IPv4 and IPv6 addresses. The default HOSTS file for Windows Vista and Server 2008, seen in Figure 2.52, contains the loopback addresses for both IPv4 (127.0.0.1) and IPv6 (::1) by default.

Figure 2.52 The HOSTS File

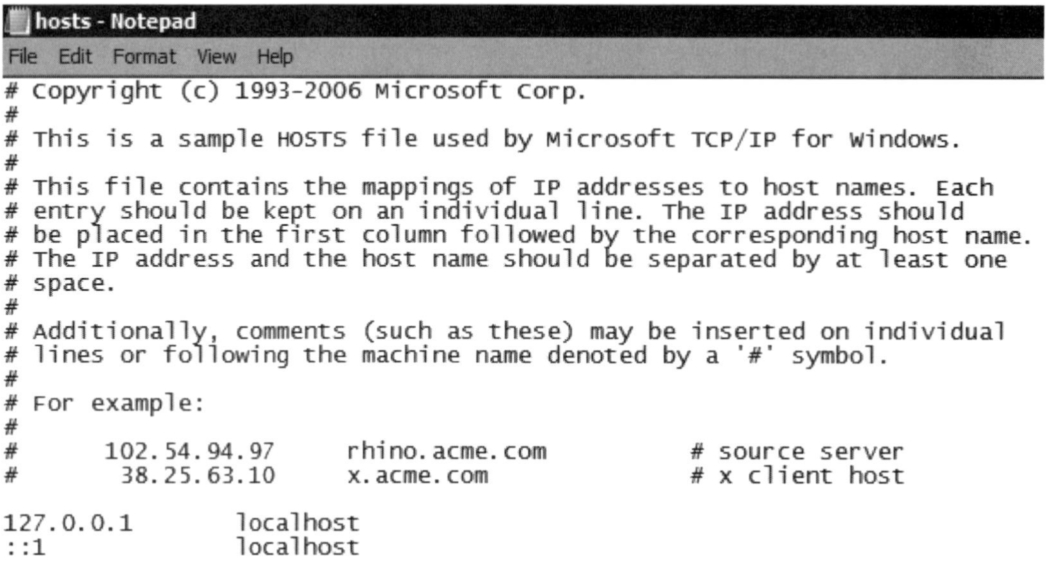

```
hosts - Notepad
File  Edit  Format  View  Help
# Copyright (c) 1993-2006 Microsoft Corp.
#
# This is a sample HOSTS file used by Microsoft TCP/IP for Windows.
#
# This file contains the mappings of IP addresses to host names. Each
# entry should be kept on an individual line. The IP address should
# be placed in the first column followed by the corresponding host name.
# The IP address and the host name should be separated by at least one
# space.
#
# Additionally, comments (such as these) may be inserted on individual
# lines or following the machine name denoted by a '#' symbol.
#
# For example:
#
#     102.54.94.97      rhino.acme.com          # source server
#      38.25.63.10      x.acme.com              # x client host

127.0.0.1        localhost
::1              localhost
```

Table 2.3 shows some sample HOSTS file entries. More detailed information is available in Windows Help and Microsoft's online documentation.

Table 2.3 Common LMHOSTS Entries

LMHOSTS Entry	Effect
192.168.2.1 Server1.syngress.com #Major server	This is a basic HOSTS file entry. When the HOSTS file is examined for the host name Server1.syngress.com, the IP address 192.168.2.1 will be returned. In this case, the text after the # sign is a comment inserted by an administrator.
192.168.2.1 Server1.syngress.com DNS.syngress.com #Major server	This entry adds an alias to the primary host name. It will resolve both Server1.syngress.com and DNS.syngress.com.

Configuring the NetBIOS Node Type

With Windows Vista, there are several ways that NetBIOS name resolution can occur. The NetBIOS node type determines the order in which these name resolution methods are used. The following methods can be used for NetBIOS name resolution:

- **Local NetBIOS computer name.** This method of name resolution examines the local computer name to see if it matches the name of the computer with which communication is being attempted.

- **Local NetBIOS cache.** When successful NetBIOS name resolution occurs, entries are cached for a variable period, usually around 10 minutes. This method of name resolution examines this cache to see if the name of the computer with which communication is being attempted is contained in it.

- **Broadcast.** This method sends a broadcast out on the local network segment. Some routers can be configured to pass these NetBIOS messages to other segments, but typically this setting is not used because of the increase in network traffic it causes. If the computer with which communication is being attempted is within broadcast range, it will communicate back in peer-to-peer fashion and complete the name resolution process.

- **WINS server.** This method of name resolution uses WINS or NetBIOS name servers for name resolution. More information about this option is available in the *Configuring the WINS Server List* section.

- **LMHOSTS file.** Each Windows Vista computer contains a LMHOSTS file. You can enter NetBIOS names and their matching IP addresses in this file. When this type of name resolution is used, the local system checks this file to see if it contains a match for the computer with which communication is being attempted. More information about this option is available in the *Configuring the LMHOSTS File* section.

These five name resolution methods are not specified individually. Microsoft groups them into four possible configurations, known as NetBIOS node types:

- **B-Node or Broadcast Node.** In Microsoft's version of B-Node resolution, the workstation first checks its local NetBIOS name cache. If this fails it sends a broadcast. Finally, it checks the LMHOSTS file. This is the default node type if no WINS server is configured.

- **P-Node or Point-to-Point Node.** This name resolution method only queries a WINS or NetBIOS name server.

- **M-Node or Mixed Node.** This name resolution method uses B-Node followed by P-Node.

- **H-Node or Hybrid Node.** This is the default node type if at least one WINS server is configured on the client. The name resolution order for this node type is similar to a combination of P-Node followed by B-Node. Each step is tried individually, and resolution stops when one is successful:

  - The local NetBIOS name is checked

  - The local NetBIOS cache is checked

  - WINS is queried

  - A broadcast is sent

  - LMHOSTS file is checked

  - If all attempts at name resolution fail, host name resolution will be attempted for the name using the HOSTS file and DNS.

Most networks use DHCP to assign client networking information, including the NetBIOS note type. In this section, we examine the possible settings and how to configure it manually on a Windows Vista computer. Follow these steps to locally configure the NetBIOS node type for a Windows Vista computer:

1. Click **Start | Run....**
2. In the **Run** dialog box, type **regedit** and click **OK**.
3. In the left pane, expand **HKEY_LOCAL_MACHINE**.
4. Expand **SYSTEM**.
5. Expand **CurrentControlSet**.
6. Expand **Services**.
7. Expand **Netbt**.
8. Select **Parameters**.
9. On the Edit menu, select **New**, then click **DWORD (32-bit) Value**.
10. In the right pane, type **NodeType** where indicated and press **ENTER**.
11. In the right pane, right-click **NodeType**, and click **Modify....**
12. In the **Edit DWORD (32-bit) Value** dialog box, type the desired value:
    For B-Node type: 1
    For P-Node type: 2
    For M-Node type: 4
    For H-Node type: 8
13. Click **OK**.

Configuring the WINS Server List

If your network uses WINS for NetBIOS name resolution, you can configure a Windows Vista client to use one or more WINS server(s). Clients register their computer name and some of the services they provide with a WINS server. They also query WINS servers when this type of information is needed regarding other computers on the network. Typically, Windows servers are configured by administrators to provide WINS server services to clients. Follow these steps to configure Windows Vista to use one or more WINS server(s):

1. Click **Start | Control Panel | Network and Sharing Center | Manage network connections**.

2. In the **Network Connections** window's **General** tab, right-click the network connection you want to configure and select **Properties**.

3. In the **Local Area Connection Properties** dialog, select **Internet Protocol Version 4 (TCP/IPv4)** and click **Properties**.

4. In the **Internet Protocol Version 4 (TCP/IPv4) Properties** dialog box, click the **Advanced...** button.

5. In the **Advanced TCP/IP Settings** dialog box, click the **WINS** tab to bring it to the foreground.

6. In the **WINS addresses, in order of use:** section of the page, do one or more of the following (see Figure 2.53):

    ■   Reorder the existing WINS servers by placing the first one you want used at the top of the list, the second one in the second position on the list, and so forth. To accomplish this, select the name server you wish to reorder and use the up or down arrows to place it in the desired position.

    ■   Add new WINS servers to the list. To accomplish this, click the **Add...** button and enter the IP address of the new WINS server in the **TCP/IP WINS Server** dialog box, then click **Add**.

    ■   Edit the IP address of an existing server in the list. To accomplish this, click the **Edit...** button, make the desired change in the **TCP/IP WINS Server** dialog box, then click **OK**.

    ■   Remove a DNS server from the list. To accomplish this, select the WINS server you want to remove from the list and click the **Remove** button.

Figure 2.53 The WINS Tab

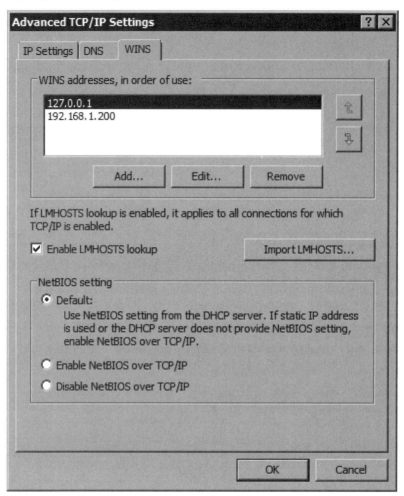

Configuring the LMHOSTS File

The LMHOSTS file can be enabled, disabled, and manually modified by administrators. To enable or disable the LMHOSTS file, use the **Enable LMHOSTS lookup** option on the **WINS** tab in the client's **Advanced TCP/IP Settings** dialog box (see Figure 2.53). By default, use of the LMHOSTS file is enabled. A sample file is provided by Microsoft. It is located in the *C:\WINDOWS\system32*

drivers\etc directory, and is named LMHOSTS.SAM. To make the file functional, the SAM file extension must be removed. Several configuration options exist, as can be seen by part of the included help text that is visible in Figure 2.54.

Figure 2.54 The LMHOSTS File

```
 lmhosts.sam - Notepad
File  Edit  Format  View  Help
# Copyright (c) 1993-1999 Microsoft Corp.
#
# This is a sample LMHOSTS file used by the Microsoft TCP/IP for Windows.
#
# This file contains the mappings of IP addresses to computernames
# (NetBIOS) names.  Each entry should be kept on an individual line.
# The IP address should be placed in the first column followed by the
# corresponding computername. The address and the computername
# should be separated by at least one space or tab. The "#" character
# is generally used to denote the start of a comment (see the exceptions
# below).
#
# This file is compatible with Microsoft LAN Manager 2.x TCP/IP lmhosts
# files and offers the following extensions:
#
#      #PRE|
#      #DOM:<domain>
#      #INCLUDE <filename>
#      #BEGIN_ALTERNATE
#      #END_ALTERNATE
#      \0xnn (non-printing character support)
#
# Following any entry in the file with the characters "#PRE" will cause
# the entry to be preloaded into the name cache. By default, entries are
# not preloaded, but are parsed only after dynamic name resolution fails.
#
# Following an entry with the "#DOM:<domain>" tag will associate the
# entry with the domain specified by <domain>. This affects how the
# browser and logon services behave in TCP/IP environments. To preload
# the host name associated with #DOM entry, it is necessary to also add a
# #PRE to the line. The <domain> is always preloaded although it will not
# be shown when the name cache is viewed.
#
# Specifying "#INCLUDE <filename>" will force the RFC NetBIOS (NBT)
# software to seek the specified <filename> and parse it as if it were
# local. <filename> is generally a UNC-based name, allowing a
# centralized lmhosts file to be maintained on a server.
# It is ALWAYS necessary to provide a mapping for the IP address of the
# server prior to the #INCLUDE. This mapping must use the #PRE directive.
```

Table 2.4 shows some sample LMHOSTS file entries. More detailed information is available by examining a LMHOSTS.SAM file and viewing the comments it contains, as well as Windows Help and Microsoft's online documentation.

Table 2.4 Common LMHOSTS Entries

LMHOSTS Entry	Effect
192.168.2.1 Server1 #Major server	This is a basic LMHOSTS file entry. When the LMHOSTS file is examined for the NetBIOS name Server1, the IP address 192.168.2.1 will be returned. In this case, the text after the # sign is a comment inserted by an adminis trator. Comments can consist of any text, as long as they do not contain a command such as #PRE or #DOM.
192.168.2.1 Server1 #PRE #Major server	This entry preloads the entry into the NetBIOS name cache. Because the name and IP are present in the cache, the LMHOSTS file does not have to be checked for this NetBIOS name to be resolved.
192.168.2.1 Server1 #PRE #DOM:Syngress	In addition to the preceding, this entry also identifies Server1 as a domain controller for the Syngress domain.

Understanding Link-Local Multicast Name Resolution (LLMNR)

Link-Local Multicast Name Resolution, also known as multicast DNS (mDNS), is a new protocol in Windows Vista and Server 2008. If these are the primary operating systems in use and hosts on a segment of the network are unable to contact a DNS server, some name resolution can still take place on a peer-to-peer basis. LLMNR is also designed to allow for host name resolution on single-segment networks that do not have DNS servers, such as very small home or office networks. Ordinarily NetBIOS name resolution is enabled by default and will handle name resolution in situations like this; however NetBIOS supports only IPv4. LLMNR works with both IPv4 and IPv6, ensuring that host name resolution can occur regardless of the version of IP in use on the network.

Managing Client Settings by Using Group Policy

A number of client DNS settings can be controlled using group policy, including those shown in Table 2.5. Generally, settings applied at the group policy level override manually configured settings on the host. This not only makes client configuration using GPOs more convenient, but also helps to ensure that settings cannot be changed at the workstations.

Table 2.5 Client DNS Group Policy Settings

Setting
Allow DNS Suffix Appending to Unqualified Multi-Label Name Queries
Connection-Specific DNS Suffix
DNS Servers
Primary DNS Suffix
Register DNS records with connection-specific DNS suffix
Register PTR Records
Dynamic Update
Replace Addresses In Conflicts
Registration Refresh Interval
TTL Set in the A and PTR records
DNS Suffix Search List
Update Security Level
Update Top Level Domain Zones
Primary DNS Suffix Devolution
Turn off Multicast Name Resolution

EXERCISE 2.5

USING GROUP POLICY TO CONFIGURE DNS SETTINGS

In this exercise you will use group policy to configure the DNS servers that will be assigned to Windows XP Professional workstations. You need to have an active directory domain and domain-level administrator access. To configure a DNS setting using group policy, follow these steps:

1. Open the GPO that will be used using the **Group Policy Management Editor** and navigate to **Computer Configuration | Policies | Administrative Templates | Network | DNS Client** as shown in Figure 2.55.

2. In the **Group Policy Management Editor**, right-click **DNS Servers** and select **Properties** (see Figure 2.55).

Figure 2.55 The Group Policy Management Editor

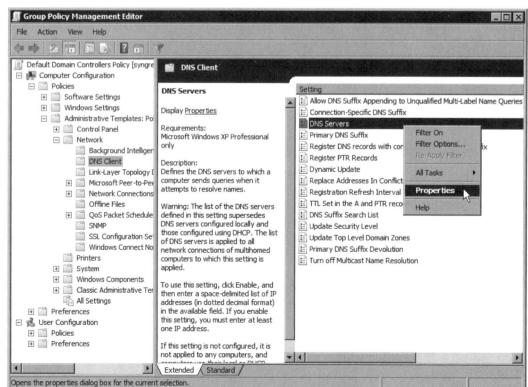

3. Each of the DNS group policy settings has slightly different configuration options, and these settings can often appear deceiving. This option configures the DNS servers the client will query during name resolution. At first glance it appears that only one can be entered, however the **Explain** tab makes it clear that multiple entries are supported in the single box, as long as they are separated by a space. In the **DNS Servers Properties** dialog, enter the IP address of one or more DNS server(s) in the **IP Addresses:** text box and click **OK** (see Figure 2.56).

Figure 2.56 The Properties Tab

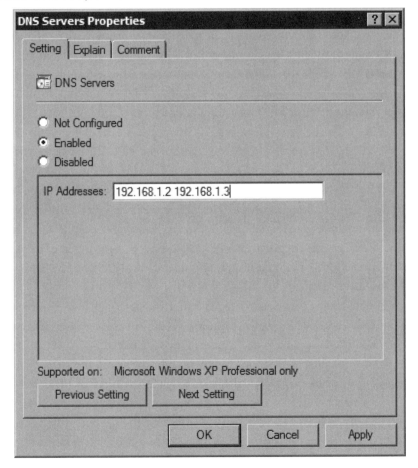

7. Close the **Group Policy Management Editor**.

Summary of Exam Objectives

DNS allows hosts and services to be located on IP networks using user-friendly, fully qualified domain names instead of IP addresses. When a user attempts to access a Web site, for example, their local DNS resolver first checks its cache followed by the local host file to see if the address of the web server is stored locally. If it isn't, the resolver then contacts a DNS server using a client-to-server query. This type of query requests an answer that either provides the needed information or informs the client that the information cannot be located. If the DNS server that the client contacts has the information, it is returned to the client. If not, the DNS server initiates a server-to-server query and asks another DNS server for any assistance it can provide. This server-to-server query is sent to the root hints that are configured on the DNS server.

The server contacted may return an answer that no information is available, at which point a negative response is sent back to the client. However, if the server contacted has the needed information, or information about one or more other DNS servers that could be of assistance in resolving the query, that information will be returned to the requesting DNS server. This process continues until the information is located, or it becomes clear that the client's query will not be resolvable. Both positive and negative responses to queries are cached for a period of time on the original DNS server, as well as the client.

You can make any Windows Server 2008 host a DNS server by installing the DNS Server role. The default installation creates a caching only DNS server with root hints that point to the Internet's root servers. You can separate all or a portion of your DNS infrastructure from the Internet by designating private, internal DNS servers as root hints DNS servers. Generally these should be the DNS servers that are at the top of the organization.

Forwarding can be used instead of root hints when a DNS server needs to contact other DNS servers to resolve a query. When a DNS server sends a query to a forwarder, the query is similar to a client-to-server query in that it asks the receiving server to do all the work and return only a complete answer to the query. This can be used to minimize the bandwidth involved in recursive queries on portions of an organization's network. Server level forwarding sends all queries to a single DNS server or set of servers. Conditional forwarding can be used to forward resolution requests to other DNS servers based on specific domain names.

Zones represent the physical partitioning of the DNS namespace. They store the records for one or more domains or subdomains. Forward lookup zones resolve host and service names to IP addresses, and reverse lookup zones resolve IP addresses into names. Primary zones can be changed, and secondary zones are read-only copies. Standard primary zones are traditional zones with a single server that can accept changes. AD integrated zones are exclusive to Windows 2000 Server and later, can be used only on domain controllers, and support multiple primary copies of a zone database for fault tolerance.

A master zone is any zone that a secondary or stub zone transfers records from, and can include standard primary, AD integrated, and standard secondary zones. Secondary zones transfer records via file transfer across the network. The SOA record is used to configure the interval that secondary servers use when checking for updates. Domain controllers replicate AD integrated zone information using AD directory services. These transfers are much more secure and efficient than standard zone transfers. Stub zones are a special form of read-only zone that contains the name server records for a zone. They use standard zone transfers to copy these records from a master zone.

Windows Server 2008 includes a new zone type, the GlobalNames zone. GNZs support the transition away from WINS by integrating single name resolution into DNS. Unlike WINS, GNZs support IPv6 addressing. Only Windows Server 2008 DNS servers support GNZs, and the feature must be enabled manually on each server. GNZs store static CNAME records that correspond to single name records such as NetBIOS names.

Windows Server 2008's DNS Server role is a fully compliant DNS server, with some extensions such as the GNZs to provide additional support on Windows networks. Records can be administered manually, updated automatically by hosts, or both. All standard DNS record types are supported including A, AAAA, PTR, MX, SRV, CNAME, and NS. Dynamic DNS can be used to allow hosts and DHCP servers to automatically add and modify DNS host and PTR records. When DDNS is used with AD integrated zones, additional record level security can be specified to prevent unauthorized changes to dynamic records. The aging and scavenging feature can be used to clean up DDNS records that have not been updated or refreshed within a given period and may be invalid. Scavenging can be done manually or configured to occur automatically.

There are two primary forms of naming on Windows networks, NetBIOS and host names. Recent operating system releases from Microsoft increasingly have moved away from NetBIOS toward DNS. If a network runs a variety of Windows client and server versions, it's important that both forms of name resolution are configured properly. If the network is comprised primarily of Windows XP and later clients, and Windows server 2003 and later servers, DNS is most likely supporting many of the network's name resolution needs. Although some integration is possible, the NetBIOS and host name resolution methods are very different. By default, the following name resolution steps are taken when resolving host names: the local host name => the local DNS resolver cache => the local HOSTS file => DNS => the local NetBIOS name cache => WINS => a local network broadcast => the local LMHOSTS file. By default, the following name resolution steps are taken when resolving NetBIOS names: the local NetBIOS name cache => WINS => a local network broadcast => the LMHOSTS file => the local host name => the local DNS resolver cache => DNS. Regardless of the resolution type, additional configuration is needed for all steps to be applied. Administrators have considerable control over all components involved in the process.

Exam Objectives Fast Track

An Introduction to the Domain Name System (DNS)

☑ DNS allows hosts and services to be located on IP networks using friendly names instead of IP addresses.

☑ DNS can be used to resolve public FQDNs, or used privately by organizations that wish to use its features while remaining isolated from the Internet.

☑ DNS uses an incremental query process involving client-to-server and server-to-server queries to resolve names and IP addresses.

Configuring a DNS Server

☑ When the DNS Server role is installed, a caching only DNS server is created.

☑ Root hints tell a DNS server where to look next when resolving queries for records not contained in locally stored zones.

☑ Forwarding can be used instead of root hints. Server forwarding typically involves an organization's internal DNS servers' forwarding requests for public name resolution to a DNS server that has direct access to the Internet. Conditional forwarding allows administrators to configure DNS servers to forward resolution requests to other DNS servers based on specific domain names.

Configuring DNS Zones

- ☑ Forward lookup zones resolve host names to IP addresses. Reverse look up zones resolve IP addresses to host names.

- ☑ DNS records can be changed on primary and AD integrated zones, but not on secondary or stub zones.

- ☑ Zone delegation allows a domain name space to be divided among different zones on separate servers.

- ☑ The new GlobalNames feature supports single name resolutions (such as NetBIOS computer names) on IPv6 networks using DNS.

Configuring and Managing Standard DNS Replication

- ☑ By default, primary, AD integrated and secondary zones limit the servers from which they can accept zone transfer requests.

- ☑ Administrators can manually request incremental zone updates or a complete refresh of all zone records for secondary zones using DNS Manager.

- ☑ The SOA zone record is used to configure the replication parameters for secondary zones.

Configuring DNS Records

- ☑ DNS records can be administered manually, updated automatically by hosts, or both.

- ☑ DNS record types include A, AAAA, PTR, MX, SRV, CNAME, and NS.

- ☑ Aging and scavenging is used to clean up DDNS records that have not been updated or refreshed within a given period and may be invalid.

Configuring Name Resolution for Client Computers

- ☑ Two primary forms of name resolution exist on Windows networks: NetBIOS and host names. Microsoft increasingly has moved away from NetBIOS toward DNS. If a network runs a variety of Windows client and server versions, it's important that both forms of name resolution are configured properly. If the network is comprised primarily of Windows XP and later clients, and Windows Server 2003 and later servers, DNS is most likely supporting many of the network's name resolution needs.

☑ By default, the following name resolution steps are taken when resolving host names: the local host name => the local DNS resolver cache => the local HOSTS file => DNS => the local NetBIOS name cache => WINS => a local network broadcast => the local LMHOSTS file.

☑ By default, the following name resolution steps are taken when resolving NetBIOS names: the local NetBIOS name cache => WINS => a local network broadcast => the LMHOSTS file => the local host name => the local DNS resolver cache => DNS.

☑ Regardless of the resolution type, additional configuration is needed for all steps to be applied. Administrators have considerable control over all components involved in the process.

Exam Objectives
Frequently Asked Questions

Q: What exactly is DNS and why do I need it?

A: DNS is the primary name resolution method for Windows Server 2008, making it essential to a properly functioning domain and network. It provides hosts with the actual network location of network services and other hosts. It also can be used to determine host and service information when an IP address is provided. Computers cannot find themselves using most key components of Windows Server 2008 without DNS.

Q: My organization does not wish to connect to the Internet. We are using Windows Server 2008 and Windows Vista DNS is essential for name resolution. I know that DNS was designed to work with the Internet; what can I do?

A: Although DNS originally was designed for use with the Internet and its predecessors, it is no problem to use it privately. In fact, if you have an Active Directory domain, it will be required. In this scenario you will create and configure a separate DNS environment that is very similar to the Internet, except you will control all levels of it instead of just a tiny portion.

Q: I need to specify a totally private DNS server network for my organization. How should I configure root hints?

A: When root hints don't need to point to the Internet's root name servers, typically they should point to the highest level DNS servers within an organization. A good way to think about root hints is that they are designed to point to the top of whatever DNS hierarchy is being used.

Q: I want to use forwarding, but don't want all queries to go to the same place. I need to distribute them based on the domain being asked for; how can I do this in Windows Server 2008?

A: Conditional forwarding can be used to distribute queries to forwarders based on the domain being requested.

Q: Domains and zones are very confusing to me. What is the difference between a domain and a zone?

A: Because zones use domain names, it's easy to get confused. Zones hold the actual records for part of the domain namespace. A domain like syngress.com. has records distributed across several zones. The root name servers hold the "." Portion, which is typically hidden from users at the end of the domain name. The ".com" name servers hold the zone for this portion of the namespace. Finally a server managed by the organization contains a zone for the "syngress" portion of the DNS namespace.

Q: Does Microsoft recommend standard or AD integrated zones? Why?

A: Microsoft recommends AD integrated zones. The records are stored in the AD database, which increases their security and allows for more efficient replication of the records when compared to traditional zone transfers. Using AD integrated zones also enables secure DDNS, which eases the burden of DNS administration without compromising security.

Q: My organization is implementing IPv6. Right now we use both DNS and WINS for name resolution. WINS supports only IPv4. What can I do to support NetBIOS type names for IPv6?

A: Microsoft's new GlobalNames feature can be used. When activated, DNS servers can serve manually created single name records. You can create these records to match important NetBIOS resource names, such as key servers.

Q: What is the difference between an A and AAAA host record?

A: The Windows Server 2008 DNS Server role fully supports IPv4 and IPv6. The A host record is one of the oldest in DNS and is used to resolve a host name to an IPv4 address. The newer AAAA record is used to resolve a host name to an IPv6 address.

Q: What is a PTR record used for?

A: PTR, or pointer, records are the primary records used in reverse lookup zones. These records facilitate the resolution of IP addresses into host names.

Q: My office has a lot of sales people that work on laptops in and out of the office. I've noticed that there are quite a few inaccurate DDNS records being left behind by these computers. What can be done about it?

A: Microsoft's aging and scavenging feature can be used to clean up records such as these. You can set your organization's Windows 2000 and later DNS servers to delete records automatically if they have not been kept up to date.

Q: Most of the name resolution on my network uses DNS, however all clients are still configured for WINS. When a client attempts to access a resource by using the resource's host name, what steps may occur?

A: By default, the following name resolution steps are taken when resolving host names: the local host name => the local DNS resolver cache => the local HOSTS file => DNS => the local NetBIOS name cache => WINS => a local network broadcast => the local LMHOSTS file. All these steps are at least partially configurable by an administrator.

Q: My environment uses IPv6 addresses, but NetBIOS broadcasts are supported only for IPv4. What can I do?

A: Microsoft has included a new protocol in Windows Vista and Server 2008 to solve this problem: Link-Local Multicast Name Resolution. If these are the primary operating systems in use and hosts on a segment of the network are unable to contact a DNS server, some name resolution can still take place on a peer-to-peer basis using either IPv4 or IPv6.

Q: I'm responsible for several hundred Windows XP and Vista clients. Is there an easy way to automate their DNS configuration?

A: Many DNS settings can be managed centrally using group policy. In most cases, settings applied with group policy will override settings that are configured manually on the client. Not all settings work with all client types, however. It's important to carefully read the description of each to determine how and where it can be applied.

Self Test

1. You are the administrator for a Windows Server 2008 network. You've been tasked with designing a secure facility and have recommended that it be isolated from the Internet. Which of the following do you recommend for DNS? (Select all that apply.)

    A. You recommend a private DNS infrastructure with internal root hints servers.

    B. You recommend the use of AD integrated zones.

    C. You recommend the use of secure dynamic updates.

    D. You recommend the use of secondary zones.

2. You are the administrator for a small organization's network. The network is connected to the Internet. Both servers run Windows Server 2008 and all clients run Windows Vista Enterprise. Your manager has asked you to explain how her computer finds web servers on the Internet. Which of the following do you tell her? (Select all that apply).

    A. You tell her that her local resolver sends a recursive query to the organization's local DNS server.

    B. You tell her that her local resolver sends a query to the Internet's root DNS servers.

    C. You tell her that the local DNS server sends a server-to-server query to the Internet's root DNS servers.

    D. You tell her that the local DNS server returns the requested record from its zone files.

3. You have recently been transferred to the DNS team at a large multinational company, and are working feverously learn about DNS. Lately you've been working on the difference between client-to-server and server-to-server queries. Which of the following are true? (Select all that apply).

    A. Client-to-server queries are all-or-nothing requests.

    B. Client-to-server queries are also known as recursive queries.

    C. Server-to-server queries ask for FQDN resolution.

    D. Server-to-server queries ask for as much information as can be provided about the FQDN.

4. You are the DNS administrator for a mid-sized organization. As part of the upgrade process, you put in a request to transition all DNS services to AD integrated zones. When your manager asks about the key features involved, what do you tell her? (Select all that apply).

   A. You tell her that AD integrated zones are stored in Active Directory.

   B. You tell her that all zone records are stored as AD objects and have object level security.

   C. You tell her that it enables secure dynamic updates.

   D. You tell her that replication is much more efficient and secure.

5. You are the administrator of a small Windows Server 2008 network. Your organization has a single AD domain with a standard primary zone. Using DNS Manager, you enabled DDNS and enabled the **Scavenge stale resource records** checkbox in the properties of the server. Stale records are not being cleaned up. Which two actions do you take to resolve the problem?

   A. You manually delete the stale records.

   B. You alter the refresh and no-refresh intervals.

   C. You select **Scavenge stale resource records** in the properties of the zone.

   D. You select the **Enable automatic scavenging of stale records** box.

6. You are the administrator for a small office. Until now you have used your ISP's DNS server, however your slow WAN link to the Internet is becoming congested and you've been working to optimize the traffic that passes over it. The users in the office use the Internet heavily, and you decide that one thing you'd like to minimize is DNS traffic. You install the DNS Server role on your only file server, a Windows Server 2008 workgroup server. Which one of the following do you configure?

   A. You configure a forward lookup zone.

   B. You configure a reverse lookup zone.

   C. You configure it as a server forwarder.

   D. You configure it as a conditional forwarder.

7. You are the administrator of a Windows Server 2008 network for a regional organization. The organization has small offices in several states that connect to headquarters with slow WAN connections. Each of these small offices has its own server with DNS and AD installed on it. You've noticed that users in the

small office spend a lot of time surfing the Internet. You've taken some measures to manage that traffic, however the DNS queries from the small office servers still generate excessive traffic. Which of the following steps can you take to minimize that traffic? (Select two).

A. You can install a server at headquarters for the small office servers to forward their DNS queries to.

B. You can configure the small office servers as forwarders.

C. You can alter the root hints on the small office servers.

D. You can alter the root hints on the new server at headquarters.

8. You are the administrator of a small Windows Server 2008 network. When you installed your first domain controller, you had the DCPROMO wizard also install and configure the DNS Server role. While adding your second domain controller, you did not select the option to install the DNS Server role. A few days later you installed the DNS Server role on the server. When you opened DNS Manager and looked at the configuration for the server, which one of the following did you see?

A. You saw that the server had no zones.

B. You saw that the server had a secondary forward lookup zone for the AD domain automatically created on it.

C. You saw that the server had a standard primary forward lookup zone for the AD domain automatically created on it.

D. You saw that the server had an AD integrated zone for the AD domain automatically created on it.

9. You are the Windows Server 2008 administrator for a small office at a large multinational company. The company's DNS environment is huge, spanning not only many domains and subdomains but also many different types of DNS servers. The DNS administrators have been asked by the network and routing group to reduce the traffic load DNS is placing on the network. As part of this effort, you've been asked to configure conditional forwarding for several, disjointed, internal domain name spaces that your company uses. Which of the following do you do? (Select all that apply.)

A. In DNS manager, you right-click the appropriate server node and open its properties.

B. In DNS manager, you right-click the **Conditional Forwarders** node and select to create a new forwarder.

C. In the **Properties** tab, you configure the DNS servers to forward to.

D. In the **New Conditional Forwarder** dialog you specify the domain and the DNS server to send queries to.

10. You are the Windows Server 2008 administrator for a mid-sized organization. You have decided to implement conditional forwarding on one of your Windows Server 2008 DNS servers. For some reason, you've been unable to create the forwarder. Which one of the following is the most likely reason?

A. The configuration dialog cannot locate the IP address of the server to be forwarded to.

B. The configuration dialog cannot locate the host name of the server to be forwarded to.

C. You already have a zone configured for the domain you're trying to forward to.

D. The DNS Server role has become corrupt on the server and should be reinstalled.

Self Test Answer Key

1. **A, B**

2. **C**

3. **A, C, D**

4. **A, B, C, D**

5. **C, D**

6. **C**

7. **A, B**

8. **D**

9. **B, D**

10. **C**

## Chapter 3

MCTS/MCITP
Exam 642

Configuring Network Access

Exam objectives in this chapter:

- Configuring Routing
- Configuring Remote Access
- Configuring Wireless Access

Exam objectives review:

- ☑ Summary of Exam Objectives
- ☑ Exam Objectives Fast Track
- ☑ Exam Objectives Frequently Asked Questions
- ☑ Self Test
- ☑ Self Test Quick Answer Key

Introduction

Organizations rely on networking and communications to meet the challenging requirements necessary to compete in the global marketplace. All members of these organizations need to have constant access to the files. This requires the ability to connect to the network wherever they may be and from any device that they have available to them at the time. In addition, those outside the vendor's network will require the ability to interact smoothly with the key resources they require. Partners and clients want to be able to also conduct quick and fluid transactions through the network. Security is more important than ever in networking, due to the constant threat of infiltration and exposure to the Internet. Successfully navigating all of these concerns relies on the knowledge of how to configure network access efficiently and provide the most secure yet accessible connection possible to your organization and its members.

As an administrator, you must accommodate these needs using the latest and most practical tools in your arsenal. To help accomplish this there have been a number of networking and communications enhancements made to Windows Server 2008 to address connectivity. This will help you to improve the ease of use, reliability, management, and security of your organization's assets. By applying what Windows Server 2008 has to offer with its latest features you will have more flexibility when managing your network infrastructure. Windows Server 2008 allows for a total system health by deploying settings for authenticated wireless and wired connections through Group Policy or scripts, and deploying protected traffic scenarios. In order to take on this task, a number of features from former versions of Windows Server have been improved upon or replaced with new updated features, which will allow you to provide the highest level of efficiency and security to your organization. For your exam, you will need to be familiar with the new and updated changes that Windows Server 2008 provides and how to best utilize these tools to manage and maintain your network.

The three main areas of focus or objectives for your exam will be configuring routing, remote access, and wireless access. This chapter will include a brief overview of the latest features available in Windows Server 2008 as well as detailed descriptions of the fundamental principals of these objectives and how to apply them to the newest version of Windows Server.

In this chapter, we will discuss the many new and powerful changes to Microsoft Windows Server 2008 that include innovative enhancements to networking technologies and network access configuration. We will go over the latest changes to protocols and core networking components, wireless and 802.1X-authenticated wired technologies. This will include network infrastructure components and services that can be applied when using Windows Server 2008. Before moving on in detail concerning the exam and what you will be required to know, let us take a more detailed overview of the latest features that Windows Server 2008 has to offer in terms of routing, remote access, and wireless access.

Windows Server 2008 and Routing

Routing is one element that helps to ensure successful network traffic flow. It has always been the framework for a functional logical network regardless of which version of Windows Server you may be working on. Because of this, Microsoft has taken some time to improve the overall ease of use for routing with this latest version. As you are probably aware, Windows Server 2003 used the Routing and Remote Access Service (RRAS) to handle many of the configuration needs for routing in the past. Windows Server 2008 also uses the RRAS, but features a number of changes to it when compared to older versions of Windows. Many former encapsulation protocols have been made obsolete or revised for Windows Server 2008. Here is a brief summarization of what changes and omissions to expect in this build.

- Bandwidth Allocation Protocol (BAP) is no longer supported by Windows Server 2008.

- X.25 is also no longer supported.

- Serial Line Internet Protocol (SLIP), an encapsulation of Internet Protocol (IP) meant for use over serial ports and modems, has also been excluded due to infrequency of use. All SLIP-based connections will automatically be updated to Point-to-Point Protocol (PPP)-based connections.

- Asynchronous Transfer Mode (ATM), which was used to encode data traffic into small fixed cells, has been discarded.

- IP over Institute of Electrical & Electronics Engineers (IEEE) 1394 is no longer supported.

- NWLink IPX/SPX/NetBIOS Compatible Transport Protocol has been omitted.

- Services for Macintosh (SFM).

- Open Shortest Path First (OSPF) routing protocol component in Routing and Remote Access is no longer present.

- Basic firewall in Routing and Remote Access has been replaced with a new Windows Firewall feature.

- Static IP filter application program interfaces (APIs) for Routing and Remote Access are no longer viable and have been replaced with Windows Filtering Platform APIs.

- SPAP, EAP-MD5-CHAP, and MS-CHAP authentication protocols for PPP-based connections are no longer used by Windows Server 2008.

Exam Warning

Some of the old familiar aspects of Windows Routing and Remote Access have changed since Windows Server 2003. Be sure to familiarize yourself with the improvements and discontinuations to these features before test day.

Don't get caught off guard by confusing old functionality with new functionality, such as the differences between Windows Firewall with Advanced Protection and the old Windows Firewall. Also be aware of technology that is no longer supported in this new build. This will help you to stay focused and result in better retention for the exam.

Window Server 2008 and Remote Access

As with past versions of RRAS, Windows Server 2008 offers exceptional ease of use and configuration for remote access. All features previously available are featured in this version of Windows Server. There is also the additional replacement of Internet Authentication Service (IAS) with Network Policy Server and Network Access Protection (NAP).

The change to Windows Server 2008 in regards to remote access is the addition of Secure Socket Tunneling Protocol (SSTP). SSTP is the latest form of VPN tunnel created for use with Windows Server 2008. It contains many new features that enable traffic to pass through firewalls that block Point-to-Point Tunneling Protocol (PPTP) and Layer 2 Tunneling Protocol (L2TP)/Internet Protocol Security (IPSec) traffic. In addition, SSTP uses the Secure Sockets Layer (SSL) channel of the Hypertext Transfer Protocol Secure (HTTPS) protocol by making use of a process that encapsulates PPP traffic. PPP is very versatile. It enables you to use strong authentication methods such as Extensible Authentication Protocol-Transport Layer Security (EAP-TLS), which were not possible in past versions of Windows for VPN. All traffic will be channeled through the TCP port 443, which is typically used for Web access, because of the use of HTTPS. Security features include transport level security with enhanced key negotiation, encryption, and integrity checking capabilities by using SSL.

Windows Server 2008 and Wireless Access

Windows Server 2008 includes the following changes and enhancements to IEEE 802.11 wireless support:

- Native Wi-Fi architecture
- User interface improvements for wireless connections
- Wireless Group Policy enhancements
- Changes in Wireless Auto Configuration
- WPA2 support
- Integration with Network Access Protection when using 802.1X authentication
- EAPHost infrastructure
- 802.11 wireless diagnostics
- Command-line support for configuring wireless settings
- Network Location Awareness and network profiles
- Next Generation Transmission Control Protocol (TCP)/IP stack enhancements for wireless environments
- Single Sign On

Configuring Routing

Routing is a sometimes-confused aspect of networking, which can be complicated due to lack of fundamental understanding and training. All information that travels through a network has two things in common: a device that sent it and a required routing decision. The decisions for these routes are conducted by comparing the destination address to a list of entries located on a routing table or stored in a remote location. The routing table is normally configured and built by the network administrator or from information gathered by the TCP/IP system. These configurations can take place in a number of ways to ensure the best and most secure transport of information. Windows Server 2008 has a number of features that previous versions of Windows Servers possessed as well as some new added updates. Before reviewing changes to the system let's take a better look at the fundamentals of routing.

Routing Fundamentals

When attempting to select a path in a network by which to send data or physical traffic, an administrator has many options available to him. There are a number of ways to send packets from one destination to another based on intermediary hardware or nodes. This can include a number of different hardware devices including bridges, gateways, routers, firewalls, and switches. Even computers with multiple network cards are capable of routing packets. There are different types of routing algorithms or protocols that can be used to organize the signal flow between these devices.

These algorithms rely on what is called a *routing metric*, a value used by a routing algorithm to determine whether one route should perform better than another. Metrics can include a number of different parameters to judge performance by, as configured by the administrator.

On the simplest level, the system will select an entry from the routing table and use the netmask from that entry (see Figure 3.1). The system then performs a comparison of this value and the destination address. The resulting value is cross-referenced to the network address in the table entry. If the two values match, the information can arrive at the destination through the gateway in that entry. If the two values do not match, the routing system continues along the routing table to the next entry and performs the same check again. If the "no matching entry" is found on the table, the routing system discards the packet and generates a message notifying the sender that the destination network cannot be reached.

Otherwise, when a routing table entry is found that matches the network value, the packet is sent based on the information in the table entry via the destination listed. If the destination exists on a portion of the network directly connected to the routing system, the packet is delivered to the destination system. If it does not exist on the same segment, the packet is sent to a gateway system for delivery. This is a very complicated way of describing what is referred to as *static routing*.

Figure 3.1 Routing Tables

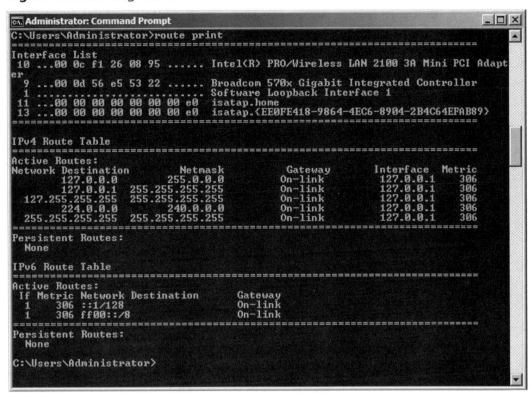

TEST DAY TIP

Take advantage of the fundamentals of routing by practicing with routing tables and configuring your traffic flow. Remember that even the most complicated networks can find a need for the use of static routing. Be aware of how static routing can affect a system as opposed to dynamic routing.

EXERCISE 3.1

WORKING WITH THE ROUTING TABLE ON WINDOWS SERVER 2008

When working with Windows Server 2008, you can configure the static routing table in many ways. With Internet Protocol version 4 (IPv4), you can configure the table with routes by removing or changing them. For example:

1. To display the entire contents of the IP routing table you can type **route print**.

2. To display the routes in the IP routing table that begin with 10. type **route print 10.***

3. To add a default route with the default gateway address of 192.168.10.1, type **route add 0.0.0.0 mask 0.0.0.0 192.168.10.1**.

4. To add a route to the destination 10.40.0.0 with the subnet mask of 255.255.0.0 and the next hop address of 10.20.0.1, type **route add 10.41.0.0 mask 255.255.0.0 10.20.0.1**.

5. To add a persistent route to the destination 10.41.0.0 with the subnet mask of 255.255.0.0 and the next hop address of 10.20.0.1, type **route -p add 10.40.0.0 mask 255.255.0.0 10.27.0.1**.

6. To add a route to the destination 10.40.0.0 with the subnet mask of 255.255.0.0, the next hop address of 10.20.0.1, and the cost metric of 7, type **route add 10.40.0.0 mask 255.255.0.0 10.20.0.1 metric 7**.

7. To add a route to the destination 10.40.0.0 with the subnet mask of 255.255.0.0, the next hop address of 10.20.0.1, and using the interface index 0x3, type **route add 10.40.0.0 mask 255.255.0.0 10.20.0.1 if 0x3**.

8. To delete the route to the destination 10.40.0.0 with the subnet mask of 255.255.0.0, type **route delete 10.40.0.0 mask 255.255.0.0**.

9. To delete all routes in the IP routing table that begin with 10. type **route delete 10.***

10. To change the next hop address of the route with the destination of 10.40.0.0 and the subnet mask of 255.255.0.0 from 10.20.0.1 to 10.20.0.25, type **route change 10.40.0.0 mask 255.255.0.0 10.20.0.25**.

If using IPv6, you can add a route just as easily. For example:

11. To display the entire contents of the IP routing table you can type **route print -6**.

12. To add a route, type **route add 3ffe::/32 3ffe::1**.

Test Day Tip

When using Windows Server 2008, remember that the output of the route command will now show IPv6 options by default. For the exam, make sure that you are familiar with the options of IPv6 and the route command.

Static Routing

Static routing describes a system that does not implement adaptive routing in its configuration. In these systems, routes through a network are defined by set paths referred to as *static routes*, which are inserted into the router manually by the system administrator. This is accomplished via the route command, which can be used to manipulate local routing tables. There is no fault tolerance in regards to static routing. Changes to the network or a failure between two statically defined nodes will cause any traffic between those points to not be rerouted. This means any packets that are awaiting transport between the affected paths will be forced to wait for repairs to the failure, or for an updated static route by the administrator. This also leaves open the issue of the request timing out before repairs can be made to the route.

Static routing is considered the simplest form of routing and requires excessive manual processes. It often is the least efficient way of routing in cases where information paths have to be changed frequently. This is also the case for configurations that require a large number of routing devices, because each one must be manually entered. Static routing is also the least preferred method of dealing with outages or down connections, because any route that is configured manually must be reconfigured manually to fix or repair any lost connectivity.

There may be many downsides to static routing, but there are many incidents where a static route is the most logical and efficient method for routing. Static routing is the opposite of dynamic routing, which is a system in which routers will automatically adjust to changes in network topology or traffic. *Dynamic routing* is used by most modern routers, but some amount of programming is still available for customizing routes if necessary.

As we mentioned earlier, you as an administrator will need to deal with clients and employees of your company attempting to access the network and Internet. The Internet and Local Area Networks (LANs) are referred to as *packet switching networks*.

The idea of packet switching networks is defined by the ability to optimize the use of the channel capacity available in a network. This helps to minimize transmission latency. This also requires the use of specific protocols for directing traffic through them. There are two major classes of routing protocols used in packet switch networking today:

- **Distance-vector Routing Protocol** A distance-vector routing protocol requires that a router contact and transmit to its neighbors of topology changes to the network. The frequency of this must be periodic and in most instances when a change is detected. Routing Internet Protocol (RIP) is the most popular example of this type of protocol.

- **Link State Protocol** The simplest explanation of link-state routing is that every node (router) is given a map of the topology of the network. This map is in graph form and shows the connectivity of nodes in the network. Then each individual node calculates the next best hop from every node in the network. This information then forms the routing table for each individual node based on its calculations. No other communication occurs between nodes. The most popular version of this is the OSPF.

Routing Internet Protocol (RIP)

The RIP was once the most commonly used Interior Gateway Protocol (IGP) on internal networks. It was also commonly used on networks connected to the Internet. RIP was used to help routers dynamically adapt to the variety of changes made to network connections. It accomplished this by relaying information about which networks each router had access to, and the distance those networks were from each other.

Although RIP is still actively used and has an important place in some networks, it is generally considered a dying protocol, which has been replaced by other routing protocols such as OSPF. RIP is a distance vector routing protocol that employs the hop count as a routing metric. RIP allows a maximum of 15 hops. The total hold down time for transfer is 180 seconds. Most traffic at the time RIP was commonly used was not significant, so each RIP router had an update time of 30 seconds by default, which was common practice. This proved to be a poor configuration and was later changed to randomized updates.

RIP is limited in a number of ways due to its lack of scalability. It prevents routing loops from continuing indefinitely, by implementing a limit on the number of hops allowed in a path from the source to a destination. It also limits the size of the network that RIP can support by design.

On the other hand, RIP is easier to configure than many other protocols, because it uses one of the smallest amounts of settings of any routing protocols. RIP does not require the use of any parameters on a router, and it can be ideal for small networks. RIP can be configured through the RRAS, which we will discuss later.

NOTE

Microsoft Windows Server 2008 supports RIP version 2 within RRAS.

Open Shortest Path First (OSPF)

OSPF was the natural successor to the RIP. OSPF protocol is a hierarchical IGP that uses a link state in the individual areas that make up the hierarchy. A link state database (LSDB) creates a tree-image of the network topology. It then sends copies of the LSDB periodically to update all routers in the area of the OSPF network.

OSPF is the most widely used IGP in regards to large enterprise networks. It has a much larger network size range than RIP. The OSPF protocol can determine the best path by communicating with other routers and then saving the routes in their LSDBs securely.

An OSPF network is divided into *areas*, which contain *area identifiers*. These identifiers are 32-bit and are usually written in the format of an IP address. Be aware that area identifiers are not IP addresses, and may often times duplicate any IP address without conflict occurring. These areas are logical groupings of routers whose information may be communicated to the rest of the network. There are several types of areas in an OPSPF network:

- **Backbone Area** The backbone area forms the central hub of an OSPF network. All other areas are connected to it, and inter-area routing happens via routers connected to the backbone area and to their own non-backbone areas. The backbone area distributes all routing information between the non-backbone areas. The backbone must be adjacent to all other areas, but does not need to be physically contiguous. Connectivity can be established and maintained through virtual links. All OSPF areas must connect to the backbone area. This connection, however, can be through a virtual link.

- **Stub Area** The stub area is an area that does not receive external routes except the default route, but does receive inter-area routes. All routers in the area need to agree they are stub, so that they do not generate types of LSA not appropriate to a stub area. Stub areas do not have the transit attribute and thus cannot be traversed by a virtual link.

■ **Not-so-stubby area (NSSA)** The Not-so-stubby area (NSSA) is a type of stub area that can import autonomous system (AS) external routes and send them to the backbone, but cannot receive AS external routes from the backbone or other areas. The NSSA is a non-proprietary extension of the existing stub area feature, which allows the injection of external routes in a limited fashion into the stub area.

Exam Warning

As of this writing, the OSPF routing protocol component is no longer present in Windows Server 2008. Although this may not be covered in the exam extensively, knowledge regarding this protocol will help you better understand RIP and other routing protocols by comparison, and will help with real-world applications that may occur as a consequence of the removal of this element.

Configuring Remote Access

Remote access is commonly used by many companies today to allow access to a computer or a network from a remote location. Most corporations include people at branch offices, telecommuters, and people who are traveling that will need to be able to gain access to network resources. Even clients using your company's services from home need to gain access to the Internet through an Internet Service Provider (ISP). *Dial-up connection* through desktop, notebook, or handheld computer modem over regular telephone lines was a common method of remote access in the early years of its inception.

It is also possible to gain remote access using a dedicated line between a computer or a remote local area network and the central or main LAN. This tends to be a less flexible and more expensive method, but does offer faster data exchange rates and fewer configurations. Integrated Services Digital Network (ISDN) is a compromise between the two other common methods of remote access, since it combines dial-up access with faster data exchange rates. The most growing trends in remote access in recent years have included wireless, cable, and digital subscriber line (DSL) technologies, which offer more convenient and efficient methods for remote access.

A remote access server is comprised of a computer with a remote access application installed, which is configured to handle the authentication and authorization of clients seeking access to a network remotely. This can also be referred to as a *communication server*. A remote access server usually includes or is associated with a firewall server to ensure security, and a router that can forward the remote access request to another part of the network. A single remote access server may also be used as part of a much larger VPN.

Like past versions, Windows Server 2008 has included a wide array of options for configuring remote access for you company. You will be required to be familiar with the workings of how to set up a remote access server and all of the methods of connectivity available in a modern networking environment. Like its previous versions, Windows Server 2008 houses most of its remote access tools in the RRA role. This role is crucial to the successful deployment of remote access services for your company, and will be used heavily in the exam.

EXAM WARNING

Remote access is an important part of the exam, and will weigh heavily into the overall grade. Be sure to familiarize yourself with all of the aspects of the objective. Also be sure to familiarize yourself with usage of MMC, Network Policy Server (NPS), and NAP, which are additional tools that maybe be covered in a small portion of the exam. Remember, every question counts and a comprehensive knowledge of the subject matter will ensure total retention for usage in real-world environments.

Routing and Remote Access Services (RRAS)

Most of the major functions of network access and the objectives that you will be required to know for your examine, revolve around the RRAS role. This is not a new feature to Windows Server 2008, but has many omissions and additions since Windows Server 2003. From this role, you can access configuration tools for routing, connection manager, and remote access service all of which will be very helpful in setting up remote access on your machines and managing policies.

Let's install the RRAS role. This will help you to configure most of the remote access features available in Windows Server 2008 that we will be discussing. Be sure to start with a clean install of Windows Server 2008, and review all guidelines and requirements for the system you are using.

EXERCISE 3.2

INSTALLING RRAS

To begin installing RRAS, follow these steps:

1. Open the Server Manager by clicking on the **Administrative Tools** menu.

2. Scroll down to the **Roles Summary** section of the details pane.

3. Click **Add Roles** to launch the **Add Roles Wizard**, as seen in Figure 3.2.

Figure 3.2 Add Roles Wizard

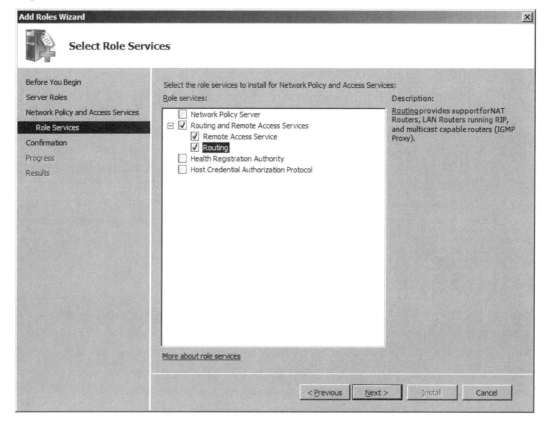

4. Click **Next** to bypass the Welcome screen.

5. Select the **Network Access Services** checkbox.

6. Click the **Next** button.

7. Click **Next** again to bypass the Network Access Service screen description.

8. Select the **Network Access Services** components that you want to install. Select the check boxes for **Network Policy Server (NPS)** and **Routing and Remote Access Services (RRAS)**.

9. When you select the Routing and Remote Access Services check box, the Remote Access Service, Routing, and Connection Manager Administration Kit check boxes will be selected automatically.

Network Policy Server and Network Access Protection

In the RRAS there are a number of snap-in roles that can be used in configuring and setting up your network access needs for Windows Server 2008. In previous incarnations of Windows Server 2003, Internet Authentication Service (IAS) snap-in was Microsoft's implementation of a Remote Authentication Dial-in User Service (RADIUS) server and proxy. It was capable of performing localized connection AAA Protocol for many types of network access, including wireless and VPN connections.

For Windows Server 2008, Microsoft has replaced IAS with a new snap-in called Network Policy Server (NPS). NPS is the Microsoft implementation of a RADIUS server and proxy in Windows Server 2008, and promises to be even simpler to use than IAS. For your exam, you will be required to be familiar with NPS.

NPS is not just a replacement for IAS; it does what IAS did but also offers another role called Network Access Protection (NAP). When you install NPS you will find that you have a lot of new functionality.

NPS does many of the same things that IAS did such as:

- Routing of LAN and WAN traffic.

- Allow access to local resources through VPN or dial-up connections.

- Creating and enforcing network access through VPN or dial-up connections.

For example, NPS can provide these functions:

- VPN services

- Dial-up services

- 802.11 protected access

- RRAS

■ Offer authentication through Windows Active Directory

■ Control network access with policies

What NPS does that is new, are all the functions related to NAP. NAP when used in unison with NPS creates a "total system health policy enforcement platform," which helps in the creation of health policies for your network, as shown in Figure 3.3.

Figure 3.3 NPS and NAP Health Policy Overview

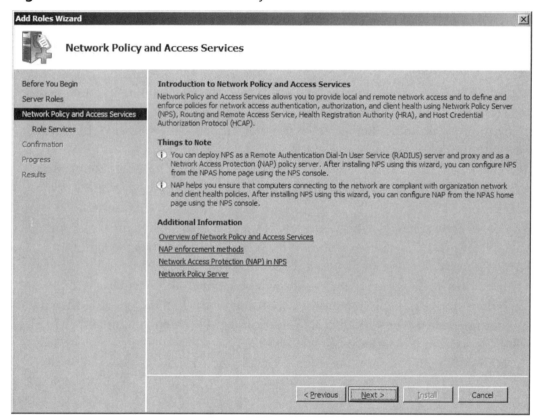

NAP is designed to enhance a corporate VPN. This is accomplished when clients establish a VPN session with a Windows Server 2008 system that is running the RRAS. Once a connection is made, a NPS will validate the remote system and determine the status of its health. The NPS collects information and compares the remote computer's configuration against a pre-determined network access policy that can be customized by the administrator. Policies can be configured to either monitor or isolate based on the administrators preference as, shown in Figure 3.4.

Figure 3.4 NPS Policy Configuration

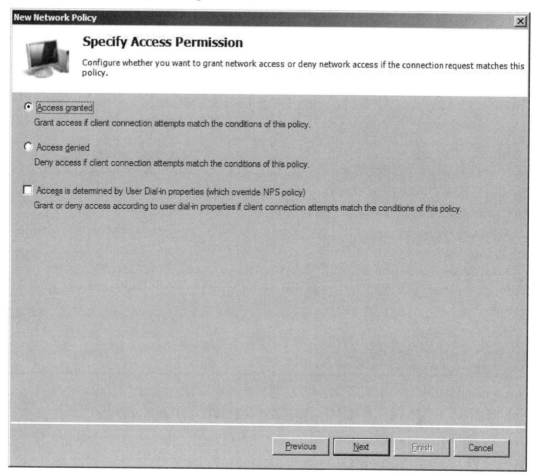

Although monitoring will not prevent any PCs from gaining access to your network, each PC logging on to the network will be recorded for compliance. Isolation will put non-compliant users onto an isolated segment of the network, where it cannot interfere with production or resources. Of course, the administrator is ultimately responsible for configuring what access non-compliant computers will be allowed.

If you are already familiar with Windows Server 2003 and the IAS snap-in, you will notice many changes to the NPS snap-in:

- Network policies have replaced remote access policies and have been moved to the policies node.

- RADIUS Clients and Servers node has replaced the RADIUS Client node.

- There is no Connection Request Processing node.

- Policies and the Remote RADIUS Server Groups node have been moved under RADIUS Clients and Servers.

- Remote access policy conditions and profile settings have been reorganized on the Overview, Conditions, Constraints, and Settings tabs for the properties of a network policy.

- The Remote Access Logging folder has been renamed the Accounting node, and no longer has the Local File or SQL Server nodes.

In addition, the System Health Validators node allows you to set up and adjust all NAP health requirements. The Remediation Server Groups node allows you to set up the group of servers that restricted NAP clients can access for the VPN and Dynamic Host Configuration Protocol (DHCP) NAP enforcement methods. Last, the Accounting node allows you to set up how NPS stores accounting information for the network.

The NAP wizard automatically configures all of the connection request policies, network policies, and health policies. Knowing how to set up and configure this feature will put you steps ahead of the competition.

EXERCISE 3.3

CONFIGURING POLICIES AND SETTINGS FOR NAP ENFORCEMENT METHODS IN NPS

To configure policies and settings for NAP enforcement methods in NPS:

1. Select **Network Access Protection** in the Standard Configuration drop-down box.

2. Click Configure NAP.

To configure policies and settings for VPN or dial-up network access:

3. Select RADIUS server for Dial-Up or VPN Connections from the drop-down box.

4. Click **Configure VPN** or **Dial-Up**.

    To configure policies and settings for 802.1X-authenticated wired or wireless access:

5. Select **RADIUS server for 802.1X Wireless** or **Wired Connections** from the drop-down box.

6. Click **Configure 802.1X**.

The wizard will guide you through the configuration process for your chosen scenario. The NAP wizard for VPN enforcement has a number of policy creation options, including ones for compliant NAP clients, noncompliant NAP clients, and non–NAP capable clients. It also includes two health policies for compliant and noncompliant NAP clients. The new NAP wizards and other wizards contained within will help you with creating RADIUS clients, remote RADIUS server groups, connection request policies, and network policies. Overall, this will make it that much easier to configure NPS for a variety of network access scenarios, and this will make your job and exam all the more simple.

Dial-Up

Dial-up by definition is the method used to connect a device to a network using a modem and a public telephone service. Dial-up access works in the same exact manner as a telephone connection does. The only true difference is that the two ends of the connections have computer devices communicating rather than people. Dial-up access utilizes normal telephone lines and because of this, the quality of the connection can suffer. Data rates are also limited. The maximum data rate with dial-up access for many years was 56Kbph. ISDN provides faster rates but are still limited compared to cable and DSL.

Dial-up networking using Windows Server 2008 include some of the following components:

- **Dial-up Networking Servers** You can configure a server running RRAS to provide dial-up networking access to an entire network, or restrict access to the shared resources of the remote access server only.

- **Dial-up Networking Clients** Remote access clients must be running Windows Server 2008, Windows Server 2003, Windows XP, Windows 2000, Windows NT to have access to the RRAS.

- **Remote Access Protocols** Remote access protocols are used to negotiate connections and provide framing for LAN protocol data that is sent over a wide area network (WAN) link. RRAS supports LAN protocols such as TCP/IP, which enable access to the Internet. RRAS supports remote access protocols such as PPP.

- **WAN Options** Clients can dial in by using standard telephone lines and a modem or modem pool. Faster links are possible by using ISDN. You can no longer connect remote access clients to remote access servers by using X.25 or ATM with Windows Server 2008.

- **Security Options** Windows Server 2008 provides logon and domain security, support for security hosts, data encryption, RADIUS, remote access account lockout, remote access policies, and callback for secure network access for dial-up clients.

Remote Access Policy

Remote access policies are an ordered set of rules that define how connections are either authorized or rejected. For each rule, there are one or more conditions, a set of profile settings, and a remote access permission setting. If a connection is authorized, the remote access policy profile specifies a set of connection restrictions. The dial-in properties of the user account also provide a set of restrictions. Where applicable, user account connection restrictions override the remote access policy profile connection restrictions.

For servers running the RRAS that are configured for the Windows authentication provider, remote access policies are administered from RRAS and apply only to the connections of the RRAS server. Centralized management of remote access policies is also used when you have remote access servers that are running RRAS. Remote access policies validate a number of connection settings before authorizing the connection, including the following:

- Remote access permission
- Group membership
- Type of connection
- Time of day
- Authentication methods
- Advanced conditions such as access server identity, access client phone number, or Media Access Control (MAC) address
- Whether user account dial-in properties are ignored
- Whether unauthenticated access is allowed

After the connection is authorized, remote access policies can also be used to specify connection restrictions, including the following:

- Idle timeout time
- Maximum session time
- Encryption strength
- IP packet filters

Advanced restrictions:

- IP address for PPP connections
- Static routes

Additionally, you can vary connection restrictions based on the following settings:

- Group membership
- Type of connection
- Time of day
- Authentication methods
- Identity of the access server
- Access client phone number or MAC address
- Whether unauthenticated access is allowed

For example, you can have policies that specify different maximum session times for different types of connections or groups. Additionally, you can also specify restricted access for business partners or unauthenticated connections. All of this can be configured using the RRAS panel on the client computer, as shown in Figure 3.5. This is accessible as follows:

1. Open **Server Manager** and expand the **Roles** tab.
2. Expand the **Network Policy and Access Service** tab, as seen in Figure 3.5.

Figure 3.5 Network Policy and Access Tab

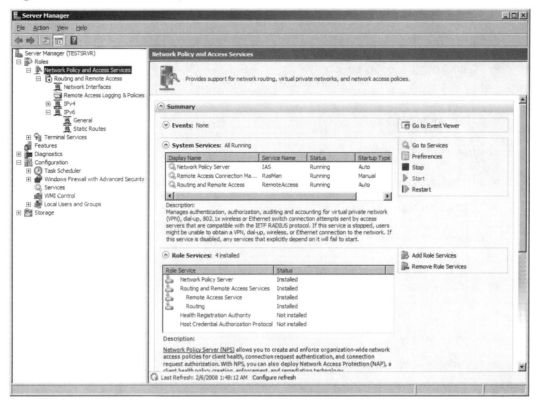

3. Expand the **Routing and Remote Access** panel and right click for **Properties**.

This will allow you to set up configurations for your remote access policies.

Network Address Translation (NAT)

Windows Server 2008 provides network address translation (NAT) functionality as part of the RRAS. NAT provides a method for translating the IPv4 addresses of computers on one network into IPv4 addresses of computers on a different network. A NAT-enabled IP router works as a translation service when deployed at the boundary where a private network meets a public network. This allows computers on the private network to access computers on the public network.

The whole reasoning behind the development of NAT technology was as a place holder solution for a greater issue that administrators faced. This problem was IPv4 address-depletion that plagued the Internet community. Due to a huge and continuing rise in computer usage, the number of available globally unique (public) IPv4 addresses was far too small to accommodate the need to access to the Internet. A long-term solution for the problem was well under way in the development of Internet Protocol version 6 (IPv6) addresses, which are supported by Windows Server 2008. Unfortunately, IPv6 is not yet widely adopted and would require extensive reconfiguring to deploy large scale in most organizations. The technology has been in use for more than a decade, but the practical deployment still remains an issue. This is why NAT is still in use, because it allows computers on any network to use reusable private addresses to connect to computers with globally unique public addresses on the Internet.

Small- to medium-sized organizations with private networks to access resources on the Internet or other public networks, use NAT for this reasoning. They configure reusable private IPv4 addresses while the computers on the public servers are set up with globally unique IPv4 addresses. The most useful deployment of NAT is in a small office or home office (SOHO) or a medium-sized business that uses RRAS. NAT technology enables computers on the internal corporate network to connect to resources on the Internet without having to deploy a proxy server.

NAT is a good solution for situations where ICS is not an option, such as when using a VPN or when the clients are using static IP addresses. A real benefit of NAT becomes apparent when dealing with Administration duties. For example, NAT makes it fairly simple to move your Web server or File Transfer Protocol (FTP) server to another host computer without having to worry about broken links. If you merely change the inbound mapping at the router, you can set it to reflect the new host. The same holds true of changes to your internal network. This is because the only external IP addresses either belong to the router or come from a pool of global addresses.

EXERCISE 3.4

ENABLING AND CONFIGURING NAT

Now that you understand how NAT works, let's look at how to enable and configure NAT:

1. In the left pane of the **Server Manager**, expand the **Routing and Remote Access** node, as shown in Figure 3.6.

2. Expand the **IPv4** node.

3. Click on the **NAT** node.

4. In the **NAT** node, right click on the external network server that you wish to enable NAT for on the middle pane of the console. For example, the external interface could be **Local Area Connection**.

5. Click **Properties** and select **NAT** and click **OK**, as shown in Figure 3.6.

Figure 3.6 Enabling NAT

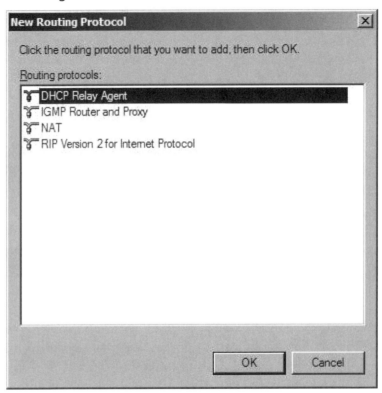

Internet Connection Sharing (ICS)

Internet Connection Sharing (ICS) is a feature that permits you to use Windows Server 2008 to connect a small office network or home network over the Internet. Not much has changed in this version of Windows Server 2008, and you may find that most of the features and set up procedures are very similar to that of Windows Server 2003. As it always has, ICS provides NAT, IP addressing, and name resolution services for all the computers on a small network. This method is best used for sharing an Internet connection among a small business network.

ICS routes TCP/IP packets that are present in a small LAN environment to the Internet. ICS will calculate and map individual IP addresses belonging to the clients of the LAN to unused port numbers in the TCP/IP stack. Because it uses NAT, IP addresses belonging to the local computer will not be visible on the Internet. All packets leaving or entering the LAN are sent from or to the IP address of the external adapter on the ICS host computer. This IP address is static and will always be 192.168.0.1, and will provide NAT services to the whole 192.168.0.x subnet.

ICS is not customizable in terms of which addresses are used for the internal subnet. It does not contain provisions for bandwidth limiting or other features common to more advanced systems. ICS is also not compatible and cannot be combined with Wi-Fi and dial-up mobile modems. ICS does offer limited configuration for other standard services and some configuration of NAT.

Configuring & Implementing...

Configuring ICS When Dealing with VPNs

Virtual private networks (VPNs), which we discuss later, are common in most companies today. When configuring an ICS, there are several things you should bear in mind concerning these types of connections and hazards that may occur if the proper precautions are not met.

Never create a VPN connection to a corporate network from the ICS computer. By doing so, you will cause the default setting for all traffic from the ICS computer to be forwarded over the VPN connection to the corporate network. This includes traffic from LAN clients. This will suspend Internet resources across the network and all the client computers will be sending data over the logical connection created with the credentials of the ICS computer user.

Never configure ICS on a computer that is a VPN server. If your Windows Server 2008-based computer is serving as a VPN server, you must use Windows Server 2008 NAT role.

These are very important configuration mistakes that, if avoided, can save wasted time and energy for you as an administrator.

Here is a list of required hardware and software for enabling ICS:

- A DSL or cable modem with an ISP connected to it and an active DSL or cable account.

- Two network adapters installed in the ICS machine.

- A network already configured with functioning TCP/IP.

Due to the nature of the way ISC works and its drawbacks, you should never install ICS on a machine that incorporates any of the following stipulations:

- Uses static IP addresses

- Has a domain controller

- Uses other DNS servers, gateways, or DHCP servers

ICS creates a static IP address for your network adapter and allocates IP addresses to other computers on your network. This means you will lose your connection to the rest of the network if other network computers already provide those services. If any of these conditions already exist in your network, you must use Windows Server 2008 NAT server instead of ICS.

Also bear in mind these other warnings:

- Do not create a VPN connection to a corporate network from the ICS computer. If you do, by default all traffic from the ICS computer, including traffic from local area network clients, will be forwarded over the VPN connection to the corporate network. This means that Internet resources will no longer be reachable, and all the client computers will be sending data over the logical connection created with the credentials of the ICS computer user.

- Do not configure ICS on a computer that is a VPN server. If your Windows Server 2008-based computer is serving as a VPN server, you must use Windows Server 2008 NAT role.

EXERCISE 3.5

CONFIGURING ICS

The ICS host computer provides a connection through the second network adapter to the existing TCP/IP network. Log on as member of the Administrators group to set up the ICS host computer.

1. Click **Start**.
2. Click **Control Panel.**
3. Click **Network Connections**.

4. Right-click **Local Area Connection** (for the installed network card) and rename it "Internet Connection."

5. In the **Network and Dial-up Connections** dialog box, two connections are displayed (for different network adapters): the Internet Connection and Local Area Connection.

6. Right-click **Internet Connection** and then click **Properties**.

7. Click the **General** tab, and then verify that **Client for Microsoft Networks** and **Internet Protocol** (TCP/IP) are displayed.

8. Click the **Advanced** tab, and then click to select the **Enable Internet Connection Sharing for this Connection** check box.

NOTE

Make sure that firewall software or other Internet-sharing software from any third-party manufacturer has been removed.

9. Click **OK**

Remote Access Protocols

Setting up remote access servers and connections in Windows Server can be somewhat overwhelming and confusing if you don't understand the protocol configuration options available to you. You have a number of remote access protocol options to choose from, and deciding which ones to use will be based on the exact task and functionality you seek to accomplish. This will depend on your system configurations, your hardware, you're your communications capabilities.

You must try to organize and make sense of all these options. To start, let's take a look at the categories of protocols and the advantages and disadvantages of the various protocols within each one.

Microsoft's PPTP is most commonly used for voluntary authenticated and encrypted tunneling between dial-up clients and a PPTP Network Server located just inside the customer's network.

The PPTP Network Server authenticates the tunnel user with Challenge-Handshake Authentication Protocol (CHAP) and negotiates data compression and encryption as dictated by security policies. PPTP offers payload privacy, but does not encrypt session control traffic.

The L2TP consolidates the best of other protocols within a single standard. L2TP Access Concentrators terminate PPP Link Control Protocol (LCP) and carry out dial session authentication. L2TP can be used with a separate LAC at the ISP NAS, or with a LAC Client on the end-user's PC. L2TP Network Servers terminate PPP NCP, provide routing and bridging for the PPP session, and make the user appear directly connected to the "home" network.

L2TP is transparent in compulsory mode, multiprotocol support, and leaving authentication, authorization, and addressing responsibility within the customer's network. L2TP is a tunneling protocol, not an encryption protocol. If customers require data confidentiality, you'll need to run L2TP over IPSec.

Features have been added to the IP protocol to provide greater security for IP packets that transit public networks. The Encapsulating Security Payload (ESP) encrypts packets, usually by encapsulating a private IP packet inside an outer public IP packet. Another standard known as Internet Security Association and Key Management Protocol (ISAKMP) can be used for strong authentication of tunnel endpoints and key management. Collectively, these extensions are called IPSec.

IPSec supports Site-to-Site VPNs by building security associations between gateways at the edge of customer networks. Every packet that enters or leaves each network will be tunneled according to customer-defined policy, with filtering down to the individual host and port level. IPSec-compatible encryption and packet authentication algorithms support a wide variety of security policies, allowing customers to strike their own balance between security and performance.

IPSec can also be used to support Remote Access VPNs, by tunneling from an individual host to a security gateway, topologically similar to voluntary PPTP tunnels. IP packets sent by an IPSec host to a protected network are encrypted and delivered to the security gateway for that network. IP packets to public destinations are sent without the addition of IPSec protocols.

Windows Server 2008 has offered many new upgrades. Their newest to the realm of VPNs is the addition of SSTP, which is the latest alternative form of VPN tunnel. SSTP is an application-layer protocol. It uses a synchronous communication, which works in unilateral motion between two programs allowing a constant exchange and comparison of data. By doing this, it allows for many application endpoints over a single network connection. This allows for a very efficient usage of the communication resources that are available to that network. SSTP is based on SSL as opposed to IPSec or PPTP, and thereby uses port 443 for traffic.

New & Noteworthy...

Microsoft's Development Direction of SSL

When developing SSTP to be a viable and improved VPN tunneling protocol, Microsoft had many available resources to build upon. Two of the most commonly used were IPSec and SSL. Both had benefits, but it took much consideration to determine which would provide the better ground work to allow the most benefits. At the conclusion of their decision-making process, SSL was chosen as the basis for the SSTP, which is used in Windows Server 2008.

There are many obvious reasons for this choice. Most become apparent when you examine the downsides of IPSec. IPSec main function is supporting site-to-site VPN connectivity and no roaming. SSL was obviously a better base for SSTP development, as it supports roaming. Besides the obvious, there are several other reasons for not basing SSTP on IPSec:

- Strong authentication is not required.
- User Clients must be present.
- No sense of conformity in regards to support and coding from one vendor to the next.
- No Default non-IP protocols.
- Remote users attempting to connect via a site with limited IP addresses would cause problems due to the inherent site-to-site secure connections design.

With SSL, VPN static IP addresses are not required, clients are unnecessary in most cases, and since connections are made via a browser over the Internet, the default connection protocol is TCP/IP. This makes connections transparent to the user. Microsoft hopes that this sort of forethought in their development will ensure more user friendly interactions when using SSTP in Windows Server2008.

SSTP allows for the passage of traffic through firewalls that would normally inhibit PPTP and L2TP/IPSec traffic. SSTP is able to incorporate PPP traffic over the SSL channel of the HTTPS protocol. By using PPP, SSTP can utilize well-protected authentication methods such as EAP-TLS. By involving HTTPS, traffic is directed and flows through TCP port 443. This port is commonly used for Web access, which is why the SSTP is so versatile compared to past VPN protocols. Key negotiation, integrity checking, and encryption are handled via SSL VPN. This also allows for transport-level security when dealing with these functions.

TEST DAY TIP

As you can see there are many similarities between the new features available in Windows Server 2008 and previous versions of Windows Server. Try to be certain of the distinguishing elements that separate the two. Although two features may have similar uses and applications, their exact functionality may be very different.

For example, you should remember that although STTP may be closely related to SSL, no cross comparison can be made between the two. You should be sure not to confuse the two, as SSTP is only a tunneling protocol, unlike SSL.

SSL uses a cryptographic system. This system uses two encrypted keys to secure data. One is the public key and the other is the private key. The public key is recognizable to everyone and the private key can only be identified by the recipient. A secure connection between a client and a server is created by this method of encryption. You can thereby establish secure remote access from almost any Internet connected to a Web browser, which was not possible using traditional VPN. Thanks to this new method, there are not issues with instability in connection and loss of service due to connectivity issues for the client. The added bonus is that with SSL VPN, the session is completely secured.

Remember that while SSTP is a strong method for client-to-site VPN connections, it is not designed for site-to-site VPN connections. Let's review the assets that SSTP can provide to you and your organization:

- SSTP takes advantage of HTTPS to establish a secure and stable connection.

- The SSTP (VPN) tunnel will function over Secure-HTTP. This means that Web proxies, firewalls, and NAT routers present on the path between clients and servers will no longer block VPN connections.

- Port blocking is greatly decreased.

- Clients will be able to connect from anywhere on the Internet.

- SSTP is built into Windows Server 2008, providing higher compatibility.

- SSTP allows simpler training procedures, because the end-user VPN controls are identical to previous versions.

- The SSTP-based VPN tunnel will directly plug into the current interfaces for Microsoft VPN client and server software.

- IPv6 is fully supported.

- It takes advantage of the new integrated network access protection support for client health-check.

- MS RRAS client and server are strongly supported, allowing for two-factor authentication capabilities.

- VPN coverage is expanded from limited points of access to almost any Internet connection.

- The use of port 443 for SSL encapsulation.

- Acts as a full network VPN solution over all applications.

- NAP integration.

- SSL tunnel is created in s single session.

- Stronger forced authentication process than other methods like IPSec.

- Supports non-IP protocols.

- No additional costs or hard-to-configure hardware firewalls that do not support Active Directory integration and integrated two-factor authentication.

Now that we know the benefits of using Secure Socket Protocol, lets examine the data flow for an SSTP-based VPN connection in action:

If a user on a computer running Windows Server 2008 initiates an SSTP-based VPN connection, the following occurs:

1. A TCP connection between the STTP client and the SSTP server is made. This happens between a dynamically allocated TCP port on the SSTP client. The same connection occurs on the TCP port 443 on the SSTP server.

2. An SSL Client-Hello message is sent by the SSTP client. This Client-Hello Message acts as an invitation from the SSTP client to create an SSL session with the SSTP server.

3. The SSTP server responds by providing and sending its computer certificate to the SSTP client.

4. The computer certificate is validated by the STTP client.

5. Next, the STTP determines the encryption method for the SSL session.

6. Then the SSTP Client creates an SSL session key.

7. This SSL session key is then encrypted with the public key of the SSTP server's certificate.

EXAM WARNING

SSL uses a cryptographic system, which uses two encrypted keys to secure data. One is the public key and the other is the private key. The public key is recognizable to everyone and the private can only be identified by the recipient. A secure connection between a client and a server is created by this method of encryption. You can thereby establish secure remote access from almost any Internet-connected Web browser, which was not possible using traditional VPN.

Please remember that while SSTP is a strong method for client-to-site VPN connection, it is not designed for site-to-site VPN connections. If you need a site-to-site VPN connection, you should use a traditional VPN.

8. The SSL session key is then sent as the encrypted form of the SSL session key to the SSTP server.

9. The SSTP server decrypts the encrypted SSL session key with the private key of its computer certificate. Now any further communication between the SSTP client and the SSTP server will be encrypted with the negotiated encryption method and SSL session key.

10. The SSTP client sends an HTTP over SSL request message to the SSTP server.

11. The SSTP client attempts to negotiate for an SSTP tunnel with the SSTP server.

12. The SSTP client attempts to negotiate a PPP connection with the SSTP server. All user credentials are negotiated at this time with a PPP authentication method. Also during the negotiation they configure settings for IPv4 or IPv6 traffic.

13. Once negotiation is completed, the SSTP client begins sending IPv4 or IPv6 traffic over the PPP link.

Configuring & Implementing…

Taking Advantage of Virtual Networking

Microsoft Windows 2008 has a variety of new networking options available to you, but it also offers other peripheral roles that can helpful in a variety. One huge trend in today's networking is virtual networking. This allows you to more efficiently economize and consolidate the number of physical machines by replacing them with virtual ones. While testing out different aspects of networking in this chapter such as creating a VPN using SSTP protocol, it will be helpful to you to work in real-world testing environments. Normally, in previous editions of Windows, this would require many physical computers to create an accurate test case or a program like Virtual PC 2007 to simulate this.

Using the Hyper V role of Windows Server 2008, you can create the same test scenario with only one or two physical computers and still accurately test your deployment cases. This will allow you to more effectively test a variety of VPN configurations using only a limited number of physical machines. It will also familiarize you with other aspects of the Windows Server 2008 roles that are available to you as an administrator, and also gain more proficiency with the operating system (OS).

By utilizing all of the new features of Windows Server 2008 in unison, you can take advantage of the full power of real-world networking benefits that Windows Server 2008 has to offer your organization. This will also present the option of virtualization and the benefits it can bring to your organization.

EXERCISE 3.6

CONFIGURING SSTP ON WINDOWS SERVER 2008

Now that we understand how STTP using the SSL VPN works, let's go over the steps required to set up an SSTP connection in Windows Server 2008.

1. On **SSTP client**, click on **Network and Sharing Center**.
2. Click **Manage network connections**.

3. Double-click the **VPN Connection**, and then click on **Properties**.
4. Click on the **Networking** tab and find the **Type of VPN** drop-down list.
5. Select **Secure Socket Tunneling Protocol** (SSTP) from the **Type of VPN** drop-down list.
6. Click **OK.**
7. Click **Connect** on the **Connect VPN Connection** dialog box. The Client will then connect to the VPN server using the SSTP connection.

Virtual Private Networks

VPNs use public wires to join nodes to create a network. This network allows the user to create their own private networks for the transfer of data. There are a large number of security systems at play within the VPN, such as encryption and other security measures. This makes certain that no data is intercepted by unauthorized users. VPN has been used successfully for several years, but has recently encountered problems. Many organizations have widely increased the number of roaming users that have access to their networks. Because of this, other methods have been in development to accomplish this same type of access. IPSec and SSL VPN are two such methods commonly in use by many organizations.

VPNs typically use an encrypted tunnel that keeps data confidential within the tunnel. By doing this, when the tunnel routes through typical NAT paths, the VPN tunnel fails to remain active and stops working completely. VPNs will most often connect a node directly to an endpoint. If the node and the endpoint have the same internal LAN address and NAT is involved, many problems and complications will arise causing a lack of service to your end client.

TEST DAY TIP

Be familiar with all of the tools available to you in Server Manager. Windows Server 2008 provides a number of roles and snap-in features that help immensely with your job as an administrator. When you are prepping the day of the exam, make sure you can identify and locate roles like RRAS and Network protection and Access roles. This will help you gain a better understanding of the design structure for Windows Server 2008, and help you to apply what you know on your exam.

Installing and Configuring a SSL VPN Server

Now that you have an idea of how SSTP and new SSL VPNs work, we will explain how to use the RRAS panel to install and configure a VPN. Before beginning, be sure that you have a clean version of Windows Server 2008 installed. Also, you must not have RRAS installed yet to set up the SSL VPN. Before installing RRAS, you must request a machine certificate server.

The VPN server needs a machine certificate to create the SSL VPN connection with the SSL VPN client computer. The name on the certificate should match the name that the VPN client will use to connect to the SSL VPN gateway computer. This means that you will need to create a public DNS entry for the name on the certificate, so that it will resolve to the external IP address on the VPN server or the IP address of a NAT device in front of the VPN server, as described earlier in this chapter. This will forward the connection to the SSL VPN server.

EXERCISE 3.7

REQUESTING AND INSTALLING THE MACHINE CERTIFICATE ON THE SSL VPN SERVER

Perform the following steps to request and install the machine certificate on the SSL VPN server:

1. Open **Server Manager**. Expand the **Roles** node in the left pane.

2. Expand the **Web Server** (IIS) node. Click on **Internet Information Services (IIS) Manager**.

3. Locate the **Internet Information Services Manager** console and find the pane to the right of the left pane, and click on the **name** of the server you are using.

4. Click on the **Server Certificates** icon in the right pane of the IIS console.

5. In the right pane of the console, click the **Create Domain Certificate** link.

6. Fill out the information on the **Distinguished Name Properties** page. Remember to correctly enter the **Common Name** entry as mentioned previously. This name is the name that VPN clients will use to connect to the VPN server. You will need a public Domain Name Server (DNS) entry for this name, so that it resolves either to the external interface of the VPN server, or the public address

of a NAT device in front of the VPN server (e.g., the common name *sstp.msexamfirewall.org*). The VPN client computer should have Host files created so that it can resolve this name later.

7. When finished click **Next**.

8. On the **Online Certification Authority** page, find and click the **Select** button.

9. In the **Select Certification Authority** dialog box, click the name of the **Enterprise CA** and click **OK**.

10. Enter a name for the certificate in the Friendly name text box (e.g., the name SSLVPN).

11. Click **Finish** on the Online Certification Authority page.

When the Wizard completes its work, you will see the certificate appear in the IIS console:

12. Double click on the **certificate** and you can see the common name in the "Issued to" section, and that we have a private key that corresponds to the certificate.

13. Click **OK** to close the Certificate dialog box.

Once you have a certificate, you can then install the RRAS Server Role as described earlier in this chapter. It is critical that you install the certificate first, before you install the RRAS Server Role. If you do not, you will have to use a fairly complex command-line routine to bind the certificate to the SSL VPN listener.

To set up a VPN, proceed with the following steps. Once RRAS is installed, you must first enable RRAS.

Perform the following steps to enable the RRAS service:

1. Open Server Manager and expand the **Roles** node in the left pane of the console.

2. Expand the **Network Policy and Access Services** node and click on the **Routing and Remote Access** node. Right-click on the **Routing and Remote Access** node and click **Configure and Enable Routing and Remote Access**, as shown in Figure 3.7.

Figure 3.7 Configure and Enable Routing and Remote Access

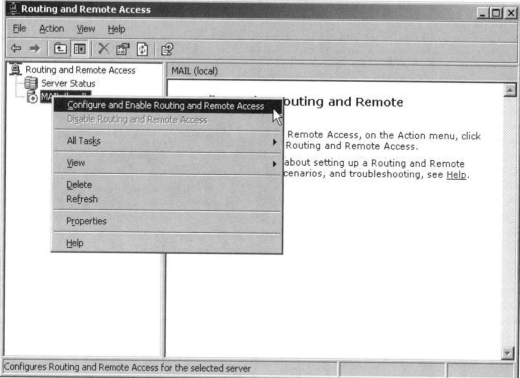

3. Click **Next** on the **Welcome to the Routing and Remote Access Server Setup** Wizard page.

4. On the **Configuration** page shown in Figure 3.8, select the **Virtual private network (VPN) access and NAT** option.

5. Click **Next**.

Figure 3.8 Routing and Remote Access Server Setup Wizard

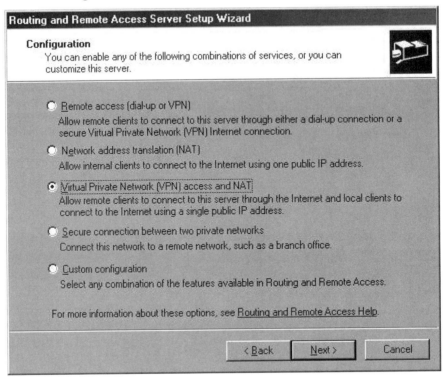

6. On the **VPN Connection** page, select the **NIC** in the **Network interfaces** section that represents the external interface of the VPN server.

7. Click **Next**.

8. On the **IP Address Assignment** page, select the **Automatically** option if you have a DHCP server. If you do not have a DHCP server, select the **From a specified range of addresses** option and provide a list of addresses that VPN clients would use when connecting to the network through the VPN gateway.

9. Click **Next**.

10. On the **Managing Multiple Remote Access Servers** page, select **No, use Routing and Remote Access to authenticate connection requests**. Use this option when there is no NPS or RADIUS server available. If the VPN server is a member of the domain, you can authenticate users using domain accounts. If the VPN server is not a member of the domain, then only local accounts on the VPN server can be used.

11. Click **Next**.

12. Review the summary information on the **Completing the Routing and Remote Access Server Setup** Wizard page for accuracy and click **Finish**.

13. Click **OK** in the Routing and Remote Access dialog box telling you that relaying of DHCP messages requires a DHCP relay agent.

14. Expand the **Routing and Remote Access node** and then click on the **Ports** node. In the middle pane you will see that WAN Miniport connections for SSTP are now available.

EXAM WARNING

There are a number of server types that can be set up in a given real-world situation. It is up to you to determine which suits your clients' needs the best. For the exam, however, you must be aware of what type of information concerning what type of access is being asked of you. Remember that RRAS and NPS are two different means of setting up many of the available services. Be sure to double check the type of server information the question is calling for.

Inbound/Outbound Filters

Windows Server 2008 features a variety of inbound and outbound features that you will need to be able to implement for your exam. The old version of Windows Firewall has been upgraded and is now called Windows Firewall with Advanced Security (WFAS).

This new version of WFAS has a number of advanced components that will help with you security needs.

- **New GUI Interface** MMC is a snap-in that is available to help configure the advanced firewall.

- **Bi-directional Filters** Unlike past versions of Windows Firewall, WFAS filters both outbound traffic as well as inbound traffic.

- **Better IPSec Compatibility** WFAS rules and IPSec encryption configurations are both integrated into the same singular interface.

- **Enhanced Rules Generation** Using WFAS, you can create firewall rules for Windows Active Directory service accounts and groups. This includes source/destination IP addresses, protocol numbers, source and destination TCP/User Datagram Protocol (UDP) ports, Internet Control Message Protocol (ICMP), IPv6 traffic, and interface all on the Windows Server.

With the addition to having inbound and outbound filters, the WFAS has advanced rules configuration.

The first concern of any server administrator in using a host-based firewall is "What if it prevents critical server infrastructure applications from functioning? While that is always a possibility with any security measure, WFAS will automatically configure new rules for any new server roles that are added to the server. However, if you run any non-Microsoft applications on your server that need inbound network connectivity, you will have to create a new rule for that type of traffic.

By using the advanced windows firewall, you can better secure your servers from attack and secure your servers from attacking others, and really nail down what traffic is going in and out of your servers.

Configuring Remote Authentication Dial-In User Service (RADIUS) Server

RADIUS is protocol used for controlling access to network resources by authenticating, authorizing, and accounting for access, and is referred to as an AAA protocol. RADIUS is the unofficial industry standard for this type of access. It is more common today than ever before, being employed by ISPs, large corporations that need to manage access to the Internet, and also internal networks that operate across a large variety of access providing technologies such as modems, DSL, wireless and VPNs. To better understand what RADIUS does, let's try to understand each of its required functions as an AAA protocol.

- **Authentication** The server seeking access sends a request to NAS. The NAS then creates and sends a RADIUS Access Request to the RADIUS Server. This request acts as an authorization to grant access. Typically, a user name and password or some other means of establishing identity is requested for this process, which must then be provided by the user seeking access. The request will also contain other means of verification that the NAS collected, such as physical location of the user and/or the phone number or network address of the user.

- **Authorization** Upon receipt of the request, the RADIUS server processes the new request for access. Most times, the RADIUS server will have access to a list of accounts or be able to query an external database to cross reference the provided information on the user. RADIUS will verify the user information and, if configured to do so, other information such as the user's network address or phone number that it has access to against the information it has stored. Based on the result of the check, the RADIUS server will respond with one of three responses to the NAS responsible for enforcing the access decision of the RADIUS server:

- **Access Accept** This result indicates that the user is granted access. The terms of access are based on the information the RADIUS server has on file, and is conveyed to the NAS, which allows the conditional access based on these terms. A variety of terms could be stipulated, such as time restrictions, bandwidth restrictions, security access control restrictions, and others.

- **Access Challenge** This requests further verification from the user before access will be granted. These types of verification can include a secondary password, PIN, or token card challenge response.

- **Access Reject** This indicates that there has been a failure to prove the user's identity or that their account is inactive or unusable. This means that the user has been completely denied access to all network resources requested.

- **Accounting** If network access is granted to the user by the NAS based on the authentication and authorization phases, NAS then sends an *Accounting Start* request to the RADIUS Server to indicate that the user has begun accessing the network. These types of records will contain a variety of information concerning the identity, point of attachment, and unique session ID for the user. Active session may have periodic updates sent out called *Interim Accounting* records. These records may update the session duration and information on current data usage. When the user exits the network and the access point (AP) is again closed, the NAS will send a final *Accounting Stop* record to the RADIUS server. This informs it of the final information related to the user's network access.

NAS devices communicate with the RADIUS via the link-layer protocol, using PPP for example. The RADIUS server responds using the RADIUS protocol. The RADIUS server authenticates using security schemes such as PAP, CHAP or EAP.

Remember that just because the user is authenticated, it does not give him or her total access to all resources the network has to offer, so the RADIUS server will often check that the user is authorized to use the network service requested. There are a number of specifications that access can be based on once authenticated. These include:

- The specific IP Address that will be assigned to the user.

- The total amount of time that the user is permitted to remain connected.

- Limited access or priority based access to certain resources.

- L2TP parameters.

- Virtual Local Area Network (VLAN) parameters.

- Other Quality of Service (QoS) parameters.

In previous incarnations of Windows Server 2003, Internet Authentication Service (IAS) was Microsoft's implementation of a RADIUS server and proxy. IAS performed centralized connection AAA Protocol for many types of network access, including wireless and VPN connections.

For Windows Server 2008, Microsoft has replaced IAS with a new feature called NPS. NPS is the Microsoft implementation of a RADIUS server and proxy in Windows Server 2008, and promises to be even simpler to use than IAS. You will need to know how to set up a RADIUS server using NPS. Begin by installing NPS and setting up your RADIUS Server.

EXERCISE 3.8

INSTALLING NPS AND SETTING UP YOUR RADIUS SERVER

1. Open **Server Manager** and click on the **Add Roles.**

2. Choose the **Network Policy and Access Services** shown in Figure 3.9, and review the overview screen (see Figure 3.10).

Figure 3.9 Choosing the NPS Role

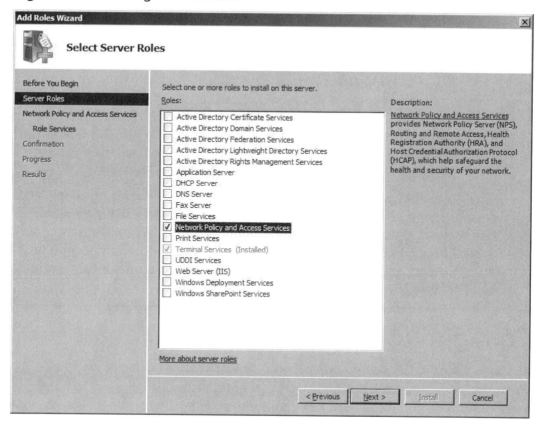

Figure 3.10 Overview Screen on NPS

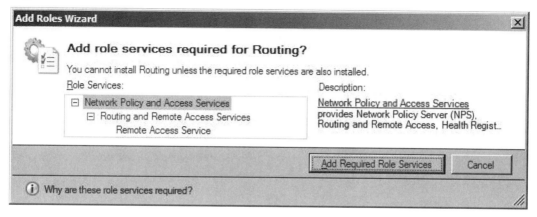

3. Select the **Network Policy Service** role. You may notice that the Network Policy Service is actually the RADIUS server that you are used to seeing with previous versions of Windows Server in IAS.

4. Click **Next**. You will see a final confirmation screen, as seen in Figure 3.10.

5. Click **Install**.

6. Once the software has been loaded, click on **Network Policy Server** under administrator tools. You will see that the RADIUS Client and Server Tabs are available and can be configured according to your needs by right-clicking on them and selecting **Properties**.

NPS can be used as a RADIUS proxy to provide the routing of RADIUS messages between RADIUS clients (access servers) and RADIUS servers that perform user AAA for the connection attempt. When used as a RADIUS proxy, NPS is a central switching or routing point through which RADIUS access and accounting messages flow. NPS records information about forwarded messages in an accounting log.

Configuring Wireless Access

Increased use of laptop computers and other wireless access devices within an enterprise along with an increase in worker mobility, have fuelled the demand for wireless networks in recent years. Up until recently, wireless technology was plagued with incompatibility issues and vendor-specific products. The technology was slow, expensive, and reserved for mobile situations or hostile environments where cabling was impractical or impossible. In recent years, the maturing of industry standards has caused a leveling point. This is thanks to industry-enforced compatibility standards and the deployment of lightweight wireless networking hardware. All of these factors have allowed wireless technology to come of age in the modern company.

Wireless networking hardware requires the use of technology that deals with radio frequencies as well as data transmission. The most widely used standard is 802.11 produced by the IEEE. This is a standard defining all aspects of radio frequency wireless networking. There have been several amendments to the 802.11 standard, the most recent being 802.11i.

Many Wireless networks use an AP to gain connectivity. In this type of network, the AP acts like a hub, providing connectivity for the wireless computers. It can connect the wireless LAN to a wired LAN, allowing wireless computer access to LAN resources. This includes such resources as file servers or existing internet connectivity. This type of wireless network is said to run in infrastructure mode.

An ad hoc or peer-to-peer wireless network is one in which a number of computers each equipped with a wireless networking interface card, can connect without the use of an AP. Each computer communicates with all of the other wireless-enabled computers directly. This allows for the sharing of files and printer services, but may not be able to access wired LAN resources. The exception to this is if one of the computers acts as a bridge or AP to the wired LAN using special software.

As you might be familiar with in Windows Server 2003, Wireless Auto Configuration will attempt to pair up configured preferred wireless networks with the wireless networks that are broadcasting their network name. If no such available networks exist that match a preferred wireless network, Wireless Auto Configuration will then send a number of probe requests to attempt to find a match. These are to try and determine if the preferred networks in the ordered list are non-broadcast networks. The end result of this total process should be that broadcast networks are connected to before non-broadcast networks. This even includes situations where a non-broadcast network is higher in the preferred list than a broadcast network. A big downside of this method, however, is that a Windows XP or Windows Server 2003 wireless client has to advertise its list of preferred wireless networks when sending probe requests. This leaves clients vulnerable while sending these probe requests.

Windows Server 2008 presents a better option. By configuring the wireless networks as broadcast, the wireless network names will be included in the Beacon frames sent by the wireless AP. If you set the wireless network as non-broadcast, the Beacon frame contains a wireless network name. This name is set to NULL, which results in Wireless Auto Configuration attempting connection to the wireless networks in the preferred network list order. This is regardless of whether they are broadcast or non-broadcast. By explicitly marking wireless networks as broadcast or non-broadcast, Windows Server 2008 wireless clients only send probe requests for non-broadcast wireless networks. This reduces wireless client side vulnerability and enhances security.

Previously, if a preferred wireless network could not be connected to and the wireless client was configured in a way that prevented automatic connections not in the preferred list by default, then Wireless Auto Configuration would create a random wireless network name. Then it would place the wireless network adapter in infrastructure mode. The random wireless network does not have a security configuration, making it possible for all kinds of malicious users to connect to the wireless client, thereby using the random wireless network name.

For computers running Windows Server 2008 that use updated wireless drivers designed for Windows Vista, Wireless Auto Configuration will remove this vulnerability by parking the wireless network adapter in a passive listening mode. A parked wireless device does not send probe request frames for a random wireless network name. It also does not allow for any other names, so malicious users cannot connect to the wireless client.

If you are using a wireless network adapter driver that was designed for Windows XP, computers running Windows Vista or Windows Server 2008 will use the behavior of the Wireless Client Update for Windows XP with Service Pack 2 (a random wireless network name with a security configuration).

Windows Server 2008 troubleshooting wireless connections is made much easier through the following features:

- **Network Diagnostics Framework** The Network Diagnostics Framework is an extensible architecture that provides users with a means to recover from and troubleshoot problems with network connections. In the case of a failed wireless connection, Network Diagnostics Framework will give the user the option to identify and correct the problem. Wireless support for the Network Diagnostics Framework tries to discover the source of the failed connection and will automatically fix the problem. Also based on your security considerations, it can be made to prompt the user to make the appropriate configuration change themselves.

- For a failed wireless connection attempt, the wireless components of Windows Server 2008 now records detailed information about the connection attempt in the Windows event log. Support professionals can now access and use these records to perform troubleshooting tasks, and attempt to resolve the problem quickly if the wireless diagnostics either could not resolve the problem or when it could resolve the problem, but the problem cannot be fixed by changing wireless client settings. This will cut down on the time needed to resolve wireless connection support problems. These can also be automatically collected by network administrators using Microsoft Operations Manager, to be analyzed for patterns and wireless infrastructure design changes.

- You can now gain access to in-depth information about the computer's state and wireless components in Windows, and their interaction when the problem occurred. This can be done using information from *wireless diagnostics tracing* in Windows Server 2008. To use wireless diagnostics tracing, you must start tracing, reproduce the problem, stop tracing, and then collect the tracing report. To view the tracing report, in the console tree of the Reliability and Performance Monitor snap-in open **Reports | System | Wireless Diagnostics**.

Windows Server 2003 and Windows XP do not have a command-line interface that allows you to configure the wireless settings that are available from the wireless dialog boxes in the Network Connections folder, or through the Wireless Network (IEEE 802.11) Policies Group Policy settings. Command-line configuration of wireless settings can help deployment of wireless networks in the following situations:

- **Automated script support for wireless settings without using Group Policy Wireless Network (IEEE 802.11) Policies Group Policy settings only apply in an Active Directory domain.** For an environment without Active Directory or a Group Policy infrastructure, a script that automates the configuration of wireless connections can be run either manually or automatically, such as part of the login script.

- **Bootstrapping of a wireless client onto the protected organization's wireless network.** A wireless client computer that is not a member of the domain cannot connect to the organization's protected wireless network. Furthermore, computers are not able to join the domain until a successful connection has occurred to the organization's secure wireless network. A command-line script provides a method to connect to the organization's secure wireless network to join the domain.

In Windows Server 2008, you can use **Netsh** commands in the **netsh wlan** context to do the following:

- Save all wireless client settings in a named profile including general settings (the types of wireless networks to access), 802.11 settings (SSID, type of authentication, type of data encryption), and 802.1X authentication settings (EAP types and their configuration).

- Specify the list of allowed and denied wireless network names.

- Specify the order of preferred wireless networks.

- Display a wireless client's configuration.

- Remove the wireless configuration from a wireless client.

- Migrate a wireless configuration setting between wireless clients.

Many applications are not network aware, resulting in customer confusion and developer overhead. For example, an application cannot automatically adjust its behavior based on the currently attached network and conditions. Users might have to reconfigure application settings depending on the network to which they are attached (their employer's private network, the user's home network, the Internet).

To remove the configuration burden, application developers can use low-level Windows APIs, data constructs, and perhaps even probing the network themselves to determine the current network and adjust their application's behavior accordingly.

To provide an operating system infrastructure to allow application developers to more easily reconfigure application behavior based on the currently attached network, the Network Awareness APIs in Windows Server 2008 make network information available to applications and enables them to easily and effectively adapt to these changing environments. The Network Awareness APIs allow applications to obtain up-to-date network information and location change notification.

Let's take a look at how to deal with the variety of elements available with Windows Server 2008 in regards to wireless network access and how they will be applied to your exam.

Set Service Identifier (SSID)

The Service Set Identifier (SSID) is a 32-character unique identifier attached to the header of packets that are sent over a Wireless Local Area Network (WLAN). The SSID acts as a password when a mobile device tries to connect to the BSS. The SSID differentiates one WLAN from another. This way all APs and all devices attempting to connect to a specific WLAN must use the same SSID in order to succeed. No device will be permitted to join the BSS unless it can provide the unique SSID. SSID is not a security measure, because it can very easily be sniffed due to being stored in plain text.

In Windows Server 2008, an additional wireless network configuration setting has been added that can indicate whether a wireless network is broadcast or non-broadcast. This setting can be configured locally through the "Manually connect to a wireless network" dialog box, the properties of the wireless network, or through Group Policy. The "Connect even if the network is not broadcasting" check box determines whether the wireless network broadcasts or does not broadcast its SSID. Once selected, Wireless Auto Configuration sends probe requests to discover if the non-broadcast network is in range.

Configured wireless networks are now openly marked as broadcast or non-broadcast. Windows Server 2008-based wireless clients only send probe requests for wireless networks that are configured for automatic connection and as non-broadcast.

This method allows Windows Server 2008-based wireless clients to detect non-broadcast networks when they are in range. Therefore, even though they are not broadcasting the name of their wireless network, they will appear in the list of available wireless networks when they are in range. The wireless client detects whether the automatically connected, non-broadcast networks are in range based on the probe request responses. Then Wireless Auto Configuration attempts to connect to the wireless network in the preferred networks list order. This is regardless of whether they are configured as broadcast or non-broadcast. By only sending probe requests for automatically connected, non-broadcast networks, Windows Server 2008-based wireless clients reduce the number of situations in which they disclose their wireless network configuration.

You can also configure manually connected, non-broadcast wireless networks. In doing so, you can control exactly when to send probe requests. Manually connected, non-broadcast wireless networks are always displayed in the list of available networks, allowing users to initiate connections as needed.

Despite the improvements in non-broadcast network support in Windows Server 2008, Microsoft recommends against using non-broadcast wireless networks.

Wi-Fi Protected Access (WPA)

Wi-Fi Protected Access (WPA) was designed to provide a much higher level of security for wireless users than existing WEP standards provide. The WPA specification makes allowances both for network-based authentication for corporate networks, and for a special home mode for use in a SOHO or home-user environment. WPA is capable of interoperating with WEP devices, although in cases of interoperability, the default security for the entire wireless infrastructure reverts to the WEP standard. WPA's network-based authentication can make use of existing authentication technologies such as RADIUS servers, so adding the secure technology that WPA represents won't disrupt existing network infrastructures too much. Windows Server 2008 offers full support and configuration for WPA through the Wireless Group Policy settings.

Test Day Tip

Remember to know your hardware. The installed wireless network adapter must be able to support the wireless LAN or wireless security standards that you require. For example, Windows Server supports configuration options for the Wi-Fi Protected Access (WPA) and Wi-Fi Protected Access 2 (WPA2) security standards. However, if the wireless network adapter does not support WPA2, you cannot enable or configure WPA2 security options.

Wi-Fi Protected Access 2 (WPA2)

Windows Server 2008 includes built-in support to configure WPA2 authentication options with both the standard profile (locally configured preferred wireless networks), and the domain profile with Group Policy settings. WPA2 is a product certification available through the Wi-Fi Alliance that certifies wireless equipment as being compatible with the IEEE 802.11i standard. WPA2 in Windows Server 2008 supports both WPA2-Enterprise (IEEE 802.1X authentication) and WPA2-Personal (pre-shared key authentication) modes of operation.

Windows Server 2008 also includes full support for WPA2 for an ad hoc mode wireless network including the *Fast Roaming* settings. Fast roaming is an advanced capability of WPA2 wireless networks that allow wireless clients to more quickly roam from one wireless AP to another by using pre-authentication and pair wise master key (PMK) caching in infrastructure mode. With Windows Server 2008, you can configure this feature using the Wireless Group Policy settings.

Ad Hoc vs. Infrastructure Mode

To set up an ad hoc wireless network, each wireless adapter must be configured for ad hoc mode versus the alternative infrastructure mode. In addition, all wireless adapters on the ad hoc network must use the same SSID and the same channel number.

An ad hoc network tends to feature a small group of devices all in very close proximity to each other.

Performance suffers as the number of devices grows, and a large ad hoc network quickly becomes difficult to manage. Ad hoc networks cannot bridge to wired LANs or to the Internet without installing a special-purpose gateway.

Ad hoc networks make sense when needing to build a small, all-wireless LAN quickly and spend the minimum amount of money on equipment. Ad hoc networks also work well as a temporary fallback mechanism if normally available infrastructure mode gear (APs or routers) stop functioning.

Most installed wireless LANs today utilize infrastructure mode that requires the use of one or more APs. With this configuration, the AP provides an interface to a distribution system (e.g., Ethernet), which enables wireless users to utilize corporate servers and Internet applications.

As an optional feature, however, the 802.11 standard specifies ad-hoc mode, which allows the radio network interface card (NIC) to operate in what the standard refers to as an independent basic service set (IBSS) network configuration. With an IBSS, APs are not required. User devices communicate directly with each other in a peer-to-peer manner.

Ad hoc mode allows users to form a wireless LAN with no assistance or preparation. This allows clients to share documents such as presentation charts and spreadsheets by switching their NICs to ad hoc mode to form a small wireless LAN within their meeting room. Through ad hoc mode, you can easily transfer the file from one laptop to another. With any of these applications, there's no need to install an AP and run cables.

The ad hoc form of communications is especially useful in public-safety and search-and-rescue applications. Medical teams require fast, effective communications when attempting to find victims. They can't afford the time to run cabling and install networking hardware.

Before making the decision to use ad hoc mode, you should consider the following:

- **Cost Efficiency** Without the need to purchase or install an AP, you'll save a considerable amount of money when deploying ad hoc wireless LANs.

- **Rapid Setup Time** Ad hoc mode only requires the installation of radio NICs in the user devices. As a result, the time to set up the wireless LAN is much less than installing an infrastructure wireless LAN.

- **Better Performance Possible** The question of performance with ad hoc mode is very debatable. Performance can be higher with ad hoc mode because there is no need for packets to travel through an AP. This only applies to a small number of users, however. If you have many users, then you will have better performance by using multiple APs to separate users onto non-overlapping channels. This will help to reduce medium access contention and collisions. Also, because of a need for sleeping stations to wake up during each beacon interval, performance can be lower with ad hoc mode due to additional packet transmissions if you implement power management.

- **Limited Network Access** There is no distribution system with ad hoc wireless LANs. Because of this, users have limited effective access to the Internet and other wired network services. Ad hoc is not a good solution for larger enterprise wireless LANs where there's a strong need to access applications and servers on a wired network.

- **Difficult Network Management** Network management can become a nightmare with ad hoc networks, because of the fluidity of the network topology and lack of centralized devices. The lack of an AP makes it difficult for network managers to monitor performance, perform security audits, and manage their network. Effective network management with ad hoc wireless LANs requires network management at the user device level. This requires a significant amount of overhead packet transmission over the wireless LAN. This again disqualifies ad hoc mode away from larger, enterprise wireless LAN applications.

Infrastructure mode requires a wireless AP for wireless networking. To join the WLAN, the AP and all wireless clients must be configured to use the same SSID. The AP is then cabled to the wired network to allow wireless clients access to, for example, Internet connections or printers. Additional APs can be added to the WLAN to increase the reach of the infrastructure and support any number of wireless clients.

Compared to the alternative, ad hoc wireless networks, infrastructure mode networks offer the advantage of scalability, centralized security management, and improved reach.

The disadvantage of infrastructure wireless networks is simply the additional cost to purchase AP hardware.

Wireless Group Policy

New technology makes it easier for mobile workers to connect to hotspots or corporate LANS, by eliminating the need for manual configuration of the network connection. Enterprises can better manage guest access on their network and provide payment plans such as pay-per-use or monthly Internet access to customers, but in order to do so a strict wireless group, policy must be maintained to better control access.

Wireless network settings can be configured locally by users on client computers, or centrally. To enhance the deployment and administration of wireless networks, you need to take advantage of Group Policy. In doing so, you can create, modify, and assign wireless network policies for Active Directory clients and members of the wireless network. When you use Group Policy to define wireless network policies, you can configure wireless network connection settings, enable IEEE 802.1X authentication for wireless network connections, and specify the preferred wireless networks that clients can connect to. By default, there are no Wireless Network (IEEE 802.11) policies.

EXERCISE 3.9

CREATING A NEW POLICY

To create a new policy:

1. Right-click **Wireless Network (IEEE 802.11) Policies** in the console tree of the **Group Policy** snap-in.

2. Click **Create Wireless Network Policy**.

3. The Create Wireless Network Policy Wizard is started, from which you can configure a name and description for the new wireless network policy. You can create only a single wireless network policy for each Group Policy object.

4. To modify the settings of a **Wireless Network Policy**, double-click its name in the details pane.

5. Locate the **General** tab for the **Wireless Network Policy** you wish to update.

6. Click on the **General** tab and configure the following:

   ▪ **Name** Specifies a friendly name for the wireless network policy.

   ▪ **Description** Provides a description for the wireless network policy.

   ▪ **Check for Policy Changes Every…** Specifies a time period in minutes, after which wireless clients that are domain members will check for changes in the wireless network policy.

   ▪ **Networks to Access** Specifies the types of wireless networks with which the wireless client is allowed to create connections to. Select either **Any available network** (AP preferred), **Access point** (infrastructure) networks only, or **Computer-to-computer** (ad hoc) networks only.

7. Select the **Windows to configure wireless network settings for clients** check box if you wish to enable the Wireless Auto Configuration.

8. Click the **Automatically connect to non-preferred networks** check box if you wish to allow automatic connections to wireless networks that are not configured as preferred networks.

9. Click the **Preferred** tab of the **Wireless Network Policy** pane to configure these options:

   ▪ **Networks** Displays the list of preferred wireless networks.

   ▪ **Add/Edit/Remove** Creates, deletes, or modifies the settings of a preferred wireless network.

   ▪ **Move Up/Move Down** Moves preferred wireless network up or down in the Networks list.

10. Click on a **Preferred Wireless Network** to open up advanced configuration options.

Summary of Exam Objectives

The main objectives covered in this chapter deal with the routing and configuration of network access in a windows Server 2008 environment. It includes all of the new features that have been introduced, as well as old technology no longer supported in this build.

This also includes the routing of network topography using static and dynamic routing, and the differences between the two. You should now be familiar with the fundamentals of routing and the protocols used in its practice. This will also include RIP and OSPF protocols. Windows Server 2008 has chosen not to support OSPF for this build.

You should be aware of the need for remote access in the business environment. This includes what features of remote access are supported such as dial up, VPNs, NAT, and RADIUS, and how each of these aspects can be configured and installed. You should also be aware of the newest VPN protocol for Windows Server 2008, SSTP, and how it compares to other VPN protocols. You should now be able to set up a SSL VPN network from start to finish using the RRAS, NPS, and NAP. Additionally, you should be aware of all of the necessary installation methods for these snap-in features.

Lastly you should have a good grasp of wireless access methods such as infrastructure mode and ad hoc mode, and be able to distinguish which of these options is best for the situation you are presented with. This also includes the security methods that are supported for wireless access in Windows Server 2008, such as WEP, WPA, and WPA2. You should be confident in how to distinguish the advantages and disadvantages of each of these methods and also be able to Group Policy for each of them.

Exam Objectives Fast Track

Configuring Routing

- ☑ **Static Routing** Describes a system that does not implement adaptive routing in its configuration. In these systems, routes through a network are defined by set paths referred to as static routes. These types of routes are inserted into the router manually by the system administrator. This is accomplished via the route command, which can be used to manipulate local routing tables.

- ☑ **Distance-vector Routing Protocol** A distance-vector routing protocol requires that a router contact and transmit to its neighbors any topology changes to the network. The frequency of this must be periodic and in most instances when a change is detected. RIP is the most popular example of this type of protocol.

☑ **Link State Protocol** The simplest explanation of link-state routing is that every node (router) is given a map of the topology of the network. This map is in graph form, and shows the connectivity of all the nodes in the network. Then each individual node calculates the next best hop from every node in the network. This information then forms the routing table for each individual node based on its calculations. No other communications occur between nodes. The most popular version of this is the OSPF.

☑ OSPF routing protocol component in Routing and Remote Access is no longer present.

Configuring Remote Access

☑ Remote access is commonly used by many companies today to allow access to a computer or a network from a remote location. Most corporations include people at branch offices, telecommuters, and people who are traveling that will need to be able to gain access to network resources. Even clients using your companies services from home need to gain access to the Internet through an ISP.

☑ Most of the major functions of Network Access and the objectives that you will be required to know for your examine, revolve around the RRAS role.

☑ Remote access policies validate a number of connection settings before authorizing the connection, including the following: Remote access permission, Group membership, Type of connection, Time of day, and Authentication methods.

☑ Small- to medium-sized organizations with private networks to access resources on the Internet or other public network, use NAT for this reasoning. They configure reusable private IPv4 addresses while the computers on the public servers are set up with globally unique IPv4 addresses. The most useful deployment of NAT is in a SOHO or a medium-sized business that uses RRAS.

☑ SSTP is the latest alternative form of VPN tunnel. SSTP is an application-layer protocol. It uses a synchronous communication, which works in unilateral motion between two programs, allowing a constant exchange and comparison of data. It allows for a very efficient usage of the communica-tion resources available to a network. SSTP is based on SSL as opposed to IPSec or PPTP, and thereby uses port 443 for traffic.

☑ VPN uses public wires to join nodes to create a network. This network allows the user to create their own private networks for the transfer of data. There are a large number of security systems at play within the VPN, such as encryption and other security measures. This makes certain that no data is intercepted by unauthorized users.

☑ RADIUS is protocol used for controlling access to network resources by authenticating, authorizing, and accounting for access, referred to as an AAA protocol. RADIUS is the unofficial industry standard for this type of access.

☑ Windows Server 2008 Microsoft has replaced IAS with a new feature called NPS. NPS is the Microsoft implementation of a RADIUS server and proxy in Windows Server 2008, and promises to be even simpler and more secure to use than IAS.

☑ NAP, when used in unison with NPS, creates a "total system health policy enforcement platform." NAP is designed to enhance a corporate VPN. This is accomplished when clients establish a VPN session with a Windows Server 2008 system that is running the RRAS. Once a connection is made, a NPS will validate the remote system and determine the status of its health.

Configuring Wireless Access

☑ The SSID is a 32-character unique identifier attached to the header of packets that are sent over a WLAN. The SSID acts as a password when a mobile device tries to connect to the BSS. The SSID differentiates one WLAN from another. This way all access points and all devices attempting to connect to a specific WLAN must use the same SSID in order to suc-ceed. No device will be permitted to join the BSS, unless it can provide the unique SSID. SSID is not a security measure, because it can very easily be sniffed due to being stored in plain text.

☑ In Windows Server 2008, an additional wireless network configuration setting has been added that can indicate whether a wireless network is broadcast or non-broadcast. This allows Windows Server 2008-based wire-less clients to detect non-broadcast networks when they are in range. Even though they are not broadcasting the name of their wireless network, they will appear in the list of available wireless networks when they are in range.

☑ Windows Server 2003 and Windows XP do not have a command-line interface that allows you to configure the wireless settings that are available from the wireless dialog boxes in the Network Connections folder, or through the Wireless Network (IEEE 802.11) Policies Group Policy settings. Windows Server 2008 has a command-line configuration of wireless settings that can help deployment of wireless networks.

☑ WPA was designed to provide a much higher level of security for wireless users than existing WEP standards provide. The WPA specification makes allowances both for network-based authentication for corporate networks, and for a special home mode for use in a SOHO or home-user environment. WPA is capable of interoperating with WEP devices.

☑ Windows Server 2008 includes full support for WPA2 for an ad hoc mode wireless network, including the Fast Roaming settings. Fast roaming is an advanced capability of WPA2 wireless networks, that allows wireless clients to more quickly roam from one wireless AP to another by using pre-authentication and PMK caching.

☑ On wireless computer networks, ad hoc mode is a method for wireless devices to directly communicate with each other. Operating in ad hoc mode allows all wireless devices within range of each other to discover and communicate in peer-to-peer fashion without involving central access points (including those built in to broadband wireless routers).

☑ Infrastructure mode requires a wireless AP for wireless networking. To join the WLAN, the AP and all wireless clients must be configured to use the same SSID. The AP is then cabled to the wired network to allow wireless clients access to, for example, Internet connections or printers. Additional APs can be added to the WLAN to increase the reach of the infrastructure and support any number of wireless clients.

Exam Objectives
Frequently Asked Questions

Q: What is Static Routing?

A: Static routing describes a system that does not implement adaptive routing in its configuration. In these systems, routes through a network are defined by set paths referred to as static routes.

Q: What changes have been made to Windows Server 2008 in regards to routing?

A: These are the major changes present in Windows Server 2008 in regards to routing:

- BAP is no longer supported by Windows Server 2008.

- X.25 is also no longer supported.

- SLIP, an encapsulation of IP meant for use over serial ports and modems, has also been excluded due to infrequency of use. All SLIP-based connections will automatically be updated to PPP-based connections.

- ATM, which was used to encode data traffic into small fixed cells, has been discarded.

- IP over IEEE 1394 is no longer supported.

- NWLink IPX/SPX/NetBIOS Compatible Transport Protocol has been omitted.

- Services for Macintosh (SFM).

- OSPF routing protocol component in Routing and Remote Access is no longer present.

- Basic Firewall in Routing and Remote Access has been replaced with the new Windows Firewall feature.

- Static IP filter APIs for Routing and Remote Access are no longer viable, and have been replaced with Windows Filtering Platform APIs.

- SPAP, EAP-MD5-CHAP, and MS-CHAP authentication protocols for PPP-based connections are no longer used by Windows Server 2008.

Q: Is IAS still a feature of Windows Server 2008 and if not, what has replaced it?

A: In previous incarnations of Windows Server 2003 IAS snap-in was Microsoft's implementation of a RADIUS server and proxy. It was capable of performing localized connection AAA Protocol for many types of network access, including wireless and VPN connections. For Windows Server 2008, Microsoft has replaced IAS with a new snap in called NPS. NPS is the Microsoft implementation of a RADIUS server and proxy in Windows Server 2008, and promises to be even simpler to use than IAS.

Q: What is an SSL VPN?

A: An SSL VPH is a VPN that uses SSTP as its tunneling protocol. With SSLVPN, static IP addresses are not required, clients are unnecessary in most cases, and since connections are made via a browser over the Internet, the default connection protocol is TCP/IP. This makes connections transparent to the user.

Q: How is Windows Firewall with Advanced Security better than previous versions?

A: This new version of WFAS has a number of advanced components that will help with your security needs.

- **New GUI Interface** MMC is a snap-in that is available to help configure the advanced firewall.

- **Bi-directional Filters** Unlike past versions of Windows Firewall, WFAS filters both outbound traffic and inbound traffic.

- **Better IPSec Compatibility** WFAS rules and IPSec encryption configurations are both integrated into the same singular interface.

- **Enhanced Rules Generation** Using WFAS, you can create firewall rules for Windows Active Directory service accounts and groups. This includes source/destination IP addresses, protocol numbers, source and destination TCP/UDP ports, ICMP, IPv6 traffic, and interface all on the Windows Server.

Q: When does ad hoc mode work best for wireless access?

A: Ad hoc networks work best when building a small, all-wireless LAN quickly, with the lowest cost possible for equipment. Ad hoc networks also work well as a temporary fallback mechanism if normally available infrastructure mode gear (APs or routers) fail to function.

Self Test

1. You are asked by your employer to set up a LAN using Windows 2008 Server RRAS. Which of these types of routing algorithms or protocols cannot be used to organize the signal flow between the devices in the network, according to the supported Windows Server 2008 features?

   A. RIP

   B. RIP2

   C. OSPF

   D. None of the Above

2. You are asked to configure a routing table based on information gathered to optimize the network. You find that a static route with the IP destination 10.40.0.0 and the subnet mask of 255.255.0.0 requires deleting. Which of the following commands would successfully accomplish this routing change?

   A. route delete 10.40.0.0 mask 255.255.0.0

   B. route delete 10.*

   C. route change 10.40.0.0 mask 255.255.0.0 10.20.0.25

   D. route add 10.41.0.0 mask 255.255.0.0 10.20.0.1

3. You are troubleshooting a network system that has applied a number of static routes. After reviewing the information used to make these routes, you determine that an error was made while entering the routes into one of the gateways. Which of the following choices best defines your actions as a result of this error?

   A. No effect because the Static Routes act the same way dynamic ones do, and will auto correct itself.

   B. An immediate change must be made because there is no fault tolerance in regards to static routing.

   C. A system reboot should be performed to clear all persistent routes.

   D. None of the above.

4. You are responsible for upgrading and configuring a large enterprise's LAN network to Windows Server 2008. It will include a high number of physical machines and will need to be scalable for aggressive growth over the next year

as the company expands. Which of the following answers best describes why you should not use a Distance Vector Routing protocol like RIP for this task?

A. Distance Vector Routing Protocols like RIP are not scalable for large networks.

B. Distance Vector Routing Protocols like RIP are not usable for LAN configurations.

C. RIP does not understand VLSM.

D. All of the Above.

5. You are about to set up and configure a VPN for your client's communications server using Windows Server 2008. Before going through the set up and configuration process, which of the following steps need to be taken before you can configure the connection on the machine to ensure the best possible outcome?

A. Ensure a clean install of Windows Server 2008 has been installed.

B. Enter Add Roles Wizard and ensure that the RRAS role has been installed.

C. Both A and B.

D. Configure the SSTP protocols for the VPN.

6. You are working with a server running the RRAS that is configured for the Windows authentication provider. You have administered several policies from RRAS to the server. Which of the following connection settings cannot be validated before authorization occurs by the policies you set up?

A. Advanced conditions such as access server identity, access client phone number, or MAC address.

B. Remote access permission.

C. Whether user account dial-in properties are ignored.

D. None of the above.

7. Your company has begun a migration from Windows Server 2003 to Windows Server 2008 throughout their network. The RADIUS configurations for the old build were configured through IAS for Windows Server 2003. The new build for Windows Server 2008 will be using NPS. Which of the following statements would be true in regards to NPS?

A. The Connection Request Processing node still exists.

B. The Remote Access Logging folder still contains the Local File or SQL Server nodes.

C. The Network policies have replaced Remote Access policies and have been moved to the Policies node.

D. All of the Above.

8. You are the administrator of a network employing the Network Access Protection snap-in in conjunction with NAP. You have configured a set of monitoring policies in NAP for use on the network. Which of the following options will the new NAP monitor policies of Windows Server 2008 be able to accomplish?

A. Recording for compliance of each PC logging in to the system.

B. Isolation of non-compliant users.

C. Restricting access of non-compliant users.

D. None of the above.

9. You are asked to reconfigure a cheap and efficient access solution using the newly installed Windows Server 2008's RRAS role for your company. The access solution must have medium data transfer rates and reliable connection stability. The company's existing method of connection is ISDN and is utilizing the X.25 protocols for transfer. Which of the following changes in regards to Windows Server 2008 would need to be made to the existing system to make these adjustments?

A. The connection type should be downgraded, because the data transfer rate for ISDN is very unstable.

B. The connection type should be improved to Cable or DSL, because ISDN has the slowest data transfer rate.

C. The X.25 protocol needs to be changed because it is not supported by Windows Server 2008.

D. None of the above.

10. You are setting up a communications server for your small- to medium-sized organization with private networks to handle their need to access resources on the Internet and other public networks. You have installed Windows Server 2008 and are using IPv4 currently. You need more globally unique (public) IPv4 addresses to accommodate the need to access to the Internet. Which of the following solutions is the most simple and cost effective?

A. Plan a conversion of the existing setup to accommodate IPv6, because it is supported by Windows Server 2008.

B. Enable the NAT technology on the computers of the corporate network.

C. Deploy a Proxy server.

D. None of the Above.

Self Test Quick Answer Key

1. **C**

2. **A**

3. **A**

4. **A**

5. **C**

6. **D**

7. **C**

8. **A**

9. **C**

10. **B**

## Chapter 4

MCTS/MCITP Exam 642

Configuring File and Print Services

Exam objectives in this chapter:

- Configuring a File Server
- Configuring Distributed File System (DFS)
- Configuring Shadow Copy Services
- Configuring Backup and Restore
- Managing Disk Quotas
- Configuring and Monitoring Print Services

Exam objectives review:

- ☑ Summary of Exam Objectives
- ☑ Exam Objectives Fast Track
- ☑ Exam Objectives Frequently Asked Questions
- ☑ Self Test
- ☑ Self Test Quick Answer Key

Introduction

The entire point of creating a computer network is to allow users to share the various resources that are located on the network. File shares allow users to collaborate on documents, and printer shares keep you from having to purchase every employee his or her own individual printer. As important as it is to be able to share files and printers, though, it is equally important to be able to put certain restrictions in place to prevent the files or printers from being used in an unauthorized manner. After all, your file servers likely contain sensitive information, and you need to protect that information from accidental disclosure.

Security is important for printers as well. Although there is generally no harm in allowing an employee to print a document, you may need to limit some printers for use by only specific employees. For example, if your organization has a printer that's dedicated to the task of printing checks, you probably would not want casual users to have access to that printer. You may also want to restrict access to special-purpose printers that use expensive supplies. This chapter will show you how to configure Windows Server 2008 to act as a file or print server. It will also discuss some of the various security implications of doing so.

Configuring a File Server

Windows Server 2008 provides many powerful features for centralized control, administration, security, and sharing of resources. To share and secure files that multiple users on the network will access, configure your server by adding the File Services role in Server Manager. In this section, we will look at how to share folders, enable Offline Files for laptops and remote users, secure files and control user access, and encrypt sensitive or confidential files.

Windows Server 2008 introduces many new ways to perform administrative tasks using the command line instead of the GUI. At first, many network administrators think there is no good reason to use the command line and that Microsoft is reminiscing in the old DOS days. Well, you might be pleasantly surprised to learn that there are many good reasons to use the command line to perform administrative tasks! Command-line tools allow an administrator to script, automate, and schedule tasks. Let's say, for example, that you need to configure Windows Server

2008 to run a full system backup. "No problem," you might be thinking, "I can use the GUI to configure and run a full backup." Now imagine having to do this on 12 different servers—this is where the power of using the command line and writing a small script really comes in handy. You may also be tested on the command lines in your exam. Look for *Exam Warnings* throughout this chapter to learn the command-line equivalent of the administrative tasks we discuss.

TEST DAY TIP

To help you clear and ready your mind for optimal concentration, get a good full night's sleep the night before and eat a balanced breakfast the morning of your test.

File Share Publishing

To configure a server for file sharing, you must add the **File Services** role in **Server Manager**. To open Server Manager, navigate to **Start Menu | Server Manager**. Server Manager is a preconfigured console designed to handle the most common administrative tasks. **Server Manager** allows you to:

- Add, remove, configure, and manage roles
- Manage users and groups
- Add/remove features
- View the event logs
- Monitor server performance
- And much more
- For more on adding roles, see Exercise 4.1.

Windows Server 2008 supports two file-sharing models: Standard (in-place) File Sharing and Public Folder Sharing. Table 4.1 explains the differences between these two models.

Table 4.1 Comparison of Sharing Models

Sharing Model	Explanation
Standard (in-place) File Sharing	Allows you to share a folder and all of its contents (files and sub folders) with users on the network. Standard File Sharing does not require you to move the files and folders to share them.
Public Folder Sharing	Allows you to use a common folder (%SystemDrive%\Users\Public) to share files and folders with other local users on the server and option ally network users as well. Requires you to place any files and folders you want to share out in the Public folder.

Sharing folders on your server is like opening a door (share) directly to a room (folder) to allow others to enter (network users to access the folder). In this analogy, a room may contain other rooms that are accessible once you have walked through the door just as a folder that is shared on the network can contain multiple subfolders that are accessible once you have connected to the file share. In Exercise 4.2, we will add the **File Services** role to a Windows 2008 Server.

EXERCISE 4.1

ADDING THE FILE SERVICES ROLE IN SERVER MANAGER

To enable file sharing and install the management tools in Windows Server 2008 follow these steps:

1. Launch the **Server Manager** console by navigating to **Start Menu | Server Manager**.

2. In the **Roles Summary** section of **Server Manager**, you will be presented with a list of the roles that are currently installed on your server, as seen in Figure 4.1. Click on the **Add Roles** hyperlink.

Figure 4.1 Roles Summary Section in the Server Manager Console

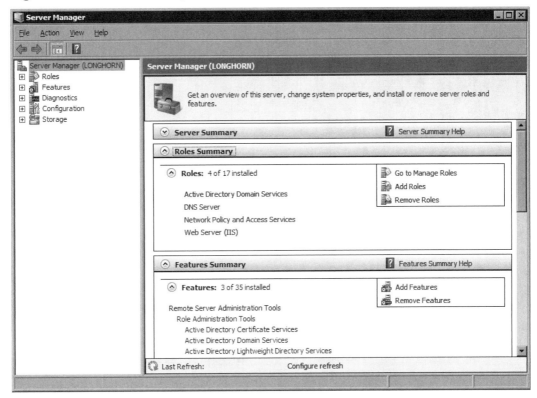

3. The **Add Roles Wizard** will open. Click the **Next** button if you are presented with a **Before You Begin** page.

4. On the **Select Server Roles** page shown in Figure 4.2, put a **checkmark** in the box next to **File Services**.

Figure 4.2 List of Available Roles on the Select Server Roles Page in the Add Roles Wizard

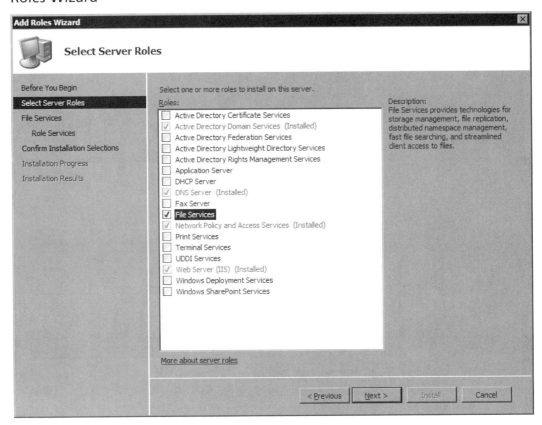

5. You will be presented with an **Introduction to File Services**; click the **Next** button.

6. On the **Select Role Services** page, verify that **File Server** is checked and click the **Next** button. You can add more Role Services at any time, so it is not necessary to select them at this time.

7. A summary of the options selected for installation will appear. Click on the **Install** button to start the installation process.

Additional Role Services

When you install the **File Services** role, Windows Server 2008 allows you to install a subset of roles called **Role Services**. Table 4.2 explains the **Role Services** available for the **File Services** role.

Table 4.2 Explanation of Role Services for the File Services Role

Role Service	Explanation
File Server	Enables the Server Message Block (SMB) protocol and the ability to share folders with other users on the network
Distributed File System	Enables the Distributed File System (DFS) and installs DFS management tools
DFS Namespace	Allows an administrator to share folders from multiple servers into one central share name (namespace)
DFS Replication	Allows an administrator to replicate files and folders among multiple servers
File Server Resource Manager	Installs the File Server Resource Manager, a useful tool for configuring and managing file screening and quotas, and for generating storage reports
Services for Network File System	Installs Services for the Network File System (NFS). The NFS protocol allows an administrator to share out folders to UNIX clients.
Windows Search Service	The new indexing service from Microsoft that allows clients to rapidly search for files on the target server. Windows Search Service works by creating an index of the most common files and other data types (such as e-mail, contacts, calendar appointments, documents, pictures, and multimedia) on the target server. The client-side search for Windows Search Service is built into Windows Vista. You can add it onto Windows Server 2003 and Windows XP by downloading and installing Windows Desktop Search from www.microsoft.com/windows/products/winfamily/desktopsearch/getitnow.mspx.

Continued

Table 4.2 Continued. Explanation of Role Services for the File Services Role

Role Service	Explanation
Windows Server 2003 File Services	Installs optional services for backward compatibility with Windows 2003 servers in a mixed environment
File Replication Service	Installs the File Replication Service (FRS). FRS is the older, less efficient service for replicating files and folders among multiple servers. This service is included for backward compatibility with Server 2003 R1. DFS replication is far more efficient (it's faster and uses less band width) than FRS. However, DFS replication is available only on Server 2003 R2, Windows Server 2008, and later.
Indexing Service	Installs the legacy (older) Microsoft Indexing Service on the target server. This service has been replaced by the Windows Search Service and it is recom mended that you install the Windows Search Service instead, unless you have a customized or non-Microsoft applica tion that requires the legacy Indexing Service. The Indexing Service is slower and does not have as many features as the new Windows Search Service. You cannot install both the Indexing Service and Windows Search Service on the same server.

To add role services, navigate to **Start Menu | Server Manager | Roles | File Services** and click on the **Add Role Services** hyperlink, as shown in Figure 4.3.

Figure 4.3 Role Services Configuration for the File Services Role

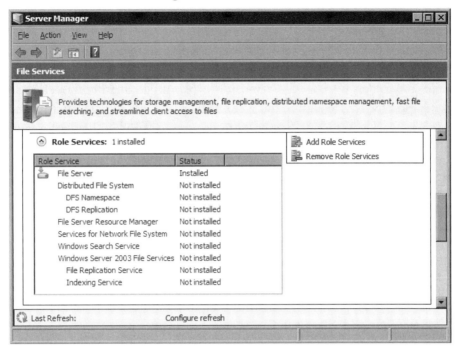

File Screening

New to Windows Server 2008 is the ability to prevent users from copying and saving specified file types to the server. For example, you may notice that your server's backups are starting to run out of space. Upon further inspection, you notice that one of your users is storing 20 GB of funny videos and TV shows in a shared folder on the server. As this is not important company data, it should not be taking up precious space on the server and consuming backup drive space. With Windows Server 2008 File Screening, you can actually configure each shared folder to block specified file types such as Music and Videos.

Figure 4.4 shows the error message a user will get if he or she attempts to copy a restricted file (in this case the file is called Music.mp3) to a share that has **File Screening** enabled and is blocking music files.

Figure 4.4 Error When Attempting to Copy a Restricted File

We will be given the option to configure File Screening in Exercise 4.2.

Sharing a Folder

Windows sharing uses the SMB protocol, which is also known as Common Internet File System (CIFS); Microsoft's open standard based on SMB. The preferred method for sharing files and folders is to use the Standard (in-place) File Sharing model. As a means to simply sharing for novice administrators or to be run in conjunction with Standard (in-place) File Sharing, Windows Server 2008 also supports Public Folder Sharing.

TEST DAY TIP

Read the questions thoroughly and do not select an answer until you have read all possible choices. Microsoft is known to make the certification exams tricky and if you miss an "and, not, or, etc." it can change the entire meaning of the question.

To enable Public Folder sharing (optional), navigate to **Start Menu | Control Panel | Network and Sharing Center** and turn on **Public folder sharing**. Select the first option (see Figure 4.5) if you would like to share the public folder to network users using read-only access. Or you can select the second option to allow network users to modify and write to the public folder as well. Be sure to click the **Apply** button to enable your changes.

Figure 4.5 Public Folder Sharing Options in the Network and Sharing Center

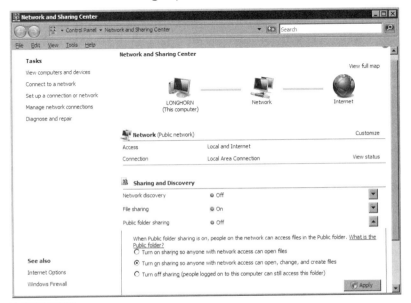

Once **Public Folder Sharing** is turned on, you can easily share files and folders by opening **Windows Explorer** and moving files and folders via drag and drop to the **Public** folder shown in the left pane folder list. In Figure 4.6, the first Public folder in the left pane folder list is the local Public folder. Figure 4.6 also shows that same Public folder and its contents as viewed through the network.

Figure 4.6 Accessing the Public Folder Share Using Windows Explorer

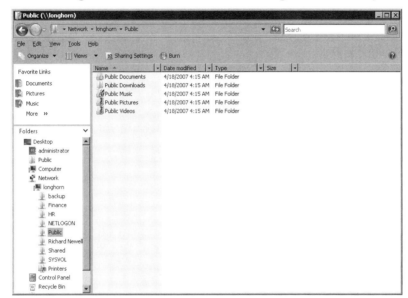

We will walk through the steps to configure shared folders and permissions using the Standard (in-place) File Sharing method in Exercise 4.2 in this chapter, but first we will briefly discuss the concepts of Share Permissions, NTFS permissions, and Offline Files.

Share Permissions

As you remember from earlier, sharing a folder is like opening a door to network users directly into that folder. Share Permissions are like posting a security guard at that door (share). As people (network users) attempt to enter the room, the security guard checks his list (Share Permissions) to see who is allowed in and who is not. If a user is allowed in with Full Control, the security guard lets him in and lets him do whatever he wants. If a user is allowed in with Read, the security guard lets him in but watches him as he is in the room to make sure he "looks but doesn't touch." Table 4.3 shows the available Share Permissions and their function.

Table 4.3 Overview of Share Permissions

Share Permission	Explanation
Full Control	The highest level of access to the folder. Allows users to view, modify, add, and delete files and folders, plus modify permissions.
Change	Allows users to view, modify, add, and delete files
Read	Allows users to view files and list folder contents

Windows Server 2008 and previous versions have both Share and NTFS permissions to support sharing on non-NTFS volumes such as FAT, or File Allocation Table, where only Share Permissions are available to control network access.

Test Day Tip

For the optimal combination of security and simplicity, it is a best practice to remove the Everyone group from the Share Permissions and **Allow** the Authenticated Users group Full Control. Then set your permissions and restrict access using NTFS instead of Share Permissions. If a user or their group is not granted NTFS permissions they will be blocked from accessing the share.

Exercise caution when using the **Deny** permission, as it will override and block any user or group even if they have the **Allow** permission elsewhere.

NTFS Permissions

Using NTFS permissions allows administrators a lot more control over access than Share Permissions. NTFS permissions also allow you to control access to files as well as folders whereas Share Permissions can only be set on the first-level folder (the folder being shared out).

Configuring & Implementing...

Locking Down Files from Local Access

In addition to securing files and folders accessed over the network, NTFS permissions also secure files and folders when users access them locally by logging directly into the workstation or server where the data resides. It is a best practice to use NTFS on all workstations that support it (Windows NT, 2000, XP, Vista, or Windows Server).

Using the room and door analogy (you can tell that we really like this analogy), NTFS permissions are like putting a padlock and chain on the individual items in the room (files and folders), desks, filing cabinets, chairs, and so on (Word documents, Excel spreadsheets, PowerPoint presentations, etc.). Only the people you gave a key to can unlock those items, just as with NTFS permissions only the users you granted permissions to can access the files and folders. Keep in mind that users are also restricted by the Share Permissions (security guard at the door) for that folder when connecting through the network. For example, if the Share Permissions on a folder were set to **Everyone – Read**, users connecting through the network would be restricted to read-only access even if they had Full Control in NTFS (i.e., the security guard at the door is restricting them to "look but don't touch" even though they have a key).

NTFS permissions also give an administrator very granular control over how users can access files and folders. You can control all of the permissions listed in Table 4.4.

Table 4.4 Overview of NTFS Permissions

NTFS Permission	Explanation
Full Control	Allows the same permissions as Modify, plus the ability to take ownership, change NTFS permissions, and delete files and folders
Modify	Allows the same permissions as both Read & Execute and Write permissions. Also gives the user the ability to delete the folder.
Read & Execute	Allows users to view all files, folders, and subfolders as well as open or run the files or programs
List Folder Contents	Allows users to view the contents of the folder
Read	Allows users to view and open the files in a folder and view the properties of the files
Write	Same as Read permission; plus the user can create and edit files and subfolders
Special Permissions	Allow you to set the advanced and extremely granular permissions that make up the permissions above, such as "Traverse folder / execute file" and "Read extended attributes". For more information, see the Windows Server 2008 help topic titled "Permission Entry Dialog Box".

To modify or view NTFS permissions, right-click the file or folder you want to set permissions on and click on **Properties**, then navigate to the **Security** tab.

EXAM WARNING

You may be required to know command-line operations for administrative tasks. To modify NTFS permissions (also called access control lists or ACLs) using the command line, use the *ICACLS* command. For more information, type in **ICACLS /?** at the Windows command prompt.

By default, permissions assigned to a folder using NTFS are automatically passed down to (or inherited by) subfolders and files (also known as *descendants*) within that parent folder. This concept is called *inheritance*. To disable inheritance for a specific folder or file, see Step 6 in Exercise 4.2.

Offline Files

The Offline Files feature in Windows gives users the ability to access the files from a network share, or shared folder on a network location, even when they are off the network. This is extremely useful when traveling with a laptop or connecting to a folder over a virtual private network (VPN) or WAN link. Offline Files works by caching (or making a local copy of) the files on a shared location (i.e., a server). If the network resource is unavailable, the user can still open and work on these files. When the shared resource is once again available, the user's changes are synchronized with the network share.

Offline Files support is available in Microsoft's client operating systems such as Windows XP and Windows Vista.

Now that we have discussed Share Permissions, NTFS permissions, and Offline Files, it is time to put File Sharing into action. Exercise 4.2 will lead you through the two primary methods for setting up Standard (in-place) File Sharing.

EXERCISE 4.2

CONFIGURING SHARED FOLDERS AND PERMISSIONS

Using Share and Storage Management:

1. Navigate to **Start Menu | Server Manager | Roles | File Services** and click on the **Share and Storage Management** node.

2. Share and Storage Management gives you an overview of folders that are currently being shared out on the network as well as the local paths to the shared folders, as seen in Figure 4.7.

Figure 4.7 Share and Storage Management

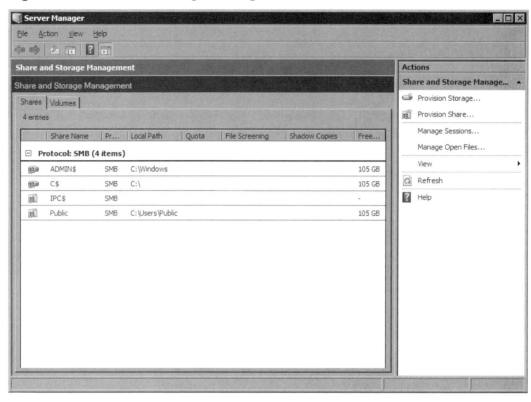

3. Click on the **Provision Share** hyperlink to launch the **Provision a Shared Folder Wizard**.

4. On the **Shared Folder Location** page click the **Browse** button and select the folder you would like to share. You can use the **Make New Folder** button if you need to create a new folder to share. Click **OK** when you have selected a folder and then click **Next**.

5. On the **NTFS permissions** page, select the **Yes, change NTFS permissions** option and click **Edit Permissions** to control which users and groups will have access to this folder.

6. Click the **Advanced** button and uncheck the **Include inheritable permissions from the object's parent** checkbox, as shown in Figure 4.8. This will allow us to remove users and groups that are currently allowed access via inheritance from a parent folder. When prompted, choose to **Copy** the permission entries that were previously applied from the parent.

Figure 4.8 Advanced Security Settings for the HR Share

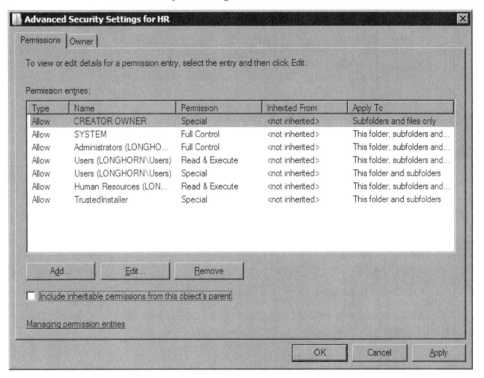

7. Click **OK** to get back to the Permissions screen and remove all users and groups except Administrators and/or Domain Admins.

8. Click the **Add** button to add the users or groups that will require access to this shared folder. In this example, we add the Human Resources group and grant them Modify access, as shown in Figure 4.9.

Figure 4.9 NTFS Permissions for the HR Share

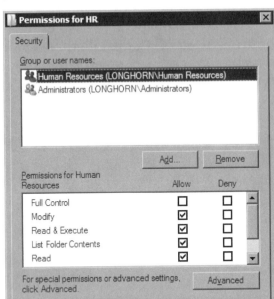

9. Click **OK** to return to the Provision a Shared Folder Wizard and then click **Next**.

10. On the **Share Protocols** page, choose **SMB** and verify the share name that you would like; then click **Next**.

11. The **SMB Settings** page allows you to configure options for Offline Files, Access-based enumeration, and connection limit. Click the **Next** button to continue.

12. On the **SMB Permissions** page, select the **Users and groups have custom share permissions** option and click the **Permissions** button. Set permissions using the best practice of **Authenticated Users – Full Control** and click **OK**, then **Next**.

13. The **Quota Policy** page allows you to configure a limit to the amount of disk space a user can consume. We will discuss quotas in more depth later in this chapter. Click the **Next** button to continue.

14. The **File Screen Policy** page allows us to configure file screening using templates from the File Server Resource Manager. Click **Next** to continue.

15. The **DFS Namespace Publishing** page allows us to add this share under a DFS namespace. We will discuss DFS in more depth later in this chapter. Click the **Next** button to continue.

16. Next click the **Create** button and then **Close**. Congratulations, you have just shared a folder in Windows Server 2008!

Alternatively, you can use Windows Explorer to share a folder using the following steps:

1. Launch Windows Explorer by navigating to **Start Menu | All Programs | Accessories | Windows Explorer**.

2. Using the **Folders** list in the left pane, locate the folder you would like to share (i.e., **Computer | Local Disk (C:) | Shares | Finance**).

3. Right-click on the target folder and select **Properties**.

4. Configure the NTFS permissions on the **Security** tab, as shown in Figure 4.10.

Figure 4.10 NTFS Permissions for a Folder

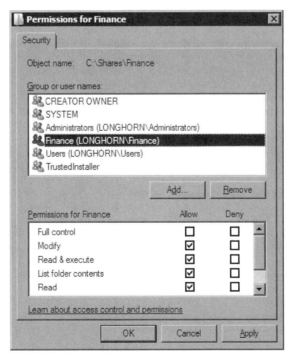

5. Use the **Sharing** tab and click on the **Advanced Sharing** button to configure share name (see Figure 4.11) and Share Permissions (see Figure 4.12).

Figure 4.11 Advanced Sharing

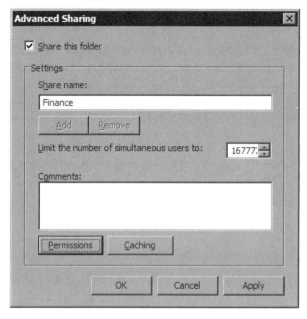

Figure 4.12 Share Permissions

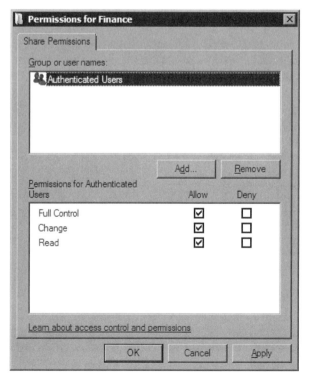

EXAM WARNING

You may be required to know command-line operations for administrative tasks. To share folders using the command line, use the *NET SHARE* command. For more information, type in **NET SHARE /?** at the Windows command prompt.

Encrypting File System (EFS)

Now we will look at securing your files using the built-in encryption feature found in Windows Server 2008. Encrypting File System (EFS) is a feature that scrambles the data in your file to the point that it is not usable or viewable by an outside party. When you open an encrypted file Windows will automatically decrypt the data using a transparent process so that you can work with it. When you are finished working with the file Windows will automatically re-encrypt it for you using a transparent process. The simplicity of checking a box makes EFS very easy for Windows users to use.

Head of the Class...

Why Encrypt Files?

If you have ever wondered why you would want to encrypt your files, here is a true story. Of course, the names have been changed to protect the innocent.

My friend Gwendolyn was the coordinator of a charity golf tournament. The day of the big event, she arrived early and set down her laptop in a seemingly secure downstairs room in the clubhouse. In fact, this room was so secure (or appeared to be), it even had staff members from the golf course guarding the entrance. Gwendolyn immediately started running around coordinating the event and ensuring that every detail of this golf tournament would run smoothly. The weather was great and the tournament could not have gone better, except for one detail—Gwendolyn's laptop had been stolen. To her surprise, that sinking feeling in her stomach was not really about having lost a laptop worth

Continued

$1,500; no, she had lost much more. That sinking feeling was about her data—in the hands of a thief. PowerPoint presentations, Word documents, Excel spreadsheets that she had worked on for months, even years, were on that laptop. Sensitive and confidential data from her company, credit card numbers, passwords, bank account information, e-mails—all in the hands of a thief. We searched for that laptop for more than an hour, asking everyone we had seen enter the room and interrogating the staff. The laptop was long gone, and Gwendolyn never did get it back.

The good news is that Gwendolyn backed up her data frequently. Nearly all of it was recovered. The bad news is that none of her files was encrypted. Was the thief a kid who saw a laptop sitting out, and said to himself, "Hey look, a free laptop?" Or was it someone with plans to grab Gwendolyn's data? After all, I have even heard of thieves actually buying used hard drives on eBay to see what kind of confidential data they can pull off the drives—this could easily lead to identity theft.

It is a good practice to encrypt any important or private files.

When you are browsing in Windows Explorer, the names of encrypted files and folders are displayed in green instead of black (compressed files and folders are in blue). You can only use Microsoft's EFS on Windows NTFS volumes. If you copy an encrypted file to a non-NTFS volume, Windows will copy the file in decrypted form. Marking a folder for encryption does not actually encrypt the folder itself; instead, it encrypts every file within the folder.

Working with EFS

EFS encrypts files using a public/private key that is automatically generated and stored in the user's profile. If a user logs into multiple computers, the EFS Private Keys should be copied to each computer using a certificate backup and restore procedure to ensure that the user can access encrypted data transferred from one computer to another. An alternative option to using the same EFS Private Key on multiple computers is to use a roaming profile for that user. When using a roaming profile, the EFS Private Key is stored on the server that contains the profile as opposed to the workstation a user logs into. For more information on backing up EFS Private Keys and EFS best practices, look at Microsoft knowledgebase article 223316, "Best practices for the Encrypting File System," at http://support.microsoft.com/kb/223316/EN-US/.

You may be required to know command-line operations for administrative tasks. To configure and manage EFS using the command line, use the *CIPHER* command-line utility. For more information, type **CIPHER /?** at the Windows command prompt.

If a user is unable to open an encrypted file or his account is deleted, the file can be decrypted by a designated recovery agent. In an Active Directory domain environment, the default recovery agent is the Administrator account for the domain. In Exercise 4.3, we will enable encryption on a file or folder in Windows Server 2008.

EXERCISE 4.3

ENCRYPTING FILES AND FOLDERS USING EFS

1. Right-click on the target file or folder and choose **Properties**.
2. On the **General** tab, click the **Advanced** button.
3. In the **Advanced Attributes** dialog, click on the checkbox next to **Encrypt contents to secure data**, as shown in Figure 4.13.

Figure 4.13 Encrypting a File or Folder Using Advanced Attributes

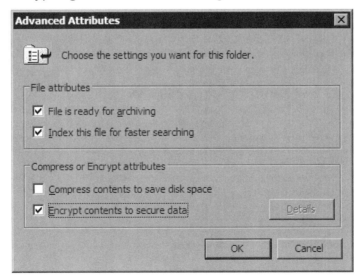

EXAM WARNING

In Windows Server 2008, you can either compress or encrypt a file, but not both. If you try to compress an encrypted file, Windows will decrypt the file and compress it. If you try to encrypt a compressed file, Windows will decompress the file and encrypt it.

New & Noteworthy...

How to Hack Right Past Your Password

Your password does not protect you *nearly* as much as you would think. To gain access to all of your unencrypted files, hackers can take the hard drive out of your computer or laptop and install it into a computer over which they have administrative rights. This can also be used for good—if Windows fries and you need to recover files or one of your users has important data on her home computer (not a member of the domain) and forgot her password.

A handy device that all IT people should have is a USB to IDE/SATA cable. This device allows you to turn *any* IDE, SATA, or laptop hard drive into an external USB2.0 device. That means without shutting down your computer or even rebooting, you can plug in a hard drive from a failed computer and access all the files (except, of course, encrypted files, which require that you have the certificate or are a recovery agent). My USB to IDE/SATA cable is one of the best IT purchases I have ever made.

Making a backup of your encryption keys is critical to prevent against accidental loss. In environments where you do not have access to log in as a recovery agent or there are no recovery agents configured, you will be unable to decrypt your data if something happens to your keys. These environments include:

- Peer-to-peer networks
- Laptops that are not joined to the Active Directory domain
- Home offices

Events and situations that can lock you out of your EFS-encrypted files include the following:

- Your account password is reset.

- You attempt to access your encrypted files from a different computer than the one you used to encrypt the files.

- You reformat and reinstall Windows, and then try to access the encrypted files on a backup drive or network share.

To protect yourself from being locked out of your encrypted files, you can use the simple procedure in Exercise 4.4 to back up your keys to a secure location.

EXERCISE 4.4

BACKING UP YOUR EFS CERTIFICATE TO PROTECT AGAINST ACCIDENTAL LOSS

1. Start Internet Explorer.

2. From the **Tools** menu, choose **Internet Options**.

3. On the **Content** tab, click the **Certificates** button.

4. On the **Personal** tab, select each certificate listed (if more than one appears) until you find the one that displays **Encrypting File System** in the **Certificate intended purposes** section. Windows automatically creates this certificate the first time you encrypt a file using this computer.

5. Select the proper certificate for Encrypting File System and click on the **Export** button, as shown in Figure 4.14.

Figure 4.14 Backing Up Your EFS Certificate

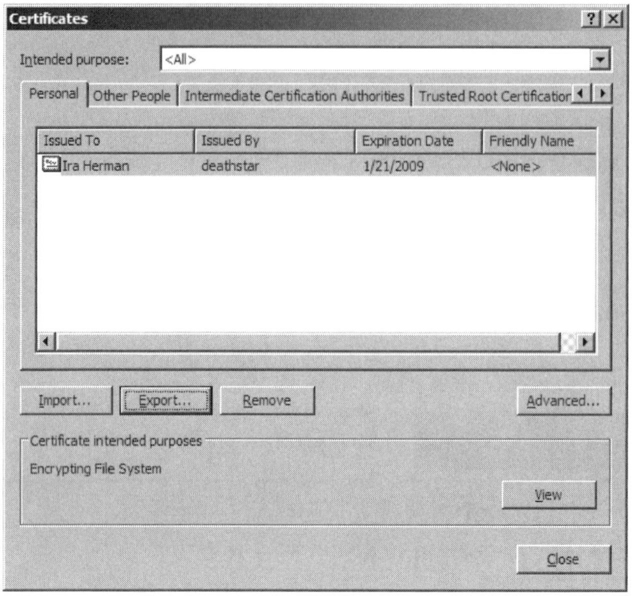

6. The **Certificate Export Wizard** will open. Click the **Next** button to continue.

7. Choose **Yes, export the private key** and click **Next**.

8. Verify that **Enable strong protection** is checked and click **Next**.

9. Type in a password to protect the exported EFS key and click **Next**.

10. Specify the location to save the key. It is a best practice not to store this on your hard drive, as it will be lost in the event of a drive failure or format. Make sure you store your key backup on an external drive, disk/disc, or server that will be kept in a secure location.

An exciting new feature in Windows Server 2008 is BitLocker Drive Encryption. BitLocker provides full-volume encryption on computers that have Trusted Platform Module (TPM) hardware. This feature is excellent for ensuring server data security in the event of a physical drive or server theft.

Configuring & Implementing...

Third-Party Encryption

Although Windows Server 2008 offers an excellent set of encryption features, you can use third-party encryption software to avoid some of the limitations and accomplish the following:

- Encrypt files on non-NTFS formats such as FAT
- Encrypt data on CDs or DVDs
- Use a passphrase instead of a key to decrypt your data

One of my favorites for this is TrueCrypt, which is freely available at www.truecrypt.org.

Configuring Distributed File System (DFS)

If you have more than one server on your network, you can use Microsoft's incredibly handy Distributed File System (DFS) features to extend the functionality of file sharing and replication. In Windows Server 2008, DFS can allow users to access shared network folders without having to remember on which server they reside. You can also configure DFS replication to copy and synchronize the files and folders on multiple servers. This is a very useful feature if your company has multiple locations, branch offices, or even just multiple servers in the same location. We will explore these features in more depth by looking at DFS namespaces, configuration and application, creating and configuring targets, and DFS replication.

DFS Namespaces

A DFS namespace is a virtual shared folder that contains shared folders from multiple servers. This allows users to access shared folders using the Universal Naming Convention (UNC) path \\[Domain]\[Namespace] instead of remembering the name of each server to which to connect. This also allows multiple servers to host a copy of the same shared folder. To create a DFS namespace, first add the **File Services** role in

Server Manager and then add the Distributed File System Role Services, as shown in Figure 4.15.

Figure 4.15 Adding DFS Role Services

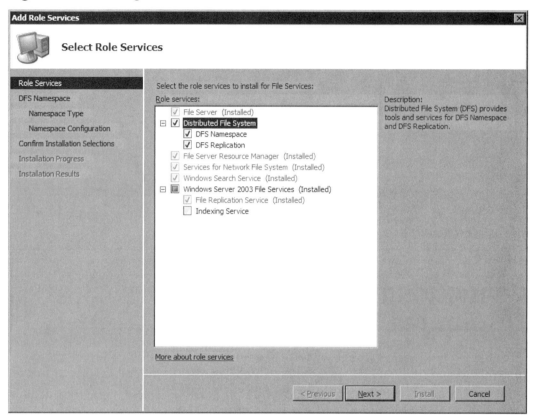

DFS Configuration and Application

You can configure DFS using the **Namespaces** and **Replication** tools located under **DFS Management** in Server Manager. When adding a DFS namespace, you will be asked whether you would like to use a domain-based namespace or stand-alone namespace. A domain-based namespace can be replicated to multiple servers for DFS availability if the host server fails. Domain-based namespaces are limited to 5,000 DFS folders. Stand-alone namespaces can support up to 50,000 DFS folders; however, the namespace is not replicated to other servers unless you are using a failover cluster and have configured replication on the cluster.

In Exercise 4.5, we will walk through the steps required to create a DFS namespace.

EXERCISE 4.5

CONFIGURING A DFS NAMESPACE

In this exercise, we will create a DFS namespace. Be sure to add the DFS Role Services to the File Services role on your server before continuing.

1. In Server Manager, navigate to **Roles | File Services | DFS Management | Namespaces**.

2. Click on the **New Namespace** hyperlink to launch the **New Namespace Wizard**.

3. When asked for the server that will host the namespace, type in the name of your server and click **Next**.

4. On the **Namespace Name and Settings** page, type in the name you would like to call the namespace. The name you type in will appear as a virtual shared folder within which all the DFS shares (shared folders under one virtual namespace that really exist on multiple servers) are shown. In Figure 4.16, we use the name **Shared**. You can also create a different DFS namespace for each business unit within your organization (e.g., HR, Finance, IT, etc.).

Figure 4.16 Namespace Name and Settings in New Namespace Wizard

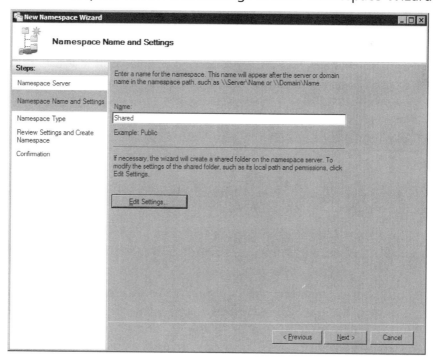

5. Be sure to click the **Edit Settings** button and set the appropriate **Share Permissions**, then click **Next**.

6. On the **Namespace Type** page, it is preferable to select *Domain-based namespace*. This will allow users to type in \\[*domain*]\ [*namespace*] (e.g., \\2k8.local\Shared) instead of remembering a specific server name. Click **Next** to continue, then **Create** to complete the wizard.

7. Now users can browse to \\[*domain*] and see the namespace you just created as a virtual shared folder. Although it is currently empty, in the next exercise we will add a shared folder to the \\[*domain*]\Shared namespace.

Creating and Configuring Targets

A DFS target is simply a shared folder that is located on one or more servers. You can increase the availability of a shared folder by hosting it on multiple servers (i.e., specifying multiple targets for the same shared folder) and replicating the data between servers using DFS replication. Placing identical shares on multiple DFS servers is also a good idea from a server maintenance perspective. It allows you to take a file server down for maintenance without the users even knowing that the server was offline.

Earlier in this chapter, we used the Share and Storage Management tool to create a shared folder, and during this process we were given the option to configure DFS for that share as well. In Exercise 4.6, we take a look at using the DFS Management | Namespaces tool to add a shared folder to our namespace.

EXERCISE 4.6

Adding Shared Folders to a DFS Namespace

In this exercise, we will add a shared folder to the \\[*domain*]\Shared DFS namespace.

1. In Server Manager, navigate to **Roles | File Services | DFS Management | Namespaces** and select the namespace we created in the previous exercise.

2. Click on the **New Folder** hyperlink to launch the **New Folder** dialog. Type in the name of the shared folder and click on the **Add** button to point this folder to one or more locations of this shared folder (targets) on one or more servers. In Figure 4.17,

we created the **Finance** folder and pointed it to a shared folder that is replicated on two different servers.

Figure 4.17 Selecting DFS Targets in the New Folder Dialog

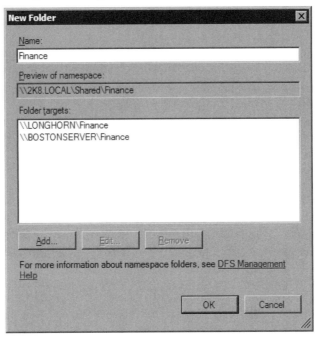

3. Now users can connect to \\[*domain*]\[*namespace*] (e.g., \\2k8.local\ Shared) and access the Finance share through DFS. If one of the targets (locations for a copy of the share) is offline, DFS will automatically point the user to one of the alternative locations.

EXAM WARNING

You may be required to know command-line operations for administrative tasks. To configure and manage DFS using the command line, use the *DFSCMD* and *DFSUTIL* command-line utilities. For more information, type **DFSCMD /?** and **DFSUTIL /?** at the Windows command prompt.

DFS Replication

DFS replication is one of the best features for creating fault tolerance in case one of your servers or sites goes offline. You can use DFS replication to:

- Replicate/synchronize a folder or folders among multiple servers in a single location

- Replicate/synchronize a folder or folders with a remote location to create an off-site backup for business continuity in case a disaster such as fire, flood, hurricane, or theft interferes with business or destroys data in your office

- Create a Branch Office Box (BOB) at branch office locations to speed up local file access (also known as *caching*) with a share that replicates with the head office

DFS replication is different from FRS in versions of Windows Server prior to 2003 R2. The primary difference is a major improvement in the efficiency of replication by copying only the "differences" or changes to a file instead of the FRS method of copying *entire files*, even if only a small portion has been changed. DFS replication makes this possible by using a technology called Remote Differential Compression (RDC). Windows Server 2008 also supports FRS for backward compatibility in a mixed environment where it is necessary to replicate with Windows Server 2000 or 2003 R1 servers.

To create a new DFS Replication group, use the **New Replication Group** hyperlink in **Server Manager | Roles | Files Services | DFS Management | Replication**.

Configuring & Implementing...

DFS Replication and DFS Namespace
DFS does not require you to set up a DFS namespace to use DFS replication. You can use DFS replication and DFS namespaces independently of each other.

Configuring Shadow Copy Services

One of the greatest innovations introduced in Windows Server 2003 has now been improved in Server 2008 and is even included with Windows Vista. When files are shared on a network, all kinds of whacky things are bound to happen. A user may accidentally delete someone else's file. A user may accidentally delete her own file. A user might change a few paragraphs in her Word document only to realize she was in "insert" mode and overwrote another page. The list goes on and on, but when these things happen (and they *do* happen), a user will ask her network administrator to restore the file from backup. This can be very time-consuming, and if the user waits too long before realizing she needs a file restored, it may be gone for good. Enter the magic of Shadow Copies.

Test Day Tip

Expect more than multiple choice questions. Microsoft has Hot area questions, Active screen questions, Drag-and-drop questions, Build list and reorder questions, Create a tree questions, Testlet exam format, and simulation questions. To try out these question formats and get used to using them, visit www.microsoft.com/learning/mcpexams/policies/inno-vations.mspx and click on the **MCP Exam Demos** download link on the right side of the page.

The Windows Shadow Copy Service creates point-in-time backup copies of files located on a Shadow Copy-enabled volume. This puts the power of restore in the user's hands. Even if a user does not realize or understand how to restore using Shadow Copies, I have used it on many occasions to roll a file back to previous versions or even restore an entire deleted folder. It is much faster and easier than loading up the backup software and finding the backup containing the correct file(s).

To enable Shadow Copy on a Server Volume, navigate to **Start Menu | Computer**, **Right-click** on the target volume and select the **Configure Shadow Copies** menu item. In the **Shadow Copies** dialog box, click on the **Enable** button to enable Shadow Copies for that volume (see Figure 4.18).

Figure 4.18 Shadow Copies Enabled

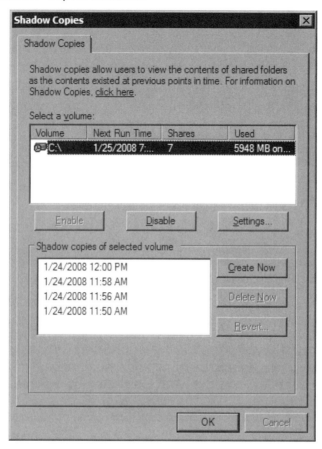

Recovering Previous Versions

Using Shadow Copies you can recover a previous version of a file on the server or a workstation using the Properties dialog of a file or folder. In Exercise 4.7, we will recover a previous version of a file and folder.

EXERCISE 4.7

USING SHADOW COPY TO RECOVER FILES AND FOLDERS

Once Shadow Copies have been enabled on a server, the Shadow Copy Service will take point-in-time snapshots on a regular basis (twice a day by default). To restore a file to its previous version:

1. Right-click on the file or folder and choose **Restore previous versions**.

Alternatively, you can right-click on the file and choose the **Properties** command from the shortcut menu. The **Properties** sheet contains a **Previous Versions** tab you can use to restore files and folders.

2. In the **Previous Versions** tab you will see a list of Shadow Copies that have been made of the file or folder (see Figure 4.19). If no Shadow Copies appear, changes may not have been made recently or the Shadow Copy Service may not be running. You can force a Shadow Copy in the **Volume Properties | Shadow Copies Dialog** (shown in the previous section) by clicking on the **Create Now** button.

Figure 4.19 Previous Versions Tab

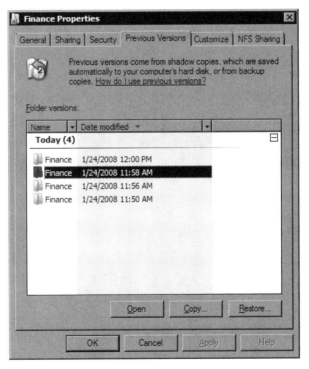

3. To restore a previous version of the file or folder, select the version you would like and click on the **Restore** button, as shown in Figure 4.20. If you would like to restore a copy instead of over-writing the existing file or folder, click the **Copy** button. To view one of the versions and make sure it is the one you are looking for before restoring you can use the **Open** button.

Figure 4.20 Restoring a Previous Version Using Shadow Copy

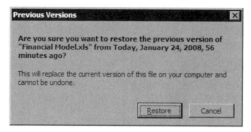

Windows Server 2008 features an enhanced version of Shadow Copy that supports restoring an entire volume to a previous state. To revert a volume to its previous state, navigate to **Start Menu | Computer, Right-click** the target volume and click **Configure Shadow Copies**. Select a previous Shadow Copy (date and time) and click on the **Revert** button, as shown in Figure 4.21.

Figure 4.21 Reverting an Entire Volume Using Shadow Copy

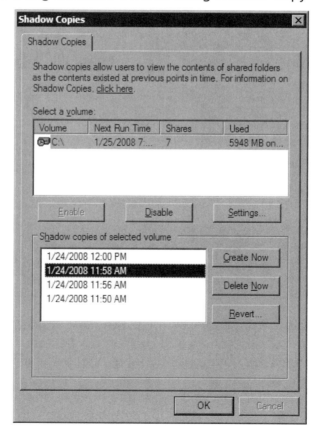

Exam Warning

Shadow Copy does not support performing a full-volume restore on the system volume (the volume that Windows Server 2008 installed on to it). To restore a system volume, use the Windows Backup utility (see the "Configuring Backup and Restore" section later in this chapter for more information).

Setting the Schedule

To control the frequency and schedule with which Windows creates Shadow Copies:

1. Navigate to **Start Menu | Computer**.

2. Right-click the target volume and click **Configure Shadow Copies**.

3. Click on the **Settings** button and then click on **Schedule**.

You will be able to set the schedule using the dialog box shown in Figure 4.22.

Figure 4.22 Setting the Schedule for Shadow Copies

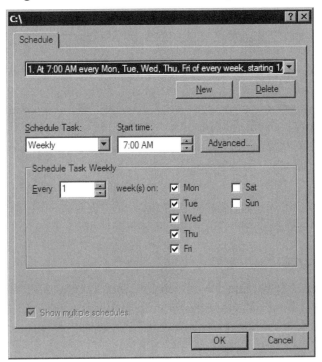

Setting Storage Locations

You can view and configure the storage location of the Shadow Copies using the **Settings** dialog available in the Shadow Copies configuration. The Shadow Copies configuration is the same screen we used to enable Shadow Copies and is available from the **Right-click | Configure Shadow Copies** menu option.

EXAM WARNING

You may be required to know command-line operations for administrative tasks. To configure and manage Shadow Copies using the command line, use the *VSSADMIN* command-line utility. For more information, type **VSSADMIN /?** at the Windows command prompt.

Configuring Backup and Restore

Hard drives fail. Natural disasters such as floods, fires, and hurricanes happen. Backup is the single most important measure you can take to recover from such an incident. As I consultant, you would not believe how many times I have walked into a new client's office to find that either backups have stopped working and have not been running for months, or there is no backup at all. Microsoft has completely revamped the Backup utility in Windows Server 2008. The new Windows Server Backup has many improvements over the old NTBACKUP, including the ability to back up to DVD, multitarget backup for off-site rotation, faster backups, and the ability to maintain multiple versions to restore back to.

The new backup APIs make a shadow copy snapshot image of everything being backed up prior to actually starting the backup. This ensures that open files, databases, and so forth will be consistent in the backup.

Backup Types

The traditional types of backup have been full, incremental, and differential. The new Windows Server Backup uses a combination of full and incremental backups using block-level backup for improved speed. Table 4.5 explains full backups and incremental backups:

Table 4.5 Explanation of Backup Types

Backup Type	Explanation
Full backup	Creates a backup of the entire volume(s).
Incremental backup	Used in conjunction with a full backup; an incremental backup backs up only the changes that have been made since the last full or incremental backup.
Differential backup	No longer used in Windows Server Backup. This backup type copies all the changes that have been made since the last full backup.

Although this is a powerful new system, the interface has been simplified in the new Windows backup utility. If you require more control over how the backups are run, you may want to buy a third-party backup utility.

Test Day Tip

There is really no replacement for good hands-on practice. Run Server 2008 and practice the exercises using it. You can create an entire Virtual Lab on a single computer using Microsoft Virtual Server (available at www.microsoft.com/windowsserversystem/virtualserver/default.aspx) or VMware Server (available at www.vmware.com).

Backup Schedules

To create a scheduled backup, you must first make sure Windows Server Backup is installed in the **Server Manager | Features | Add Features** Wizard. Although you can create an ad hoc or one-time backup to a network share, internal disk, external hard drive, or DVD, you can only run *scheduled* backups using one or multiple external USB 2.0 or IEEE 1394 drive(s). It is recommended that you use a drive that is at least 2.5 times the size of the volume you plan to back up.

Exam Warning

Windows Server Backup supports only external USB 2.0 and IEEE 1394 drives for scheduled backups. Tape drives are not supported.

In Exercise 4.8, we will configure a backup schedule in Windows Server Backup to run to an external USB 2.0 or IEEE 1394 hard drive.

EXERCISE 4.8

CONFIGURING A BACKUP SCHEDULE USING WINDOWS SERVER BACKUP

1. Connect a USB 2.0 or IEEE 1394 external hard drive to your server.

2. Launch the **Backup Schedule Wizard** by navigating to **Server Manager | Storage | Windows Server Backup | Backup Schedule**.

3. Click **Next** to move past the **Getting Started** page.

4. On the **Select Backup Type** page choose **Custom** and click **Next**. This allows us to select the volume(s) we would like to back up.

5. On the **Select Custom Backup Items** page, select only the volume you would like to back up. In this example, we back up the C: drive.

6. On the **Specify Backup Time** page, you can choose to back up the server either at a specified time once per day, or multiple times per day. In this example, we chose **Once a day** at **11:00 P.M.** (see Figure 4.23). Click the **Next** button to continue.

Figure 4.23 Specify Backup Time in Backup Schedule Wizard

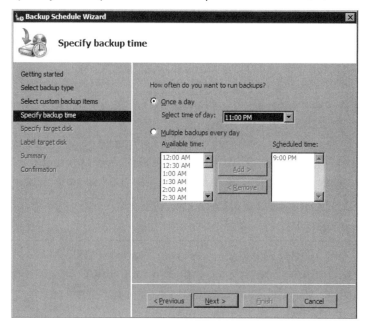

7. Select the USB 2.0 or IEEE 1394 disk or disks you would like to back up to and click **Next**. *Warning: Completing this wizard will format your external hard drive. Make sure you do not have any important data on your external hard drive before continuing.*

8. Click **Next** and then **Finish** to complete the **Backup Schedule Wizard**.

9. After the wizard formats your external hard drive, your backup schedule appears in the Windows Server Backup management tool, as shown in Figure 4.24.

Figure 4.24 Scheduled Backup Displayed in the Windows Server Backup Management Tool

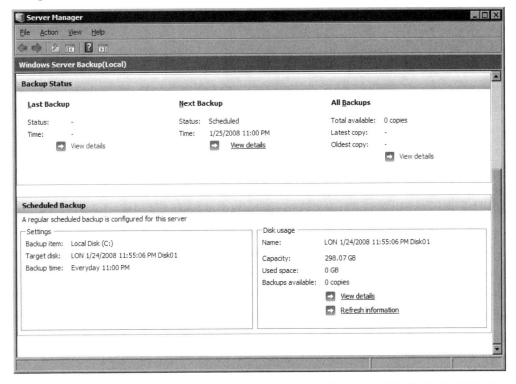

Managing Remotely

To manage backups from a remote computer, use the Backup Snap-in in the Microsoft Management Console (MMC). To launch MMC, click on **Start Menu | Run**, type **MMC**, and press the **Enter** key on your keyboard. From the **File Menu | Add/ Remove Snap-in** menu option you can select one or more management snap-ins from a list, as shown in Figure 4.25.

Figure 4.25 Add or Remove Snap-ins Window

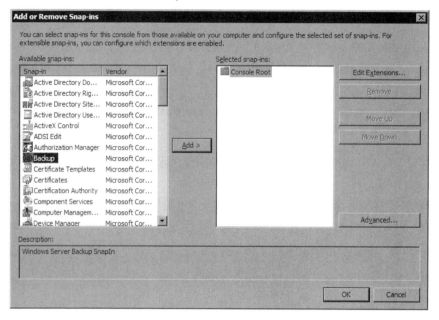

When adding the Backup Snap-in, you will be prompted to enter which server you would like to manage, as shown in Figure 4.26.

Figure 4.26 ComputerChooser When Adding Backup MMC Snap-in

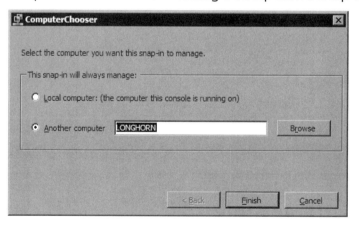

Restoring Data

The new Windows Server Backup greatly improves the restore interface in the old **NTBACKUP**. To restore incremental backups in **NTBACKUP** an administrator was required to load and restore each backup archive manually. In the new Windows Server Backup, you simply choose the point in time you would like to restore to and it takes care of loading the incremental backups for you automatically. In addition, you can perform a full-system restore without having to first reinstall Windows Server from the setup discs, as was the case in previous versions.

EXAM WARNING

You may be required to know command-line operations for administrative tasks. To configure and manage backups using the command line, use the *WBADMIN* command-line utility. For more information type in **WBADMIN /?** at the Windows command prompt.

To restore from backup you can use one of the following options:

- Restore individual files and folders to their original or an alternative location using the **Recover** hyperlink in the **Server Manager | Storage | Windows Server Backup** management tool.

- Perform a complete server recovery using the **Windows Complete PC Restore** option. To perform a full server recovery boot from the **Windows Server 2008 setup disc** and choose **Repair your computer**. On the **System Recovery Options** page choose **Windows Complete PC Restore**.

The new **Windows Server Backup** application no longer uses .bkf files. Instead, **Windows Server Backup** writes backups to a virtual hard drive file. This means that if you perform a full backup of a volume, you can actually mount the backup as a virtual hard drive. Incidentally, Microsoft offers a free utility for Windows Server 2008 and Windows Vista that allows you to restore .bkf files made with NTBACKUP. The "Windows NT Backup Restore Utility" is available for download at www.microsoft.com/downloads/details.aspx?FamilyID=7da725e2-8b69-4c65-afa3-2a53107d54a7&DisplayLang=en.

For more information on the new Windows Server Backup, check out Microsoft's "Windows Server 2008 Backup and Recovery Step-by-Step Guide" at http://technet2.microsoft.com/WindowsServer2008/en/library/00162c92-a834-43f9-9e8a-71aeb25fa4ad1033.mspx.

Managing Disk Quotas

Are you running out of storage space on your server because specific users are dumping more than their fair share on the server? Then you are going to like Disk Quotas. Disk Quotas allow you to monitor and limit server disk space on a per-volume or per-user basis. If the user hits his or her disk quotas, it will appear to that user as though that server hard drive is completely full and no more files can be copied to it. You also can configure Disk Quotas to warn users that they are reaching their limit.

Quota by Volume or Quota by User

As with many features, Microsoft has made improvements to Disk Quotas in Windows Server 2008. The most significant improvements are the addition of the File Server Resource Manager (FSRM), which allows an administrator to manage quotas and generate storage reports, and the ability to now apply a quota to a folder.

EXAM WARNING

You can enforce Disk Quotas only on end-users. Administrator accounts are impervious to Disk Quota limitations.

Microsoft has included both the older NTFS Disk Quotas system from previous Windows Server versions and the new enhanced Resource Manager Disk Quotas system in Windows Server 2008 because they each have different functionality. Although it is possible to configure both Disk Quota systems, it is recommended that you use only one of the systems on your Windows Server 2008 system. FSRM is installed as a Role Service for the File Services role.

To manage quotas by volume or user, use the NTFS Disk Quotas system. To enable the NTFS Disk Quotas system, navigate to **Start Menu | Computer** and on the target volume **Right-Click | Properties**. Click on the **Quota** tab and **Enable quota management**, as shown in Figure 4.27.

Figure 4.27 Enabling Quota Management in Volume Properties

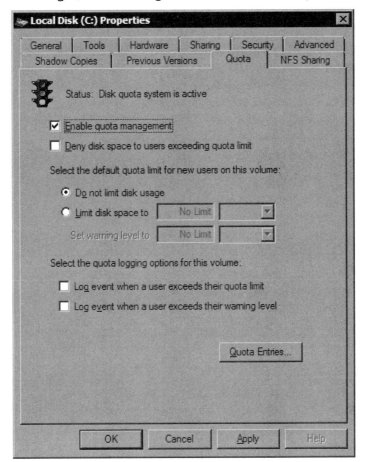

You must do this for each volume on which you want to activate NTFS Disk Quotas.

Hard Quotas prevent a user from exceeding the limit, and Soft Quotas allow users to exceed the limit and are used for monitoring and reporting. Using Resource Manager Disk Quotas you can also create a flexible quota. A flexible quota works by notifying users via e-mail when they have exceeded their quota and will temporarily extend their quota to give them flexibility to delete unnecessary files and get back into compliance.

To enable Hard Quotas in the NTFS Disk Quotas system navigate to **Start Menu | Computer** and on the target volume **Right-Click | Properties**. Click on the **Quota** tab and check the box next to **Deny disk space to users exceeding quota limit**. We will learn how to set Hard, Soft, and Flexible quotas in the next section of this chapter.

Quota Entries

To view and edit quota entries using the NTFS disk quotas system, navigate to **Start Menu | Computer** and on the target volume **Right-Click | Properties**. Click on the **Quota** tab and click on the **Quota Entries** button. In Figure 4.28, we see that user John Matzek has a Quota Limit of 1 GB, has a Warning Level of 900 MB, and is currently using 41.38 MB (or 4%) of his quota.

Figure 4.28 Quota Usage and Limits in Quota Entries Window on Volume C

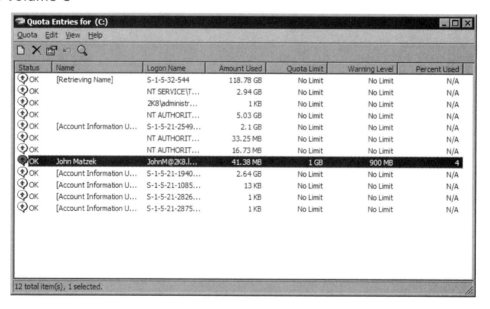

Disk quotas are tracked by file owner. If John modifies a file that is owned by another user, it will not affect his disk quota. To add a quota for a specific user, click on the **Quota Menu | New Quota Entry**. To edit the quota parameters for a user listed in the Quota Entries window, double-click the user's entry. This will bring up the **Quota Settings for [User]** dialog shown in Figure 4.29.

Figure 4.29 Modifying Quota Settings for a Specific User

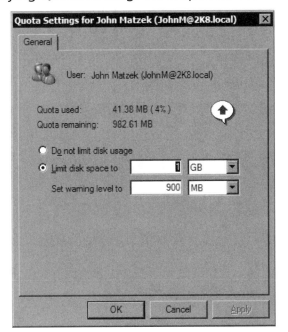

Configuring Quotas Using FSRM

Resource Manager disk quotas allow an administrator to track and enforce quotas on a per-folder basis as opposed to the **NTFS disk quotas** method of tracking per user per volume. To configure disk quotas using FSRM follow the steps in Exercise 4.9.

EXERCISE 4.9

CONFIGURING DISK QUOTAS USING FILE SERVER RESOURCE MANAGER

1. Navigate to **Server Manager | Roles | Files Services | Share and Storage Management | Quota Management | Quotas** and click on the **Create Quota** hyperlink. The **Create Quota** dialog box is displayed.

2. Click on the **Browse** button and locate the folder you would like to manage using a quota. In this example, we browse to C:\Shares\Sales.

3. Verify that **Create quota on path** is selected. Instead of using a predefined template in this example, we will select **Define custom quota properties**. Then click the **Custom Properties** button.

4. The **Quota Properties** window is displayed, as seen in Figure 4.30.

Figure 4.30 Quota Properties Window

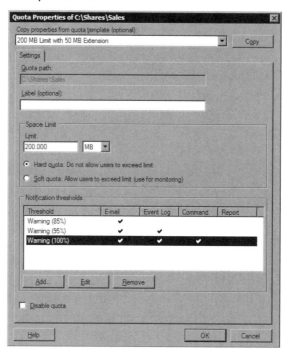

5. In the Quota Properties window, use the combo box in the **Copy properties from quota template (optional):** section to choose the **200 MB Limit with 50 MB Extension** and click **Copy**. This option sets a hard quota of 200 MB, but acts as a flexible quota to extend to 250 MB temporarily if users exceed the 200 MB limit. This is accomplished using the **Run this command or script** option in the **100% Notification threshold** actions which you can find by clicking on **Warning (100%) | Edit… | Command**. Note the option to select either a hard or a soft quota.

6. Click **OK** and then click on **Create** to create the Quota for the Sales folder. When prompted, choose not to save the options as a template. We will discuss templates in the next section.

Note that you can also apply a quota policy to a shared folder in the Provision a Shared Folder Wizard.

Quota Templates

It is recommended that all quota entries you configure using the Resource Manager disk quotas be configured using templates. This makes it easy to update or change quota settings for a large number of folders by changing a setting only once in the template that is applied instead of editing the quota properties for each individual folder. To manage quota templates, navigate to **Server Manager | Roles | Files Services | Share and Storage Management | Quota Management | Quota Templates**. From this management tool you can create, delete, and modify quota templates using the hyperlink options on the right pane.

Exam Warning

You may be required to know command-line operations for administrative tasks. To configure and manage NTFS disk quotas using the command line, use the *FSUTIL* command-line utility. For more information, type **FSUTIL QUOTA** at the Windows command prompt.

To configure and manage Resource Manager disk quotas use the *DIRQUOTA* command-line utility.

Configuring and Monitoring Print Services

In understanding printer management and configuration in Windows Server 2008, it is important to understand printer sharing, publishing printers to Active Directory, printer permissions, deploying printer connections, installing printer drivers, exporting and importing print queues and printer settings, and adding counters to Performance Monitor to monitor print servers, print pooling, and print priority. In this section, we will discuss these in detail.

Printer Share

Sharing a printer from a Windows Server 2008 machine allows multiple users on the network to access the same physical printer using print spooling, a process of queuing up documents to be printed one at a time. Users can install the printer without worrying about downloading or installing a driver as it is automatically copied from the print server. In addition, printer sharing allows administrators to centrally control and manage the printers and print queues. For clarity it is important to understand the difference between a printer and a print device. A printer is the virtual printer created within Windows to represent the driver, configuration, and print queue. A print device is the physical printer that is hooked up to the network or a server. To enable printer sharing on your Windows 2008 Server install the **Print Services** role in the **Add Roles Wizard**. This allows you to use the Print Management administration tool to manage shared printers.

EXAM WARNING

Know the difference between a printer and print device, and read your exam questions carefully. In the past, Microsoft has been known to try to trip people up with this terminology.

You can also enable printer sharing using the **Control Panel | Network and Sharing Center** and change the **Printer sharing** setting to "On."

Use the **Add Printer Wizard** in **Control Panel | Printers** to set up a new printer. On the **Printer Sharing** page select **Share this printer so that others on your network can find and use it**, as shown in Figure 4.31.

Figure 4.31 Printer Sharing Configuration in Add Printer Wizard

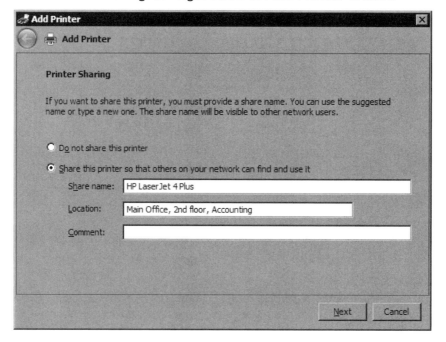

Publishing Printers to Active Directory

Publishing a printer to Active Directory allows network users to search for printers on the network by name or location instead of worrying about which server the printer lives on. To publish a printer to Active Directory, enable the **List in the directory** checkbox on the **Sharing** tab of the **Printer Properties**, as shown in Figure 4.32.

Figure 4.32 List in the Directory Option on the Sharing Tab

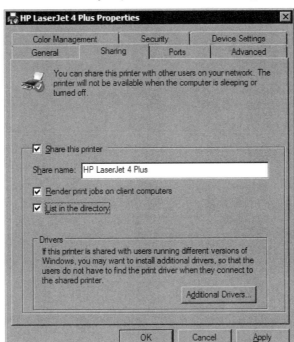

EXAM WARNING

You may be required to know command-line operations for administrative tasks. To manage print queues using the command line, use the *NET PRINT* command-line utility.

Printer Permissions

You configure printer permissions on the **Security** tab in Printer Properties; they operate in a fashion very similar to Share Permissions. Figure 4.33 shows the

Security tab in Printer Properties. Table 4.6 shows the available printer permissions and their function.

Figure 4.33 Modifying Printer Permissions

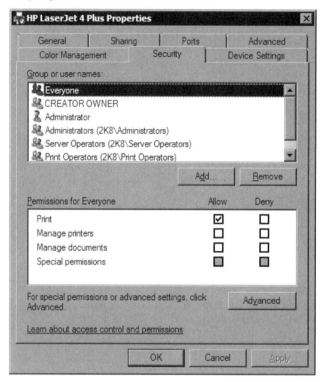

Table 4.6 Overview of Printer Permissions

Printer Permission	Explanation
Print	Allows users to connect and print to the printer
Manage printers	Allows users to perform administrative functions including adjusting printer permissions, pausing, restarting, and changing printer settings. This setting gives users more control than **Manage documents**.
Manage documents	Allows users to act as print operators. Lets them cancel, restart, reorder, pause, and resume documents in the print queue.
Special permissions	Use the **Advanced** button to configure special permissions including **Manage printers, Manage documents, Read permissions, Change permissions,** and **Take ownership**.

Deploying Printer Connections

Installing a network printer on a client Windows computer is relatively easy. Now imagine you need to install a network printer on 500 Windows computers. Fortunately, Windows Server 2008 is all about working smarter rather than harder. You can easily install printers on client workstations by deploying them using Group Policy. In Exercise 4.10, we will deploy printer connections.

EXERCISE 4.10

USING THE PRINT MANAGEMENT UTILITY TO DEPLOY PRINTER CONNECTIONS

1. Open **Print Management** in **Server Manager**.

2. Expand **Print Servers** and expand your target server in the left pane.

3. Click on the **Printers** node to view a list of installed printers, as shown in Figure 4.34.

Figure 4.34 Managing Printers in the Print Servers Console

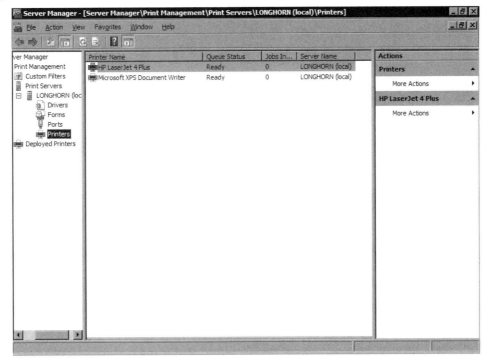

4.   Right-click on the printer you would like to deploy and click the **Deploy with Group Policy** menu item.

For more information on how to deploy printer connections for Windows Vista and Windows XP clients, visit http://technet2.microsoft.com/windowsserver2008/en/library/8433a76a-0a5d-48f4-893d-35442aa8765e1033.mspx.

Installing Printer Drivers

To enable point and print (the automatic installation of print drivers) for clients running a different version of Windows (x86 versus x64 versus Itanium) you must install the drivers for that version of Windows. Install additional drivers by clicking the **Additional Drivers** button on the **Sharing** tab in the **Printer Properties**. This brings up the **Additional Drivers** window, where you can select the types of drivers you would like to install, as shown in Figure 4.35. After you select the types of drivers and click **OK**, you will be prompted for a location to copy files from, as shown in Figure 4.36.

Figure 4.35 Selecting Additional Printer Drivers to Install

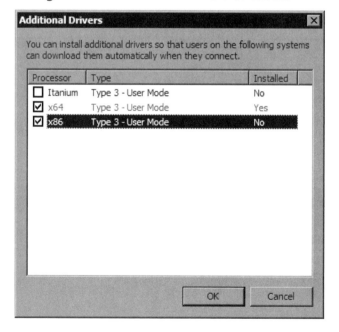

Figure 4.36 Install Additional Printer Drivers Dialog

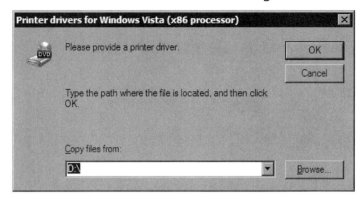

Exporting and Importing Print Queues and Printer Settings

Windows Server 2008 provides a facility for moving printers from one server to another by exporting and importing printer settings, drivers, print queues, and ports. This can be useful in consolidating printers from multiple servers or replacing an existing server with newer hardware. To export printer settings use the **Printer Migration Wizard** by right-clicking the server you would like to export from in **Print Management** (see Figure 4.37), and then click **Export printers to a file**. Figure 4.38 shows an export using the Printer Migration Wizard.

Figure 4.37 Export Printers to a File Option in Printer Management

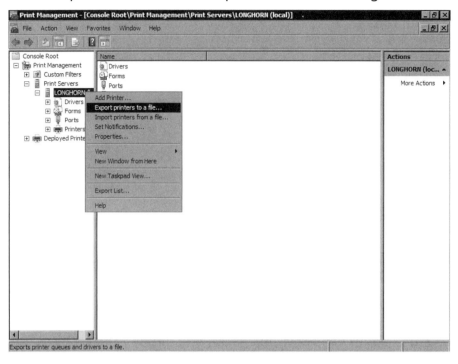

Figure 4.38 Exporting Printer Settings Using the Printer Migration Wizard

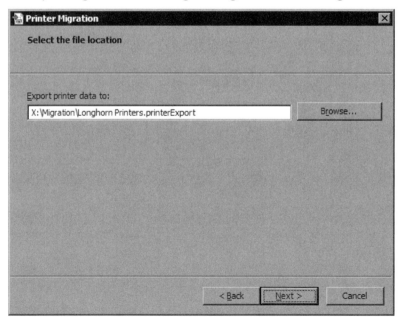

To import the printer settings on the destination server use the **Printer Migration Wizard** by right-clicking the destination server in **Print Management**, and then click **Import printers to a file**. Figure 4.39 shows print queues, drivers, and processors being imported to a new server using the Printer Migration Wizard.

Figure 4.39 Importing Printer Settings Using the Printer Migration Wizard

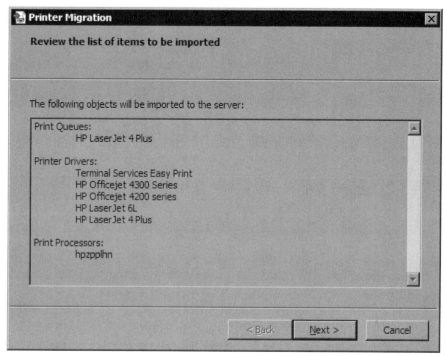

Adding Counters to Reliability and Performance Monitor to Monitor Print Servers

By using Performance Monitor, a network or server administrator can identify bottlenecks on a wide variety of server and network components. As an administrator, you can also use Performance Monitor to capture performance counters over time and identify baselines and trends.

In Windows Server 2008, Performance Monitor includes many counters that enable administrators to keep an eye on many network printers at the same time or even capture data for later analysis. You can view these performance counters in a Line Graph, Histogram, or Report view. Launch Performance Monitor by navigating to **Server Manager | Diagnostics | Reliability and Performance | Monitoring Tools | Performance Monitor**. Figure 4.40 shows the Report view in Performance Monitor.

Figure 4.40 Monitoring Printer Statistics in Report View Using Performance Monitor

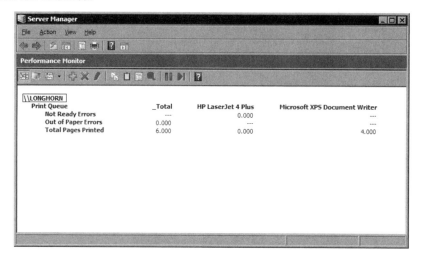

To monitor printing statistics such as **Bytes Printed/sec, Jobs Spooling,** and **Out of Paper Errors** in real time, add counters by clicking the plus button and then expand the **Print Queue** counters, as shown in Figure 4.41.

Figure 4.41 Adding Print Queue Counters to Performance Monitor

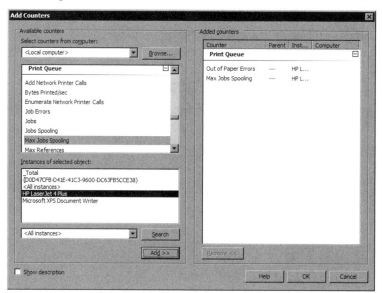

Printer Pooling

Printer pooling allows you to install a single printer to print to one of multiple print devices. For example, if Pablo is printing a 350-page document while Steve attempts to print a one-page spreadsheet to the same printer, with a single print device Steve would have to wait for Pablo's 350-page document to finish before his one-page spreadsheet is printed. With Print Pooling both documents will print on separate print devices in the pool at the same time.

To enable printer pooling:

1. Connect more than one print device of the same type to your server.

2. Open the **Printer Properties** for your printer and click on the **Ports** tab.

3. Click the checkbox next to **Enable printer pooling**.

4. Select the ports that are connected to the printers you would like to pool together (see Figure 4.42).

Figure 4.42 Enabling the Printer Pooling Option on the Ports Tab

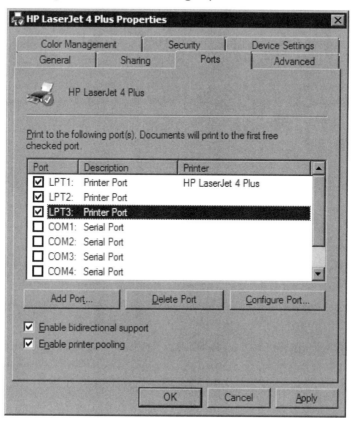

Print Priority

You can use the **Advanced** tab in **Printer Properties** to set a priority, as shown in Figure 4.43.

Figure 4.43 Boosting the Priority on a Printer

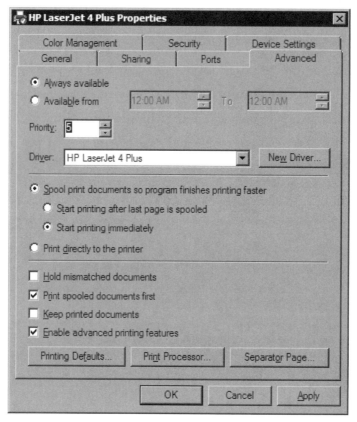

Print jobs with a higher-priority (numeric value) print before jobs with a lower priority. By configuring multiple printers with different priority levels to print to the same print device, an administrator can ensure that users in a specific department always get higher printing priority than others. For example, you can create a FinancePublic printer with default Printer Permissions and a FinanceOnly printer where only members of the Finance group have access. Configuring the FinanceOnly printer with higher priority ensures members of the Finance group who submit jobs will always get them printed first.

Summary of Exam Objectives

Out of the box, Windows Server 2008 does not include the File and Printer sharing services or tools. To install these tools use the Add Roles hyperlink in Server Manager. The File Services role installs file and folder sharing and the Share and Storage Management console, which is the preferred method for administering shared folders. There are two models:

- Standard (in-place) file sharing
- Public folder sharing

You can add additional components of the File Services role such as DFS, NFS (for UNIX), Windows Search Service, and File Server Resource Manager by using the Add Role Services hyperlink in Server Manager.

A user's effective permissions when accessing a shared folder over the network are the result of both NTFS and Share Permissions. The effective permission is the *more restrictive* of these two components:

- The *least* restrictive NTFS Permission
- The *least* restrictive Share Permission

Remember that a Deny permission will always override any allow permission for that user or group.

EFS encrypted and decrypted files use a process that is transparent to the user. EFS works only on NTFS volumes and users should use a roaming profile or backup and copy their public/private keys (which are stored in their user profile) if they use multiple computers.

DFS has two main components that can be used independently of each other:

- DFS namespaces
- DFS replication

DFS namespaces are virtual shared folders that contain shared folders from multiple servers. This simplifies access to shares and creates redundancy if a server is offline. A "target" is a pointer to a shared folder on one server. You can have multiple targets for each shared folder in a DFS namespace.

DFS replication synchronizes the changes between folders located on different servers. This can work in conjunction with DFS namespaces or be used to create a backup of a shared folder that is synchronized after changes occur.

Shadow Copy allows users and administrators a point-in-time restore or rollback to previous versions of a file or folder. Shadow Copies must be enabled on a per- volume basis and previous versions are restored using the Previous Versions tab in the properties of a file or folder located on a Shadow Copy-enabled volume.

NTBACKUP has been replaced with Windows Server Backup. You can create a backup schedule and/or ad hoc (one-time) backups in Windows Server Backup. Ad hoc backups can be made onto DVD or a network shared folder. Scheduled backups work with USB 2.0 and IEEE 1394 hard drives and first create a full backup, then incremental backups using block-level copy on a scheduled basis. You can perform a point-in-time restore without having to manually load each incremental backup.

To manage a remote Windows Server 2008 full or core server, use the Microsoft Management Console and add snap-ins. When adding a snap-in you will be prompted for which computer you want to manage.

Disk quotas can be enabled using the per-volume per-user system from previous versions of Windows Server or a per-folder basis using Resource Manager disk quotas. Resource Manager disk quotas can e-mail users and perform actions when limits are reached. FSUTIL is used to manage quotas from the command prompt and can be used to script actions.

To share printers, add the Print Services role in Server Manager. This also installs the Print Management console which allows you to import/export printers/settings, deploy printers to clients using group policy, and manage printers, ports, and drivers. A printer is the virtual printer in Windows and a print device is the physical printer.

By default, users are granted the Print permission. To allow a user or group to manage the queue and cancel, restart, pause, reorder, and resume a printer grant them the "Manage documents" print permission. The "Manage printers" print permission is similar to the "Full Control" share permission and allows a user to manage the queue and the printer itself (i.e., change permissions and printer settings).

Printer pooling is set up by enabling multiple ports in the printer properties. If a document is sent to that printer, it prints to the first port. If a second document is sent while the first print device is busy printing, the second document will be sent to the next port in the list.

You can create multiple printers that point to the same print device. This allows you to set different priorities on each printer and grant different users and groups access based on which priority they will need. The higher the numeric value, the higher the priority that will be given to that printer.

Exam Objectives Fast Track

Configuring a File Server

☑ Add the File Services role in Server Manager to enable file sharing and install the management tools.

☑ The effective permission for a user to access a shared folder is the *more* restrictive of the least restrictive Share Permission and the least restrictive NTFS Permission.

☑ A Deny permission for a user or a group they are a member of *always* overrides Allow permissions.

☑ Use the Share and Storage Management console to create and manage shared folders.

☑ Encrypting File System (EFS) is transparent to the user and works only on NTFS; you cannot both encrypt and compress a file.

Configuring Distributed File System (DFS)

☑ A DFS namespace is a virtual shared folder that contains shared folders located on multiple servers.

☑ Use the Namespaces and Replication tools in DFS Management to create namespaces and manage DFS.

☑ A DFS target is a pointer to a shared folder on a server and DFS folders can point to multiple targets (copies of the same folder on different servers).

☑ DFS replication synchronizes the changes between multiple copies of the same folder located on different servers.

Configuring Shadow Copy Services

☑ Shadow Copies are point-in-time backups of files that can be restored by the user or admin using the Previous Versions tab in the properties of the file or folder.

☑ To control the snapshot schedule and storage locations, open the **Volume (Drive C, D, E, etc) Properties | Shadow Copies** tab or right-click the volume in my computer and choose **Configure Shadow Copies**.

☑ Use the **Shadow Copies** in the Volume Properties tab to change the schedule, force Shadow Copy to run immediately, delete a snapshot, and change the storage location.

Configuring Backup and Restore

☑ Windows Server Backup replaces the old NTBACKUP and improves backup speed, simplifies the user interface, includes full and incremental backup types, and allows an ad hoc backup to DVD or a network share.

☑ Scheduled backup creates a full backup and then incremental backups using block-level copy, and supports only USB 2.0 and IEEE 1394 hard drives (no tape).

☑ Windows Server Backup can be managed remotely with the Backup snap-in in the MMC or the command line *WBADMIN*.

☑ Data can be restored to a point-in-time and will automatically load the incremental backups without user intervention.

Managing Disk Quotas

☑ You can configure disk quotas using the new system of Resource Manager disk quotas or the old system of NTFS disk quotas.

☑ Resource Manager disk quotas enable quotas on a per-folder basis. NTFS disk quotas allow you to manager quotas by user on a per-volume basis.

☑ Resource Manager disk quotas allow you to set up templates with hard or soft limits and different actions at different percent utilizations.

Configuring and Monitoring Print Services

☑ Deploy printers to clients using group policy with the Print Management console, right-click the **Printers** node, and choose **Deploy with Group Policy**.

☑ Export and import printer settings, queues, and ports using the Export Printer Wizard or Import Printer Wizard in Print Management.

☑ Add counters to the Reliability and Performance Monitor to monitor printers for out of paper errors and other statistics.

☑ Attach multiple print devices to a single printer for print pooling or multiple printers to a single print device for different printing priorities.

Exam Objectives
Frequently Asked Questions

Q: I want to add services for NFS (UNIX) but I cannot find Add/Remove Programs. Where do I install it?

A: The networking components in Add/Remove Programs have been replaced with adding Roles and Role Services in Server Manager.

Q: What is the difference between setting Share Permissions to Everyone - Full control and Authenticated Users – Full Control?

A: The "Everyone" group is just as the name implies; it includes "everyone," including guest accounts and "null sessions" (computer-to-computer sessions). The Authenticated Users group is more secure as it excludes these groups while including users on the domain.

Q: Does File Screening examine the contents of every file copied to a shared folder?

A: File screening does not examine the contents of files. It works by restricting files based on extensions (e.g., .mp3, .wma, .wmv, etc.). Users can "hack" past file screening by renaming the extension of a file to an allowed extension before copying the file to a share. If the user attempts to rename it back once it is on the server, it will be intercepted by the file screen and deleted.

Q: What is the difference between special permissions and the standard NTFS permissions?

A: The NTFS special permissions are actually the more granular permissions that make up the standard NTFS permissions. For example, the Read standard permission is actually composed of the List Folder / Read Data, Read Attributes, Read Extended Attributes, and Read Permissions special permissions.

Q: Why would I want to disable Offline Files on a network share?

A: A couple of reasons to disable Offline Files from the server are that you have confidential information that is not to leave the building and you do not want users syncing it onto a laptop, or a shared folder is heavily used for collaboration and you do not want multiple people editing the same file offline and running into a conflict when they attempt to sync it back up.

Q: What is the command-line utility for working with EFS?

A: To encrypt, decrypt, view, and manage EFS using the command-line utility CIPHER.exe.

Q: How can I tell in Windows Explorer which files and folders are encrypted or compressed?

A: In Windows Explorer, encrypted files and folders are indicated by the color green and compressed files and folders are indicated by the color blue. Regular files will show up in black.

Q: What if I do not back up my encryption keys and lose my computer or profile, or I need to reset my password?

A: By default, the first administrator account on the domain is a recovery agent and can decrypt any domain user's files in this case. It also can come in handy if an employee quit or was terminated and had encrypted his or her files. You can also configure additional recovery agents on the domain. If your password was reset and this caused you to lose your EFS keys, you can change your password back and it should restore your ability to decrypt your files.

Q: I do not see a DFS role. How do I install DFS?

A: DFS is installed by adding the Distributed File System Role Services to the File Services role in Server Manager.

Q: Can I use DFS replication without configuring a DFS namespace?

A: Yes, DFS replication can be configured to synchronize folders located on multiple servers. It does not require a DFS namespace.

Q: How do I maintain an off-site backup copy of our shared folders using a server at a remote site for business continuity planning?

A: Although it is also critically important to have a full off-site backup solution, you can use DFS replication as part of your business continuity plan (keeping the business running in case of a disaster) by setting up DFS replication between servers at different physical/geographic locations.

Q: We have branch offices that connect over the WAN link to the main file server(s). It is excruciatingly slow. How do we speed this up without buying an expensive WAN link?

A: Set up a BOB or Branch Office Box at each branch office to speed up local access by "caching" the shared folders from the main server. To accomplish this, use Windows Server 2008 (or Windows Server 2003 R2) and DFS replication.

Q: My users are running Windows 2000 or Windows XP and do not have a "previous versions" tab to access Shadow Copies. How do I fix this?

A: Newer versions of Windows, such as Windows Vista, include the Shadow Copy client. To access the previous versions (Shadow Copies) tab on Windows 2000 and XP, you must install the Shadow Copy client which is available for download at http://technet.microsoft.com/en-us/windowsserver/bb405951.aspx.

Q: I deleted a file and want to recover it using Shadow Copies. Because the file is gone and I cannot right-click on it to get the Previous Versions tab, how do I get the file back?

A: To recover a deleted file, right-click and go to the properties of the folder in which that file was located. You will be able to restore the file from the Previous Versions tab.

Q: Can I revert my entire C: volume to a previous version?

A: Not if Windows Server 2008 is installed on the C: volume. You can only revert nonsystem volumes using Shadow Copy.

Q: How come the differential backup type is no longer available in Windows Server Backup?

A: The differential backup type was useful when you had to back up to tapes, because if a tape went bad you would not lose all the data from that "increment" of the backup if you used differential. Also if you needed to restore backups, using the differential backup type took fewer steps because you did not need to manually locate and load each incremental backup—just the full and the latest differential. Because Windows Server Backup uses external hard drives instead of tape and can automatically load the appropriate incremental backups during a restore, the differential type is no longer necessary.

Q: How come DAT, DLT, Travan, and other tape drives are not recognized in Windows Server Backup?

A: Windows Server Backup does not support tape drives. To back up to tape use third-party backup software.

Q: I am trying to back up to DVD or a network share but am not given the option when I schedule a backup. How do I accomplish this?

A: To back up to DVD or a network share, create an ad hoc or one-time backup instead of a scheduled backup.

Q: What is the difference between NTFS disk quotas and Resource Manager disk quotas?

A: NTFS disk quotas is the system that also existed in previous versions of Windows Server. It allows you to set quotas on a per-volume basis and set limits for each user. Resource Manager disk quotas is a new system that allows you to control space used on a per-folder basis and is managed in File Server Resource Manager.

Q: What is the difference between hard and soft quotas?

A: A hard quota prevents users from exceeding the limit and a soft quota allows the user to exceed the limit, but is used for monitoring and reporting.

Q: I set my warning level using NTFS disk quotas but it is not e-mailing users a warning when they reach that threshold. Why not?

A: The warning level in NTFS disk quotas will not contact a user; instead, it will warn the administrator by logging to the event logs. To e-mail users based on quota usage, use Resource Manager disk quotas instead.

Q: How do I manage a network printer using the command line?

A: Use the *NET PRINT* command to manage a network printer from the command line.

Q: Why would I publish a printer to Active Directory?

A: Publishing a printer to Active Directory allows users to search for the printer closest to them and is useful to find printers on the same floor in the building or at the user's branch office location.

Q: I am used to managing printers in Control Panel | Printers. What is the new tool in Windows Server 2008 to manage printers?

A: The new tool for managing printers in Windows Server 2008 is the Print Management console and can be found in Server Manager or added to the MMC as a snap-in.

Q: I am running the 64-bit edition of Windows Server 2008. How do I install print drivers for 32-bit clients so that they can install the printer without manually install the drivers?

A: You can install additional drivers using the Additional Drivers button on the Sharing tab in the Printer Properties.

Self Test

1. Employees at your company work with sensitive medical information including Social Security numbers and patient medical history on their laptops. You want to make sure that if a laptop is lost or stolen this data is not compromised. Which security measure is the best option to secure the files on the employee laptops?

    A. NTFS permissions

    B. EFS

    C. SSL

    D. Shared Folder Permissions

2. You have just installed a new Windows 2008 Server on your network and joined it to the domain. This server will handle all of the files the Finance department will work with and you need to add the File Services to the new server to allow users to store their timesheets on the new server. Which tool do you use to add the File Services role to this server?

    A. Server Manager

    B. Share and Storage Management

    C. Add/Remove Programs

    D. Network and Sharing Center

3. Your user account is configured to use a roaming profile that is stored on the server LONGHORN. You sit down and log on using your user account to a workstation named HR13. You map a drive to a shared folder on the server FINANCESVR1, create a folder on that share, encrypt the contents of that folder, and then log off. On which computer is your EFS private key stored?

    A. The Active Directory domain controller that authenticated your logon

    B. FINANCESVR1

    C. HR13

    D. LONGHORN

4. You would like to encrypt the file D:\Shares\Finance\Timesheets.xls to protect it from unauthorized use or theft. Using the command prompt on your Windows 2008 Server, what would you type to accomplish this task?

   A. *CIPHER /C D:\Shares\Finance\Timesheets.xls*

   B. *CIPHER /E D:\Shares\Finance\Timesheets.xls*

   C. *CIPHER D:\Shares\Finance\Timesheets.xls*

   D. *CIPHER /X D:\Shares\Finance\Timesheets.xls*

5. You want to grant the user BillG full control to the D:\Shares\HR folder. What command should you type in at the command prompt to accomplish this task?

   A. *ICACLS D:\Shares\HR /grant billg:(F)*

   B. *ICACLS D:\Shares\HR /grant billg:(M,RX,R,W)2*

   C. *NET SHARE sharename=D:\Shares\HR /GRANT billg,FULL*

   D. *NET SHARE D:\Shares\HR /grant billg:(M,RX,R,W)*

6. You are running a Windows 2008 Server called FINANCESVR1 in core mode and would like to configure the Windows Server Backup remotely using a GUI. You log into the server LONGHORN, running a full GUI installation of Windows Server 2008. Which utility do you run to accomplish this task?

   A. **Start Menu | Run | NTBACKUP**

   B. **Server Manager | Roles | File Services | Share and Storage Management | Disk Management**

   C. **Start Menu | Run | MMC** and add the **Backup** snap-in

   D. **Start Menu | Run | WBADMIN enable backup**

7. A network administrator tells you she has enabled NTFS disk quotas for three different users on a Windows 2008 Server but they are not working. Your server has a C: volume that contains the operating system and a D: volume that contains the shared folders. What is most likely the issue?

   A. Enable Quotas is not checked in the Properties of the D volume

   B. Enable Quotas is not checked in the Properties of the C volume

   C. The File Services Role has not been installed

   D. A Quota Template has not been configured in Quota Management

8. Users are complaining that they are no longer able to add files to the shared folder \\LONGHORN\Sales on your Windows 2008 Server and you suspect they have run out of space in their quota. The users tell you they are able to

add files to the \\LONGHORN\Public share, which is located on the same volume as the Sales share. Where should you go to increase the quota for the \\LONGHORN\Sales share?

A. **Properties** on the volume, **Quota** tab, **Quota Entries**

B. **Server Manager | Roles | File Services | Share and Storage Management | File Resource Manager**

C. **Server Manager | Roles | File Services | Share and Storage Management | File Resource Manager | Quota Management | Quotas**

D. **Server Manager | Roles | File Services | Share and Storage Management | File Resource Manager | Storage Reports Management**

9. You have enabled NTFS disk quotas on the D: drive of your Windows 2008 Server. You would like to increase the amount of space user BillG is allocated to 2 GB. Where should you go to increase BillG's quota?

A. **Server Manager | Roles | File Services | Share and Storage Management | File Resource Manager | Quota Management | Quotas**

B. Disk Management

C. BillG's user properties in Active Directory Users and Computers

D. Open the **Quota Entries** window from the **D: volume properties**, **Quota** tab

10. You have just connected a [print device to your network and added the printer on your Windows 2008 Server. You would like to share the printer on the network and administer the Print Permissions. Which of the following utilities will let you accomplish this task? (Select two.)

A. **Start Menu | Control Panel | Printers**

B. The **Print Management** console

C. The printer drivers disk from the manufacturer

D. The Network and Sharing Center

Self Test Quick Answer Key

1. **B**

2. **A**

3. **D**

4. **B**

5. **A**

6. **C**

7. **A**

8. **C**

9. **D**

10. **A, B**

## Chapter 5

MCTS/MCITP
Exam 642

Monitoring and Managing a Network Infrastructure

Exam objectives in this chapter:

- Configuring Windows Server Update Services Server Settings
- Capturing Performance Data
- Monitoring Event Logs
- Gathering Network Data

Exam objectives review:

- ☑ Summary of Exam Objectives
- ☑ Exam Objectives Fast Track
- ☑ Exam Objectives Frequently Asked Questions
- ☑ Self Test
- ☑ Self Test Quick Answer Key

Introduction

One of the most critical functions of a network administrator is the ability to properly monitor and manage the network for which he or she is responsible. This chapter will introduce you to some tools in Server 2008 that help you more easily monitor and manage your network. We will discuss setting up and using Windows Server Update Services (WSUS) to ensure that your servers and workstations remain properly updated with the latest security fixes from Microsoft. We will also look at collecting and using performance data as well as review event logs to assist you in troubleshooting problems. Finally, we will take a look at the Simple Network Management Protocol (SNMP), the Microsoft Baseline Security Analyzer (MBSA), and Network Monitor (netmon).

Configuring Windows Server Update Services Server Settings

Windows Server Update Services (WSUS) is Microsoft's out-of-the-box solution for managing updates and security fixes to Microsoft operating systems, Office products, and several other server applications. WSUS allows you to easily review, test, and send updates to servers and workstations on your network. You may be familiar with the Windows update software already installed on your server or client operating system. The Windows update software allows you to download the latest software updates and security patches from Microsoft. This works fine for home PCs and even some small businesses; however, can you imagine hundreds or thousands of computers in a large company connecting to Microsoft to download updates? This could pose obvious problems for your company's Internet bandwidth. This is where WSUS comes into play. WSUS allows you to download updates to a central repository on your network and distributed those updates at a time you schedule. Not only does this save your Internet connection from being brought to its knees, but it also allows you to centrally manage updates as well as test them before deploying. This section will walk you through installing, configuring, and using WSUS. Before we begin setting up WSUS, let's take a look at how it works.

WSUS is installed on a server in your corporate network. This server contacts Microsoft update servers over the Internet to download new updates. The WSUS administrator then must approve or deny updates that should be installed. Corporate servers and workstations are configured to download updates from the WSUS server instead of the Windows Update Web site. After the administrator approves updates for installation, servers and workstations download and install the approved updates (see Figure 5.1).

Figure 5.1 A Simple WSUS Architecture

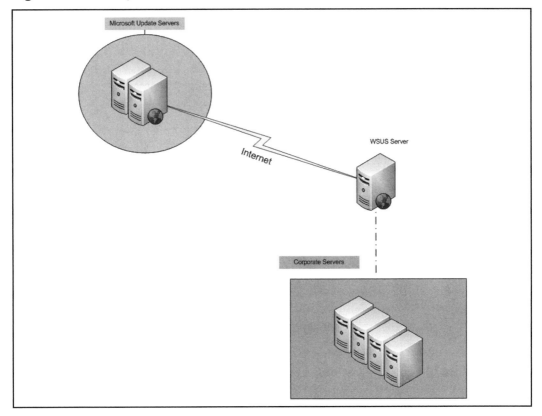

Installing Windows Server Update Services

Now that we've gotten a quick overview of how WSUS works, let's install this role. You install WSUS just as you would any other role in Windows Server 2008 (see Exercise 5.1)—by choosing the Add Server Role option in Server Manager.

Before deploying WSUS, it is important to design and plan the deployment. Just jumping in and installing WSUS could lead to a misconfiguration and cause unwanted problems on your network. Always use a lab environment to test the product and ensure that you fully understand its functionality. Use network drawings and checklists to create your deployment plan. After you feel comfortable with the plan, go forward with deployment.

EXERCISE 5.1

INSTALLING WINDOWS SERVER UPDATE SERVICES

To install WSUS perform the following steps:

1. Open Server Manager by selecting **Start | Administrative Tools | Server Manager**.

2. Click the **Add Roles** link, as shown in Figure 5.2. This will launch the **Add Roles Wizard**.

Figure 5.2 Server Manager

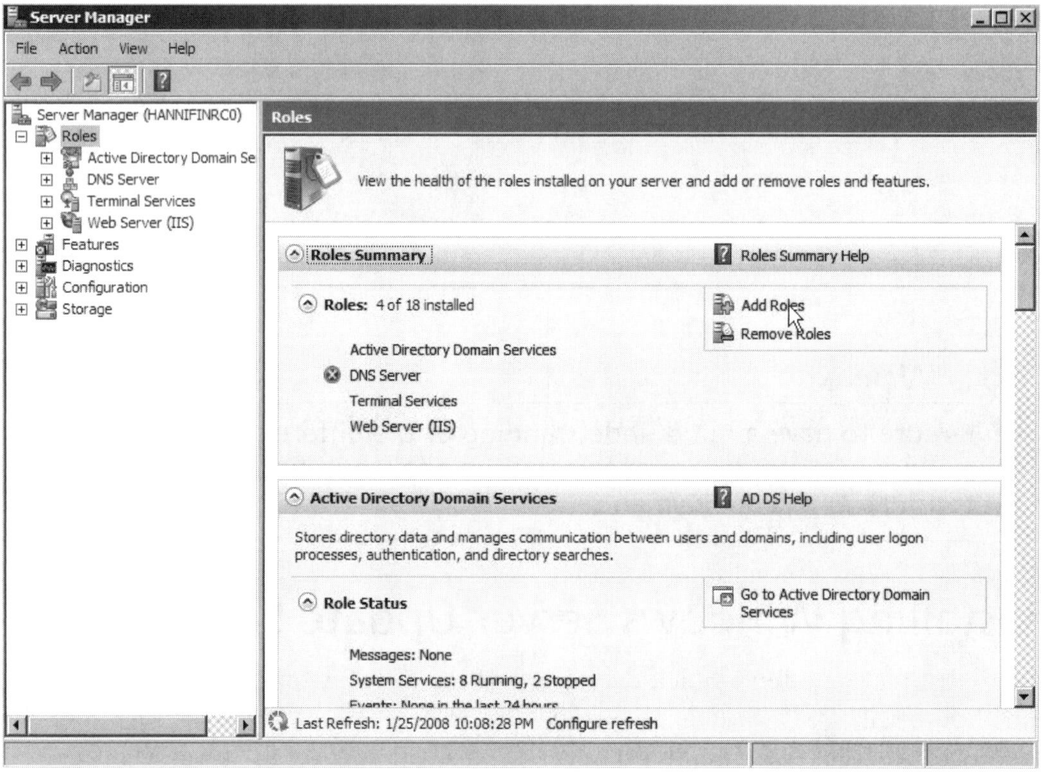

3. Click **Next** to proceed to add a new role.

4. Check the checkbox next to the **Windows Server Update Services** option and click **Next** (see Figure 5.3). The WSUS Install Wizard will launch.

Figure 5.3 Selecting Server Roles

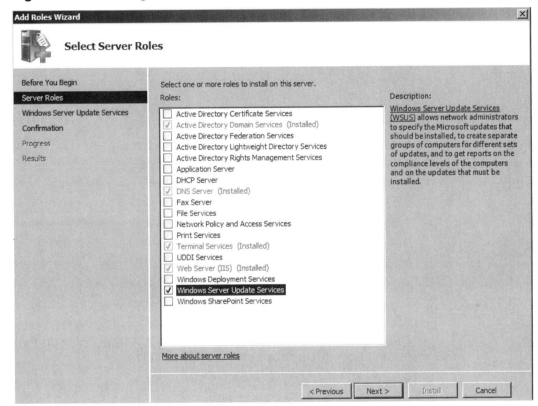

5. Click the **Next** button to proceed to the summary and confirmation screen. Click the **Install** button to begin installation (see Figure 5.4).

Figure 5.4 Confirming Install Selections

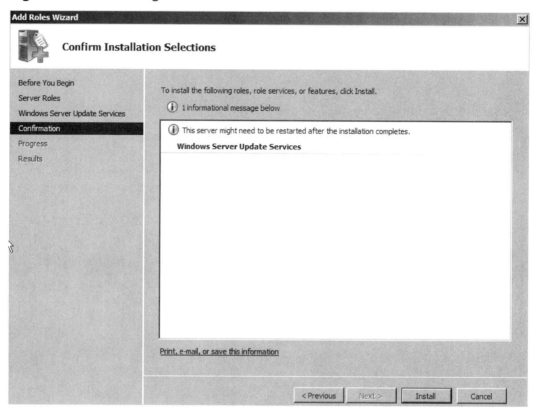

6. The wizard will then download the WSUS components and launch the **Windows Server Update Services Setup Wizard**.

7. Click the **Next** button to begin WSUS Setup. Read and accept the license agreement and click **Next** again.

8. You may receive a warning that the Microsoft Report Viewer is not installed, as shown in Figure 5.5.

Figure 5.5 The Microsoft Report Viewer Warning

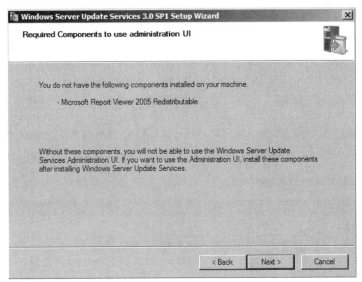

9. Choose the disk drive and folder where you want to store downloaded updates, and then click **Next**. It is recommended that you do not use the same drive as the operating system. The wizard states that you must have at least 6 GB of free disk space for the update. Depending on the size and types of updates selected, you may need a lot more than the recommended minimum. You may want to be safe and use a drive with 20 GB or more (see Figure 5.6).

Figure 5.6 Selecting the Update Source

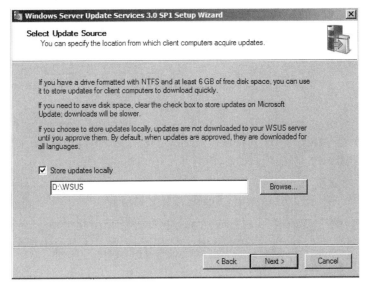

10. Choose a location to install the Windows Internal Database used by WSUS. This can be any drive with at least 2 GB of free space (see Figure 5.7). If you already have a SQL Server 2005 server set up on your corporate network, you may choose the **Using an existing database server on a remote computer** option for the database location. This will create a new WSUS database on that server instead of the WSUS server. This option may be useful if you have dedicated SQL 2005 servers that are managed by database administrators. Once you have chosen a location, click **Next**.

Figure 5.7 Database Options

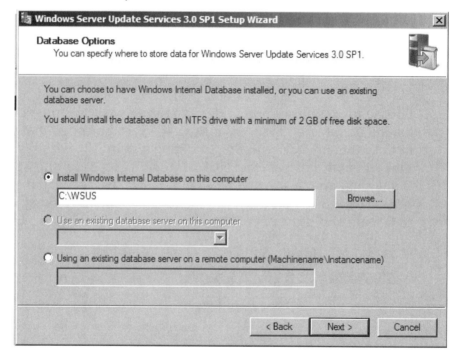

11. The next step is to create a new Internet Information Server (IIS) Web site to host WSUS. Select the **Use the existing IIS Default Web site** option, and then click **Next**.

12. You will now see a summary screen displaying the steps that the wizard is about to perform. Click **Next**.

13. The WSUS role will now take a few minutes to complete setup. After setup completes successfully click the **Finish** button, as shown in Figure 5.8.

Figure 5.8 WSUS Setup Wizard Success

14. The WSUS Configuration Wizard will now launch so that we can properly configure the server. Click the **Next** button to begin configuring the server.

15. In the next step of the wizard, choose whether you want to participate in the customer experience program and click the **Next** button.

16. We now need to decide whether the WSUS server will be downloading updates from Microsoft directly or from another WSUS server on the corporate network. Larger enterprises may need multiple WSUS servers in various locations due to network bandwidth or security boundaries. Some organizations may also choose to deploy separate WSUS servers in DMZs or perimeter networks. For now, we will assume that this is the first WSUS server in our deployment, so go ahead and choose to download updates directly from Microsoft, as shown in Figure 5.9. Then click **Next**.

Figure 5.9 Choosing the Upstream Server

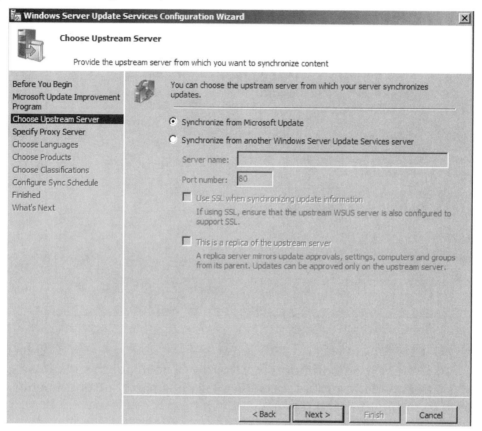

17. If your network requires that you use a proxy server to access the Internet, enter the proper information in this step. Otherwise, just click the **Next** button to continue to the initial connection step of the wizard.

18. The Configuration Wizard now needs to connect to Microsoft update servers to determine products that can be updated via WSUS, languages supported, and the types of updates available. Click the **Start Connecting** button, as shown in Figure 5.10. After the wizard completes the initial connection, click the **Next** button to continue.

Figure 5.10 The Initial Connection to the Upstream Server

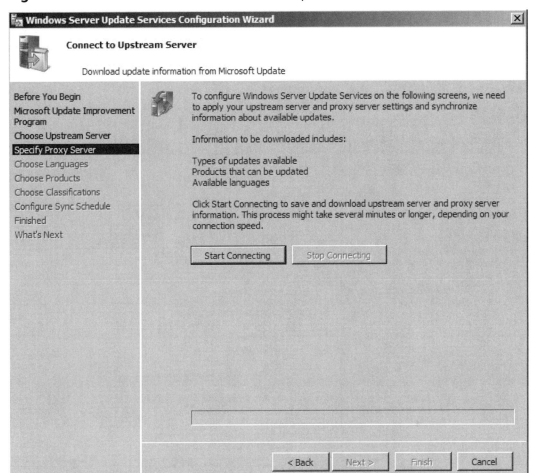

19. We now need to select the languages for which we wish to download updates. If your organization supports applications and operating systems in multiple languages, you will need to download patches for all supported languages. By choosing only the languages that you need, you will use less disk space and your download will be faster. Select the languages your organization supports, and then click the **Next** button to proceed to the next step.

20. In this step of the wizard, we need to select the products for which we want to download updates (see Figure 5.11). You can select to download updates for all products available or only those that you have installed on your network. By selecting only

the products currently installed on your network, you use less disk space to store updates and update downloads from Microsoft require less time. You can always change this configuration in the future if you add new Microsoft products to your network. Select the products you wish to keep updated by WSUS and click the **Next** button.

Figure 5.11 WSUS Product Selection

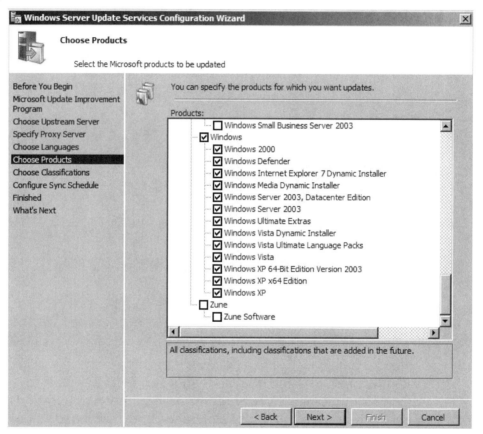

21. We now must select classifications or types of updates we wish to download to WSUS. For example, you may not wish to perform service pack installs or hardware driver updates manually and not via WSUS. Here you can choose not to select those types of updates if you plan to install them manually or by some other method (see Figure 5.12). You can change this configuration later if your update needs change. Select the classification types you wish to download to WSUS and click the **Next** button.

Figure 5.12 WSUS Classification Selection

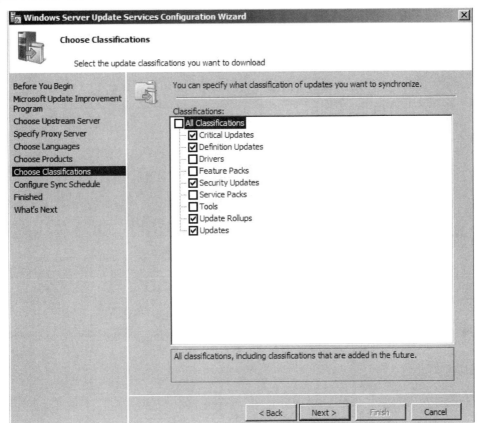

22. We now need to choose whether to sync the WSUS server with Microsoft manually or at a scheduled time every day. In most cases, you will probably want to sync on a regular schedule to ensure that the most current updates are downloaded from Microsoft. Downloading updates may use a significant amount of bandwidth depending on your network's Internet connection speed. You may want to schedule your WSUS server to download updates during hours of low network usage, such as during the night. Go ahead and set a schedule for update downloads and click the **Next** button.

23. Finally, we need to perform an initial synchronization with the Microsoft servers. You can select to do that now in this step or defer until later. Because we have not synchronized our WSUS server with Microsoft yet, it may take a significant amount of

time and bandwidth to download updates for the first time. Select whether you want to perform the initial sync now and click the **Next** button.

24. A summary to steps left to perform to complete WSUS configuration will be displayed. Go ahead and click the **Finish** button.

25. You should now see the WSUS role displayed in Server Manager (see Figure 5.13).

Figure 5.13 The WSUS Role in Server Manager

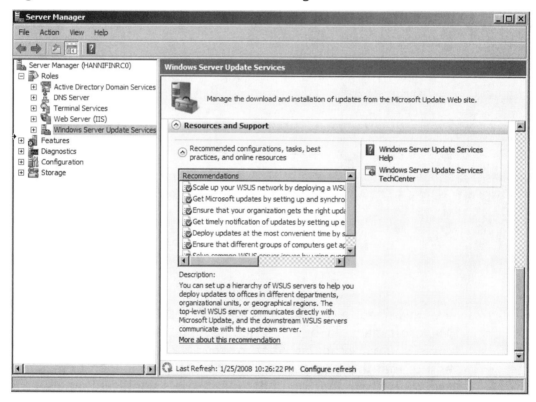

Now that we have explored the setup and initial configuration process for WSUS, let's take a closer look at the server role. In the following sections, we will set up other servers and workstations to download updates from the WSUS server, approve and deploy updates, and discuss WSUS in disconnected networks.

Update Type Selection

During WSUS installation and setup we briefly discussed choosing update types and classifications. It is important to review updates and classifications, as Microsoft regularly adds new products for download and distribution via WSUS. In Exercise 5.2, we'll take a look at how to monitor and manage the update types we are downloading via WSUS.

EXERCISE 5.2

UPDATING TYPE SELECTION

1. Open **Server Manager** by selecting **Start | Administrative Tools | Server Manager**.

2. Expand the **Windows Server Update Services** node then click on the **Options** node.

3. Click the **Products and Classifications** link in the middle pane (see Figure 5.14). This will open the **Products and Classifications** window.

Figure 5.14 WSUS Options

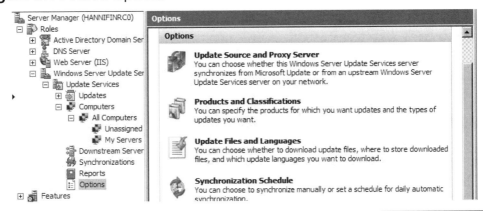

4. You can now select existing or new products and update classifications you wish to distribute to your servers and workstations. You can also deselect any products or update types you will not be distributing via WSUS (see Figure 5.15). After updating your selections, click the **OK** button.

Figure 5.15 Products and Classifications Selection

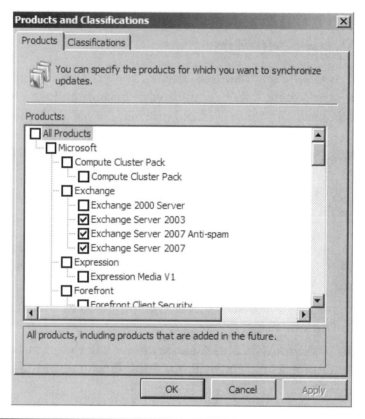

Client Settings

After installing and configuring your WSUS server, you'll need to set up your other workstations and servers to connect to WSUS for their updates. Configuring clients to connect to a WSUS server requires a change to the Windows Update software on those clients. The easiest way to accomplish this change is by using Group Policy. If your clients are in a domain environment, you can create a Group Policy Object (GPO) and link it at the domain or organizational unit (OU) level. This ensures that all clients on the network are properly configured to download updates from your WSUS server. In Exercise 5.3, we'll walk through an example of setting up a GPO that will automatically configure servers to connect to WSUS for Windows updates.

New & Noteworthy...

Client Settings with Multiple WSUS Servers

If your environment contains multiple WSUS servers, you can set up Group Policies to configure clients in different sites, domains, or OUs to report to a specified WSUS server for updates. You can use this design to avoid overloading your WSUS servers and network bandwidth.

EXAM WARNING

Be sure you have a good general understanding of Group Policy for the exam. The exam will very likely try to trip you up on GPO overrides and application order.

EXERCISE 5.3

CREATING WSUS COMPUTER GROUPS

Before we jump into our Group Policy Management Console and create a GPO, we need to configure a couple of options in WSUS:

1. First, open **Server Manager** by selecting **Start | Administrative Tools | Server Manager**.

2. Expand the **Roles | Windows Server Update Services | Computers | All Computers** nodes.

3. Right-click the **All Computers** node and choose **Add Computer Group**, as shown in Figure 5.16.

Figure 5.16 Adding a New Computer Group

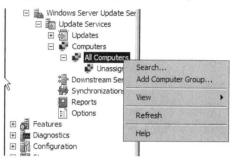

4. In the **New Computer Group** dialog box, enter a name for your new computer group—for example, **My Servers** (see Figure 5.17). Then click the **Add** button.

Figure 5.17 Entering a Computer Group Name

Exam Warning

Be sure to not confuse WSUS computer groups with Active Directory Groups or OUs. The exam may include questions that test your knowledge in knowing the difference.

Configuring WSUS Computer Group Assignment Settings

We now need to configure WSUS to assign computers to this newly created group via Group Policy (see Exercise 5.4). This allows computer group assignment within WSUS to take place automatically. If you do not change this setting, you will have to manually assign all clients to the appropriate computer group after they contact WSUS for the first time.

EXERCISE 5.4

CHANGING COMPUTER GROUP ASSIGNMENT SETTINGS

1. Click the **Options** node in the WSUS role configuration.
2. Click the **Computers** link in the center pane (see Figure 5.18).

Figure 5.18 The WSUS Console Options Pane

3. In the **Computers** window, select the option to **Use Group Policy or registry settings on computers** (see Figure 5.19). Then click the **OK** button. This setting will instruct WSUS to automatically assign client computers to our newly created computer group based upon the GPO applied to those clients.

Figure 5.19 WSUS Computer Assignment Options

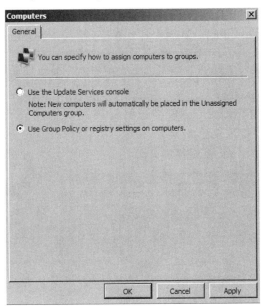

TEST DAY TIP

If none of the answers seem to fit a particular test question, don't panic. Sometimes the questions can be worded to try to trip you up. Take a deep breath and read each answer one word at a time. You'll usually find a word meant to trip you up in some of the answers. This can help you when trying to eliminate incorrect answers.

Group Policy Objects (GPOs)

We are now ready to create our GPO to manage client settings. In our example, we will create a new GPO and link it to a Servers OU within Active Directory. If you have not done so already, create a new OU named "Servers" in Active Directory Users and Computers. After creating the new OU, you will be ready to create and link a GPO. To do this, follow along with Exercise 5.5.

EXERCISE 5.5

SETTING UP A GROUP POLICY TO CONFIGURE CLIENT SETTINGS

1. Select **Start | Administrative Tools | Group Policy Management**. This will open the Group Policy Management Console (GPMC).

2. Within the GPMC, expand the nodes of the forest and domain in which you want to create a new GPO.

3. Locate and right-click on the newly created **Servers** OU. Choose the option to **Create a GPO in this domain, and Link it here**, as shown in Figure 5.20.

Figure 5.20 Creating a New GPO

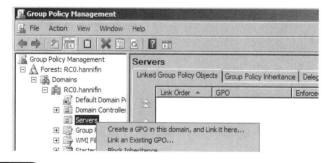

4. The **New GPO** dialog box will appear. Enter a name for the GPO and ensure that **Source Starter GPO** is set to **None**. Then click the **OK** button.

5. Right-click the new GPO you created and choose **Edit**, as shown in Figure 5.21. The Group Policy Editor window will open.

Figure 5.21 Editing the New GPO

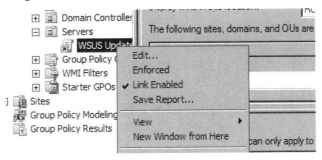

6. Select the **Computer Configuration | Administrative Templates | Windows Components | Windows Update** node. This will display the Windows Update settings that you can configure via GPO. Open each of the following settings by double-clicking on that policy setting. Set each of the following settings as shown in Table 5.1.

Table 5.1 Windows Update GPO Settings

Group Policy Option	Setting(s)
Configure Automatic Updates	• **Enabled**
	• Configure Automatic Updating: **4 – Auto Download and Schedule the install**
	• Schedule Install Day: **7 – Every Saturday**
	• Schedule Install Time: **02:00**

Continued

Table 5.1 Continued. Windows Update GPO Settings

Group Policy Option	Setting(s)
Specify intranet Microsoft update service location	• **Enabled** • Set the intranet update service for detecting updates: **http://*nameof yourWSUSserver* • Set the intranet statistics server: **http://*nameofyourWSUSserver***
Automatic Updates detection frequency	• **Enabled** • Check for updates at the following interval (hours): **12**
Enable Client Side Targeting	• **Enabled** • Target group for this computer: **My Servers**

EXAM WARNING

Be sure to review the all of the Windows Update GPO settings. Each setting should provide a brief explanation of what the setting does.

7. After configuring the appropriate GPO settings, close the **Group Policy Editor**. Then close the **Group Policy Management Console**. This policy will apply to any new clients added to the My Servers OU in Active Directory. In our example, we'll move our WSUS server to this OU.

8. After your clients perform a Group Policy update, they will check in and register with the WSUS server. You should see the clients appear in the My Servers computer group within WSUS role management, as shown in Figure 5.22. You can now easily set up any Windows client to register with your WSUS server for updates simply by placing them in the My Servers OU.

Figure 5.22 A New Computer Automatically Assigned to the WSUS Computer Group

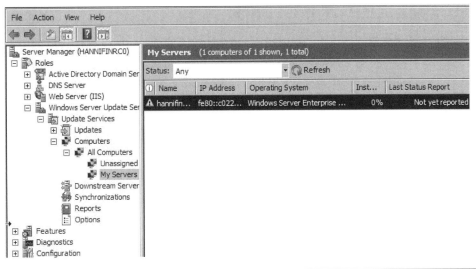

We have just walked through an example of how to use Group Policy to configure your clients to connect to WSUS for update management. You can easily apply these GPO settings to multiple OUs or domains, depending on the needs within your organization.

Client Targeting

In the preceding section, you learned how to use a GPO to automatically configure the Windows Update settings for computers that you want to connect to the WSUS server for updates. From the preceding exercise, you saw how we can use GPO settings to instruct a client computer to become a member of a particular computer group within WSUS. This prevents you from having to manually add computers to computer groups within WSUS.

Software Updates

Now that your clients are configured to connect to WSUS for Windows updates, we need to take a look at how to review, manage, and deploy updates from the WSUS management console. In Exercise 5.6, we'll take a look at viewing and managing software updates.

EXERCISE 5.6

EXPLORING SOFTWARE UPDATES

1. Open **Server Manager** by selecting **Start | Administrative Tools | Server Manager**.

2. Expand the **Roles | Windows Server Update Services | Updates** nodes.

3. Click to highlight the **Updates** node. This will display the Updates Dashboard in the middle pane. The dashboard displays a high-level status of updates, as shown in Figure 5.23. This is a quick way to see the deployment status of updates in your environment.

Figure 5.23 The WSUS Updates Dashboard

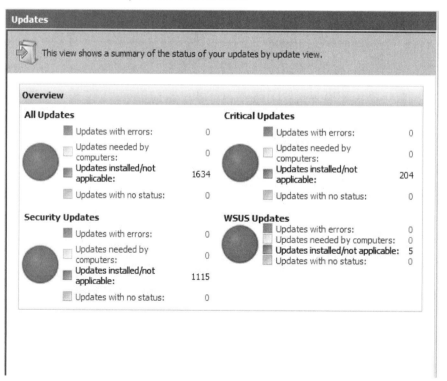

4. Expand the **Updates** node to see predefined views of updates. These views allow you to easily inspect updates for review and deployment. For example, you can easily review and deploy critical updates by using the **Critical Updates** view. Go ahead and

click the **All Updates** view, choose **Unapproved** from the Approval drop-down menu, and then click **Refresh** (see Figure 5.24). After the view is refreshed, you should see a list of all unapproved updates available for deployment.

Figure 5.24 The Updates | All Updates View

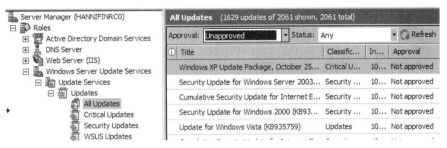

5. You can see more information on any update simply by clicking and highlighting that update in the center pane. Click on any update and notice that the details of this update appear in the bottom half of the view, as shown in Figure 5.25. Notice that this detailed information even provides a link to the Microsoft Knowledgebase article that references the update.

Figure 5.25 The Update Details Window

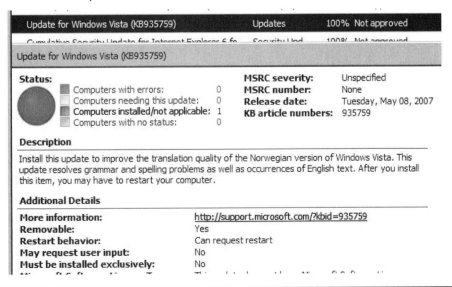

In this section, you saw how using the predefined views allows you to quickly review updates available for deployment via your WSUS server. We will now discuss the process to test updates and then deploy those updates to your production clients.

Test and Approval

You are finally ready to begin rolling out updates to your workstations and servers. However, it is always good practice to deploy updates to a test environment before pushing them out to your production systems. In this section, we will walk through the process of deploying updates to a test environment and then to a production environment. In our example, we will be using two WSUS computer groups. The My Servers group contains all production servers. The Test Lab group contains our test lab servers and workstations. Figure 5.26 depicts the example environment.

Figure 5.26 The WSUS Example Environment

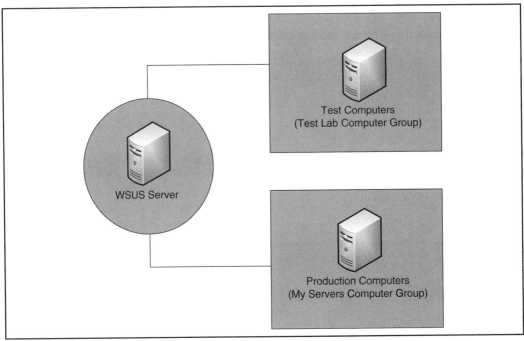

We have one WSUS server that downloads updates from Microsoft. Within WSUS we have two computer groups defined. These groups are named Test Lab and My Servers. Our example computers exist within one of two OUs named Test Lab Computers and My Servers. A GPO is applied to each OU. The GPO configures computers to connect to the WSUS server and assigns them to the correct computer group within WSUS. A GPO applied to the Test Lab Computers OU schedules computers in the OU to install updates Mondays at 11:00 P.M. Another GPO applied to the My Servers OU schedules computers to install updates Thursdays at 11:30 P.M. In Exercise 5.7, we'll walk through the process of testing an update and then deploying that update to our production servers.

EXERCISE 5.7

APPROVING WSUS UPDATES

1. Open **Server Manager** by selecting **Start | Administrative Tools | Server Manager**.

2. Expand the **Roles | Windows Servers Update Services | Update Services | Updates** nodes.

3. Click to highlight the **All Updates** view.

4. In the middle pane, click on an update that you wish to deploy. Then, in the Actions pane, click the **Approve** link (see Figure 5.27). The **Approve Updates** window will open.

Figure 5.27 Update Selection

5. Right-click the **Test Lab** computer group and select **Approved for Install**, as shown in Figure 5.28. Then click the **OK** button. The next time the clients in the Test Lab Computers OU check in with WSUS they will begin downloading the approved update. After downloading the update, the client computers will then wait until the scheduled install time of Monday at 11:00 P.M., and then install the update. After the update is installed, the computers will reboot.

Figure 5.28 The Approve Updates Window

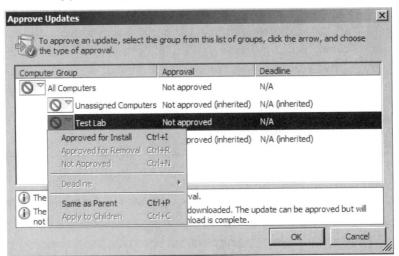

6. Now that we have deployed the update to our test lab, we can confirm that there are no compatibility issues that might impact our production environment. After deploying to the Test Lab and confirming that there are no problems with the update, we can deploy to production systems. Locate the update in the **All Updates** view.

7. Right-click the same update you just deployed and choose **Approve**.

8. In the **Approve Updates** window, right-click the **My Servers** computer group and then click **Approved for Install**. Now click the **OK** button. The next time the client computers in the My Servers OU connect to WSUS they will begin downloading the approved update. The computers will then wait until the scheduled time to install the update and reboot.

We have now deployed the update to our test lab and production environment. You can follow the same steps to deploy multiple updates at the same time. Remember that it is generally a good practice to deploy updates to a test environment before deploying to your production environment.

Disconnected Networks

WSUS provides a great way to centralize the management and deployment of updates to your Windows workstations and servers. But what if you want to deploy your WSUS server in a network disconnected from the Internet? Some networks must remain disconnected from the Internet for security reasons. In this situation, you can deploy a WSUS server on a network that does have Internet connectivity and download updates to that server. You can then copy those updates to removable media (CD, DVD, etc.). Those updates can then be imported to the WSUS server in the disconnected network via the removable media. The updates will then appear in the WSUS console and can be deployed to clients on that network via WSUS. To transfer updates to your disconnected WSUS server follow along with Exercise 5.8.

EXERCISE 5.8

IMPORTING WSUS UPDATES IN A DISCONNECTED NETWORK

1. Open **Server Manager** on your Internet-connected WSUS server by selecting **Start | Administrative Tools | Server Manager**.

2. Expand the **Windows Server Update Services | Update Services** node.

3. Click to highlight the **Options** node.

4. Click the **Updates Files and Languages** link in the center pane of the console.

5. Click the **Update Files** tab and check the box to **Download express installation files** (see Figure 5.29). Then click the **OK** button.

Figure 5.29 The Update Files and Languages Pane

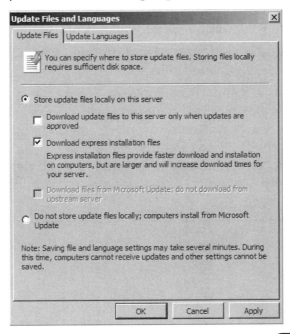

6. Log on to the disconnected server and ensure that the Updates and Files settings are configured exactly the same as the Internet-connected server.

7. You are now ready to export the files and metadata from the Internet-connected server and copy those to your media. To do this, first copy the folder ***WSUSInstallDrive\WSUSUpdatesFolder* WSUSContent** (C:\WSUS\WSUSContent) to your removable media. Depending on the size of the updates available, this folder could be very large.

8. Next, you need to run **WSUSUtil.exe** to export the metadata from the Internet-connected server. Open a command prompt and change to the directory **C:\Program Files\Update Services\Tools**.

9. Run the command **wsusutil.exe export transfer.cab transfer.log**. Then press **Enter**. The metadata export process will begin.

10. After the export completes, copy the **transfer.cab** and **transfer.log** files to the media that will be used to transfer data to the disconnected network server.

11. We are now ready to import the updates and metadata to our disconnected WSUS server. First, copy the **WSUSContent** folder to ***WSUSInstallDrive\WSUSUpdatesFolder*** (C:\WSUS). If prompted, you can replace existing files.

12. Finally, you need to import the metadata to the disconnected WSUS server. Copy the **transfer.cab** file to the directory **C:\ Program Files\Update Services\Tools** on the disconnected server.

13. Open a command prompt and change to the **C:\Program Files\ Update Services\Tools** directory.

14. Enter the command **wsusutil.exe import transfer.cab transfer. log**. This will import the metadata to your disconnected server. This process can take an extended amount of time. After the process completes, you can approve and deploy updates from the disconnected WSUS server. You will need to perform this process anytime you download new updates to your Internet-connected WSUS server.

Capturing Performance Data

Collecting and analyzing performance data is necessary to ensure that your servers and systems are running in optimal condition. It is important that you understand how your servers are performing during normal conditions to establish baselines. This type of information can be crucial when trying to troubleshoot performance problems. Collecting this data can also help you to proactively find bottlenecks and correct them before system performance is severely impacted.

Data Collector Sets

Data Collector Sets are groups of components that collect data to be used by the Reliability and Performance Monitor. Data Collector Sets can contain information from performance counters, trace events, and configuration data. You can then view this data in the Reliability and Performance Monitor or use it to create reports. In Exercise 5.9, we'll look at some of the predefined system Data Collector Sets as well as creating our own.

EXERCISE 5.9

RUNNING A DATA COLLECTOR SET

1. Open the Reliability and Performance Monitor in Server Manager by selecting **Start | Administrative Tools | Server Manager**.

2. Expand the **Diagnostics | Reliability and Performance | Data Collector Sets** nodes (see Figure 5.30).

Figure 5.30 Data Collector Sets

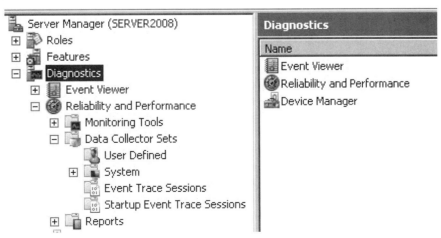

Now let's explore the system-defined sets. These contain pre-defined counters and log monitoring to provide some key statistics that help to determine the health of your server. Let's take a look at these Data Collector Sets.

3. Expand the **System** node under **Data Collector Sets**. You should see several predefined sets, such as System Performance, LAN Diagnostics, and Active Directory Diagnostics.

4. Click to highlight the **System Performance** set. Notice that the Data Collector Set contains an NT Kernel trace and Performance Counter item (see Figure 5.31).

Figure 5.31 The System Performance Data Collector Set

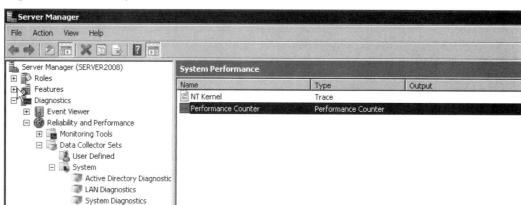

5. Right-click the **Performance Counter** item and choose **Properties**. This will open the **Performance Counter Properties** window. Here you can see a list of all performance counters that this Data Collector Set will gather (see Figure 5.32). Click the **OK** button to close the window.

Figure 5.32 Performance Counter Properties

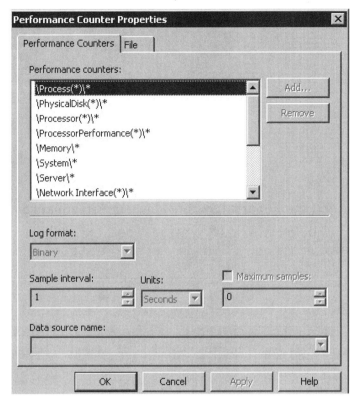

6. We now need to start the Data Collector Set. This will start the process of gathering data. Right-click the **System Performance** set and choose **Start**. This will start data collection. You should see a green arrow on top of the set (see Figure 5.33). This indicates that the collector is running. The Data Collector Set will run for one minute and then stop. After stopping, a report will automatically be generated under the Reports node.

Figure 5.33 Running the Data Collector Set

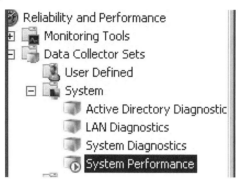

7. Expand the **Reports | System | System Performance** nodes.

8. You should see a newly created report under the System Performance node. Click on that report to open it in the center pane, as shown in Figure 5.34.

Figure 5.34 The System Performance Report

New & Noteworthy...

Data Collector Sets

Data Collector Sets are a new addition to the Windows Server product. The included Data Collector Sets provide some best-practice troubleshooting stats. You may already have experience troubleshooting performance problems in previous versions of Windows. If this is the case, you probably know how tough it can sometimes be to remember what performance counters or logs to look at when tackling a performance issue. Data Collector Sets use predetermined *best-practice* counters and logs provided by Microsoft. The included Data Collector Sets are also a great way to regularly ensure that your servers are running in an optimal condition. If you decide you need additional data, you can always create your own Data Collector Set using custom counters and logs.

The resultant report displays detailed information about system performance. This type of report can be very valuable when troubleshooting performance problems. We can see at the bottom of our report that memory is being reported as busy and only 126 MB are available. We also received a warning that the system is experiencing excessive paging. We could easily use this report to determine whether we need to upgrade the memory on this system. Now that we've looked at the built-in system Data Collector Sets, let's create a custom set of our own (see Exercise 5.10).

EXERCISE 5.10

CREATING A CUSTOM DATA COLLECTOR SET

1. Right-click the **User Defined** node under **Data Collector Sets**. Then choose **New | Data Collector Set**. This will launch the **Create New Data Collector Set Wizard**.

2. In the first step of the **Create New Data Collector Set Wizard**, enter a name for your set and make sure the **Create from a template** option is selected; then click the **Next** button (see Figure 5.35).

Figure 5.35 The Create New Data Collector Set Wizard

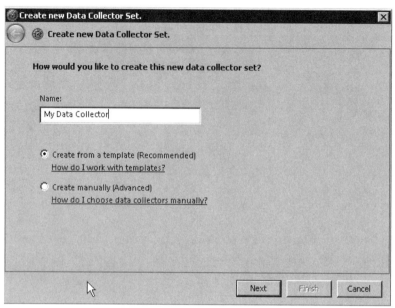

3. We now need to choose which template to use. Select the **Basic** template, and then click the **Next** button.

4. In the next step of the wizard, you need to enter a location to store the data. Enter **C:\MyDataCollector** and then click the **Next** button.

5. Finally, you can choose to run the Data Collector Set as a certain account. Go ahead and leave the **RunAs** setting at **default**. Choose the **Save and Close** option. Then click the **Finish** button.

    You should now see the new Data Collector Set under the **User Defined** node, as shown in Figure 5.36. We now need to configure the **My Data Collector** to collect the data we wish to review. Go ahead and perform the following to set up our data collection options.

Figure 5.36 The New Data Collector Set

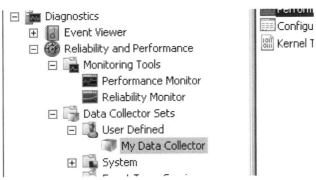

6. Click **My Data Collector** to highlight the set.

7. Next, right-click the **Performance Counter** item in the center pane and choose **Properties**. This will open the **Performance Counter Properties** window (see Figure 5.37).

Figure 5.37 Performance Counter Properties

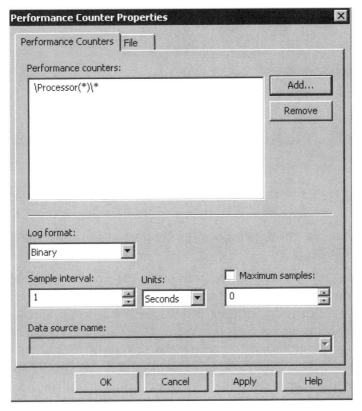

8. In the **Performance Counter Properties** window, click the **Add** button. This will open the **Performance Counter Selection** window.

9. Select the counter **Logical Disk | Avg. Disk Queue Length**. Then select the **C:** instance and click the **Add** button (see Figure 5.38).

Figure 5.38 Performance Counter Selection

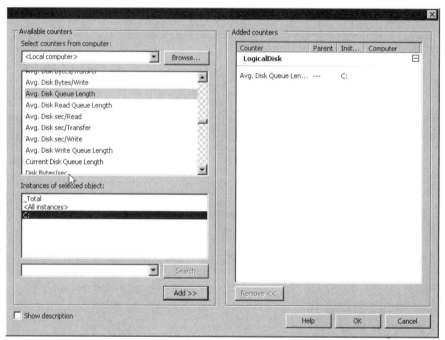

10. Go ahead and add the **Current Disk Queue Length** and **Avg. Disk Read Queue Length** counters. Then click the **OK** button.

11. In the **Performance Counter Properties** window, click the **OK** button.

12. Now right-click the **My Data Collector** node and choose **Properties**. This will open the **Collector Set Properties** window. You can set various options for your data collector in this window. For example, you could use the Schedule tab to schedule a date and time for the data collector to begin collecting data. This will allow you to collect data when you are not logged on to the server. For now, we just want to set the stop condition for our data collector.

13. Click the **Stop Condition** tab.

14. Ensure that the **Overall duration** option is selected. Then set the **duration** to **5 minutes** (see Figure 5.39). Then click the **OK** button.

Figure 5.39 The Data Collector Set Properties Window

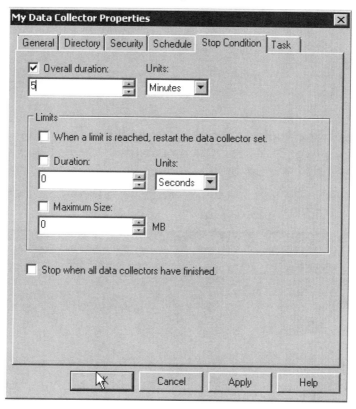

15. Now that the Data Collector Set is set up, go ahead and start the data collector and wait for five minutes for the collector to stop.

16. After the collector stops, locate the newly created report in the **Reports | Use Defined | My Data Collector** node. Right-click the new report and choose **View | Performance Monitor**.

17. In the center pane, click the **Add** button, as shown in Figure 5.40.

Figure 5.40 Adding a Performance Counter

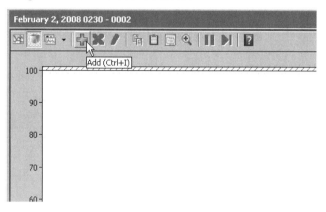

18. Select the **Logical Disk | Avg. Disk Queue Length** and **Logical Disk | Avg. Disk Read Queue Length** counters (see Figure 5.41). Then click the **OK** button.

Figure 5.41 The Add Counters Pane

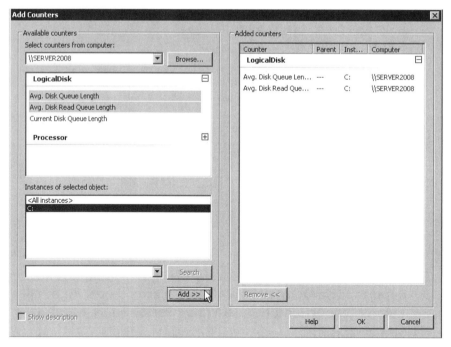

19. You will now see a graph of the performance data collected by the Data Collector Set (see Figure 5.42).

Figure 5.42 The Data Collector Set Graph

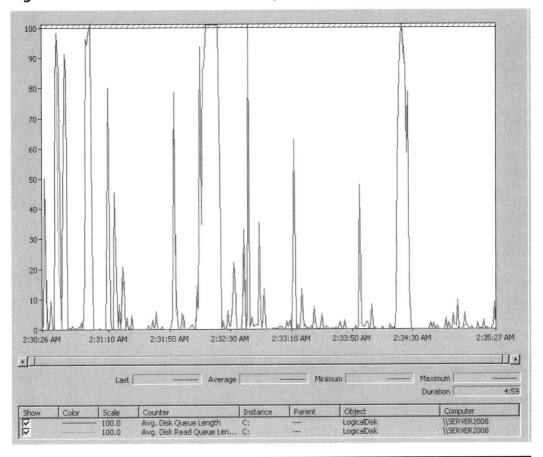

We just discovered how to set up and review Data Collector Sets in Windows Server 2008. As you can see, these sets provide an easy way to capture performance and log data to troubleshoot system performance issues. You should collect and review performance data on a regular basis to ensure that your servers are running at optimal performance. For example, you may want to schedule a Data Collector Set to run between 8:00 A.M. and 10:00 A.M. to monitor the load on your servers during peak logon hours at your company. In the next section, we will cover Performance Monitor in a little more depth. Keep in mind that running Data Collector Sets can increase the load on your server. Typically, the load caused by Data Collector Sets is very small; however, if you are running them on a highly utilized server, the collection job could impact server performance.

Performance Monitor

Now that we've explored Data Collector Sets, let's take a look at Performance Monitor in a little more depth. You can use Performance Monitor to review system performance data collected by Data Collector Sets as well as in real time. Performance Monitor also allows you to view the data in different formats. It is important to understand some of the key performance counters in Performance Monitor. Table 5.2 lists a few counters you should become familiar with. The table includes the counter name, a brief description, and the threshold value.

Table 5.2 Performance Counters

Counter	Description	Threshold Value
Memory\Pages/sec	Pages/sec is the number of memory pages written to disk every second. High pages/sec can indicate memory problems with your server.	20
Processor\% Processor Time	This is the percentage of the processor time spent executing tasks.	85%
System\Processor Queue Length	This counter tracks the number of threads queued and waiting to be processed.	2
Physical Disk\Current Disk Queue Length	This counter collects the current number of waiting requests for the physical disk.	Number of Disk Spindles + 2

In Exercise 5.11, we'll take a closer look at Performance Monitor.

EXAM WARNING

Be sure you review all of the settings in Performance Monitor. Performance Monitor has been part of Microsoft certification exams since the Windows NT days. Microsoft still believes this tool is important enough to include in exam questions.

EXERCISE 5.11

EXPLORING PERFORMANCE MONITOR

1. Open **Server Manager** by selecting **Start | Administrative Tools | Server Manager**.

2. Expand the **Diagnostics | Reliability and Performance | Monitoring Tools** nodes.

3. Click on the **Performance Monitor** node to display Performance Monitor in the center pane of the console.

4. Performance Monitor uses what is known as *counters*. Counters are the different types of data collection you can add to Performance Monitor. Go ahead and click the **Add** button, as shown in Figure 5.43. The **Add Counters** window will open.

Figure 5.43 The Add Button in Performance Monitor

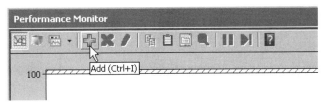

5. Expand the **Processor** heading and then click the **% Processor Time** counter. Choose the **_Total** instance and click the **Add** button (see Figure 5.44). You can also check the **Show description** checkbox to display a description of any of the counters. Go ahead and also add the **%Idle Time** counter too. Then click the **OK** button.

Figure 5.44 Selecting Data to Display

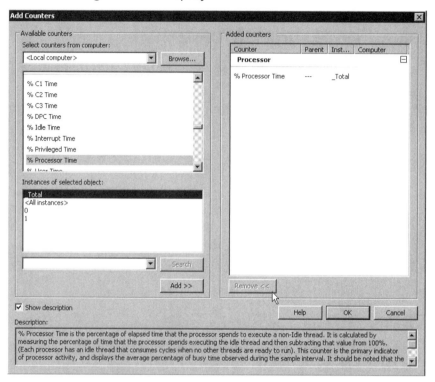

6. The **Performance Monitor** window will immediately begin to display data from the selected counters. Notice that this data is being displayed in real time. Performance Monitor lets us view this data in a few different formats. If you want to view the raw numbers being collected, you can change the view to **Report** (see Figure 5.45).

Figure 5.45 The Report View

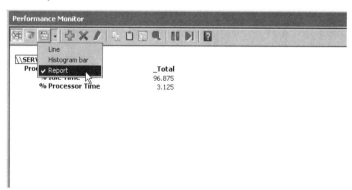

7. You can quickly change your data view from real time to data from a Data Collector Set. Click the **Data Collector** icon in the toolbar of the **Performance Monitor** window. Choose the **Log files** option and add the data directory for any existing Data Collector Sets (see Figure 5.46). Then click the **OK** button. You will now see performance data from an existing Data Collector Set.

Figure 5.46 Viewing Data from a Data Collector Set

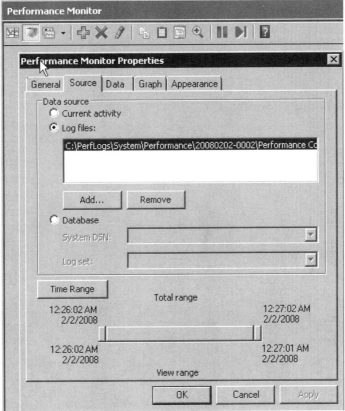

In this section, we discovered how to use Performance Monitor to review system performance data in real time, or that collected by Data Collector Sets. Performance Monitor is a great way to troubleshoot performance issues and find bottlenecks with server hardware and software. Some common performance counters to watch are % Processor Time, Avg Disk Queue Length, and Memory Pages/Sec. Now let's take a look at Reliability Monitor.

Reliability Monitor

Reliability Monitor is a new feature introduced in Windows Vista and Windows Server 2008. Reliability Monitor keeps track of system stability over time and reports on events that could cause the system to become unreliable. Reliability Monitor keeps track of software installs, uninstalls, system failures, application failures, and hardware failures. These failures are logged and displayed in the Reliability Monitor window. You can access Reliability Monitor by opening **Server Manager** and expanding the **Diagnostics | Reliability and Performance | Monitoring Tools** nodes and then selecting **Reliability Monitor** (see Figure 5.47). You should review Reliability Monitor on a regular basis to check for system or application failures. This is also a quick and easy way to see what new software that has been installed or removed from the system.

Figure 5.47 Reliability Monitor

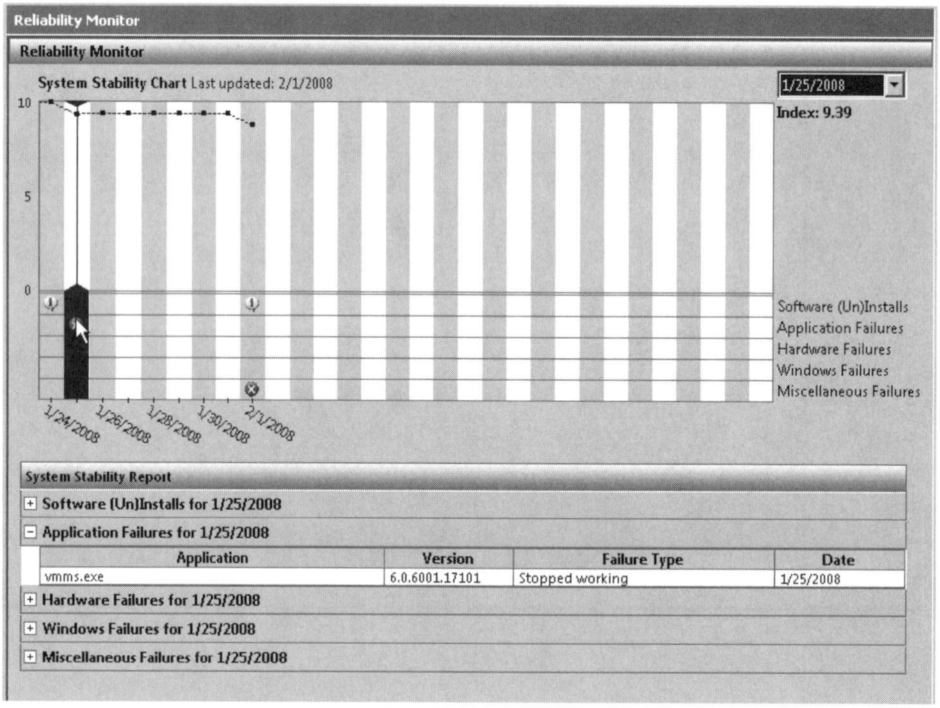

In Figure 5.47, you can see that on 1/25/2008 this system experienced an issue with the vmms.exe application. If this failure continues to take place, you should troubleshoot this application, as it may be impacting the overall stability of the system. Next we'll discuss the System Stability Index.

Monitoring the System Stability Index

The System Stability Index is a measurement that indicates the overall reliability of the server. The index is a number between 1 and 10, with 1 being the least stable and 10 being the most stable. As application or system failures occur, they negatively impact the System Stability Index. Recent failures have more impact on the overall index than historical failures. The more time the system goes without failures, the more the index increases. The System Stability Index is a great way to understand the overall stability of the system over time. To see the System Stability Index open Reliability Monitor by opening **Server Manager** and expanding the **Diagnostics | Reliability and Performance | Monitoring Tools** nodes and then selecting **Reliability Monitor** (see Figure 5.48). The System Stability Index is displayed in the upper-right-hand corner of Reliability Monitor. You can view the index for a single day or for the system over time.

TEST DAY TIP

Be sure to always read all of the answers to a test question. It's easy to prematurely select the wrong answer that may appear to be correct on the surface.

Figure 5.48 The System Stability Index

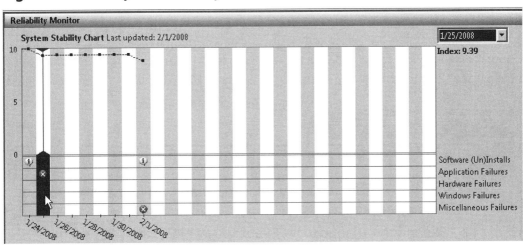

If you begin to see a decline in the System Stability Index over time, you should determine the root cause of the issue based on application and system failures. A decrease in the System Stability Index could imply that the reliability of the entire server is being impacted. This, of course, impacts user's ability to access applications that may be running on this system.

Monitoring Event Logs

Event logs have been a valuable tool for troubleshooting Windows operating system and application problems for years. Windows has traditionally provided three main log categories. These categories are System, Application, and Security. The System log contains entries, also known as *events*, related to the Windows operating system and components that make up the OS. The Application log contains events related to applications running on top of the operating system. Third-party applications typically write to this log. Finally, the Security log is a source of security-related events, such as logons, attempts to access files, and privilege use. Windows Server 2008 introduces two new log categories: Setup logs and Forwarded Events logs. The Setup log keeps events related to application installs. The Forwarded Events log contains logged events forwarded from other systems' Event logs. This allows you to provide simple centralized log management and monitoring of remote servers. Finally, Application and Services logs provide logs for specific applications. For example, a database application could write events to a log specifically available for that application. Let's take a closer look at Event logs.

Custom Views

You can create custom views of Event logs to easily filter events and save the filter for use the next time you access the Event Viewer. For example, maybe you need a quick way to log on and view only critical events on a particular server. You can create a custom view for critical events and simply click on that view anytime you need to see those events in the future. In Exercise 5.12, we will create a custom view.

EXERCISE 5.12

CREATING A CUSTOM EVENT VIEW

1. Open **Server Manager** by selecting **Start | Administrative Tools | Server Manager**.

2. Expand the **Diagnostics | Event Viewer | Custom Views** nodes (see Figure 5.49).

Figure 5.49 Custom Views

3. Right-click the **Custom Views** node and choose **Create Custom View**. This will open the **Create Custom View** window.

4. Select the checkboxes for **Critical** and **Warning** events. Then click the drop-down list next to **Event Logs**. Choose the **Windows Logs** main heading, as shown in Figure 5.50. Then click the **OK** button.

Figure 5.50 Creating a Custom Event View

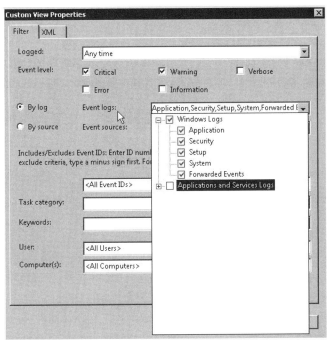

5. In the **Save Filter to Custom View** window, enter **All Critical and Warning Events** for the name of your view. Click to highlight **Custom Views** (see Figure 5.51). Then click the **OK** button.

Figure 5.51 Saving a Filter to a Custom View

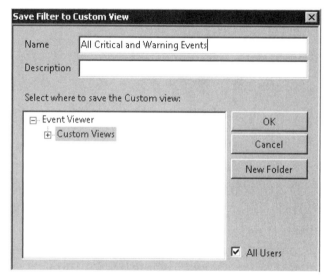

6. The view is now displayed under the **Custom Views** node. Click the view to see all events with a severity of Warning or Critical (see Figure 5.52).

Figure 5.52 The All Critical and Warning Events Custom View

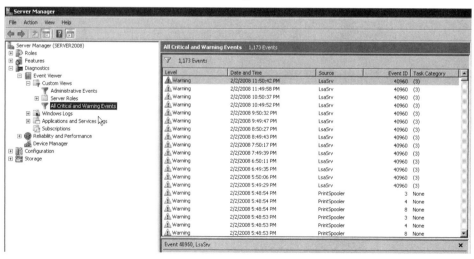

You can create custom views to filter events from various Event logs. Custom views allow you to easily save commonly used filters.

TEST DAY TIP

As you perform the exercises in this book, take some of your own screenshots. Screenshots provide a ton of information with just a glance. Keep these screenshots handy and use them as part of your "cram" session before the exam.

Application and Services Logs

Application and Services logs is a new feature introduced in Windows Server 2008. Application and Services logs are logs focused on monitoring specific applications instead of events that have an impact on the entire server. Application and Services logs contain four types of logs per application. These types are Admin, Operational, Analytic, and Debug.

Admin Logs

Admin logs contain information typically useful to system administrators. These logs usually contain the error that occurred and details of that error. The events also will typically contain steps an administrator can take to resolve the error.

Operational Logs

Operational logs contain information for diagnosing problems. These events contain fewer error descriptions and more diagnostic data than the Admin logs, but administrators can still use them to determine the root cause of the problem. Some of the events in the Operational logs may be useful to application developers when debugging program bugs.

Analytic Logs

Analytic logs contain information that is not useful for most server administrators. Microsoft support personnel can use these logs when contacting Microsoft Support Services.

Debug Logs

Debug logs contain very detailed information that can be useful to developers when debugging application code.

Subscriptions

Windows Server 2008 and Windows Vista provide the ability to forward event logs to another computer. This allows you to centralize the collection of events from remote computers. By centralizing events, you can review and monitor logs from multiple computers in one location. To collect events from remote computers, you must set up subscriptions. To create subscriptions we must first configure source computers, also known as *sources*, to forward events and the central computer, also known as the *collector*, to receive events. In Exercise 5.13, we will use the computer names Chost1 and Chost2. Chost2 will be our source and Chost1 will be our collector.

EXERCISE 5.13

SETTING UP AN EVENT LOG SUBSCRIPTION

On all computers whose events you wish to forward to a collector computer, you need to set up event forwarding. To set up the source computers we need to configure winrm, which allows remote management, and open the appropriate port on the host firewall to allow inbound and outbound winrm traffic. To do this, log on to each source computer and perform the following:

1. Log on to Chost2.

2. Open a command prompt and type the command **winrm quickconfig**.

3. When prompted whether you want to make changes to the WinRM listener and Windows Firewall, enter **Y**. You will receive a confirmation that these changes were successful.

    On the collector computer, you need to set up event collection. In this task, we will enable and start the collector service on the central server. Perform the following on the central collection server to configure and enable the event collector service:

4. Log on to Chost1.

5. Open a command prompt and type the command **wecutil qc**. Then, when prompted to change the service startup mode, choose **Yes**. You should see a confirmation that the collector service was set up properly.

    Now that we have properly set up event forwarding and collection, we need to create subscriptions for the events we wish to forward to the collector. Subscriptions are set up on the collector computer. Perform the following to create a subscription:

6. Log on to Chost1 (Collector).

7. Open **Server Manager** by selecting **Start | Administrative Tools | Server Manager**.

8. Expand the **Diagnostics | Event Viewer** nodes.

9. Right-click the **Subscriptions** node and choose **Create Subscription**.

10. In the **Subscription Properties** window, enter the text **All Critical and Warning Events** in the **Subscription Name** text box.

11. Choose the **Collector Initiated** option. This option will instruct the collector to connect to the source computers to gather events.

12. Click the **Select Computers** button.

13. In the **Computers** window, click the **Add domain computers** button. Enter the name **Chost2** and click the **OK** button. Click the **OK** button in the **Computers** window to return to the **Subscription Properties** window.

14. Click the **Select Events** button.

15. Select the **Critical** and **Warning** options and then choose all **Windows Logs**, as shown in Figure 5.53. Then click the **OK** button.

Figure 5.53 The Query Filter Window

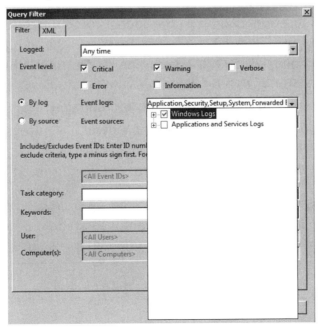

16. Click the **Advanced** button to open the **Advanced Subscription Settings** window.

17. Select the option **Specific User** and click the **User and Password** button.

18. Enter a username and password with sufficient access to the event logs on the source computer. Then click the **OK** button.

19. Click the **OK** button two more times to close all windows.

20. You will now see the subscription active in the center pane, as shown in Figure 5.54.

Figure 5.54 An Active Subscription

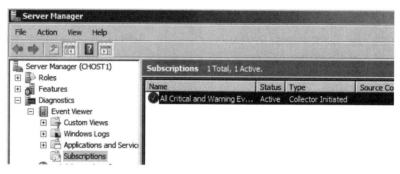

21. Now that we have successfully set up a subscription, let's test our configuration. Log on to the source computer, Chost2.

22. Open a command prompt and enter the command **EVENTCREATE /T Warning /ID 500 /L Application /D "Testing Subscription"**. This will create a warning event on Chost2.

23. Log on to Chost1 and open **Server Manager**.

24. Click on the **Diagnostics | Event Viewer | Windows Logs | Forwarded Events** node.

25. The Warning Event you created on Chost2 should be displayed in the Forwarded Events log on Chost1. You may need to click the **Refresh** button if the event does not appear. There is a short delay between the time an event is logged on a local computer and the time it is forwarded to the collector server.

Now that we have successfully created a subscription, we can set up multiple computers for event forwarding. We can then use subscriptions to centralize log collection. The collector server can then be used to troubleshoot problems for computers throughout the enterprise from a central location.

DNS Event Log

You can view the DNS logs by opening the DNS management console. The DNS Event log is used to capture and monitor domain name system (DNS)-specific events, and can provide detailed information about errors or the health of DNS on your server. You should review the DNS Event log on a regular basis for error events.

Gathering Network Data

Gathering network data is an important step in both managing and troubleshooting your network infrastructure. Microsoft provides several tools and services to allow you to more easily gather data from your Windows servers.

Simple Network Management Protocol (SNMP)

The Simple Network Management Protocol (SNMP) has been used for years to manage and monitor network devices such as switches, routers, and firewalls. Windows servers also provide the capability for management systems to connect and monitor them. In Exercise 5.14, we'll walk through setting up SNMP on a server.

EXERCISE 5.14

CONFIGURING SNMP

1. Log on to the server and open **Server Manager**.

2. Click the **Features** node. Then click the **Add Features** link in the center pane.

3. Choose to add **SNMP Service** and **SNMP WMI Provider** (see Figure 5.55). Then click the **Next** button. This will install the SNMP core services.

Figure 5.55 The Add Features Wizard

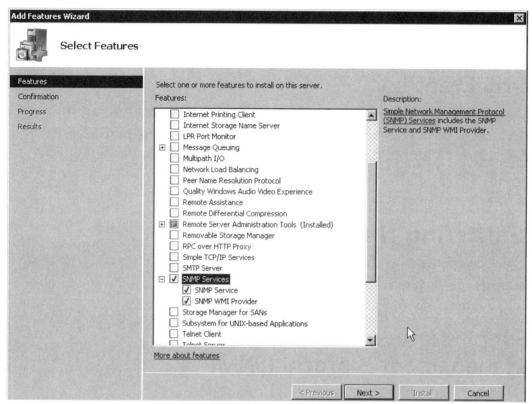

4. After the install completes, return to **Server Manager** and click on the **Configuration | Services** node.

5. Locate and double-click the **SNMP Service** to open the Properties window.

6. Click the **Agent** tab. On this tab, you configure what information you want to provide via SNMP, such as application, network, and hardware information. You can also enter system contact information on this tab. Go ahead and enter contact information and select all options on this tab (see Figure 5.56). Then click on the **Traps** tab.

Figure 5.56 SNMP Service Properties

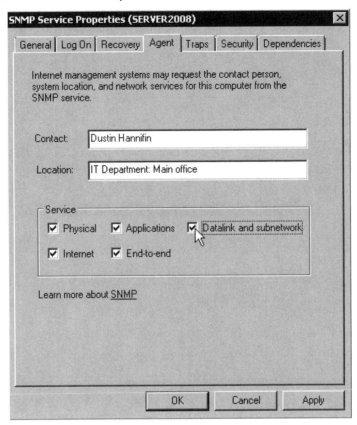

7. On the **Traps** tab, you can set up the trap destination and community name used by that system. The trap destination is the server or device with the SNMP monitoring software installed. This is where the server will send SNMP alerts, also known as *traps*. You will also need to enter a community name. Community names are simple passwords used to secure SNMP data. Without the SNMP community name, a system cannot send or receive SNMP data from other devices that use a community name. You will need to specify the community name of your monitoring server on the **Traps** tab (see Figure 5.57). After entering trap information, click on the **Security** tab.

Figure 5.57 SNMP Trap Properties

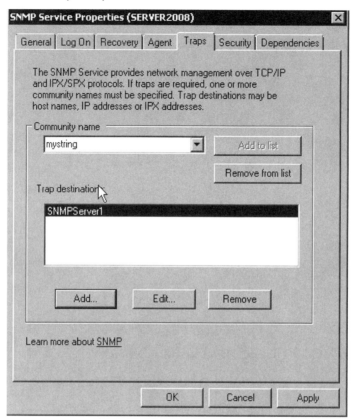

8. On the **Security** tab, you can secure SNMP data on this system by only allowing SNMP access from specified hosts, as well as requiring that a specific community string be presented to your server. Here you can enter the host name of your SNMP monitoring system as well as the community string this system will be presenting to your server. Notice that you can also specify what level of access the SNMP monitoring system has to your server (see Figure 5.58). For example, you could only allow the SNMP monitoring system to read data from your server. After entering the proper SNMP security information, click the **OK** button.

Figure 5.58 SNMP Service Security Settings

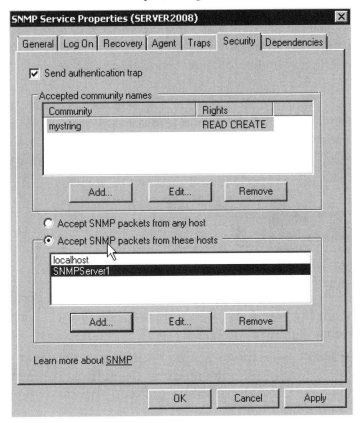

Windows does not include an SNMP monitoring application; however, some SNMP applications can be installed on Windows Server 2008. Depending on the type of SNMP monitoring application installed, you may need to enable the SNMP Trap service. By enabling this service, you are allowing it to receive SNMP traps from other servers or devices.

SNMP is an industry standard used by many network monitoring applications. Windows Server 2008 can also be monitored and managed by these systems via SNMP.

Baseline Security Analyzer

The Microsoft Baseline Security Analyzer (MBSA) is a free tool provided by Microsoft for scanning your servers and workstations for possible security vulnerabilities. These vulnerabilities can range from lack of security updates to accounts with blank passwords. The MBSA allows you to scan a single or multiple computers and then create a vulnerability report based on the scan. You can download the MBSA from Microsoft's Download Center Web site at www.microsoft.com/downloads/details.aspx?FamilyID= f32921af-9dbe-4dce-889e-ecf997eb18e9&DisplayLang=en.

After downloading and installing the MBSA, follow along with Exercise 5.15 to run a scan.

EXERCISE 5.15

SCANNING A COMPUTER WITH THE BASELINE SECURITY ANALYZER

1. Launch the **MBSA** by selecting **Start | All Programs | Microsoft Baseline Security Analyzer**.

2. The MBSA main menu will be displayed. Notice that you can choose to scan a single computer or multiple computers at the same time (see Figure 5.59). Go ahead and click the link to **Scan a computer**.

Figure 5.59 The MBSA Main Menu

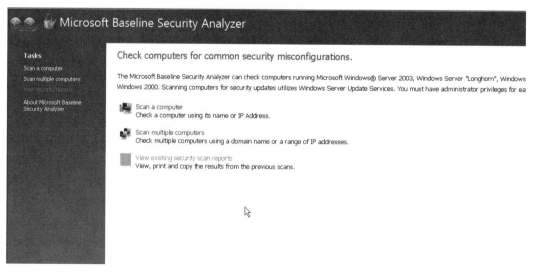

3. Next, choose the computer you wish to scan, along with the scan **Options**. For our scan, you should see the local computer already selected. Go ahead and select all options and click the **Start Scan** button (see Figure 5.60).

Figure 5.60 The MBSA Scan Options

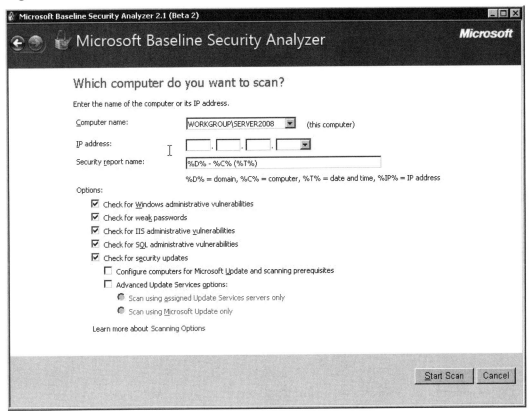

4. After the scan completes, you should be presented with a report of the scan results. Notice the overall security assessment of the system. If the assessment is **severe risk** you should take steps to immediately resolve reported issues. You can see from our report in Figure 5.61 that we were given a severe risk rating because we do not have Automatic Updates enabled. As the system administrator, we should immediately configure Automatic Updates to ensure that the server receives proper security patches from Microsoft or our WSUS server.

Figure 5.61 The MBSA Scan Report

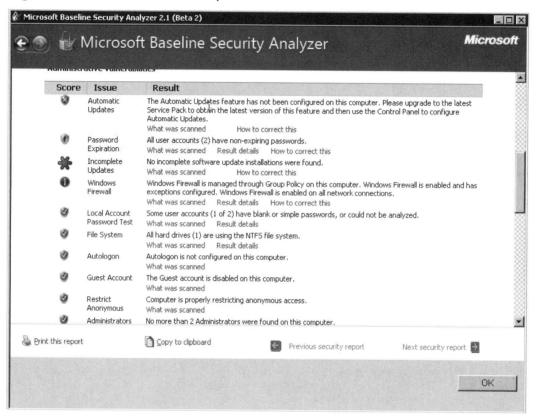

5. After reviewing the report, you can click the **OK** button to close it.

You can use the MBSA to scan multiple servers at once. You should scan servers on a regular basis to ensure that they are properly secured and updated. You can rerun the MBSA to ensure that any remediation steps you take properly resolve security vulnerabilities.

Network Monitor

Network Monitor is a tool used to capture network packets for analysis. Network Monitor is a free tool provided by Microsoft and you can download it from the Microsoft Download Center at www.microsoft.com/downloads/details.aspx? FamilyID=18b1d59d-f4d8-4213-8d17-2f6dde7d7aac&DisplayLang=en.

Network Monitor is also included in the Systems Management Server (SMS) and System Center Configuration Manager (SCCM) 2007. Network Monitor can be a useful tool when you suspect network issues may be impacting your server and network. In Exercise 5.16, we'll take a closer look at Network Monitor.

EXERCISE 5.16

EXPLORING NETWORK MONITOR

1. Open **Network Monitor** by selecting **Start | All Programs | Network Monitor 3.1**.

2. There are several configuration options you can change to instruct Network Monitor on what type of traffic to capture. The main configuration step we need to perform is to ensure that the appropriate network adapter is chosen. Select your primary network adapter from the **Select Networks** section of the main window (see Figure 5.62). Then click the **Create a new capture tab** button.

Figure 5.62 Network Monitor 3.1

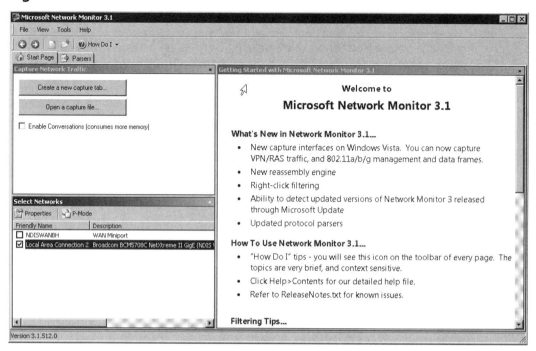

3. Each capture session uses a new tab. This allows you to quickly switch among multiple capture sessions running on the server. From the **Capture1** tab in Figure 5.63, you can see we can filter out certain data during capture or after capture. For now, we won't filter any data, so go ahead and click the **Play** button to start capturing data.

Figure 5.63 Capture Setup

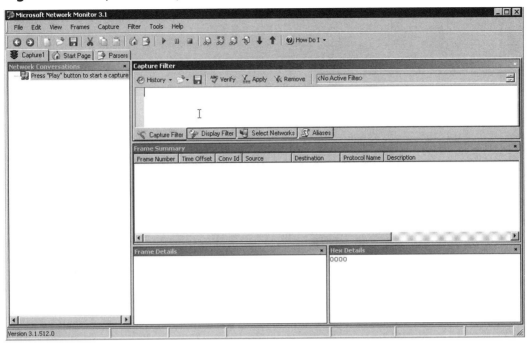

4. Let the capture process run for several minutes, and then click the **Stop** button.

5. After the packet capture completes, you will see a list of all network conversations on the left-hand side of the window. Go ahead and click the **My Traffic** node. This will filter the packet results to only display data to and from your server.

6. You can review and analyze the packets in the **Frame Summary** window, as shown in Figure 5.64.

Figure 5.64 The Frame Summary Window

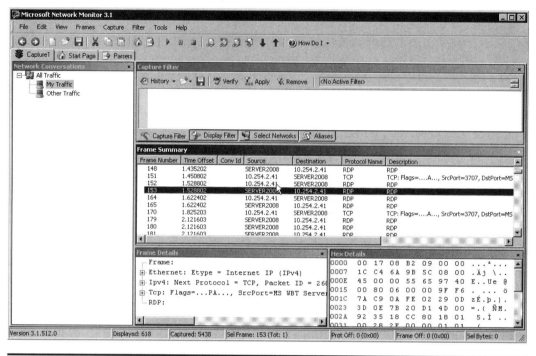

By reviewing the packets, you can see what type of traffic is being sent and received by your server as well as the devices your server is talking to on the network. This information can be useful if you see traffic going to or from another system that you don't recognize. For example, you could have a situation where your network is performing very slowly. By running Network Monitor, you notice that a workstation is sending and receiving a lot of data to and from the server. Network Monitor pinpoints the workstation's name and Internet Protocol (IP) address. You log on to the workstation and notice the network adapter is misconfigured. After you properly configure the network adapter, network performance returns to normal.

Summary of Exam Objectives

It is important for any network administrator to have a good understanding of the tools available to monitor, manage, and troubleshoot the network for which he or she may be responsible. This chapter provided detailed information and exercises on installing, configuring, and using Windows Server Update Services (WSUS) for update management. This chapter also covered Data Collector Sets and Performance Monitor. You discovered how you can use Data Collector Sets and Performance Monitor to capture diagnostic and performance data from your servers. This chapter introduced two features new to Server 2008: Reliability Monitor and the System Stability Index. Both of these tools allow you to see the overall reliability of your server at a glance. In this chapter, we also covered Event logs and Subscriptions. Event logs are a great source for information when trying to debug or troubleshoot problems. Subscriptions allow you to forward events from remote servers to a centrally managed server. This allows you to review and maintain Event log events from one server console. We also looked at capturing network data using features such as SNMP and Network Monitor. SNMP allows Windows to report to SNMP-compliant monitoring systems, and Network Monitor allows you to collect and review network traffic going to and from your servers. Finally, this chapter introduced us to the Microsoft Baseline Security Analyzer (MBSA). The MBSA is a tool that provides details about security misconfigurations or missing security updates. The MBSA allows you to proactively look for errors in your server security configurations. This chapter should have provided you with detailed information and exercises on the toolsets available to properly monitor and manage your Windows network.

Exam Objectives Fast Track

Configuring Windows Server Update Services Server Settings

☑ WSUS is available in Windows Server 2008 via a Server Role.

☑ Group Policy can be used to configure WSUS clients.

☑ WSUS can be used in disconnected networks by importing updates from another source.

Capturing Performance Data

☑ Data Collector Sets collect log and performance data and generate a summary report.

☑ Performance Monitor can be used to troubleshoot performance bottlenecks.

☑ Reliability Monitor can be used to determine the cause of system failures.

Monitoring Event Logs

☑ Custom views allow you to save a standard view of filtered Event log items.

☑ Application logs provide specific codes and events related to applications instead of the operating system.

☑ Subscriptions can be used to forward events to a central server for ease of reviewing.

Gathering Network Data

☑ Windows Server 2008 supports SNMP for monitoring.

☑ The Baseline Security Analyzer can be used to determine security vulnerabilities on a single or multiple computers.

☑ Network Monitor is used to capture network packets when troubleshooting system or network problems.

Exam Objectives
Frequently Asked Questions

Q: Can I use Windows Server Update Services to deploy updates to servers in a "disconnected" network?

A: Yes, You an import updates from another server to a WSUS server on the disconnected network.

Q: What is the difference between Performance Monitor and Data Collector Sets?

A: Performance Monitor only collects performance data from the system. Data Collector Sets allow collection of data from Performance Monitor, logs, and so on.

Q: Does Windows Server 2008 include the Reliability and Performance Monitor, like Windows Vista does?

A: Yes, Windows Server 2008 includes the same Reliability and Performance Monitor features as Windows Vista.

Q: Can you automate WSUS computer group membership?

A: Yes, you can use Group Policy to assign group membership to WSUS clients.

Q: How is the System Stability Index number determined?

A: System error events negatively impact the System Stability Index, whereas time passing without system error increases the System Stability Index number.

Q: Do Data Collector Sets replace Performance Monitor?

A: Data Collector Sets actually use Performance Monitor when gathering data. Data Collector Sets just provide best-practice counters and logs already set up by Microsoft.

Self Test

1. As the network administrator for Contoso, you have been tasked with ensuring that all servers and workstations are properly up-to-date with patches and security fixes. You currently must ensure that the company's 200 workstations and 50 servers have the most recent security fixes on a monthly basis. You decide that WSUS is the best method to update computers in your company. You just received a new Windows Server 2008 server to host WSUS. What is the best method to install WSUS on this server?

   A. Download WSUS from the Microsoft Web site and install using the setup wizard

   B. WSUS is already preinstalled with Windows Server 2008

   C. Use the Add Role option from Server Manager and add the WSUS role

   D. Install IIS on the server and then download WSUS from the Microsoft Web site and install using the setup wizard

2. You have just deployed WSUS to provide updates to your network workstations. You want to automate the configuration of your workstations by creating a Group Policy and applying it to the Corp Workstations OU. You then move the workstations into the Corp Workstations OU. Within 30 minutes, you notice that all clients except one are properly connecting to WSUS. What is the first troubleshooting step you should perform to figure out why the workstation is not connecting to WSUS?

   A. Ensure that the Group Policy has been applied to the workstation by logging on to the workstation and running *gpupdate* from the command line

   B. Log on to the workstation and manually configure Windows Update settings

   C. Create a new OU and move the workstation into that OU

   D. Reboot the WSUS server

3. You notice that Microsoft has released a Service Pack for Windows Vista. However, when you open the WSUS console and review updates, you do not see any service packs listed. You do see recent security updates available. What is the most probable cause that no service packs are available?

   A. Microsoft does not provide the ability to deploy service packs using WSUS

   B. Service packs are available only for Windows Server operating systems

C. WSUS is not properly downloading updates from Microsoft update servers

D. The Service Packs update type is not selected in the WSUS options

4. You notice that a new critical security update has been released to the Microsoft update site. You want to download this update to your WSUS server and install it on all of your corporate computers as soon as possible. You approve the update for install to the All Computers computer group and set an install deadline of 11:00 P.M. of the same day. When you return to the office the next morning you notice that the update was not installed on any computers. What is the most likely cause that the update was not installed?

A. The WSUS server lost connectivity to the Internet

B. You must approve the update for each computer individually

C. The Automatic Updates Detection Frequency is set to a period longer than the amount of time that has elapsed since you approved the update

D. The client computers need to be rebooted before the update can be installed

5. As the network administrator for your company, you have been tasked with managing security updates for the company's 500 servers. Three hundred of these servers are used to support the company's production environment and the other 200 servers are used by programmers for application development and testing. Several of the development servers mimic the production application environment. Due to the complexity of certain mission-critical applications, all security updates must be tested before being deployed to the production servers. What is the easiest and fastest method to test updates and then deploy them to production servers?

A. Set up two WSUS servers. Create two GPOs. Prod_GPO will be assigned to the OU containing the production servers. Dev_GPO will be assigned to the OU containing Dev Servers. Prod_GPO will configure servers to connect to WSUS1. Dev_GPO will configure servers to connect to WSUS2. Log on to WSUS2 and approve security updates for development servers. After testing the updates on development servers, log on to WSUS1. Approve the same updates for the production servers.

B. Set up one WSUS server. Create two computer groups in WSUS. Name one group Production Servers and the other group Development Servers. Create two GPOs. Prod_GPO will be assigned to the OU containing production servers. Dev_GPO will be assigned to the OU containing development servers. Prod_GPO will configure servers to report to WSUS1 and assign them to the Production Servers computer group. Dev_GPO will configure servers to report to WSUS1 and assign them to the Development Servers computer group. Approve new updates for the Development Servers computer group. After testing the updates, approve them for deployment to the Production Servers computer group.

C. Set up one WSUS server. Create one computer group named Servers. Create two GPOs. Prod_GPO will be assigned to the OU containing production servers. Dev_GPO will be assigned to the OU containing development servers. Both GPOs will configure servers to connect to WSUS1 and assign them to the Servers computer group. Approve updates for deployment to the OU containing development servers. After successfully testing the updates, approve the same updates for deployment to the OU containing the production servers.

D. Set up one WSUS server. Create two computer groups named Production Servers and Development Servers. Create one GPO named ServerUpdates_ GPO. Assign the same GPO to both the OU containing development servers and the OU containing production servers. The GPO will configure servers to connect to the WSUS server and assign them to the proper computer group based on the server's IP address.

6. Users are complaining that the billing system is performing slowly. You remember that this system was just moved to a new server last week. You have no idea why the application is performing poorly, but you suspect it's a resource issue. What is the best tool you should use to gather a few quick diagnostics on the system?

A. Performance Monitor

B. Network Monitor

C. Data Collector Set

D. Event Logs

7. One of your mission-critical database servers keeps crashing several times per day. You suspect that one of the DBAs may have installed a new database management tool that could be causing the problem. How can you determine whether any tools were installed recently?

A. Open Reliability Monitor and look for application install events over the past week

B. Ensure that the System Stability Index is above 3

C. Look at the modified dated of the .exe file for the application

D. Search the Event logs for an installation event

8. You have set up a new WSUS server to manage updates for your Windows workstations and servers. You create two computer groups from the WSUS management console. These groups are named Servers and Workstations. You want to use Group Policy to ensure that server computers are in the Servers group and workstation computers are in the Workstations group. You create a new Group Policy and link it to the domain. When you open the WSUS management console, you notice that both servers and workstations are in the Workstations group. Which of the following is the correct way to ensure that servers are in the Servers group and workstations are in the Workstations group?

A. Edit the domain GPO and change the Target Group to Servers

B. Edit the domain GPO and change the Target Group to both Workstations and Servers

C. Unlink the current GPO from the domain. Relink the GPO to the OU containing Workstations. Create a new GPO and link it to the OU containing Servers. Ensure that the new GPO has the Target Group set to Servers.

D. Unlink the current GPO from the domain. Relink the GPO to the OU containing Workstations and the OU containing Servers.

9. You have been tasked with planning and deploying a patch management solution for your company's engineering department computers. For security reasons, these computers are connected to a network that does not have access to the Internet. The security team has also mandated that the engineering network will not have access to any other network in the company. The patch management solution you deploy must reside on the engineering network and will not have access to the Internet or other networks. You have been considering deploying WSUS; however, you know WSUS downloads updates from Microsoft. Can you deploy WSUS for patch management in this situation, and if so, how? Choose the best answer.

A. Yes. Deploy WSUS on a network that has Internet access. Download updates from Microsoft. Move the WSUS server to the engineering network to update the engineering computers.

B. Yes. Deploy two WSUS servers. Deploy the first server on the company's normal network which has access to the Internet. Deploy the second WSUS server on the engineering network. Export updates from the first WSUS server and import the updates to the second WSUS server.

C. Yes. Deploy two WSUS servers. Deploy the first server on the company's normal network which has access to the Internet. Deploy the second WSUS server on the engineering network. Configure the second server to receive updates from an upstream proxy. Specify the first WSUS server as the upstream proxy.

D. WSUS cannot be used in this situation. You will need to manually update computers on the engineering network.

10. Your company is in the process of deploying a new intranet Web site. The Web site will be accessed by thousands of people in the company. Before making the site available to the entire company, the development team would like to run load testing tools to ensure that the Web site will support normal user loads. The development team has asked you to determine whether the hardware is adequate for the new intranet site. You decide to collect CPU, memory, and disk statistics and watch them in real time while the development team performs the load tests. By doing this, you will quickly be able to see whether there are hardware bottlenecks. What tool should you use to perform this test?

A. Performance Monitor

B. Network Monitor

C. Server Manager

D. Event logs

Self Test Quick Answer Key

1. **C**

2. **A**

3. **D**

4. **C**

5. **B**

6. **C**

7. **A**

8. **C**

9. **B**

10. **A**

## Chapter 6

MCTS/MCITP
Exam 642

Network Access Protection

Exam objectives in this chapter:

- Working with NAP

Exam objectives review:

- ☑ Summary of Exam Objectives
- ☑ Exam Objectives Fast Track
- ☑ Exam Objectives Frequently Asked Questions
- ☑ Self Test
- ☑ Self Test Quick Answer Key

Introduction

Microsoft for some time has been making security its main priority with the Microsoft Trustworthy Computing initiative. Starting with Microsoft Windows 2003 Server we were introduced to Network Access Quarantine Control. This feature enabled administrators to control remote access to a private network until the remote computer was validated by a script. The components necessary to deploy this solution included Microsoft Windows 2003 remote access servers, the Connection Manager Administration Kit, and Internet Authentication Service.

The most obvious problem with Network Access Quarantine Control was that it worked with only remote computers connecting to the network using Routing and Remote Access Services (RRAS). This solution left a wide gap throughout the network infrastructure for other types of clients to cause issues and management problems for network administrators.

With Microsoft Windows 2008 Server, Windows Vista, and Windows XP Service Pack 3, Microsoft has introduced Network Access Protection (NAP). NAP can control virtual private network (VPN) connections better than Network Access Quarantine Control, but NAP can also enforce policy compliance through the following types of network access or communications:

- Internet Protocol security (IPSec) protected traffic
- IEEE 802.1x authenticated network connections
- Dynamic Host Configuration Protocol (DHCP) address configurations
- Remote access VPN connections

The key word to keep in mind when discussing NAP and its features is "compliance." With the introduction of NAP into our network, we can force Windows Server 2008, Windows Vista, and Windows XP Service Pack 3 to comply with standards set forth on our network. If for some reason a client does not comply with standards set forth by an administrator, the client could be directed to a separate network segment. On the separate network segment, a Remedial Server could update the client to the company's standards and then allow the client access to the network. Examples of these standards include but are not limited to:

- Windows update files
- Virus definitions
- Windows firewall settings

In addition, Microsoft has provided an application program interface (API) so that Network Access Protection Partners can write their own piece of software to add to the functionality of NAP. Some of the Access Protection Partners already providing add-ons include AppSense, Citrix, Intel, and Symantec. For a complete list of Access Protection Partners, go to the following Web site: www.microsoft. com/windowsserver2008/en/us/nap-partners.aspx.

In the following section, we are going to first look at all of the components of implementing NAP on a network. Once we gain a broad understanding of the components needed to build a NAP-supported network, we will look at different scenarios and implementation steps through the exercises throughout this chapter.

New & Noteworthy...

Network Access Quarantine Control vs. Network Access Protection

For the examination this text prepares you for, you will not need to know anything about the Windows 2003 Server feature Network Access Quarantine Control. We discussed it here to give you a way to associate NAP with a feature from Windows 2003 Server.

For the test objectives in this chapter, you will need to understand what each component of NAP does and how it fits into the overall design of the NAP network solution. Keep this in mind—understand the terminology of the components. Also, the management interface has been totally redesigned for Windows 2008 Server. Do not rely on your hands-on experience with Windows 2003 Server. The best advice we can give you is to perform the exercises as presented in this chapter and on the links we will provide to other step-by-step exercises that Microsoft makes available to the public. Some questions on this exam will have you demonstrating that you understand a feature by simulation and not by a multiple choice question. That is why it is imperative to actually gain hands-on experience for this exam.

As a side note: we would recommend that you download the free version of Microsoft Virtual PC 2007, get a 180-day trial copy of Windows Server 2008, build a network with Microsoft Virtual PC 2007, and practice the exercises presented not only in this chapter but throughout the whole book.

EXAM WARNING

If you have taken Microsoft exams in the past, you already know that Microsoft loves to ask more questions about new features in its products. Be assured you will get multiple questions on subjects like NAP just because it is a new feature, and Microsoft will use the exam to promote new features and changes to its products.

Working with NAP

The NAP platform main objective is to validate the state of a client computer before connecting to the private network and offer a source of remediation. To validate access to a network based on system health, NAP provides the following areas of functionality:

- Health state validation
- Network access limitation
- Automatic remediation
- Ongoing compliance

TEST DAY TIP

It would be advisable to look over the bullet points listed in this section before going into the exam. Although the exam is technical in nature, Microsoft likes to put a little marketing jargon into the exams. The agents provided by Microsoft provide the aforementioned validations for Windows Server 2008, Windows Vista, and Windows XP Service Pack 3. Other validation types will be provided by third-party vendors.

Network Layer Protection

All the components of NAP reside at the network layer. It is very important to understand where each component can reside and what the function of each component does. We are first going to look at a very general Microsoft Visio drawing and then point out each component and its function as related to NAP. Like a lot of Microsoft network designs, some servers can play multiple Windows Server 2008 roles within the NAP-enabled network architecture. Later in this chapter we will point out during the hands-on exercises where these servers with multiple Windows 2008 Server roles can reside, but for now we will concentrate on each individual function of the components and server roles (see Figure 6.1).

Figure 6.1 NAP Network Design

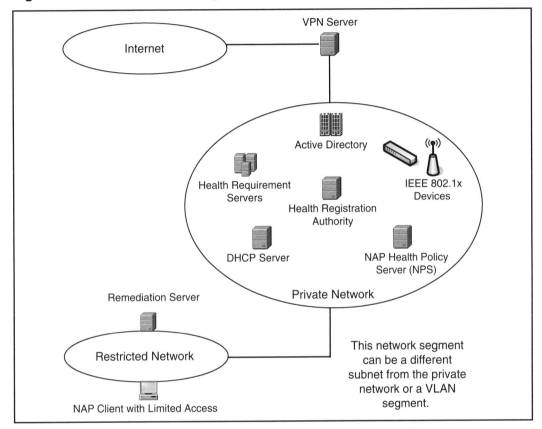

NAP Clients

NAP clients can be Windows Vista, Windows 2008 Server, or Windows XP Service Pack 3 clients. At the time of this writing these are the only operating systems that support the NAP platform for system health validated network access or communication. Microsoft does plan on supporting other operating systems through third-party software providers—independent software providers (ISVs). Microsoft is also planning to provide support to the Microsoft Windows Mobile platform, including support for handheld devices and Microsoft Windows Mobile phones.

The NAP API is really important for the adoption of NAP-based networks. The API that Microsoft is releasing for developers allows them to write code to support various other clients that are not Microsoft based. Expect to see these devices become more popular as more and more enterprises adopt Microsoft Windows Server 2008.

NAP Enforcement Points

NAP enforcement points are parts of the NAP infrastructure that determines the health and compliance of a NAP client before allowing network access. To determine if the NAP client is in compliance by the policies set forth by the administrator, the NAP Health Policy Server (NPS) evaluates the health and compliance of the NAP client. The NPS also decides the remediation process that is going to be applied to the NAP client. For instance, the client can be forwarded to restricted network where a remediation server will offer the updates or settings needed to enforce the compliance policy. NAP enforcement points include the following:

- Health Registration Authority (HRA) The HRA is a Windows 2008 Server with the roles of Internet Information Server 7.0 (IIS) and Certificate Authority (CA) role installed. This enforcement point is used primarily with IPSec Enforcement policies. The CA uses health certificates to enforce NAP compliance to the NAP client.

- Windows 2008 VPN Server A server running Windows 2008 Server Network Policy Server can enforce NAP compliance to a NAP client.

- DHCP Server Servers installed into the NAP network infrastructure running Windows 2008 Server with the DHCP server role providing Internet Protocol version 4 (IPv4) addresses to NAP clients can enforce NAP compliance to a NAP client.

- Network access devices Network hardware, such as switches and wireless access points that support IEEE 802.1 x authentication, can be used to support NAP compliance to a NAP client. Types of protocols supported include Extensible Authentication Protocol (EAP), Lightweight Extensible Authentication Protocol (LEAP), and Protected Extensible Authentication Protocol (PEAP).

Exam Warning

During the examination, Microsoft sometimes like to give you a scenario questions and ask what it is wrong with the provided solution. One of the multiple choice answers could be none—meaning the solution is correct on its own merit. At face value this may be correct. For example, a scenario question may include the addition of a DHCP server running Internet Protocol version 6 (IPv6) in a NAP client. Windows Server 2008 does support IPv6; however, NAP does not support IPv6, only IPv4. Make sure you read the scenario in its entirety and pay close attention to detail.

Active Directory Domain Services

As you already know, Active Directory Services store account and group policy information for an Active Directory Domain. NAP does not necessarily rely on Windows 2008 Server Active Directory Domain Services or Windows 2003 Server Active Directory Domain Services. NAP definitely does not need Active Directory Services to determine if a client is compliant, but other services and roles depend on Active Directory Services.

Active Directory Domain Services is needed for Network Policy Server VPN enforcement, IEEE 802.1x network device enforcement or IPSec-based enforcement. Also, as you will see later in this chapter, using group policy objects is a good way to set compliance and enforcement settings to NAP clients on your network.

NAP Health Policy Server

The NAP Health Policy Server is the heart of the NAP-supported network infrastructure. The NAP Health Policy Server runs Windows 2008 Server and has the NPS server role installed. The NPS server role is responsible for storing health requirement policies and provides health state validation for NAP.

Interestingly, the NPS server role replaces Internet Authentication Service (IAS), Remote Authentication Dial-In User Service (RADIUS), and proxy server provided by Windows 2003 Server. So NPS not only supports the NAP infrastructure but also acts as the authentication, authorization, and access (AAA) server in Windows 2008 Server. The NPS role can act as the RADIUS proxy to exchange RADIUS data packets with another NAP health policy server.

Health Requirement Server

Health requirement servers contain the data that NAP NPS servers check for current system health state for NAP NPS servers. Examples of the data that health requirement servers may provide are the latest virus DAT information files for third-party antivirus packages or updates for other software packages that the ISVs use the NAP API to develop.

Restricted Network

A restricted network is where NAP sends a computer that needs remediation services or to block access to the private network until remediation can take place. The restricted network can be a different subnet that has no routes to the private network or a different logical network in the form of a virtual local area network (VLAN). A good NAP design would place remediation servers located within the restricted network. Placing remediation servers inside the restricted network, enables NAP clients to get updated and then be allowed access to the private network.

The remediation server could be in the form of a Windows 2008 Server or Windows 2003 Server running Windows Server Update Services (WSUS). WSUS provides an easy way to update the NAP client system files using Microsoft Update Services. You could also place virus update files and other third-party critical update files on the remediation server.

Test Day Tip

A good review on the test date is to go through this book and look over the diagrams and understand different network designs. Glancing over these network diagrams is a good refresher right before entering the testing center.

Head of the Class...

Understanding VLANs

When you are working with NAP, one of the best technologies to take advantage of is working with virtual local area networks. Microsoft does not go into great detail about how VLANs work, but for any student or a well-seasoned network administrator, understanding this technology is vital.

VLANs are basically multiple networks on the same switch. The switching management software allows us to take ports from the switch and build many virtual local area networks. These virtual networks are independent networks of each other. Newer switches actually allow us to configure routing between these VLANs. This makes setting up the restricted network in NAP easy and more efficient. To read more about VLAN technology, go to this Web address: http://www.cisco.com/univercd/cc/td/doc/cisintwk/idg4/nd2023.htm#wp3280.

Software Policy Validation

Before you actually start doing some exercises, it is important to understand what actually goes on during system-compliant testing and validation. NPS uses System Health Validators (SHVs) to analyze the compliance of a client computer. SHVs determine whether a computer is getting full access to the private network or if it will be isolated to the restricted network. The client has a piece of software installed called a System Health Agent (SHA) to monitor its system health. NPS uses SHVs and SHAs to determine the health of a client computer and to monitor, enforce, and remediate the client computer.

Built into Windows Server 2008 and Windows Vista are the Windows Security Health Agent (WSHA) and Windows Security Health Validator (WSHV). These agents are used to enforce the most basic compliance settings in a NAP infrastructure. The settings provided by WSHA and WSHV are:

- The client computer has firewall software installed and enabled.

- The client computer has antivirus software installed and enabled.

- The client computer has current antivirus updates installed.

- The client computer has antispyware software installed and enabled.

- The client computer has current antispyware updates installed.

- Microsoft Update Services is enabled on the client computer.

Even without third-party SHVs and SHAs, Microsoft has built very powerful tools into Windows Server 2008, Windows Vista, and Windows XP Service Pack 3 to validate the compliance and health of computers.

DHCP Enforcement

DHCP enforcement is probably the easiest NAP infrastructure design to implement. In Exercise 6.1, we are going to show you how to implement NAP DHCP enforcement.

EXERCISE 6.1

Implementing DHCP Enforcement

In this exercise we are going to implement the DHCP and NPS server roles on the server NPS1. We will then configure NAP with the wizard and also configure the SHVs that will force any connecting client using DHCP to be network compliant. The domain name is CONTOSO.COM, Keeping with the Microsoft tradition. Figure 6.2 depicts this simple network. We are going to imply that both servers are Windows Server 2008 and Active Directory Domain Services have already been set up for the CONTOSO.COM domain.

Figure 6.2 Network Diagram for Exercise 6.1

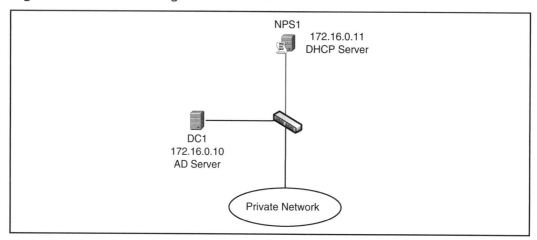

1. First we will install the NPS and DHCP server roles on NPS1. Click **Start** and then click **Server Manager**.

2. Under **Roles Summary**, click **Add Roles** and then click **Next**.

3. On the Select Server Roles page, select the **DHCP Server** and **Network Policy and Access Services** check boxes and then click **Next** twice (see Figure 6.3).

Figure 6.3 Server Roles Page

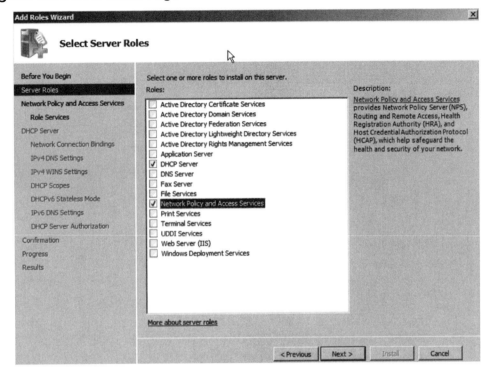

4. On the **Select Server Roles** page, select the **Network Policy Server** check box and then click **Next** twice.

5. On the **Select Network Connection Bindings** page, verify that **172.16.0.11** is selected and click **Next**.

6. On the **Specify IPv4 DNS Server Settings** page, verify that **contoso.com** is listed under **Parent Domain**.

7. Type **172.16.0.10** under the **Preferred DNS server IP address** and click **Validate**. Verify that the server was able to validate the DNS server.

8. On the **Specify WINS Server Settings**, click **Next,** accepting the default settings.

9. On the **Add or Edit DHCP Scopes** page, click **Add**.

10. In the **Add Scope** dialog box, type **NAP SCOPE** next to **Scope Name**. Add **172.16.0.20** as the **Starting IP Address** and **172.16.0.30** as the **Ending IP Address**. For the **Subnet Mask** use **255.255.255.0**. Select the **Activate this scope** check box. Notice in Figure 6.4 that we do not specify a **Default Gateway**.

Figure 6.4 Add Scope Dialog Box

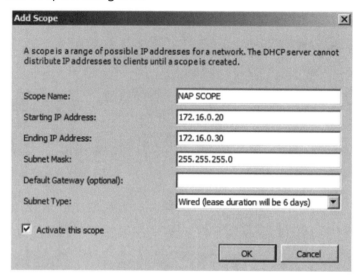

11. On the **Configure DHCPv6 Stateless Mode** page, select **Disable DHCPv6 stateless mode for this server** and then click **Next**. Remember that NAP does not support DHCPv6.

12. On the **Authorize DHCP Server** page, select **Specify,** enter **Administrator information**, and then click **Next**.

13. On the **Confirm Installation Selections** page, click **Install**.

14. Verify the installation completed with no errors and then click **Close**.

At this point, we now have our DHCP Server and NPS installed. The DHCP Server is configured and authorized for the domain CONTOSO. COM. Now we need to configure NPS as a NAP health policy server so that it can validate the clients connecting to our domain via DHCP. To do this, we will use the NAP configuration wizard.

1. Click **Start**, click **Run**, type **nps.msc** and press **Enter**.

2. Make sure that in the Network Policy Server console tree, that **NPS (Local)** is selected.

3. Under **Standard Configuration**, click **Configure NAP**. The NAP configuration wizard will start. See Figure 6.5.

Figure 6.5 NAP Configuration Wizard

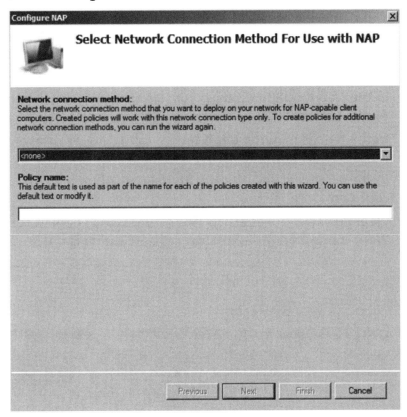

4. On the **Select Network Connection Method for Use with NAP** page, under **Network connection method**, select **Dynamic Host Configuration Protocol (DHPC)**, and then click **Next**.

5. On the **Specify NAP Enforcement Servers Running DHCP** page, click **Next**.

6. On the **Specify DHCP Scopes** page, click **Next**.

7. On the **Configure User Groups and Machine Groups** page, click **Next**.

8. On the **Specify a NAP Remediation Server Group and URL** page, click **Next**.

9. On the **Define NAP Health Policy** page, verify that **Windows Security Health Validator** and **Enable auto-remediation of client computers** check boxes are selected, click **Next**.

10. Click **Finish** on the Completing NAP **Enforcement Policy and RADIUS Configuration** page.

The only thing left to configure is our System Health Validators (SHVs). We are going to set up our new SHV to make sure that the Windows Firewall is enabled, and an antivirus application is on and up-to-date.

1. In the Network Policy Server console tree, double-click **Network Access Protection**, and then click **System Health Validators**.

2. In the details pane, under **Name**, double-click **Windows Security Health Validator**.

3. In the **Windows Security Health Validator Properties** dialog box, click **Configure**.

4. Clear all check boxes except for **A firewall is enabled for all network connections** and **An antivirus application is on**. See Figure 6.6.

Figure 6.6 Windows Security Health Validator

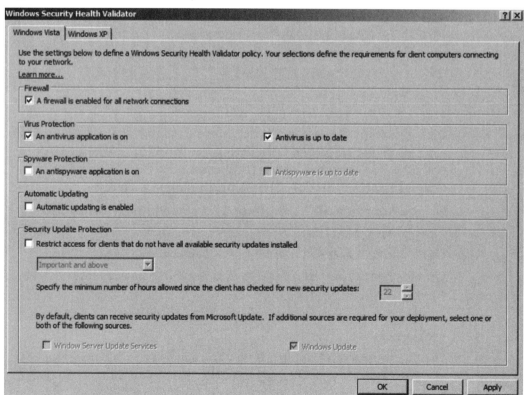

5. Click **OK** to close the **Windows Security Health Validator** dialog box, and then click **OK** to close the **Windows Security Health Validator Properties** dialog box.

6. Close the Network Policy Server console.

This was a long exercise, but it is very important to see this process from start to finish—it helps facilitate your understanding of all concepts dealing with implementing DHCP enforcement.

Exam Warning

Microsoft new exams test whether or not you understand the location of certain properties and how to implement a process—these are simulation type questions. Be sure that when you practice exercises, to take the time to notice the layout and where items are located.

VPN Enforcement

Windows Server 2008 and Network Policy Server (NPS) can facilitate NAP connections—allowing remote VPN clients to be checked for compliance and be remediated.

Communication Process with VPN Client and NAP

When a Windows Vista or Windows XP Service Pack 3 computer connects to a NPS server that is NAP enabled, the communication process is a little different than a normal VPN connection. The NAP client in this case becomes the VPN client and uses simple Point-to-Point Protocol (PPP) messages to establish a remote access VPN connection. While this is going on, Protected Extensible Authentication Protocol (PEAP) messages are sent over the PPP connection to indicate the client system current health state to the NAP health policy server. If the connecting client is not compliant, the NAP health policy server uses PEAP to send remediation instructions to the VPN client. If the client is compliant, the NAP health policy server will use PEAP messages to tell the client that it has access to the private network. Because all

PEAP messages between the VPN client and NAP health policy server are routed through the VPN server, this process is encrypted.

If the VPN client is noncompliant, the Windows 2008 Server NPS will use a set of remote access IP filters to limit the traffic of the VPN client so that it can reach only the restricted network. Once directed to the restricted network, the client can become compliant through the remediation resources provided. While the system is noncompliant, the VPN server will continue to apply the IP packet filters to the IP traffic that is received from the VPN client and silently discard all packets that do not correspond to a configured packet filter.

EXERCISE 6.2

CONFIGURE NPS FOR REMOTE VPN CONNECTIONS

In this exercise, we are going to configure NPS for use with remote VPN connections. This exercise assumes that RRAS is already configured on the server DC1 (172.16.0.10). This exercise also assumes that DC1 is an Enterprise Certification Authority (CA) for the domain CONTOSO.COM.

EXAM WARNING

Configuring an Enterprise Certification Authority is beyond the scope of this chapter, but explained in more detail in another chapter in this book. It is import to understand implementing an Enterprise CA—especially with RRAS and IPSec NAP enforcement.

1. Click **Start**, click **Run**, type **nps.msc**, and then press **Enter**.

2. In the Network Policy Server console tree, click **NPS (Local)**.

3. In the details pane, under **Standard Configuration**, click **Configure NAP**. The NAP configuration wizard will start.

4. On the **Select Network Connection Method for Use with NAP page**, under **Network connection method**, select **Virtual Private Network (VPN)** and click **Next**. See Figure 6.7.

Figure 6.7 Select Network Connection Method for Use with NAP

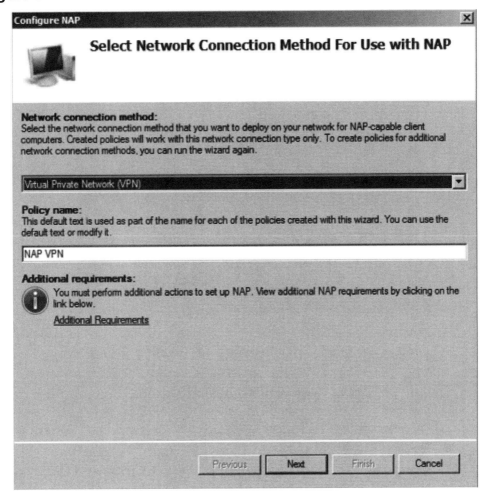

5. On the **Specify NAP Enforcement Servers Running VPN Server page**, under **RADIUS clients**, click **Add**.

6. In **the New RADIUS Client** dialog box, under **Friendly Name**, type **NAP VPN Server**. Under **Address (IP or DNS)**, type **DC1**.

7. Under **Shared secret**, type **secret**.

8. nder **Confirm shared secret**, type **secret**, click **OK** and then click **Next**. See Figure 6.8.

Figure 6.8 New RADIUS Client

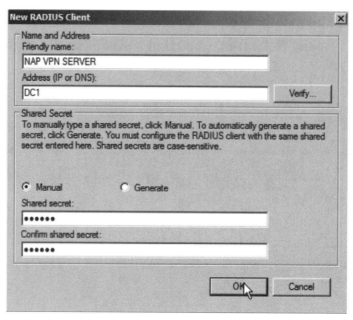

9. On the **Configure User Groups and Machine Groups** page, click **Next**.

10. On the **Configure an Authentication Method** page, confirm that a computer certificate is displayed under **NPS Server Certificate** and that **Secure Password (PEAP-MSCHAP-v2)** is selected under **EAP types**. Click **Next**.

11. On the **Specify a NAP Remediation Server Group and URL** page, click **New Group**.

12. In the **New Remediation Server Group** dialog box, under **Group Name**, type **Domain Services** and then click **Add**.

13. In the **Add New Server** dialog box, under **Friendly name**, type **DC1**.

14. Under **IP address or DNS name**, type **172.16.0.10** and then click **OK** twice.

15. Under **Remediation Server Group**, verify that the newly created remediation server group is selected and then click **Next**.

16. On the **Define NAP Health Policy** page, verify that **Windows Security Health Validator** and **Enable auto-remediation of client computers** check boxes are selected and then click **Next**.

17. On the **Completing NAP Enforcement Policy and RADIUS Client Configuration** page, click **Finish**.

18. Close the NPS console.

EXAM WARNING

Whenever you add a remediation server group to NAP—noncompliant computers are automatically granted access to the group. To deny access to a remediation group, at least one IP filter is required.

Configuring NAP Health Policies

NAP Health Policies are a combination of settings for health determination and enforcement of infrastructure compliance. Health requirement policies on the NAP health policy server determine whether a NAP client is compliant or noncompliant, how to treat noncompliant NAP clients and whether they should automatically remediate their health state, and how to treat clients that are not NAP capable for different NAP enforcement methods. The following settings make up the NAP Health Policies:

- Connection Request Policies

- Network Policies

- Health Policies

- Network Access Protection Settings

All the NAP Health Policies are configured within the Network Policy Server console, as shown in Figure 6.9. Interestingly, Microsoft recommends starting with the Configure NAP Wizard to build your initial settings for your NAP installation. To access the Configure NAP Wizard, click the **NPS (LOCAL)** node of the configuration tree and then click **Configure NAP** under the Standard Configuration in the right window. In Figure 6.9, we can see where you can access the Configure NAP Wizard within the Network Policy Server console.

Figure 6.9 The Network Policy Server Console

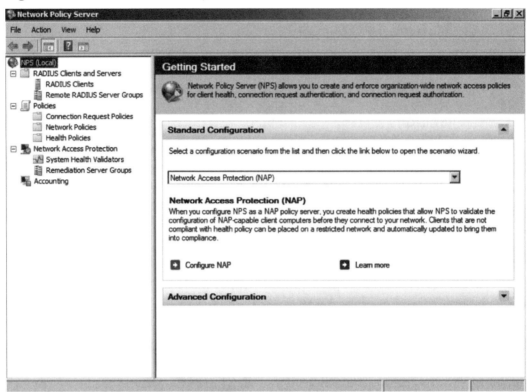

TEST DAY TIP

A couple of hours before your exam go through the Network Policy Server console and click on the different icons in the tree. Also, right-click the icons and select properties. Go through the tabs paying attention to where different settings reside. This tip is good for any exam, and we would highly recommend it. Remember, on multiple choice questions there are four possibilities. One will obviously be wrong, two will be plausible, and one answer will be the correct Microsoft answer!

Connection Request Policies

As we discussed earlier, NPS replaces IAS in Windows Server 2003. NPS handles all RADIUS activities in Windows 2008 Server—RADIUS can be configured to handle the authentication and logging locally. Also, RADIUS in Windows 2008 can be configured as a RADIUS proxy and forward all authentication request to another RADIUS server.

Connection Request Policies are a set of rules that can be processed in a set order. Connection Request Policies determine whether RADIUS request should be processed locally or forward the requests to another RADIUS server. Connection Request Policies are configured and ordered in the NPC console under the Policies node (see Figure 6.10). When the NPS server is configured for NAP health compliance and enforcement, the local server is acting as a RADIUS server locally.

Figure 6.10 Connection Request Policies

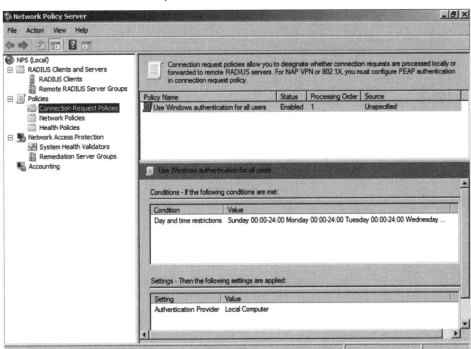

Network Policies

Network Policies either deny or grant access to network connection attempts. These policies, like Connection Request Policies, are an ordered group of rules. For each rule, there are a set of conditions, constraints, an access permission that either grants or denies access and network policy settings. For NAP, network policies specify the conditions to check for health requirements and, for computers that are not capable of NAP—the enforcement behavior.

When setting the Network Policies, you have four options for NAP Enforcement settings—these settings specify the type of network access the client will have. The four options include (also see Figure 6.11):

1. Allow full network access

2. Allow full network access for a limited time

3. Allow limited access

4. Enable auto-remediation of client computers

Figure 6.11 Compliant Properties

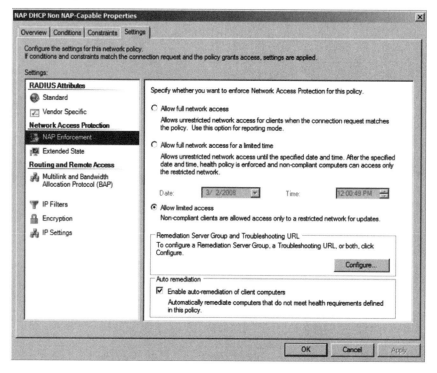

Health Policies

Health Policies check the client for compliance via the system health validators (SHVs). If you recall from earlier in this chapter, we discussed Windows Security Health Validator (WSHV). These SHVs are the ones provided with Windows 2008 Server, Windows Vista or Windows XP Service Pack 3. Other SHVs can be created by independent software vendors (ISVs) via the application programming interface provided by Microsoft. By default, the WSHV is always listed in the health policies.

EXERCISE 6.3

CREATE A HEALTH POLICY

In this short exercise, we are going to create a Health Policy on NPS1 server. Pay close attention to all of the options available to you in the exercise.

1. Click **Start**, click **Run**, type **nps.msc**, and then press **Enter**.
2. In the Network Policy Server console tree, click **Policies**.
3. In the details pane, under **Health Policies**, click **Configure Health Policies**.
4. **Right-click** the **Health Policies** node and click **New**.
5. For the **Policy Name** enter **CONTOSO Policy 1**.
6. In the **Client SHV checks** drop down menu select Client **fails one or more SHV checks**.
7. Make sure under **SHVs used in this health policy** that **Windows Security Health Validator** is **Checked**. See Figure 6.12.

Figure 6.12 Configure Health Policy Settings

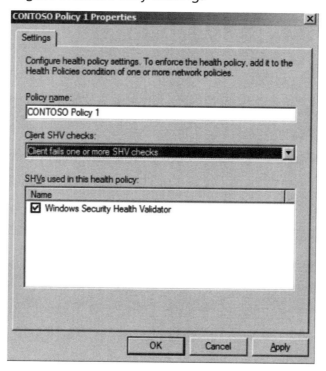

8. Click **OK**.

9. Close the NPS console.

Network Access Protection Settings

Network Access Protection (NAP) settings consist of two components. The components that make up NAP settings include:

- System Health Validators
- Remediation Server Groups

System Health Validators (SHVs) specify the configuration of installed SHVs for health requirements and error conditions. By default, Windows Server 2008, Windows Vista, and Windows XP Service Pack 3 include the Window Security Health Validator (WSHV).

Remediation Server Groups specifies the set of servers that are accessible to computers that are not NAP compliant with limited network access. If you recall Figure 6.1, these servers would be located on the restricted network.

EXERCISE 6.4

CREATE REMEDIATION SERVER GROUP

In this exercise, we are going to create a remediation server group on server NPS1 to allow computers that are not compliant with the NAP infrastructure to get updated. We will point the clients to DC1 to get updates—in a real NAP infrastructure environment, we would never point to an Active Directory Domain Server as a remediation server.

1. Click **Start**, click **Run**, type **nps.msc**, and then press **Enter**.

2. In the Network Policy Server console tree, click **Network Access Protection**.

3. In the details pane, under **Network Access Protection**, click **Configure Remediation Server Groups**.

4. **Right-click** the **Remediation Server Groups** node and click **New**.

5. Click **Add**.

6. For the **Friendly name** enter **CONTOSO Remediation Server Group**.

7. For the IP address or DNS name enter **172.16.0.10** (DC1). See Figure 6.13.

Figure 6.13 Remediation Server Groups

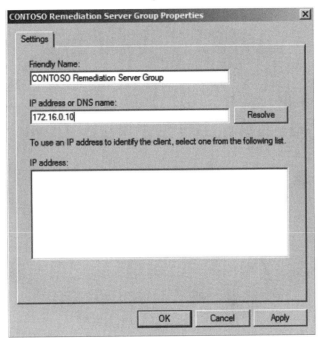

8. Click **OK** twice.
9. Close the NPS console.

IPsec Enforcement

IPsec enforcement breaks a network down to three different logical networks by using health certificates provided by the Health Certificate Server (HCS). Any computer can be a member of only one of the three networks at any given time—membership to the network is determined by the status of the computers health certificate. The logical networks are defined by which computers have valid health certificates and which computers require IPSec authentication for incoming access connections. Computers requiring IPSec authentication would normally be servers on the private network. Figure 6.14 shows a basic diagram of what an IPSec-based NAP infrastructure would look like. As you can see, there are three distinct networks:

1. Secure network
2. Boundary network
3. Restricted network

Figure 6.14 IPSec-Based NAP Network

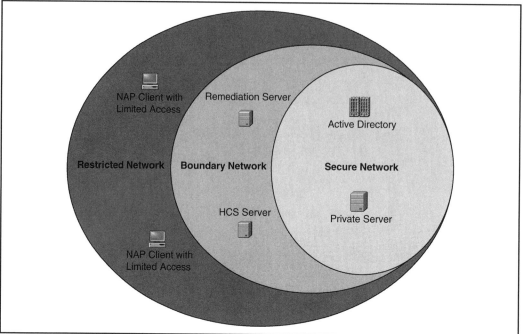

Secure Network

The secure network is where all computers have health certificates and require IPsec authentication to communicate with any other computer. If a computer tries to communicate with a computer in the secure network without a health certificate, the computer in the secure network will ignore the client's request. In a NAP infrastructure, computers in the secure network would be members of the Active Directory domain.

Boundary Network

Boundary networks are where computers that are not NAP compliant can access a remediation server and become compliant. Once compliant, they can access an HCS Server and acquire a health certificate to participate in the secure network. Computers on the boundary network will accept communication requests from computers with a health certificate or without—this is how remediation occurs. Both the restricted network and the secure network have access to the boundary network.

Restricted Network

All the computers in the restricted network do not have a health certificate. The only network they can communicate with is the boundary network—for the purpose of remediation and acquiring the appropriate health certificate to access the secure network.

Flexible Host Isolation

Flexible Host Isolation refers to the ease of network isolation provided with the IPSec method of NAP enforcement. Isolation can be performed easily on the network with no infrastructure upgrade by using NAP and health certificates. This type of isolation cannot be easily circumvented by reconfiguring the client or using hardware like hubs. Basically, healthy systems can connect to anything, as long as the NAP policy allows it, whereas quarantined systems are isolated to the restricted network.

Exam Warning

For this exam, it is very important to understand the communication between the three different types of networks in an IPSec NAP infrastructure. The secure network can communicate with any of the other networks via IPSec authentication and without it. The boundary network can communicate with the secure network via IPSec authentication and also allow nonsecured traffic with the restricted network. The restricted network can communicate with the boundary network only via an unsecured means.

EXERCISE 6.5

INSTALL THE NPS, HRA AND CA SERVER ROLES

In this exercise, we are going to install the NPS, HRA and CA server roles on NPS1 server.

1. Click **Start** and then **Server Manager**. Under **Roles Summary,** click **Add Roles** and then click **Next**.

2. On the **Select Server Roles** page, select the **Active Directory Certificate Services** and **Network Policy and Access Services** check boxes and then click **Next** twice.

3. On the **Select Role Services** page, select the **Health Registration Authority** check box, click **Add Required Role Services** in the **Add Roles Wizard** window and then click **Next**.

4. On the **Choose the Certification Authority to use with the Health Registration Authority** page, choose **Install a local CA to issue health certificates for this HRA server** and then click **Next**. See Figure 6.15.

Figure 6.15 Choose the Certification Authority to use with the Health Registration Authority

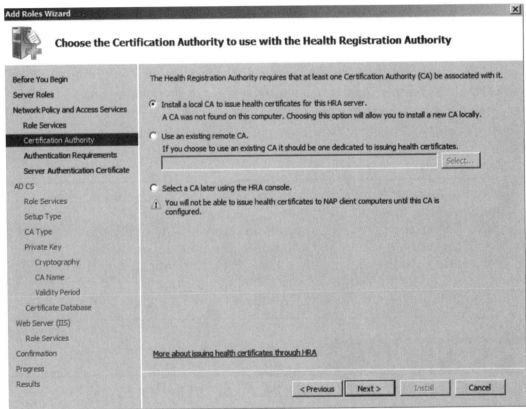

5. On the **Choose Authentication Requirements for the Health Registration Authority** page, choose **No, allow anonymous requests for health certificates** and then click **Next**. This choice allows computers to be enrolled with health certificates in a workgroup environment.

6. On the **Choose a Server Authentication Certificate for SSL Encryption** page, choose **Create a self-signed certificate for SSL encryption** and then click **Next**.

7. On the **Introduction to Active Directory Certificate Services** page, click **Next**.

8. On the **Select Role Services** page, verify that the **Certification Authority** check box is selected and then click **Next**.

9. On the **Specify Setup Type** page, click **Standalone** and then click **Next**.

10. On the **Specify CA Type** page, click **Subordinate CA** and then click **Next**.

11. On the **Set Up Private Key** page, click **Create a new private key** and then click **Next**.

12. On the **Configure Cryptography for CA** page, click **Next**.

13. On the **Configure CA Name** page, under **Common name for this CA**, type **contoso-NPS1-SubCA** and then click **Next**.

14. On the **Request Certificate from a Parent CA** page, choose **Send a certificate request to a parent CA** and then click **Browse**.

15. In the **Select Certification Authority** window, click **Contoso-DC1-CA** and then click **OK**. See Figure 6.16.

Figure 6.16 Select Certification Authority

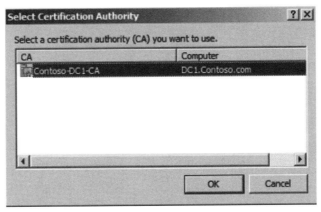

16. Verify that **DC1.Contoso.com\Contoso-DC1-CA** is displayed next to **Parent CA** and then click **Next**.

17. Click **Next** three times to accept the default database, Web server, and role services settings and then click **Install**.

18. Verify that all installations were successful and then click **Close**.

19. Exit the Server Manager.

802.1x Enforcement

IEEE 802.1x standards define an effective framework for controlling and authenticating clients to a wired or wireless protected network—in this case a NAP infrastructure. These standards define port-based authentication on supported devices. These devices could be switches or wireless access points that support the IEEE 802.1x standard. The IEEE standard is significant it has been accepted by hardware and software vendors—their products will be designed with the standards in mind. What does this mean for you and me? All hardware that is 802.1x based should work with RADIUS and NAP.

An 802.1x deployment consists of three major components that allow for the authentication process to work correctly (see Figure 6.17).

- **Supplicant** a device that requests access to our network and is connected via a pass-through authenticator.

- **Pass-through authenticator** a switch or access point that is 802.1x compliant.

- **Authentication server** when the supplicant connects to the pass-through authenticator, the request is passed to the authentication server by the pass-through authenticator. The authentication server decides whether the client is granted access or denied.

Figure 6.17 Components of 802.1x

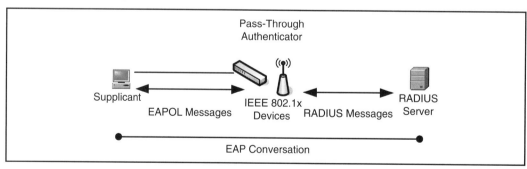

Authentication is handled using the Extensible Authentication Protocol (EAP). EAP messages used in the authentication process are transmitted between the supplicant and pass-through authenticator using EAP over LAN (EAPoL). The pass- through authenticator talks to the RADIUS using RADIUS messages and EAP.

When NAP uses IEEE 802.1x, the authenticating pass-through authenticator uses the RADIUS protocol. NPS instructs the pass-through authenticator (wireless access-point or switch) to place supplicants that are not in compliance with NPS into a restricted network. The restricted network could be a separate VLAN or a network with IP filters in place to isolate it from the secured network.

TEST DAY TIP

While studying for this exam, keep a list of new terms written down somewhere. This step will make for a great review tool on test day. Also, notice in the last section we used terminology like supplicant instead of computer or device. Always use the Microsoft terminology when studying—it will benefit you later!

EXERCISE 6.6

CONFIGURE NAP CLIENT AUTHENTICATION METHODS

In this exercise, we are going to configure a Windows Vista client authentication method.

1. Click **Start**, right-click **Network** and then **Properties**.

2. Click **Manage network connections**.

3. Right-click **Local Area Connection** and then click **Properties**. See Figure 6.18.

Figure 6.18 Windows Vista Network Properties

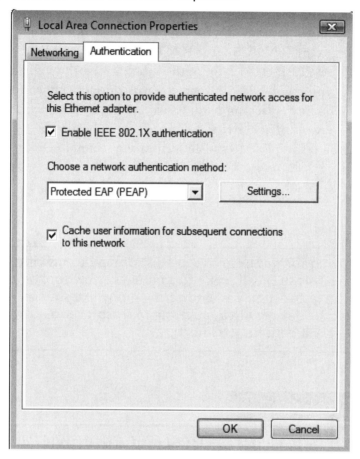

4. Click the **Authentication** tab and verify that Enable **IEEE 802.1x authentication** is selected.

5. Click **Setting**. See Figure 6.19.

Figure 6.19 Protected EAP Properties

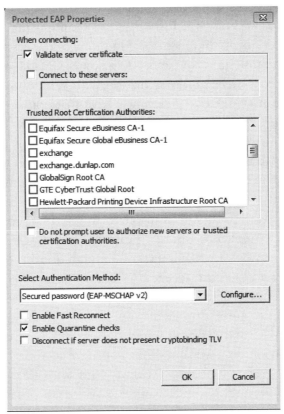

6. In the **Protected EAP Properties** dialog box, clear the **Enable Fast Reconnect** check box and verify that only the following check box is selected—**Enable Quarantine checks**.

7. Close all property sheets.

TEST DAY TIP

When you get to the test center and check in, you will be taken to your workstation and given an erasable board or paper. Use this to your advantage. Before you begin the examination, write down any network designs or acronyms you are afraid that you may forget.

Summary of Exam Objectives

The Window Server 2008 Network Infrastructure, Configuring Exam is going to contain a lot of new concepts and features—and network access protection (NAP) is going to be one of those new concepts. Microsoft has made great strides in network infrastructure compliance and remediation with Windows 2008 Server. As mentioned earlier in this chapter, it is imperative that you actually sit down and play with the Network Policy Server Console and get to know the interface. Most questions on NAP will come directly from the interface of the console.

Microsoft NAP will work with Windows 2008 Server, Windows Vista, and Windows XP Service Pack 3 at the time of this writing. More operating systems (including third-party operating systems) will be supported in the future—mostly because Microsoft is making the API available to third-party programmers.

NAP can enforce compliance through protected traffic, IEEE 802.1x authenticated network connections, Dynamic Host Configuration Protocol (DHCP) address configurations and remote access VPN connections. The main objective of NAP is to validate the state of a client computer before connecting to the private network and offer some source of remediation. It is very important to understand the drawing in Figure 6.1. Understand where each component of NAP is located—Microsoft newer exams have fewer questions but more realistic scenario questions.

The way software policy validation works is with software agents called System Health Validators (SHVs) and System Health Agents (SHAs). NPS uses SHVs to analyze the compliance of a client computer. SHVs determine whether a computer is getting full access to the private network or will it be isolated to the restricted network. The client has a piece of software installed called a SHA to monitor its system health. NPS uses SHVs and SHAs to determine the health of a client computer and to monitor, enforce and remediate the client computer. The main Microsoft SHA and SHV are—Windows Security Health Agent (WSHA) and Windows Security Health Validator (WSHV). The Microsoft agent and validator basically monitor the Microsoft Security Center.

Understand the different NAP Health Policies and where they are configured. NAP Health Policies include: Connection Request Policies, Network Policies, Health Policies and Network Access Protection Settings. All of the policies are configured with the Network Policy Server Console.

When working with NAP, understand the concept of Secure Network, Boundary Network and Restricted Network. The secure network is where all domain members should be located. The boundary network contains the remediation server and offers the client a way to become compliant. The restricted network is for clients with limited access.

802.1x enforcement relies on the access connection hardware. It is made up of three components—the supplicant, pass-through authenticator and the RADIUS server. The supplicant would be the client trying to connect to the network. The pass-through authenticator is the 802.1x device that is relaying authentication information back to the RADIUS server. The RADIUS server authenticates the network connections.

Exam Objectives Fast Track

Working with Network Access Protection

☑ The Network Access Protection (NAP) platform main objective is to validate the state of a client computer before connecting to a private network and offer a source of remediation.

☑ NAP clients include Windows Vista, Windows Server 2008 and Windows XP Service Pack 3.

☑ The NAP API will allow other ISVs to write software to be enforced by NAP.

☑ NAP provides the following areas of functionality: Health State Validation, Network Access Limitation, Automatic Remediation and Ongoing Compliance.

☑ DHCP NAP enforcement is the easiest enforcement implementation of NAP available.

☑ IPv6 is not supported with DHCP enforcement implementation.

☑ The DHCP server and NPS server can be supported on the same server by installing the 2 server roles.

☑ During the VPN connection—NPS uses PEAP messages to send NAP information to the client.

☑ All PEAP messages between the VPN client and NAP are routed through the NPS server.

☑ If the VPN client is noncompliant—the client will be directed to the restricted network with IP filters.

☑ NAP Health Policies are a combination of settings for health determination and enforcement of infrastructure compliance.

☑ The following sets of settings make up NAP Health Policies: Connection Request Policies, Network Policies, Health Policies and NAP Settings.

☑ NAP Health Policies are configured using the Network Policy Server console.

☑ NPS in Windows 2008 Server replaces IAS in Windows 2003 Server.

☑ Network Policies have four options for NAP enforcement: Allow full network access, Allow full network access for a limited time, Allow limited access and Enable auto-remediation of client computers.

☑ IPsec NAP enforcement breaks the network down to three logical networks by using health certificates provided by the Health Certificate Server (HCS).

☑ The three distinct networks are: secure network, boundary network and restricted network.

☑ Flexible Host Isolation refers to the ease of network isolation provided with the IPsec method of NAP enforcement.

☑ IEEE 802.1x standards define an effective framework for controlling and authenticating clients to a wired or wireless protected network.

☑ An 802.1x deployment consists of three major components: Supplicant, Pass-Through Authenticator and Authentication Server.

☑ Authentication is handled using the Extensible Authentication Protocol (EAP).

☑ NPS instructs the pass-through authenticator (wireless access-points or switch) to place supplicants that are not in compliance with NPS into a restricted network.

Exam Objectives
Frequently Asked Questions

Q: I have worked with Windows 2003 Server Network Access Quarantine Control extensively. Will this help me better work with Network Access Protection?

A: The short answer is no. Microsoft has totally changed the way network access is controlled in Windows Server 2008. For instance, there is no longer an Internet Authentication Service and Routing and Remote Access Service—these have been wrapped up into the Network Access Protection.

Q: You mentioned VLANs in this chapter. I am not very familiar with this technology. Should I seek other sources to help me understand this new subject?

A: Definitely! Microsoft probably does not give VLAN technology the time it deserves in its courseware or exams. In the workplace, it is almost a must to understand how VLANs work—especially if you are wanting to work (or already do work) in an enterprise environment. Earlier in this chapter, I gave you a link to a Cisco article that explains VLANs in detail. It would probably be a good idea to go out and give this article a once over.

Q: My employer has not installed or migrated to Windows Server 2008 yet. Should I get hands on experience before sitting this exam?

A: Yes! The best advice for any Microsoft exam is to actually sit down and work with the product. Go out and download the free copy of Microsoft Virtual PC 2007 and register for a 180 day trial of Windows Server 2008 Enterprise Edition. With Microsoft Virtual PC 2007, you can use multiple virtual machines to build virtual networks. This way you can setup just about any scenario in a test environment.

Q: I noticed in this chapter a lot of new acronyms that I never had heard before. This is kind of makes me nervous. Is there a way to cover them all?

A: There are a lot of new services and server roles with Windows 2008 Server. The best way to learn new acronyms and their meanings are good old fashion flash cards. Also, keeping a list with any new terms and definitions is always a good study habit.

Q: What is the technology in this material the hangs up students the most?

A: The technology that seems to always get a lot of questions has to usually deal with IP Security enforcement and 802.1x. IP Security normally causes students problems with Certificate Authorities and learning how to manage certificates. There are a lot of good whitepapers on Microsoft TechNet Web site to help you with this topic. Also, 802.1x causes some issues because the student does not understand VLANs and RADIUS. It gets a lot of attention on tests and course-ware—but a lot of students have never really got to play with this type of technology.

Q: I am having some problems understanding a specific topic in this chapter. Is there any place I can go for more help?

A: The best place to go would be the Network Access Protection Web site on TechNet. There are Web casts, whitepapers and labs out there for download. The Web site is http://technet.microsoft.com/en-us/network/bb545879.aspx. You will find an answer to just about any question concerning NAP on this site.

Self Test

1. Network Access Protection (NAP) will only work with certain operating systems at the time of Windows 2008 Server release. What operating systems will NAP support?

   A. Window XP

   B. Windows XP Service Pack 3

   C. Windows Vista

   D. Windows Server 2008

2. Network Access Protection (NAP) can provide network protection to various types of network communications. Which of the following will not support NAP?

   A. RRAS Connections

   B. DHCP Supported Network

   C. WINS Supported Network

   D. IEEE 802.11B Wireless Network

3. Network Access Protection (NAP) was designed for third-party vendors to take advantage of the infrastructure. This is really important for NAP to become popular throughout the IT community. What is the name of the item that allows third-party developers to write programs that can take advantage of the NAP infrastructure?

   A. ISV

   B. HRA

   C. API

   D. CA

4. NAP enforcement points are what determine if a client wanting to connect to a restricted network is healthy and compliant. What are the valid enforcement points listed below?

   A. Windows 2008 VPN Server

   B. HUB

   C. DHCP Server

   D. IEEE 802.1x Network Access Device

5. The NAP Health Policy Server is responsible for storing health requirement policies and provides health state validation for the NAP Infrastructure. What Windows Server 2008 roles have to be installed for the NAP Health Policy Server to be configured?

   A. Active Directory Domain Role

   B. NPS Server Role

   C. NAP Server Role

   D. DHCP Server Role

6. You have decided to implement NAP into your existing network. During the design, you need to make a decision as to how the Restricted Network will be secured from the Remediation Network. Given the options below, which one(s) would work in this scenario?

   A. Use IPsec with Health Certificates

   B. Use a secondary switch to split the networks

   C. Use IP packet filters

   D. Use VLANs

7. Using Figure 6.20 as a reference point, where would the Remediation Server be located on this network?

Figure 6.20 Network Design

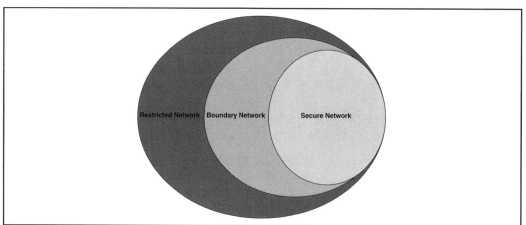

A. Secure Network

B. Boundary Network

C. Restricted Network

D. Location Does Not Matter

8. The remediation server could run Windows 2008 Server or Windows 2003 Server software. To remediate Windows Vista, Windows 2008 Server or Windows XP Service Pack 3—what other software would the remediation server need to run?

A. Windows Server Update Services (WSUS)

B. Network Protection Services (NPS)

C. Routing and Remote Access Services (RRAS)

D. Windows Security Health Validator (WSHV)

9. You instruct your junior network administrator Roger to setup a NAP enforcement point using a DHCP server. After his installation, he comes to you complaining that DHCP is working fine—but he cannot get NAP to work with Windows Vista clients. You go through the installation with him— using 802.1x certified switches, he setup a Windows 2008 Server with both the DHCP and Network Policy and Access Services server roles. Once config- ured successfully, he set the DHCP settings for DHCPv6 Stateless Mode. Once configured—he set up the NPS policies with the NAP wizard. What is the problem with this scenario?

A. The equipment needs to support 802.11 certified devices.

B. Roger did not install Routing and Remote Access Services (RRAS) on the Windows 2008 Server.

C. NAP does not support IPv6.

D. Windows Vista needs to be updated to Service Pack 1 to work in this network.

10. NAP Health Policies are a combination of settings for health determination and enforcement of infrastructure compliance. What are the sets of settings that make up the NAP Health Policies?

A. Connection Request Policies

B. Network Policies

C. Health Policies

D. Network Access Protection Settings

Correct Answer & Explanation: **A,B,C,D**. NAP Health Policies are configured within the Network Policy Server console. NAP Health Policies are made up of all of the above choices.

Self Test Quick Answer Key

1. B, C, D

2. C

3. C

4. A, C, D

5. B

6. A, C, D

7. B

8. A

9. C

10. A, B, C, D

Appendix

MCTS/MCITP
Exam 642

Self Test Appendix

Chapter 1: IP Addressing and Services

1. You need to set up a network in the lab for a training class. You want to isolate the lab network from the rest of the corporate network so students don't inadvertently do something that takes the entire network down. What IP addressing method would you use?

   A. Private network addressing

   B. Public network addressing

   C. Network Address Translation

   D. Subnet isolation through subnet mask

   Correct Answer & Explanation: **D**. If you install a router or switch and use a different subnet mask, you can isolate the subnet in the lab so that the local traffic isn't routed to the network.

   Incorrect Answers & Explanations: **A**, **B**, **C**. Answer **A** is incorrect, because your corporate network may already be using private network addresses. Without more specificity, this answer is incorrect. Answer **B** is incorrect, because a public network addressing scheme is inappropriate for a lab environment, especially one that has no need to connect to the Internet. Even if Internet connectivity was needed, a private address scheme with a router using NAT would make more sense. Answer **C** is incorrect, because network address translation is used when private IP addresses need to head out to the Internet. No mention of Internet connectivity is made and it does not solve the subnet isolation issue.

2. Your boss asked you to subnet a network in the lab for an upcoming class. He hands you a piece of paper while he's on the phone and it simply says "192.168.10.x/25. 4 subnets." What is the subnet mask and the first address in each subnet?

   A. 255.255.255.0/ 192.168.10.1, 192.168.10.32, 192.168.10.64, 192.168.10.128

   B. 255.255.255.252/ 192.168.10.0, 192.168.10.32, 192.168.10.64, 192.168.10.128

   C. 255.255.255.240/ 192.168.10.0, 192.168.16.0, 192.168.24.0, 192.168.32.0

   D. 255.255.255.128/ 192.168.10.1, 192.168.10.33, 192.168.10.65, 192.168.10.97

Correct Answer & Explanation: **D**. Using the network notation /25 indicates you need to use 25 network bits. 255.255.255.0 typically is used for the default subnet mask for Class C networks and uses 24 bits (often notated /24). Therefore, if you add one bit, you change the left-most bit in the right-most octet to 1. This equals 128, creating a subnet mask of 255.255.255.128. The starting addresses (the first assignable IP address) in each subnet would have the right-most octet set to 1, 33, 65, and 97. The network addresses themselves would be 192.168.10.0, 192.168.10.32, 192.168.10.64, and 192.168.10.96.

Incorrect Answers & Explanations: **A**, **B**, **C**. Answer **A** is incorrect, because the subnet mask is incorrect (as are the starting IP addresses). The subnet mask with zero as the last octet is the default subnet mask for a Class C network and uses only 24 bits. The network would have been notated as 192.168.10.x/24 if you were to use this subnet mask. Answer **B** is incorrect, because the bits in the last octet of the subnet mask 255.255.255.252 are set to 1111 1100 and would have to be notated as 192.168.10.x/30. Answer **C** is incorrect, because 255.255.255.240 would be notated as 192.168.10.x/28 so that the last octet would be set to 1111 0000.

3. You have a growing network that originally was configured using the private Class C address space. However, you're now about to grow beyond the maximum number of devices and need to expand but you don't anticipate needing more than a total of 290 addresses. What action would you take to solve this problem that would create the least disruption to your network?

   A. Install a router. Create two new scopes on your DHCP Server and reassign IP addresses.

   B. Change the default subnet mask to 255.255.252.0.

   C. Change the IP addressing scheme from Class C to Class B.

   D. Assign new computers on the network IP addresses from the existing address pool.

   Correct Answer & Explanation: **B**. Changing the subnet mask from the default 255.255.255.0 to 255.255.252.0 would increase your address space and allow existing computers to continue to use their IP addresses (as long as they got the new subnet mask). Your IP address space then would span from 192.168.0.x through 192.168.3.x. This potentially could slow down network traffic because these added IP addresses would be on the network as the existing ones.

However, if you don't plan on expanding much beyond about 300 devices, this would be the fastest and easiest way to go.

Incorrect Answers & Explanations: **A, C, D**. Answer **A** is incorrect, because although you could install a router to create a new subnet, the creation of a new subnet mask is probably easier. In addition, you would not need to create two new scopes on your DHCP server, and reassigning addresses could take some work if you have static IP addresses assigned. Answer **C** is incorrect, because although you could change your addressing scheme to a Class B network, that would yield far more host addresses than needed and would take more configuration than just changing the subnet mask. Answer **D** is incorrect, because if you were to allow the new computers to try to lease an IP address from the existing address pool, you would have overlapping IP addresses (depending on configuration) or a computer that could not get a lease. Either scenario would degrade the network service and availability and is the worst option of all.

4. Your company's president comes to you and says that he understands IPv6 is fully supported in Windows Server 2008. He will approve your IT budget if it includes plans to transition to Windows Server 2008 and IPv6. However, he wants to know how quickly you can transition to IPv6. What should you tell him?

   A. There is no fast and easy way to transition to IPv6. Much of the Internet's backbone is running on IPv4, so transitional technologies will be required. You'd recommend setting up IPv6 segments and using a tunneling protocol for the transition to begin.

   B. The transition to IPv6 on the Internet backbone has been completed and as soon as the company upgrades to Windows Server 2008 and replaces its routers, you're good to go.

   C. There is no reasonable way to transition to IPv6 for this organization since all hardware and software would have to be replaced to run Windows Server 2008 or Windows Vista. The cost would be prohibitive and is therefore not recommended.

   D. The transition to IPv6 requires the installation of new hardware and software on all subnets using IPv6 exclusively. In the meantime, IPv4 can be used on older subnets and IPv6 can be used on newer subnets and a specific IPv4 to IPv6 router can be installed to bridge the two.

Correct Answer & Explanation: **A**. The eventual transition to IPv6 will be gradual and will require a lot of planning at each stage. There are various transition strategies that can be employed, one of which is to create IPv6 subnets that can talk directly using IPv6 via a tunnel and then employ other transitional methods to enable IPv4 and IPv6 traffic to coexist on the network.

Incorrect Answers & Explanations: **B, C, D**. Answer **B** is incorrect, because although agencies and organizations are interested in transitioning quickly to IPv6, it is not a simple task. The transition to Ipv6 is not complete and simply replacing routers will not address the issue. Answer **C** is incorrect, because many hardware and software systems currently support IPv4 and IPv6. Not all hardware and software would have to be replaced, though it's possible some new equipment will be needed to aid in the transition to IPv6. Answer **D** is incorrect, because the transition to IPv6 does not necessarily require new hardware or software—much of the newer equipment (such as Windows Server 2003 and Windows XP) can accept IPv6 addressing. The key is planning the infrastructure transition. Though a router might be needed to help bridge mixed network traffic, this is not the best answer.

5. You open Windows Server 2008 DHCP Server role and examine the scope settings one of your staff members created, shown in Figure 1.33. Based on this information, which statement is true?

Figure 1.33 Windows Server 2008 DHCP Configuration

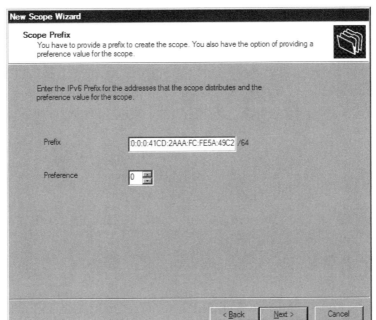

A. The Preference Value is incorrect. It must be set to 1 for all addresses that use the /64 option.

B. The Prefix Value is incorrect. It cannot begin with 0:0:0:.

C. The Prefix Value is too long. It should contain fewer digits.

D. Both B and C are correct.

E. The Prefix value and Preference values are correct.

Correct Answer & Explanation: **D**. The Prefix Value should contain the prefix for the addresses the scope distributes. The /64 indicates that there are 64 bits used for the network address. In IPv6, each digit represents 16, so /64 indicates that the prefix should be four digits. For example, FEC8: uses four 16-bit digits (hexadecimal notation).

Incorrect Answers & Explanations: **A**, **B**, **C**. Answer **A** is incorrect, because The Preference Value can be set to 0, the default value. The Preference determines the preferred order in which these addresses will be allocated to hosts. Preference 0 addresses will be handed out before Preference 1 addresses. Answer **B** is incorrect, because that would indicate a network address of 0. The issue is not with the second two zeroes, the address cannot begin with zero. Answer **C** is incorrect, because the Prefix box should contain the Prefix not a full IPv6 address as appears to be the case in this figure. Answer **E** is incorrect because the Prefix value is incorrect. The Preference value is fine as is.

6. You've asked Justin, a junior member of your IT staff, to install Windows Server 2008 on a spare computer in the lab and set up the DHCP role so you can teach a class on what's new in DHCP. Justin hesitates and asks how he should set the scope settings so it doesn't take the network down. What should you tell Justin?

A. DHCP in Windows Server 2008 cannot be installed on a computer attached to a network with a live DHCP server. Remove the server's network connection before installing DHCP.

B. Only one DHCP can exist on a network. He should configure the server as a DHCP relay agent instead.

C. A new DHCP server must be authorized in AD before it can perform the DHCP role.

D. Adding a new DHCP server could not take the network down.

Correct Answer & Explanation: **C.** You can install the DHCP server role and configure scope, reservations, and exclusions without activating the server. In addition, you must authorize the DHCP server via AD before it will be allowed to function as a DHCP server on the network. This helps prevent rogue DHCP servers from popping up, intentionally or otherwise.

Incorrect Answers & Explanations: **A, B, D.** Answer **A** is incorrect, because you can install the DHCP server role on a server attached to a network with a live DHCP server. The role can be installed and not activated, which is the default setting. Once activated, it still must be authorized in AD. Answer **B** is incorrect, because you can have more than one DHCP server on a network, though you typically have only one per subnet. DHCP relay agents are typically routers and switches designed to forward DHCP traffic. Answer **D** is incorrect, because although a new DHCP server on the network could take the network down, it could do so only if the scope settings were incorrect and it was authorized in AD. As long as Justin doesn't activate the DHCP server role or authorize it in AD, there should be no problem.

7. You need to expand your network and create a new subnet for a new research project. You want the traffic for the research group to remain local to the subnet. None of the computers for the research project are installed yet. What's the fastest and easiest way to go about creating this subnet and keeping local traffic local?

   A. Add the computers to the network, assign them a different subnet mask, enable IPSec through Group Policy, and assign it to the research project subnet.

   B. Create a scope on the DHCP server that will provide addresses to just those computers, install a router, assign it a static IP address, and use that router as the default gateway for the computers on that subnet.

   C. Install a new router and configure it as the DHCP Relay Agent for the existing scope using a static IP address. Then, connect the new computers to the network through the new router.

   D. Modify the existing scope options on the DHCP server so that the subnet addresses for the new research subnet are excluded from the scope. Install a new router and configure it with a static IP address from the same range as the excluded IP addresses. Last, connect the new computers to the subnet and check that they are configured to automatically get IP configuration data.

Correct Answer & Explanation: **B**. Creating a new scope for those computers allows you to create a distinct subnet through the use of a new subnet mask in the IP configuration data with the DHCP scope data. A router is used to physically separate the segments, keeping local traffic local to the research group, meeting the stated requirements.

Incorrect Answers & Explanations: **A, C, D**. Answer **A** is incorrect, because if you add computers to the network before you've set up the subnet isolation, they'll simply be added to the regular network and receive their IP addresses from the scope that is currently defined on your DHCP server. Answer **C** is incorrect, because assigning IP addresses from the existing scope essentially defines these new computers as part of the larger network. Although they may be separated by a router, they are still part of the network at large if they're using the same DCHP IP settings. Answer **D** is incorrect, because excluding addresses from the scope simply makes them unavailable to computers configured to get IP configuration data from that server. If those excluded addresses are not included in a scope, they are simply unavailable.

8. The company has just leased a nearby building so it can expand operations. You've been asked to configure the network infrastructure in the new building. You configure the DHCP server that will go on this new network segment with the following options:

- Scope: 192.168.10.0 to 192.168.15.0

- Subnet mask: 255.255.252.0

- Default gateway: 192.168.10.1

- Exclusions: 192.168.12.0 to 192.168.12.20

- Reservations: 192.168.10.1 DNS server, 192.168.12.2 DNS server, 192.168.12.5 WINS server, 192.168.12.6 Router8

You set Router 8 to have a static IP address of 192.168.12.6 and configure it to be a DHCP relay agent. What's wrong with your set up?

A. You can't have two DNS servers on one subnet, the scope and the subnet mask do not match, you can't set up a router as DHCP relay agent.

B. Your scope cannot have a zero in the last place, your subnet mask is wrong, your default gateway and your DNS server share the same IP address and may slow down the subnet, you don't need a WINS server.

C. Your default gateway and your DNS server use the same IP address. You cannot have a DHCP relay agent (your router) and a DHCP server on the same subnet. Your excluded range and your reservations settings are mutually exclusive.

D. The default gateway has the wrong IP address and all network traffic will be sent to the Router, causing all local traffic to be routed to the main network and back again, causing too much unneeded network traffic. You don't need a DHCP server on this subnet and should simply enable the server as a RRAS server to handle remote traffic to the main corporate site.

Correct Answer & Explanation: **C.** Your default gateway and DNS server use the same IP address. If these two functions reside on different machines, the network will not find one or the other of these devices. You should set up either a DHCP server or a DHCP relay agent, not both. If you want to isolate DHCP traffic, you need a DHCP server. If you want to have all computers from this subnet get their IP address configuration data from the main site's DHCP server, you need a DHCP relay agent. Excluded ranges are ranges of IP addresses the DHCP server cannot hand out, thus the reservations should be from within the excluded range to prevent the DHCP server from dynamically assigning those reserved IP addresses.

Incorrect Answers & Explanations: **A**, **B**, **D**. Answer **A** is incorrect, because you can have more than one DNS server on a subnet, the scope and the subnet mask could be used together, and you can have a router as a DHCP relay agent. In fact, that is the most common device for DHCP relay agents. Answer **B** is incorrect, because your network ID should end with a zero, devices cannot have a zero address, the subnet mask is correct, you probably don't want the same computer to act as default gateway and DNS server (though it is physically possible), and you don't have enough information to know if you need a WINS server or not. WINS is used for backward compatibility with older Microsoft operating systems, no data was provided on this so including or omitting a WINS server is irrelevant to this question. Answer **D** is incorrect, because the default gateway address is not wrong though it is the same as the DNS server, which may not be the best set up. Though you may not need a DHCP server on the network (you would then rely on a DHCP relay agent), you don't necessarily need to enable the server as a RRAS server. Your connection to the main corporate network is not specified.

9. You've set up a new subnet with a DHCP server. After a few days, mobile users begin complaining they can't log onto the network when they're locally connected (at their desks, for example). What would you check in your DHCP settings?

A. Scope settings

B. Exclusions

C. Subnet mask or default gateway

D. Lease duration

Correct Answer & Explanation: **D**. If mobile users are the only ones complaining about getting onto the network, you would limit your search for things related to mobile users. A long lease duration could cause IP addresses to be unavailable for mobile users. If a mobile user connects to the network and receives an IP address then disconnects from the network, it may keep the IP address even if it's disconnected from the network for an extended period of time. When mobile users log back into the network and attempt to get IP configuration settings, there may be no available IP addresses to give them. Shorter lease durations are typically better where there are many mobile users on a network or subnet.

Incorrect Answers & Explanations: **A, B, C**. Answer **A** is incorrect, because your scope settings are not necessarily incorrect. If your scope was incorrect, there would be problems with other users as well. However, if your scope did not include enough IP addresses for stationary and mobile users, you could have a problem with your scope. This would most likely be experienced by mobile users first. Although this is a possibility, this is not the best answer. Answer **B** is incorrect, because exclusions would not impact just mobile users and would essentially have no impact on users at all. Answer **C** is incorrect, because if the subnet mask or default gateway settings were wrong, all users would experience problems.

10. A recent change to the network infrastructure configuration was completed over the weekend. Monday morning, users begin complaining that the network is terribly slow. The Help Desk phones are lit up and there's a rumble in the building as users start going to others' desks asking if they're having any luck using network resources and getting out to the Internet. The new configuration is shown in Figure 1.34. What would you change in order to best resolve this problem?

Figure 1.34 New Network Configuration

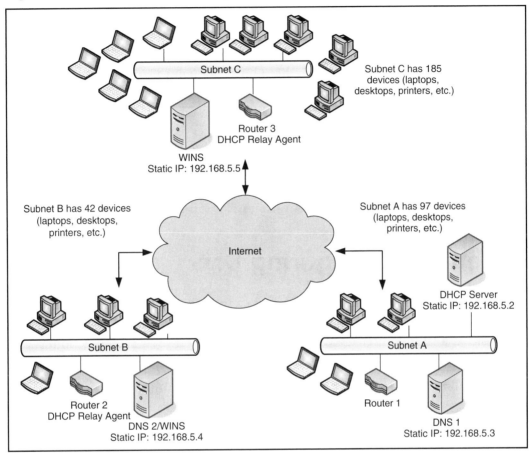

A. Add a DNS Server to Subnet C.

B. Remove the DHCP Relay Agent role from either Router 2 or Router 3.

C. Add a DHCP Server to Subnet C and remove Router 3.

D. Both A and C.

E. Add a DHCP Server to Subnet C.

Correct Answer & Explanation: **E**. If host computers have to cross a WAN link for DHCP configuration information, the link and the network can get pretty slow. If users are complaining about the response time on a subnet like C, which is the largest subnet in the company, the best solution (other than ensuring there is nothing wrong with the WAN link) is to install a DHCP server on Subnet C.

Incorrect Answers & Explanations: **A, B, C, D**. Answer **A** is incorrect, because DNS typically affects users trying to resolve domain names. It's not likely this would slow things down on the subnet. Though this is a possible answer, it's not the most likely cause. Answer **B** is incorrect, because if you remove the DHCP Relay Agent role from either router, the host computers on that subnet won't be able to get DHCP configuration settings. Answer **C** is incorrect, because although you do want to add a DHCP server to Subnet C, you should not remove the router. You should, however, remove the DHCP Relay Agent role from the router once the DHCP server is installed and authorized. Answer **D** is incorrect, because Answer **A** is not the best answer and Answer **C** is incorrect.

Chapter 2: Configuring DNS

1. You are the administrator for a Windows Server 2008 network. You've been tasked with designing a secure facility and have recommended that it be isolated from the Internet. Which of the following do you recommend for DNS? (Select all that apply.)

    A. You recommend a private DNS infrastructure with internal root hints servers.

    B. You recommend the use of AD integrated zones.

    C. You recommend the use of secure dynamic updates.

    D. You recommend the use of secondary zones.

    Correct Answers & Explanations: **A, B**. Answer **A** is correct. A DNS infrastructure that is isolated from the Internet should be configured with root hints pointing to internal servers. By default Windows Server 2008 servers point to the Internet's root name servers. Answer **B** is also correct. AD integrated zones offer additional security and fault tolerance, which are important considerations in secure environments.

    Incorrect Answers & Explanations: **C, D**. Answer **C** is incorrect. Dynamic updates should not be allowed in highly secure environments. Answer **D** is also incorrect. Secondary zones are much less secure than AD integrated zones and should be avoided.

2. You are the administrator for a small organization's network. The network is connected to the Internet. Both servers run Windows Server 2008 and all clients run Windows Vista Enterprise. Your manager has asked you to explain how her computer finds web servers on the Internet. Which of the following do you tell her? (Select all that apply.)

    A. You tell her that her local resolver sends a recursive query to the organization's local DNS server.

    B. You tell her that her local resolver sends a query to the Internet's root DNS servers.

    C. You tell her that the local DNS server sends a server-to-server query to the Internet's root DNS servers.

    D. You tell her that the local DNS server returns the requested record from its zone files.

    Correct Answer & Explanation: **C.** The local resolver sends a client-to-server query to the local DNS server. If it does not contain the needed information, by default the local DNS server queries the Internet root DNS servers, asking for any information they can provide in resolving the query. They will return any information they know of, and the local DNS server repeats this process until it eventually locates a server with the requested DNS information or fails to do so. The success or failure is then passed back to the client resolver.

    Incorrect Answers & Explanations: **A, B, D.** Answer **A** is incorrect. Local resolvers send client-to-server queries, not recursive queries. Answer **B** is also incorrect. The local resolver on the client computer does not contact the Internet root DNS servers. Finally, Answer **D** is incorrect because the local DNS server should contain only records for the organization's domain. This does not include information about web servers on the Internet, unless it is the organization's web server.

3. You have recently been transferred to the DNS team at a large multinational company, and are working feverously learn about DNS. Lately you've been working on the difference between client-to-server and server-to-server queries. Which of the following are true? (Select all that apply.)

    A. Client-to-server queries are all-or-nothing requests.

    B. Client-to-server queries are also known as recursive queries.

C. Server-to-server queries ask for FQDN resolution.

D. Server-to-server queries ask for as much information as can be provided about the FQDN.

Correct Answers & Explanations: **A**, **C**, **D**. Answer **A** is correct. Client-to-server queries are often referred to as all-or-nothing queries. They ask for their request to be successfully fulfilled, such as a host name resolved to an IP address, or they ask to be notified that the request failed. Answers **C** and **D** are also correct. Like client-to-server queries, server-to-server queries also ask for resolution of the client resolver's original request. If this is not possible, however, they ask the DNS server to provide any information that it might have that could move the resolution process forward. Usually this involves the location of the name servers for another portion of the FQDN.

Incorrect Answer & Explanation: Answer **B** is incorrect. Server-to-server queries are known as recursive queries.

4. You are the DNS administrator for a mid-sized organization. As part of the upgrade process, you put in a request to transition all DNS services to AD integrated zones. When your manager asks about the key features involved, what do you tell her? (Select all that apply.)

A. You tell her that AD integrated zones are stored in Active Directory.

B. You tell her that all zone records are stored as AD objects and have object level security.

C. You tell her that it enables secure dynamic updates.

D. You tell her that replication is much more efficient and secure.

Correct Answers & Explanations: **A**, **B**, **C**, **D**. Answer **A** is correct, because AD integrated zones have their records stored in AD directory services. Answer **B** is also correct, because the records are stored in AD and they are objects that permissions are assigned to. Answer **C** is correct, because these permissions allow for secure dynamic updates. Finally, Answer **D** is also correct. Replication of zone records occurs at the property level, and is encrypted and compressed.

5. You are the administrator of a small Windows Server 2008 network. Your organization has a single AD domain with a standard primary zone. Using DNS Manager, you enabled DDNS and enabled the **Scavenge stale resource records** checkbox in the properties of the server. Stale records are not being cleaned up. Which two actions do you take to resolve the problem?

A. You manually delete the stale records.

B. You alter the refresh and no–refresh intervals.

C. You select **Scavenge stale resource records** in the properties of the zone.

D. You select the **Enable automatic scavenging of stale records** box.

Correct Answers & Explanations: **C**, **D**. Answer **C** is correct. Standard primary zones must have the **Scavenge stale resource records** box selected at the zone level. Answer **D** is also correct. The DNS Server role needs to be configured to automatically scavenge records using the **Enable automatic scavenging of stale records** checkbox in the properties of the server object.

Incorrect Answers & Explanations: **A**, **B**. Answer **A** is incorrect. Manually deleting records does not help with configuring automatic scavenging. Answer **B** is also incorrect. Because you have records being identified as stale, these settings are configured properly.

6. You are the administrator for a small office. Until now you have used your ISP's DNS server, however your slow WAN link to the Internet is becoming congested and you've been working to optimize the traffic that passes over it. The users in the office use the Internet heavily, and you decide that one thing you'd like to minimize is DNS traffic. You install the DNS Server role on your only file server, a Windows Server 2008 workgroup server. Which one of the following do you configure?

A. You configure a forward lookup zone.

B. You configure a reverse lookup zone.

C. You configure it as a server forwarder.

D. You configure it as a conditional forwarder.

Correct Answer & Explanation: Answer **C** is correct. By installing the server you will be able to take advantage of caching queries locally. However, if you don't also configure the server as a forwarder, DNS traffic will be increased because of the recursive queries the DNS server will use by default. Each query would be sent to the root hints servers, then the next level of the namespace's DNS servers, and so forth. Configuring the server to forward requests to the ISP's DNS server allows you to take advantage of its caching features while also keeping name resolution traffic down to a minimum. The ISP's server would be left to do the bulk of the work.

Incorrect Answers & Explanations: **A**, **B**, **D**. Answers **A** and **B** are incorrect, because you don't have a local domain, so there is no reason to configure zones. Answer **C** is incorrect. All DNS queries are destined for one place, the public Internet. Conditional forwarding is used to send queries to different DNS servers based on the domains involved.

7. You are the administrator of a Windows Server 2008 network for a regional organization. The organization has small offices in several states that connect to headquarters with slow WAN connections. Each of these small offices has its own server with DNS and AD installed on it. You've noticed that users in the small office spend a lot of time surfing the Internet. You've taken some measures to manage that traffic, however the DNS queries from the small office servers still generate excessive traffic. Which of the following steps can you take to minimize that traffic? (Select two.)

   A. You can install a server at headquarters for the small office servers to forward their DNS queries to.

   B. You can configure the small office servers as forwarders.

   C. You can alter the root hints on the small office servers.

   D. You can alter the root hints on the new server at headquarters.

   Correct Answers & Explanations: **A**, **B**. Currently, each small office DNS server is most likely sending several queries across the WAN for each client lookup request. This can be minimized by configuring them to forward these queries to a central server at headquarters for resolution. By doing this, they will send only a single query across the WAN for each resource request.

   Incorrect Answers & Explanations: **C**, **D**. Answer **C** is incorrect. Modifying the root hints may have an impact on traffic but is not proper in this circumstance. Answer **D** is also incorrect. Root hints point to the Internet root name servers by default; there is no reason to modify them to properly answer this question.

8. You are the administrator of a small Windows Server 2008 network. When you installed your first domain controller, you had the DCPROMO wizard also install and configure the DNS Server role. While adding your second domain controller, you did not select the option to install the DNS Server role. A few days later you installed the DNS Server role on the server. When you opened DNS Manager and looked at the configuration for the server, which one of the following did you see?

A. You saw that the server had no zones.

B. You saw that the server had a secondary forward lookup zone for the AD domain automatically created on it.

C. You saw that the server had a standard primary forward lookup zone for the AD domain automatically created on it.

D. You saw that the server had an AD integrated zone for the AD domain automatically created on it.

Correct Answer & Explanation: Answer **D** is correct. By default, when you install the DNS Server role on a domain controller, if the AD domain has an AD integrated zone configured on at least one other DNS server, it will automatically create it after installing the DNS Server role.

Incorrect Answers & Explanations: **A**, **B**, **C**. Answer **A** is incorrect. If the DNS environment had no AD integrated zones that were replicated to the domain controller, this would be true. Because there is at least one AD integrated zone, that zone will be created and configured automatically. Answers **B** and **C** are incorrect because standard zone types are never created automatically.

9. You are the Windows Server 2008 administrator for a small office at a large multinational company. The company's DNS environment is huge, spanning not only many domains and subdomains but also many different types of DNS servers. The DNS administrators have been asked by the network and routing group to reduce the traffic load DNS is placing on the network. As part of this effort, you've been asked to configure conditional forwarding for several, disjointed, internal domain name spaces that your company uses. Which of the following do you do? (Select all that apply.)

A. In DNS manager, you right-click the appropriate server node and open its properties.

B. In DNS manager, you right-click the **Conditional Forwarders** node and select to create a new forwarder.

C. In the **Properties** tab, you configure the DNS servers to forward to.

D. In the **New Conditional Forwarder** dialog you specify the domain and the DNS server to send queries to.

Correct Answers & Explanations: **B**, **D**. Answer **B** is correct. Conditional forwarding is enabled by creating an object for each domain that DNS queries will be forwarded for under the **Conditional Forwarders** node. The objects themselves are created using the **New Conditional Forwarder** dialog, so Answer **D** is also correct.

Incorrect Answers & Explanations: **A**, **C**. Answers **A** and **C** are incorrect. They represent the configuration steps for server-level, not conditional, forwarding.

10. You are the Windows Server 2008 administrator for a mid-sized organization. You have decided to implement conditional forwarding on one of your Windows Server 2008 DNS servers. For some reason, you've been unable to create the forwarder. Which one of the following is the most likely reason?

   A. The configuration dialog cannot locate the IP address of the server to be forwarded to.

   B. The configuration dialog cannot locate the host name of the server to be forwarded to.

   C. You already have a zone configured for the domain you're trying to forward to.

   D. The DNS Server role has become corrupt on the server and should be reinstalled.

Correct Answer & Explanation: **C**. If the server has a zone that matches the forwarder you are attempting to create, your configuration attempt will fail.

Incorrect Answers & Explanations: **A**, **B**, **D**. Answers **A** and **B** are incorrect. Even though the configuration utility performs some resolution, it will allow you to create the forwarder even if these fail. Answer **D** is also incorrect, because another more viable answer exists.

Chapter 3: Configuring Network Access

1. You are asked by your employer to set up a LAN using Windows 2008 Server RRAS. Which of these types of routing algorithms or protocols cannot be used to organize the signal flow between the devices in the network, according to the supported Windows Server 2008 features?

   A. RIP

   B. RIP2

   C. OSPF

   D. None of the Above

Correct Answer & Explanation: **C.** The correct answer is **C,** because it is no longer supported in the RRAS of Windows Server 2008. RIP and RIP2 are both supported by Windows Server 2008.

2. You are asked to configure a routing table based on information gathered to optimize the network. You find that a static route with the IP destination 10.40.0.0 and the subnet mask of 255.255.0.0 requires deleting. Which of the following commands would successfully accomplish this routing change?

    A. route delete 10.40.0.0 mask 255.255.0.0

    B. route delete 10.*

    C. route change 10.40.0.0 mask 255.255.0.0 10.20.0.25

    D. route add 10.41.0.0 mask 255.255.0.0 10.20.0.1

    Correct Answer & Explanation: **A.** The correct answer is **A,** because it is the only correct command that will delete the aforementioned route. The other commands perform actions that would not accomplish the proper activity required.

3. You are troubleshooting a network system that has applied a number of static routes. After reviewing the information used to make these routes, you determine that an error was made while entering the routes into one of the gateways. Which of the following choices best defines your actions as a result of this error?

    A. No effect because the Static Routes act the same way dynamic ones do, and will auto correct itself.

    B. An immediate change must be made because there is no fault tolerance in regards to static routing.

    C. A system reboot should be performed to clear all persistent routes.

    D. None of the above.

    Correct Answer & Explanation: **A.** The correct answer is **A,** because changes to the network or a failure between two statically defined nodes will cause any traffic between those points to not be rerouted. This means any packets that are awaiting transport between the affected paths will be forced to wait for repairs to the failure or for an updated static route by the administrator.

4. You are responsible for upgrading and configuring a large enterprise's LAN network to Windows Server 2008. It will include a high number of physical

machines and will need to be scalable for aggressive growth over the next year as the company expands. Which of the following answers best describes why you should not use a Distance Vector Routing protocol like RIP for this task?

A. Distance Vector Routing Protocols like RIP are not scalable for large networks.

B. Distance Vector Routing Protocols like RIP are not usable for LAN configurations.

C. RIP does not understand VLSM.

D. All of the Above.

Correct Answer & Explanation: **A.** The correct answer is **A,** because RIP is limited in a number of ways due to its lack of scalability. It prevents routing loops from continuing indefinitely by implementing a limit on the number of hops allowed in a path from the source to a destination. It also limits the size of the network that RIP can support by design.

5. You are about to set up and configure a VPN for your client's communications server using Windows Server 2008. Before going through the set up and configuration process, which of the following steps need to be taken before you can configure the connection on the machine to ensure the best possible outcome?

A. Ensure a clean install of Windows Server 2008 has been installed.

B. Enter Add Roles Wizard and ensure that the RRAS role has been installed.

C. Both A and B.

D. Configure the SSTP protocols for the VPN.

Correct Answer & Explanation: **C.** The correct answer is **C,** because Microsoft recommends that a clean install of Windows Server 2008 be installed before configuring the RRAS role. Both of these choices are pre-requisites to setting up a VPN, and with RRAS installed you cannot proceed with the VPN configuration.

6. You are working with a server running the RRAS that is configured for the Windows authentication provider. You have administered several policies from RRAS to the server. Which of the following connection settings cannot be validated before authorization occurs by the policies you set up?

A. Advanced conditions such as access server identity, access client phone number, or MAC address.

B. Remote access permission.

C. Whether user account dial-in properties are ignored.

D. None of the above

Correct Answer & Explanation: **D.** The correct answer is **D,** None of the above. All of the listed conditions can be validated before authorization with Remote Access Policies. Advanced conditions such as access server identity access phone number or MAC address are easily accessible with Windows Server 2008.

7. Your company has begun a migration from Windows Server 2003 to Windows Server 2008 throughout their network. The RADIUS configurations for the old build were configured through IAS for Windows Server 2003. The new build for Windows Server 2008 will be using NPS. Which of the following statements would be true in regards to NPS?

A. The Connection Request Processing node still exists.

B. The Remote Access Logging folder still contains the Local File or SQL Server nodes.

C. The Network policies have replaced Remote Access policies and have been moved to the Policies node.

D. All of the Above.

Correct Answer & Explanation: **C.** The correct answer is C, because while those familiar with IAS may find much of the functionality the same, there have still been a significant number of changes to the interface that should be noted. There is no Connection Request Processing node and the Accounting node has replaced the Remote Access logging folder and no longer has the Local File or SQL Server nodes.

8. You are the administrator of a network employing the Network Access Protection snap-in in conjunction with NAP. You have configured a set of monitoring policies in NAP for use on the network. Which of the following options will the new NAP monitor policies of Windows Server 2008 be able to accomplish?

A. Recording for compliance of each PC logging in to the system.

B. Isolation of non-compliant users.

C. Restricting access of non-compliant users.

D. None of the above.

Correct Answer & Explanation: **A.** The correct answer is **A,** because NAP offers both Monitor and Isolate policies. Isolate policies would be able to accomplish choices **B** and **C,** but monitor policies would only be able to record the compliance of the PC's logging on to the network.

9. You are asked to reconfigure a cheap and efficient access solution using the newly installed Windows Server 2008's RRAS role for your company. The access solution must have medium data transfer rates and reliable connection stability. The company's existing method of connection is ISDN and is utilizing the X.25 protocols for transfer. Which of the following changes in regards to Windows Server 2008 would need to be made to the existing system to make these adjustments?

    A. The connection type should be downgraded, because the data transfer rate for ISDN is very unstable.

    B. The connection type should be improved to Cable or DSL, because ISDN has the slowest data transfer rate.

    C. The X.25 protocol needs to be changed because it is not supported by Windows Server 2008.

    D. None of the above.

    Correct Answer & Explanation: **C.** The correct answer is **C,** because Windows Server 2008 no longer supports X.25 protocol. The other options are not correct. The downgrade of the connection type would result in extremely slow data transfer rates. Improving the connection type would increase data transfer rates, but does not account for the lack of support of the X.25 protocol in Windows Server 2008.

10. You are setting up a communications server for your small- to medium-sized organization with private networks to handle their need to access resources on the Internet and other public networks. You have installed Windows Server 2008 and are using IPv4 currently. You need more globally unique (public) IPv4 addresses to accommodate the need to access to the Internet. Which of the following solutions is the most simple and cost effective?

    A. Plan a conversion of the existing setup to accommodate IPv6, because it is supported by Windows Server 2008.

    B. Enable the NAT technology on the computers of the corporate network.

    C. Deploy a Proxy server.

    D. None of the Above.

Correct Answer & Explanation: **B.** The correct answer is **B,** because NAT was designed to be the solution to for SOHO networking situations involving IPv4. It is much simpler to set up than setting up a proxy server. Although choice A is feasible with Windows Server 2008, due to its support of IPv6, it is an extremely complicated transition and not cost effective either.

Chapter 4: Configuring File and Print Services

1. Employees at your company work with sensitive medical information including Social Security numbers and patient medical history on their laptops. You want to make sure that if a laptop is lost or stolen this data is not compromised. Which security measure is the best option to secure the files on the employee laptops?

    A. NTFS permissions

    B. EFS

    C. SSL

    D. Shared Folder Permissions

    Correct Answer & Explanation: **B.** EFS or the Encrypting File System encrypts or scrambles selected files on an NTFS volume. This prevents any unauthorized user or thief who does not have the private key from opening or reading the files.

    Incorrect Answers & Explanations: **A**, **C**, **D**. Answer **A** is incorrect, because NTFS permissions can be bypassed by resetting the admin password or connecting the hard drive to another computer where you have full administrator access. Answer **C** is incorrect, because although Secure Sockets Layer (SSL) encrypts data, it is used for encrypting data while it is being transferred between two computers on the Internet, such as a Web server and Web browser client. Answer **D** is incorrect, because Shared Folder Permissions apply only to users accessing a folder through the network.

2. You have just installed a new Windows 2008 Server on your network and joined it to the domain. This server will handle all of the files the Finance department will work with and you need to add the File Services to the new server to allow users to store their timesheets on the new server. Which tool do you use to add the File Services role to this server?

    A. Server Manager

    B. Share and Storage Management

    C. Add/Remove Programs

    D. Network and Sharing Center

Correct Answer & Explanation: **A**. Server Manager allows you to add roles and role services, and manage installed roles.

Incorrect Answers & Explanations: **B**, **C**, **D**. Answer **B** is incorrect, because Share and Storage Management is used to administer file sharing and is one of the components that are installed by adding the File Services role. Answer **C** is incorrect, because although you could add File and Print Sharing in previous versions using the Add/Remove Programs Control Panel applet, this method has been removed in Windows Server 2008. Answer **D** is incorrect, because although you can enable File Sharing and Public Folder sharing in the Network and Sharing Center, it does not install the same tools and features that are included when you install the File Services role.

3. Your user account is configured to use a roaming profile that is stored on the server LONGHORN. You sit down and log on using your user account to a workstation named HR13. You map a drive to a shared folder on the server FINANCESVR1, create a folder on that share, encrypt the contents of that folder, and then log off. On which computer is your EFS private key stored?

    A. The Active Directory domain controller that authenticated your logon

    B. FINANCESVR1

    C. HR13

    D. LONGHORN

Correct Answer & Explanation: **D**. When a user with a roaming profile uses EFS his EFS keys are stored in his profile on the server that contains his roaming profile.

Incorrect Answers & Explanations: **A**, **B**, **C**. Answer **A** is incorrect, because EFS keys are stored in user profiles, not in the Active Directory or on the domain controllers. Answer **B** is incorrect, because EFS keys are stored in user profiles, not on the server containing encrypted files. Answer **C** is incorrect, because you logged in using a roaming profile. EFS keys are generally stored in the user profile on each workstation the user log into, but in the case of roaming profiles they are stored on the server in the roaming profile.

4. You would like to encrypt the file D:\Shares\Finance\Timesheets.xls to protect it from unauthorized use or theft. Using the command prompt on your Windows 2008 Server, what would you type to accomplish this task?

    A. *CIPHER /C D:\Shares\Finance\Timesheets.xls*

    B. *CIPHER /E D:\Shares\Finance\Timesheets.xls*

    C. *CIPHER D:\Shares\Finance\Timesheets.xls*

    D. *CIPHER /X D:\Shares\Finance\Timesheets.xls*

    Correct Answer & Explanation: **B**. The *CIPHER /E* command is used to encrypt files or folders.

    Incorrect Answers & Explanations: **A, C, D**. Answer **A** is incorrect, because the *CIPHER /C* command is used to display information on an encrypted file. Answer **C** is incorrect, because although *CIPHER* is the correct command, you must use a switch to perform an action. If you type in *CIPHER D:\Shares\ Finance\Timesheets.xls* it will simply show you whether the file is encrypted (indicated by an "E" in front of the filename) or unencrypted (indicated by a "U"). Answer **D** is incorrect, because *CIPHER /X* is used to back up your EFS certificate and keys into the specified filename.

5. You want to grant the user BillG full control to the D:\Shares\HR folder. What command should you type in at the command prompt to accomplish this task?

    A. *ICACLS D:\Shares\HR /grant billg:(F)*

    B. *ICACLS D:\Shares\HR /grant billg:(M,RX,R,W)2*

    C. *NET SHARE sharename=D:\Shares\HR /GRANT billg,FULL*

    D. *NET SHARE D:\Shares\HR /grant billg:(M,RX,R,W)*

    Correct Answer & Explanation: **A**. The *ICACLS* command is used to configure and modify NTFS permissions from a command prompt. The option "/grant billg:(F)" grants the user BillG full control to the folder.

    Incorrect Answers & Explanations: **A, C, D**. Answer **A** is incorrect, because this command will grant the user BillG the following permissions: Modify, Read and Execute, Read, Write; which is not the same as full control. Answer **C** is incorrect, because the *NET SHARE* command is used to control Shared Folder permissions, not NTFS permissions. Answer **D** is incorrect, because the *NET SHARE* command is used to control Shared Folder permissions, not NTFS permissions, and the syntax is not correct.

6. You are running a Windows 2008 Server called FINANCESVR1 in core mode and would like to configure the Windows Server Backup remotely using a GUI. You log into the server LONGHORN, running a full GUI installation of Windows Server 2008. Which utility do you run to accomplish this task?

    A. **Start Menu | Run | NTBACKUP**

    B. **Server Manager | Roles | File Services | Share and Storage Management | Disk Management**

    C. **Start Menu | Run | MMC** and add the **Backup** snap-in

    D. **Start Menu | Run | WBADMIN enable backup**

    Correct Answer & Explanation: **C**. Adding the Backup snap-in in the MMC allows you to choose a remote server to administer using the Backup GUI.

    Incorrect Answers & Explanations: **A, B, D**. Answer **A** is incorrect, because NTBACKUP is the older Windows backup program and is no longer included in Windows Server 2008. Answer **B** is incorrect, because the Disk Management utility can be used to administer volumes, RAID, and Shadow Copies, but not Windows Server Backup. Answer **D** is incorrect, because *WBADMIN* is the command-line utility for Windows Server Backup and in this scenario you wanted to use the GUI.

7. A network administrator tells you she has enabled NTFS disk quotas for three different users on a Windows 2008 Server but they are not working. Your server has a C: volume that contains the operating system and a D: volume that contains the shared folders. What is most likely the issue?

    A. Enable Quotas is not checked in the Properties of the D volume

    B. Enable Quotas is not checked in the Properties of the C volume

    C. The File Services Role has not been installed

    D. A Quota Template has not been configured in Quota Management

    Correct Answer & Explanation: **A**. Because the network administrator is enabling quotas on a per-user basis, she must be using NTFS disk quotas which are enabled in the properties of each volume.

    Incorrect Answers & Explanations: **B, C, D**. Answer **B** is incorrect, because the C: volume contains the operating system files, not the shared folders. Answer **C** is incorrect, because NTFS disk quotas do not rely on the File Services Role. Answer **D** is incorrect, because Quota Templates are part of the Resource Manager quotas that are independent of the NTFS disk quota system.

8. Users are complaining that they are no longer able to add files to the shared folder \\LONGHORN\Sales on your Windows 2008 Server and you suspect they have run out of space in their quota. The users tell you they are able to add files to the \\LONGHORN\Public share, which is located on the same volume as the Sales share. Where should you go to increase the quota for the \\LONGHORN\Sales share?

A. **Properties** on the volume, **Quota** tab, **Quota Entries**

B. **Server Manager | Roles | File Services | Share and Storage Management | File Resource Manager**

C. **Server Manager | Roles | File Services | Share and Storage Management | File Resource Manager | Quota Management | Quotas**

D. **Server Manager | Roles | File Services | Share and Storage Management | File Resource Manager | Storage Reports Management**

Correct Answer & Explanation: **C.** The quotas management tool allows you to manage quotas on a per-folder basis.

Incorrect Answers & Explanations: **A, B, D.** Answer **A** is incorrect, because this takes you to the NTFS disk quotas interface, which does not allow you to manage quotas on a per-folder basis. Answer **B** is incorrect, because although File Resource Manager allows you to configure quotas during the Provision a Shared Folder Wizard, it does not allow you to manage them after a folder has been shared. Answer **D** is incorrect, because Storage Reports Management allows you to monitor and run reports on disk usage but does not allow you to configure quotas.

9. You have enabled NTFS disk quotas on the D: drive of your Windows 2008 Server. You would like to increase the amount of space user BillG is allocated to 2 GB. Where should you go to increase BillG's quota?

A. **Server Manager | Roles | File Services | Share and Storage Management | File Resource Manager | Quota Management | Quotas**

B. Disk Management

C. BillG's user properties in Active Directory Users and Computers

D. Open the **Quota Entries** window from the **D: volume properties**, **Quota** tab

Correct Answer & Explanation: **D**. The Quota Entries Window allows you to configure quotas on a per-user per-volume basis.

Incorrect Answers & Explanations: **A**, **B**, **C**. Answer **A** is incorrect, because this console lets you configure Resource Manager quotas that control usage on a per-folder basis, not per user. Answer **B** is incorrect, because the Disk Management utility can be used to administer volumes, RAID, and Shadow Copies, but not to configure NTFS disk quotas without several additional steps. Answer **C** is incorrect, because quotas are not controlled in the user properties of Active Directory Users and Computers. Active Directory Users and Computer can be used to set passwords, group membership, drive mapping, and more.

10. You have just connected a [print device to your network and added the printer on your Windows 2008 Server. You would like to share the printer on the network and administer the Print Permissions. Which of the following utilities will let you accomplish this task? (Select two.)

    A. **Start Menu | Control Panel | Printers**

    B. The **Print Management** console

    C. The printer drivers disk from the manufacturer

    D. The Network and Sharing Center

    Correct Answer & Explanation: **A, B**. The Control Panel | Printers and Print Management console allows you to view printer properties and modify permissions.

    Incorrect Answers & Explanations: **C, D**. Answer **C** is incorrect, because the printer drivers disk from the manufacturer contains drivers and utilities for the printer but will not usually manage Windows printer sharing. Answer **D** is incorrect, because the Network and Sharing Center will allow you to enable Printer Sharing, but does not give a facility to configure the print permissions.

Chapter 5: Monitoring and Managing a Network Infrastructure

1. As the network administrator for Contoso, you have been tasked with ensuring that all servers and workstations are properly up-to-date with patches and security fixes. You currently must ensure that the company's 200 workstations and 50 servers have the most recent security fixes on a monthly basis.

You decide that WSUS is the best method to update computers in your company. You just received a new Windows Server 2008 server to host WSUS. What is the best method to install WSUS on this server?

A. Download WSUS from the Microsoft Web site and install using the setup wizard

B. WSUS is already preinstalled with Windows Server 2008

C. Use the Add Role option from Server Manager and add the WSUS role

D. Install IIS on the server and then download WSUS from the Microsoft Web site and install using the setup wizard

Correct Answer and Explanation: **C**. Answer **C** is correct, because Windows Server 2008 provides WSUS as a one of the standard roles which can be added via the Add Role option in Server Manager.

Incorrect Answers and Explanations: **A, B, D**. Answers **A** and **D** are incorrect, because even though it would be possible to download WSUS from the Microsoft Web site, it is not the recommended or easiest method to install and set up WSUS on Windows Server 2008. Answer **B** is incorrect, because WSUS is not preinstalled with Windows Server 2008. It must be added via the Add Role option.

2. You have just deployed WSUS to provide updates to your network workstations. You want to automate the configuration of your workstations by creating a Group Policy and applying it to the Corp Workstations OU. You then move the workstations into the Corp Workstations OU. Within 30 minutes, you notice that all clients except one are properly connecting to WSUS. What is the first troubleshooting step you should perform to figure out why the workstation is not connecting to WSUS?

A. Ensure that the Group Policy has been applied to the workstation by logging on to the workstation and running *gpupdate* from the command line

B. Log on to the workstation and manually configure Windows Update settings

C. Create a new OU and move the workstation into that OU

D. Reboot the WSUS server

1. Correct Answer and Explanation: **A**. Answer **A** is correct, because by default, Group Policy is applied to workstations within a 90-minute window. The most likely cause of this problem is that the GPO has not had time to take effect on the workstation that isn't reporting. The fact

that all workstations except one are reporting further supports the idea that the GPO has not been properly applied to this one workstation.

2. Incorrect Answers and Explanations: **B**, **C**, **D**. Answer **B** is incorrect, because you want to make sure all workstations are managed by the GPO. Manually updating the update settings would not fulfill the requirement to ensure that workstation configurations are automated when placed into the correct OU. Answer **C** is incorrect, because creating a new OU doesn't solve the problem. The problem isn't with the OU, but the fact that the GPO has not successfully applied to the workstation yet. Answer **D** is incorrect, because this is a workstation-related problem. All other workstations are connecting to WSUS properly, so the WSUS server itself is functioning properly.

3. You notice that Microsoft has released a Service Pack for Windows Vista. However, when you open the WSUS console and review updates, you do not see any service packs listed. You do see recent security updates available. What is the most probable cause that no service packs are available?

   A. Microsoft does not provide the ability to deploy service packs using WSUS

   B. Service packs are available only for Windows Server operating systems

   C. WSUS is not properly downloading updates from Microsoft update servers

   D. The Service Packs update type is not selected in the WSUS options

   Correct Answer and Explanation: **D**. Answer **D** is correct, because the most likely cause of this problem is the fact that you have not enabled update types to include Service Packs. When you enable Service Packs as an update type the Service Pack should appear in the console after the WSUS syncs with Microsoft.

   Incorrect Answers and Explanations: **A**, **B**, **C**. Answer **A** is incorrect, because Service Packs can be deployed via WSUS if selected as an update type. Answer **B** is incorrect, because Service Packs for Windows 2000, Windows Server 2003, Windows Server 2008, Windows XP, and Windows Vista all can be deployed using WSUS. Answer **C** is incorrect, because you do see recent security updates in the console. This means the WSUS server is properly contacting Microsoft servers to download new updates.

4. You notice that a new critical security update has been released to the Microsoft update site. You want to download this update to your WSUS server and install it on all of your corporate computers as soon as possible.

You approve the update for install to the All Computers computer group and set an install deadline of 11:00 P.M. of the same day. When you return to the office the next morning you notice that the update was not installed on any computers. What is the most likely cause that the update was not installed?

A. The WSUS server lost connectivity to the Internet

B. You must approve the update for each computer individually

C. The Automatic Updates Detection Frequency is set to a period longer than the amount of time that has elapsed since you approved the update

D. The client computers need to be rebooted before the update can be installed

Correct Answer and Explanation: **C**. Answer **C** is correct, because the Automatic Updates Detection Frequency is the setting configured on each workstation that instructs it to connect to the update server. Even if you set a deadline, the client will not download the new update until the detection frequency time has lapsed.

Incorrect Answers and Explanations: **A**, **B**, **D**. Answer **A** is incorrect, because you were able to see the new update in the WSUS console and approve it. If the WSUS server was unable to contact Microsoft update servers over the Internet, this update would not appear in the console. Answer **B** is incorrect, because updates are approved for computer groups and not individual computers. Answer **D** is incorrect, because no reboot is necessary to detect, download, and install new updates. Reboots are usually necessary after the update has been installed.

5. As the network administrator for your company, you have been tasked with managing security updates for the company's 500 servers. Three hundred of these servers are used to support the company's production environment and the other 200 servers are used by programmers for application development and testing. Several of the development servers mimic the production application environment. Due to the complexity of certain mission-critical applications, all security updates must be tested before being deployed to the production servers. What is the easiest and fastest method to test updates and then deploy them to production servers?

A. Set up two WSUS servers. Create two GPOs. Prod_GPO will be assigned to the OU containing the production servers. Dev_GPO will be assigned to the OU containing Dev Servers. Prod_GPO will configure servers to connect to WSUS1. Dev_GPO will configure servers to connect to WSUS2. Log on to WSUS2 and approve security updates for development servers. After testing the updates on development servers, log on to WSUS1. Approve the same updates for the production servers.

B. Set up one WSUS server. Create two computer groups in WSUS. Name one group Production Servers and the other group Development Servers. Create two GPOs. Prod_GPO will be assigned to the OU containing production servers. Dev_GPO will be assigned to the OU containing development servers. Prod_GPO will configure servers to report to WSUS1 and assign them to the Production Servers computer group. Dev_GPO will configure servers to report to WSUS1 and assign them to the Development Servers computer group. Approve new updates for the Development Servers computer group. After testing the updates, approve them for deployment to the Production Servers computer group.

C. Set up one WSUS server. Create one computer group named Servers. Create two GPOs. Prod_GPO will be assigned to the OU containing production servers. Dev_GPO will be assigned to the OU containing development servers. Both GPOs will configure servers to connect to WSUS1 and assign them to the Servers computer group. Approve updates for deployment to the OU containing development servers. After successfully testing the updates, approve the same updates for deployment to the OU containing the production servers.

D. Set up one WSUS server. Create two computer groups named Production Servers and Development Servers. Create one GPO named ServerUpdates_GPO. Assign the same GPO to both the OU containing development servers and the OU containing production servers. The GPO will configure servers to connect to the WSUS server and assign them to the proper computer group based on the server's IP address.

Correct Answer and Explanation: **B**. Answer **B** is correct, because it allows you to properly deploy new updates to a test environment prior to deploying that same update to production servers. To achieve this we must deploy two GPOs to ensure that servers report to the proper computer groups in WSUS. We need two computer groups so that we can deploy to each group of computers individually.

Incorrect Answers and Explanations: **A, C, D**. Answer **A** is incorrect, because although setting up two WSUS servers would work, it is by far not the easiest or quickest method to achieve the task requirements. Answer **C** is incorrect, because you cannot approve updates for deployment to OUs. You can only approve updates for deployment to WSUS computer groups. For this reason, you must create two WSUS computer groups instead of just one. Answer **D** is incorrect, because two GPOs are needed to properly assign the two sets of servers to their proper WSUS server. WSUS cannot use the server's IP address to autoconfigure the client settings.

6. Users are complaining that the billing system is performing slowly. You remember that this system was just moved to a new server last week. You have no idea why the application is performing poorly, but you suspect it's a resource issue. What is the best tool you should use to gather a few quick diagnostics on the system?

   A. Performance Monitor

   B. Network Monitor

   C. Data Collector Set

   D. Event Logs

   Correct Answer and Explanation: **C**. Answer **C** is correct, because you have no idea what performance stats to look at. By running the System Performance Data Collector Set, you will be able to get detailed information on where the bottleneck is and be able to determine possible root causes.

   Incorrect Answers and Explanations: **A**, **B**, **D**. Answer **A** is incorrect, because even though Performance Monitor can be used to troubleshoot performance problems, you need to have an idea of what counters to look at and what the thresholds should be. You do not need to know this information when running a Data Collector Set. Answer **B** is incorrect, because Network Monitor simply captures network packets and lets you look at the payloads for troubleshooting network connectivity problems. Answer **D** is incorrect, because Event logs are used to review errors and warnings. Event logs typically do not provide performance information.

7. One of your mission-critical database servers keeps crashing several times per day. You suspect that one of the DBAs may have installed a new database management tool that could be causing the problem. How can you determine whether any tools were installed recently?

   A. Open Reliability Monitor and look for application install events over the past week

   B. Ensure that the System Stability Index is above 3

C. Look at the modified dated of the .exe file for the application

D. Search the Event logs for an installation event

Correct Answer and Explanation: **A**. Answer **A** is correct, because Reliability Monitor tracks system configuration changes, including application installs.

Incorrect Answers and Explanation: **B, C, D**. Answer **B** is incorrect, because the System Stability Index just provides a number value of the overall stability of the computer based on previous failure events. Answer **C** is incorrect, because the modified date of the .exe file doesn't have anything to do with when the application was installed. Answer **D** is incorrect, because the installation application may not have created an install event.

8. You have set up a new WSUS server to manage updates for your Windows workstations and servers. You create two computer groups from the WSUS management console. These groups are named Servers and Workstations. You want to use Group Policy to ensure that server computers are in the Servers group and workstation computers are in the Workstations group. You create a new Group Policy and link it to the domain. When you open the WSUS management console, you notice that both servers and workstations are in the Workstations group. Which of the following is the correct way to ensure that servers are in the Servers group and workstations are in the Workstations group?

A. Edit the domain GPO and change the Target Group to Servers

B. Edit the domain GPO and change the Target Group to both Workstations and Servers

C. Unlink the current GPO from the domain. Relink the GPO to the OU containing Workstations. Create a new GPO and link it to the OU containing Servers. Ensure that the new GPO has the Target Group set to Servers.

D. Unlink the current GPO from the domain. Relink the GPO to the OU containing Workstations and the OU containing Servers.

Correct Answer and Explanation: **C**. Answer **C** is correct, because you need to create two GPOs—one that assigns workstations to the Workstations group and one that assigns servers to the Servers group. You then need to link each GPO to the appropriate OU.

Incorrect Answers and Explanations: **A, B, D**. Answer **A** is incorrect, because changing the target group of the domain GPO would just move all work-stations and servers to the Servers group. Answer **B** is incorrect, because you cannot configure a computer to connect to two computer groups in WSUS. Answer **D** is incorrect, because moving the GPO from the domain level to the individual OUs does not update the target computer group setting.

9. You have been tasked with planning and deploying a patch management solution for your company's engineering department computers. For security reasons, these computers are connected to a network that does not have access to the Internet. The security team has also mandated that the engineering network will not have access to any other network in the company. The patch management solution you deploy must reside on the engineering network and will not have access to the Internet or other networks. You have been considering deploying WSUS; however, you know WSUS downloads updates from Microsoft. Can you deploy WSUS for patch management in this situation, and if so, how? Choose the best answer.

A. Yes. Deploy WSUS on a network that has Internet access. Download updates from Microsoft. Move the WSUS server to the engineering network to update the engineering computers.

B. Yes. Deploy two WSUS servers. Deploy the first server on the company's normal network which has access to the Internet. Deploy the second WSUS server on the engineering network. Export updates from the first WSUS server and import the updates to the second WSUS server.

C. Yes. Deploy two WSUS servers. Deploy the first server on the company's normal network which has access to the Internet. Deploy the second WSUS server on the engineering network. Configure the second server to receive updates from an upstream proxy. Specify the first WSUS server as the upstream proxy.

D. WSUS cannot be used in this situation. You will need to manually update computers on the engineering network.

Correct Answer and Explanation: **B**. Answer **B** is correct, because you can deploy two WSUS servers to achieve the security requirements. You can deploy the second WSUS server to the engineering network in a disconnected network configuration. You can then download updates from the Internet on the primary WSUS server and then export those updates. Those updates can then be imported to the WSUS server in the disconnected network.

Incorrect Answers and Explanations: **A, C, D**. Answer **A** is incorrect, because moving the WSUS server between networks would prove to be unreliable and updates would fail to deploy. Also, trying to move the server on a monthly basis would be a daunting task. This answer just isn't good practice. Answer **C** is incorrect, because an engineering network is not allowed to communicate with any other networks. The secondary WSUS server would need access to the primary network where the first WSUS service resides to download updates properly. This is not permitted in this scenario. Answer **D** is incorrect, because you can use WSUS in a disconnected network deployment and import updates to the secondary WSUS server.

10. Your company is in the process of deploying a new intranet Web site. The Web site will be accessed by thousands of people in the company. Before making the site available to the entire company, the development team would like to run load testing tools to ensure that the Web site will support normal user loads. The development team has asked you to determine whether the hardware is adequate for the new intranet site. You decide to collect CPU, memory, and disk statistics and watch them in real time while the development team performs the load tests. By doing this, you will quickly be able to see whether there are hardware bottlenecks. What tool should you use to perform this test?

A. Performance Monitor

B. Network Monitor

C. Server Manager

D. Event logs

Correct Answer and Explanation: **A**. Answer **A** is correct, because you can use Performance Monitor to collect key performance statistics and view them in real time or from a log captured over time.

Incorrect Answers and Explanations: **B**, **C**, **D**. Answer **B** is incorrect, because Network Monitor is used only to capture network packets and troubleshoot networking-based issues. Network Monitor cannot be used to monitor the performance of the system's CPU, memory, and disk usage. Answer **C** is incorrect, because Server Manager is an administrative tool. Server Manager does not provide monitoring, but merely provides a console for monitoring interfaces. Answer **D** is incorrect, because the Event logs do not allow you to review CPU, memory, and disk statistics in real time. Event logs will contain error events only if application or system errors occur.

Chapter 6: Network Access Protection

1. Network Access Protection (NAP) will only work with certain operating systems at the time of Windows 2008 Server release. What operating systems will NAP support?

   A. Window XP

   B. Windows XP Service Pack 3

   C. Windows Vista

   D. Windows Server 2008

   Correct Answer & Explanation: **B,C,D**. At the time of this writing, the only operating systems that are supported by NAP are Windows XP Service Pack 3, Windows Vista and Windows Server 2008. Look for future operating system support via Independent Software Providers. Answer **A** is incorrect—Windows XP will need Service Pack 3 to support NAP.

2. Network Access Protection (NAP) can provide network protection to various types of network communications. Which of the following will not support NAP?

   A. NPS Connections

   B. DHCP Supported Network

   C. WINS Supported Network

   D. IEEE 802.11B Wireless Network

   Correct Answer & Explanation: **C**. NAP can provide network protection to the following network types: **A,B,D**. Internet Protocol security (IPsec) protected traffic, IEEE 802.1x authenticated networks, Dynamic Host Configuration Protocol (DHCP) address configurations and NPS VPN connections. All of the listed networks are supported except for the WINS Supported Network. WINS is not required on a Windows 2008 Server infrastructure unless old operating systems are in use.

3. Network Access Protection (NAP) was designed for third party vendors to take advantage of the infrastructure. This is really important for NAP to become popular throughout the IT community. What is the name of the item that allows third party developers to write programs that can take advantage of the NAP infrastructure?

   A. ISV

   B. HRA

C. API

D. CA

Correct Answer & Explanation: **C**. API stands for Application Programming Interface—this is what allows ISVs (Independent Software Vendors) tie their products in to other programs. Microsoft has provided an extensive API for NAP. Answers **B** and **D** are acronyms that are dependent on each other—but do not help third party vendors; HRA stands for Health Registration Authority which requires a Certificate Authority (CA) to work. Answer **A** is an acronym that stands for Independent Software Vendor.

4. NAP enforcement points are what determine if a client wanting to connect to a restricted network is healthy and compliant. What are the valid enforcement points listed below?

A. Windows 2008 VPN Server

B. HUB

C. DHCP Server

D. IEEE 802.1x Network Access Device

Correct Answer & Explanation: **A,C,D**. All of the devices listed can be a network enforcement point except for a hub. Answer **B** is not correct because hubs are a physical layer device and is not 802.1x compliant like most switches.

5. The NAP Health Policy Server is responsible for storing health requirement policies and provides health state validation for the NAP Infrastructure. What Windows Server 2008 roles have to be installed for the NAP Health Policy Server to be configured?

A. Active Directory Domain Role

B. NPS Server Role

C. NAP Server Role

D. DHCP Server Role

Correct Answer & Explanation: **B**. The only Windows 2008 Server Role that needs to be installed to support a NAP Health Policy Server is the Network Policy Server Role. Other Windows 2008 Server roles can be installed along with the NPS Server Role—but, NPS is the primary role that needs to be installed. So, **A,C,D** are incorrect because they are not needed to install the NPS role on the Windows 2008 Server with the NPS Server Role.

6. You have decided to implement NAP into your existing network. During the design, you need to make a decision as to how the Restricted Network will be secured from the Remediation Network. Given the options below, which one(s) would work in this scenario?

    A. Use IPsec with Health Certificates

    B. Use a secondary switch to split the networks

    C. Use IP packet filters

    D. Use VLANs

    Correct Answer & Explanation: **A,C,D**. You have a couple of options to split the secured network from the remediation network. Using IPsec and Health Certification provides an excellent way to split the network. Any client connecting to the restricted network would have to present a valid Health Certificate to authenticate to the network. IP packet filters would work— especially if you where using a RRAS VPN as an enforcement point for the restricted network. Optionally, VLANs would suffice also—a VLAN would work fine, but adding secondary switches would not help secure the restricted network from the secured network. Answer **B** is incorrect because adding a second switch would not split the networks as needed for the infrastructure.

7. Using Figure 6.20 as a reference point, where would the Remediation Server be located on this network?

Figure 6.20 Network Design

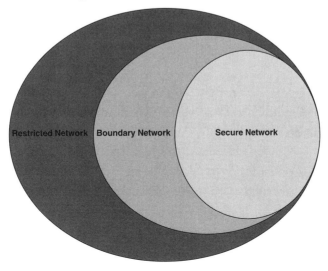

A. Secure Network

B. Boundary Network

C. Restricted Network

D. Location Does Not Matter

Correct Answer & Explanation: **B**. This network diagram represents an IPsec NAP enforcement design. The network is separated using Health Certificates. In this design, the Remediation Server would be located in the Boundary Network. This location would allow both the Secure Network to connect to the device via IPsec authentication and also allow the restricted network to connect so the clients can be remediated—then they would have access to the Secure Network. Answer **A** is incorrect because if the Remediation Server was located on the Secure Network, it would not be able to remediate noncompliant computers. Answer **C** is not correct because the Remediation Server needs to be accessible by both the Secured Network and Restricted Network. Location of the Remediation Server does matter so answer **D** is incorrect.

8. The remediation server could run Windows 2008 Server or Windows 2003 Server software. To remediate Windows Vista, Windows 2008 Server or Windows XP Service Pack 3—what other software would the remediation server need to run?

A. Windows Server Update Services (WSUS)

B. Network Protection Services (NPS)

C. Routing and Remote Access Services (RRAS)

D. Windows Security Health Validator (WSHV)

Correct Answer & Explanation: **A**. The remediation server would need to have some kind of software in place to correct clients and make them compliant to access the secured network. The Windows Security Health Validator is installed by default on clients. When these clients need to update Microsoft software—the will need Windows 2003 Server or Windows 2008 Server running Windows Server Update Services (WSUS). Answers **B** and **C** are incorrect because either service or role does not remediate an incompliant computer. The Windows Security Health Validator (WSHV) is the server side software that checks to see if the computer is compliant—it does not remediate the server; so answer **D** is incorrect.

9. You instruct your junior network administrator Heather to setup a NAP enforcement point using a DHCP server. After his installation, he comes to you complaining that DHCP is working fine—but he cannot get NAP to work with Windows Vista clients. You go through the installation with him—using 802.1x certified switches, he setup a Windows 2008 Server with both the DHCP and Network Policy and Access Services server roles. Once configured successfully, he set the DHCP settings for DHCPv6 Stateless Mode. Once configured—he set up the NPS policies with the NAP wizard. What is the problem with this scenario?

   A. The equipment needs to support 802.11 certified devices.

   B. Heather did not install Routing and Remote Access Services (RRAS) on the Windows 2008 Server.

   C. NAP does not support IPv6.

   D. Windows Vista needs to be updated to Service Pack 1 to work in this network.

   Correct Answer & Explanation: **C**. All of the information in this scenario is fine and should work except that NAP does not support IPv6. NAP only supports IPv4. Also answer **B** is incorrect, Windows 2008 Server does not have Routing and Remote Access Service or Internet Authentication Services— these services have been replaced by the Network Policy and Access Services Role. Answer **A** is incorrect because with a DHCP implementation, you do not need to have 802.1x certified devices. Answer **D** is incorrect—at the time of this writing, there is now Windows Vista Service Pack 1.

10. NAP Health Policies are a combination of settings for health determination and enforcement of infrastructure compliance. What are the sets of settings that make up the NAP Health Policies?

    A. Connection Request Policies

    B. Network Policies

    C. Health Policies

    D. Network Access Protection Settings

    Correct Answer & Explanation: **A, B, C, D**. All of the multiple choice answers are correct. NAP Health Policies are configured within the Network Policy Server console. NAP Health Policies are made up of all of the above choices.

Index

Syngress: *The Definition of a Serious Security Library*

Syn·gress (sin–gres): *noun, sing.* Freedom from risk or danger; safety. See *security*.

Syngress: *The Definition of a Serious Security Library*

Syn·gress (sin–gres): *noun, sing.* Freedom from risk or danger; safety. See *security*.

Syngress: *The Definition of a Serious Security Library*

Syn·gress (sin–gres): *noun, sing.* Freedom from risk or danger; safety. See *security*.

Phishing Exposed

Lance James, Secure Science Corporation,
Joe Stewart (Foreword)

If you have ever received a phish, become a victim of a phish, or manage the security of a major e-commerce or financial site, then you need to read this book. The author of this book delivers the unconcealed techniques of phishers including their evolving patterns, and how to gain the upper hand against the ever-accelerating attacks they deploy. Filled with elaborate and unprecedented forensics, Phishing Exposed details techniques that system administrators, law enforcement, and fraud investigators can exercise and learn more about their attacker and their specific attack methods, enabling risk mitigation in many cases before the attack occurs.

ISBN: 1-59749-030-X

Price: $49.95 US $69.95 CAN

Penetration Tester's Open Source Toolkit

Johnny Long, Chris Hurley, SensePost,
Mark Wolfgang, Mike Petruzzi

This is the first fully integrated Penetration Testing book and bootable Linux CD containing the "Auditor Security Collection," which includes over 300 of the most effective and commonly used open source attack and penetration testing tools. This powerful tool kit and authoritative reference is written by the security industry's foremost penetration testers including HD Moore, Jay Beale, and SensePost. This unique package provides you with a completely portable and bootable Linux attack distribution and authoritative reference to the toolset included and the required methodology.

ISBN: 1-59749-021-0

Price: $59.95 US $83.95 CAN

Google Hacking for Penetration Testers

Johnny Long, Foreword by Ed Skoudis

Google has been a strong force in Internet culture since its 1998 upstart. Since then, the engine has evolved from a simple search instrument to an innovative authority of information. As the sophistication of Google grows, so do the hacking hazards that the engine entertains. Approaches to hacking are forever changing, and this book covers the risks and precautions that administrators need to be aware of during this explosive phase of Google Hacking.

ISBN: 1-93183-636-1

Price: $44.95 U.S. $65.95 CAN

Syngress: *The Definition of a Serious Security Library*

Syn·gress (sin–gres): *noun, sing.* Freedom from risk or danger; safety. See *security*.

Syngress: *The Definition of a Serious Security Library*

Syn·gress (sin-gres): *noun, sing.* Freedom from risk or danger; safety. See *security*.

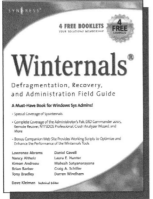

Winternals Defragmentation, Recovery, and Administration Field Guide

Dave Kleiman, Laura E. Hunter, Tony Bradley, Brian Barber, Nancy Altholz, Lawrence Abrams, Mahesh Satyanarayana, Darren Windham, Craig Schiller

As a system administrator for a Microsoft network, you know doubt spend too much of your life backing up data and restoring data, hunting down and removing malware and spyware, defragmenting disks, and improving the overall performance and reliability of your network. The Winternals® Defragmentation, Recovery, and Administration Field Guide and companion Web site provide you with all the information necessary to take full advantage of Winternals comprehensive and reliable tools suite for system administrators.

ISBN: 1-59749-079-2

Price: $49.95 US $64.95 CAN

Video Conferencing over IP: Configure, Secure, and Troubleshoot

Michael Gough

Until recently, the reality of videoconferencing didn't live up to the marketing hype. That's all changed. The network infrastructure and broadband capacity are now in place to deliver clear, real-time video and voice feeds between multiple points of contacts, with market leaders such as Cisco and Microsoft continuing to invest heavily in development. In addition, newcomers Skype and Google are poised to launch services and products targeting this market. *Video Conferencing over IP* is the perfect guide to getting up and running with video teleconferencing for small to medium-sized enterprises.

ISBN: 1-59749-063-6

Price: $49.95 U.S. $64.95 CAN

SYNGRESS®

Syngress: *The Definition of a Serious Security Library*

Syn·gress (sin–gres): *noun, sing.* Freedom from risk or danger; safety. See *security*.

How to Cheat at Designing Security for a Windows Server 2003 Network

Neil Ruston, Chris Peiris

While considering the security needs of your organiztion, you need to balance the human and the technical in order to create the best security design for your organization. Securing a Windows Server 2003 enterprise network is hardly a small undertaking, but it becomes quite manageable if you approach it in an organized and systematic way. This includes configuring software, services, and protocols to meet an organization's security needs.

ISBN: 1-59749-243-4

Price: $39.95 US $55.95 CAN

How to Cheat at Designing a Windows Server 2003 Active Directory Infrastructure

Melissa Craft, Michael Cross, Hal Kurz, Brian Barber

The book will start off by teaching readers to create the conceptual design of their Active Directory infrastructure by gathering and analyzing business and technical requirements. Next, readers will create the logical design for an Active Directory infrastructure. Here the book starts to drill deeper and focus on aspects such as group policy design. Finally, readers will learn to create the physical design for an active directory and network Infrastructure including DNS server placement; DC and GC placements and Flexible Single Master Operations (FSMO) role placement.

ISBN: 1-59749-058-X

Price: $39.95 US $55.95 CAN

How to Cheat at Configuring ISA Server 2004

Dr. Thomas W. Shinder, Debra Littlejohn Shinder

If deploying and managing ISA Server 2004 is just one of a hundred responsibilities you have as a System Administrator, "How to Cheat at Configuring ISA Server 2004" is the perfect book for you. Written by Microsoft MVP Dr. Tom Shinder, this is a concise, accurate, enterprise tested method for the successful deployment of ISA Server.

ISBN: 1-59749-057-1

Price: $34.95 U.S. $55.95 CAN

SYNGRESS®

Syngress: *The Definition of a Serious Security Library*

Syn·gress (sin-gres): *noun, sing.* Freedom from risk or danger; safety. See *security*.

Configuring SonicWALL Firewalls

Chris Lathem, Ben Fortenberry, Lars Hansen

Configuring SonicWALL Firewalls is the first book to deliver an in-depth look at the SonicWALL firewall product line. It covers all of the aspects of the SonicWALL product line from the SOHO devices to the Enterprise SonicWALL firewalls. Advanced troubleshooting techniques and the SonicWALL Security Manager are also covered.

ISBN: 1-59749-250-7
Price: $49.95 US $69.95 CAN

Perfect Passwords:
Selection, Protection, Authentication

Mark Burnett

User passwords are the keys to the network kingdom, yet most users choose overly simplistic passwords (like password) that anyone could guess, while system administrators demand impossible to remember passwords littered with obscure characters and random numerals. Author Mark Burnett has accumulated and analyzed over 1,000,000 user passwords, and this highly entertaining and informative book filled with dozens of illustrations reveals his findings and balances the rigid needs of security professionals against the ease of use desired by users.

ISBN: 1-59749-041-5
Price: $24.95 US $34.95 CAN

Syngress: *The Definition of a Serious Security Library*

Syn·gress (sin–gres): *noun, sing.* Freedom from risk or danger; safety. See *security*.

Skype Me! From Single User to Small Enterprise and Beyond

Michael Gough

This first-ever book on Skype takes you from the basics of getting Skype up and running on all platforms, through advanced features included in SkypeIn, SkypeOut, and Skype for Business. The book teaches you everything from installing a headset to configuring a firewall to setting up Skype as telephone Base to developing your own customized applications using the Skype Application Programming Interface.

ISBN: 1-59749-032-6

Price: $34.95 US $48.95 CAN

Securing IM and P2P Applications for the Enterprise

Brian Baskin, Marcus H. Sachs, Paul Piccard

As an IT Professional, you know that the majority of the workstations on your network now contain IM and P2P applications that you did not select, test, install, or configure. As a result, malicious hackers, as well as virus and worm writers, are targeting these inadequately secured applications for attack. This book will teach you how to take back control of your workstations and reap the benefits provided by these applications while protecting your network from the inherent dangers.

ISBN: 1-59749-017-2

Price: $49.95 US $69.95 CAN

SYNGRESS®

Syngress: *The Definition of a Serious Security Library*

Syn·gress (sin-gres): *noun, sing.* Freedom from risk or danger; safety. See *security*.

How to Cheat at Managing Windows Server Update Services

Brian Barber

If you manage a Microsoft Windows network, you probably find yourself overwhelmed at times by the sheer volume of updates and patches released by Microsoft for its products. You know these updates are critical to keep your network running efficiently and securely, but staying current amidst all of your other responsibilities can be almost impossible. Microsoft's recently released Windows Server Update Services (WSUS) is designed to streamline this process. Learn how to take full advantage of WSUS using Syngress' proven "How to Cheat" methodology, which gives you everything you need and nothing you don't.

ISBN: 1-59749-027-X

Price: $39.95 US $55.95 CAN

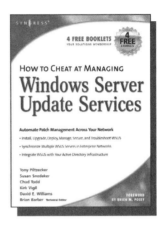

How to Cheat at IT Project Management

Susan Snedaker

Most IT projects fail to deliver – on average, all IT projects run over schedule by 82%, run over cost by 43% and deliver only 52% of the desired functionality. Pretty dismal statistics. Using the proven methods in this book, you'll find that IT project you work on from here on out will have a much higher likelihood of being on time, on budget and higher quality. This book provides clear, concise, information and hands-on training to give you immediate results. And, the companion Web site provides dozens of templates for managing IT projects.

ISBN: 1-59749-037-7

Price: $44.95 U.S. $64.95 CAN

Syngress: *The Definition of a Serious Security Library*

Syn·gress (sin–gres): *noun, sing.* Freedom from risk or danger; safety. See *security*.

Managing Cisco Network Security, Second Edition

Offers updated and revised information covering many of Cisco's security products that provide protection from threats, detection of network security incidents, measurement of vulnerability and policy compliance, and management of security policy across an extended organization. These are the tools that you have to mount defenses against threats. Chapters also cover the improved functionality and ease of the Cisco Secure Policy Manager software used by thousands of small-to-midsized businesses, and a special section on Cisco wireless solutions.

ISBN: 1-931836-56-6
Price: $69.95 USA $108.95 CAN

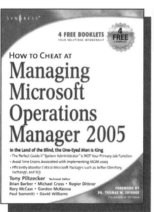

How to Cheat at Managing Microsoft Operations Manager 2005

Tony Piltzecker, Rogier Dittner, Rory McCaw, Gordon McKenna, Paul M. Summitt, David E. Williams

My e-mail takes forever. My application is stuck. Why can't I log on? System administrators have to address these types of complaints far too often. With MOM, system administrators will know when overloaded processors, depleted memory, or failed network connections are affecting their Windows servers long before these problems bother users. Readers of this book will learn why when it comes to monitoring Windows Server System infrastructure, MOM's the word.

ISBN: 1-59749-251-5
Price: $39.95 U.S. $55.95 CAN

Syngress: *The Definition of a Serious Security Library*

Syn·gress (sin–gres): *noun, sing.* Freedom from risk or danger; safety. See *security*.

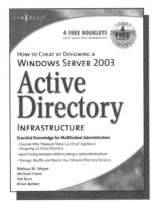

How to Cheat at Designing a Windows Server 2003 Active Directory Infrastructure

This book will start off by teaching readers to create the conceptual design of their Active Directory infrastructure by gathering and analyzing business and technical requirements. Next, readers will create the logical design for an Active Directory infrastructure. Here the book starts to drill deeper and focus on aspects such as group policy design. Finally, readers will learn to create the physical design for an active directory and network Infrastructure including DNS server placement; DC and GC placements and Flexible Single Master Operations (FSMO) role placement.

ISBN: 1-59749-058-X

Price: $39.95 US $55.95 CAN

Exam 70-291: Implementing, Managing, and Maintaining a Microsoft Windows Server 2003

ISBN: 1-931836-92-2

Price: $59.95 US

Exam 70-293: Planning and Maintaining a Microsoft Windows Server 2003 Network Infrastructure

ISBN: 1-931836-93-0

Price: $59.95 US

Exam 70-294: Planning, Implementing, and Maintaining a Microsoft Windows Server 2003 Active Directory Infrastructure

ISBN: 1-931836-94-9

Price: $59.95 US

SYNGRESS®

Syngress: *The Definition of a Serious Security Library*

Syn·gress (sin-gres): *noun, sing.* Freedom from risk or danger; safety. See *security*.

Snort 2.1 Intrusion Detection, Second Edition

Jay Beale, Brian Caswell, et. al.

"The authors of this *Snort 2.1 Intrusion Detection, Second Edition* have produced a book with a simple focus, to teach you how to use Snort, from the basics of getting started to advanced rule configuration, they cover all aspects of using Snort, including basic installation, preprocessor configuration, and optimization of your Snort system."

—Stephen Northcutt
Director of Training & Certification, The SANS Institute

ISBN: 1-931836-04-3
Price: $49.95 U.S. $69.95 CAN

Ethereal Packet Sniffing

Ethereal offers more protocol decoding and reassembly than any free sniffer out there and ranks well among the commercial tools. You've all used tools like tcpdump or windump to examine individual packets, but Ethereal makes it easier to make sense of a stream of ongoing network communications. Ethereal not only makes network troubleshooting work far easier, but also aids greatly in network forensics, the art of finding and examining an attack, by giving a better "big picture" view. *Ethereal Packet Sniffing* will show you how to make the most out of your use of Ethereal.

ISBN: 1-932266-82-8
Price: $49.95 U.S. $77.95 CAN

Nessus Network Auditing

Jay Beale, Haroon Meer, Roelof Temmingh, Charl Van Der Walt, Renaud Deraison

Crackers constantly probe machines looking for both old and new vulnerabilities. In order to avoid becoming a casualty of a casual cracker, savvy sys admins audit their own machines before they're probed by hostile outsiders (or even hostile insiders). Nessus is the premier Open Source vulnerability assessment tool, and was recently voted the "most popular" open source security tool of any kind. *Nessus Network Auditing* is the first book available on Nessus and it is written by the world's premier Nessus developers led by the creator of Nessus, Renaud Deraison.

ISBN: 1-931836-08-6
Price: $49.95 U.S. $69.95 CAN